Praise for *Myths of Coaching*

"Amy and Jenny have put together a book that might just make you stop... and think. If you are interested in growing as a coach, what's the benefit of not having more options and a better understanding of what might work when and why? Enjoy!"

~ Russell Earnshaw: Director, the Magic Academy

"By highlighting the myths within coaching, this book forces you to question the conscious and unconscious biases within your own coaching practice, and where these come from. It challenged me to differentiate between what I know and what I believe and look for ways to better align the two."

~ Sara Francis-Bayman: Director of netball for Loughborough Lightning, and Scottish Thistles assistant coach

"Myths of Sport Coaching addresses fundamental gaps in understanding, practice & expectations. This work, illuminated by leading authors, scholars & practitioners, is indispensable for anyone supporting & championing others through coaching."

~ Dr Steve Ingham: Supporting Champions

"Awesome things can happen when great people come together and this is a prime example of such an occurrence. I'll summarise; if you want to become a great coach, this book is an absolute must-read."

~ Nick Levett: Head of Coaching at UK Coaching

"It is a great collaboration of minds from both the academic and applied worlds that helps open your thinking to the many different aspects and ways of coaching. The concepts raised and some fresh perspectives offered, present useable information for coaches to take away and apply in their own practice."

~ Mel Marshall MBE: Olympic Swimming Coach, 3x Olympian and 6x Commonwealth Games Medalist

"A broad spanning volume that invites one to pause and ask the pertinent critical questions of why we do what we do within the field of sports coaching."

~ Craig Morris: Podium Technical Coach, British Canoeing

"A really interesting journey through some of the 'rules' of coaching that have become embedded within our language and the reality behind them. This book uses all the developments which have taken place in coaching understanding and knowledge in the last few years and offers really up to date advice and recommendations for those wanting their coaching practice to be both highly effective and enjoyable."

~ Dr Josephine Perry, Chartered Sport and Exercise Psychologist

"I'm fortunate to spend my days speaking with head coaches all around the world, and the questions they're pondering are answered in this book. What Whitehead and Coe have done is given us a blueprint for the next decade of coaching craft - Which myths still persist without reason? Where have we taken great ideas too far? What will take my coaching to the next level? Whether you're decades into your coaching journey or just getting started, Myths of Sport Coaching will help you become the best coach you can be."

~ Cody Royle: Former Head Coach of AFL Team Canada, Author of "The Tough Stuff" & "Where Others Won't"

Myths of Sport Coaching

Myths of Sport Coaching

Dr Amy E. Whitehead & Jenny Coe

First published in 2021 by Sequoia Books

ISBN
Print: 9781914110122
EPUB: 9781914110139

A CIP record for this book is available from the British Library

Library of Congress Cataloguing-In-Publication Data
Name: Dr Amy Whitehead & Jenny Coe, editors
Title: Myths of Sport Coaching / Dr Amy Whitehead & Jenny Coe
Description: 1st Edition, Sequoia Books UK 2021
Subjects: LCSH:. Sport Psychology. Sports-Psychological Aspects
Print: 9781914110122
EPUB: 9781914110139

Library of Congress Control Number: 2021920718

Print and Electronic production managed by Deanta Global

About the Editors

Dr Amy E. Whitehead, PhD, CPsychol, HCPC is Reader (Associate Professor) in Sport Psychology and Coaching at Liverpool John Moores University. Dr Whitehead is a sport and exercise psychologist accredited with the British Psychological Society and is registered with the Health and Care Professions Council. Dr Whitehead delivers sport psychology support and coach development to a range of athletes and coaches, and also brings this work into her teaching in the classroom.

Jenny Coe is Head of Performance and Wellbeing with West Ham United Women's Team. She also works across a number of Olympic sports as a high performance coach developer and performance analyst. Her athletic career spanned 15 years of international basketball, and she also has a wealth of experience coaching internationally. On the back of that, she is a founding member of the company Impact the Game that aims to support athletes and coaches in all areas of performance. She is an advocate for mental wealth and women in sport, and she continues to support and influence change in these areas.

Contents

CONTENTS

Contributors

Zoë Avner, Northumbria University, UK
Lee Baldock, University of South Wales, UK
Stewart Bicker, Liverpool John Moores University, UK
Alexander D. Blackett, Staffordshire University, UK
Claire Blennerhassett, Edge Hill University, UK
Ali Bowes, Nottingham Trent University, UK
Edward Coughlan, Munster Technological University, Ireland
Colum Cronin, Liverpool John Moores University, UK
Brendan Cropley, University of South Wales, UK
Diane M. Culver, University of Ottawa, Canada
Chris Cushion, Loughborough University, UK
Lauren Downham, UK Coaching, UK
Tiago Duarte, University of Ottawa, Canada
Sam Elliot, Flinders University, Australia
Anna Feiler, The George Washington University, USA
Jonathan D Foulkes, Liverpool John Moores University, UK
Sheldon Hanton, Cardiff Metropolitan University, UK
Laura C. Healy, Nottingham Trent University, UK
Patricia C. Jackman, University of Lincoln, UK
Luke Jones, University of Hull, UK
Jolan Kegelaers, Amsterdam University of Applied Sciences, Netherlands
Liz Mahon, Liverpool John Moores University, UK
Desmond McEwan, University of Bath, UK
Kristin McGinty-Minister, Liverpool John Moores University, UK
Jody McGowan, Auckland University of Technology, New Zealand
Mark O'Sullivan, Sheffield Hallam University, UK, & AIK Football, Sweden
Mark Partington, Edge Hill University, UK

CONTRIBUTORS

James R Rudd, Norwegian School of Sport Sciences, Norway

Mustafa Sarkar, Nottingham Trent University, UK

Matthew J. Schweickle, University of Wollongong, Australia

Andy Sparks, Edge Hill University, UK

Anna Stodter, Anglia Ruskin University, UK

Laura Swettenham, International Federation of Esports Coaches, Cultiv8 Academy, UK

Don Vinson, University of Worcester, UK

Amanda J. Visek, The George Washington University, USA

Chris Wagstaff, University of Portsmouth, UK

Simon Walters, Auckland University of Technology, New Zealand

Chris Whatman, Auckland University of Technology, New Zealand

Carl T. Woods, Victoria University, Australia

Introduction

Welcome to Myths of Sport Coaching, a book that is designed to challenge your thinking and current understanding of some of the key areas within sport coaching. Over the years, practitioners and researchers have questioned some of the perpetually existing ideas within coach learning and practice, and this book hopes to provide readers with new perspectives.

This book aims to bring you contemporary arguments to some key myths or common misconceptions within the sport coaching domain. These myths and misconceptions range from the vastly cited idea that athletes must engage in 10,000 hours of practice in order to develop excellence to the idea that male and females must be coached in entirely different ways.

We have provided a multi-disciplinary perspective to some of these areas, with authors from a variety of backgrounds, which all contribute to the coaching domain. For example, we have leading authors in the area of social theory, coaching pedagogy, and practice who discuss issues of gender, reflection, questioning practices, and care in coaching. We also have physiologists providing their perspective on the physiological implications of the 10,000-hour rule and early specialization. We have nutritionists, who have unravelled some of the common misconceptions within sport nutrition, which is vital information for coaches. Furthermore, we have psychologists providing insights into the myths associated with resilience, flow, and clutch performance, and also the role of the sport psychologist.

Each chapter aims to present you with an introduction of the myth(s) and an explanation for where the myth has originated or why it may currently exist. Furthermore, each author has tried to carefully unpick the reasoning for why the myth may not be correct or where there may be some truth. Each author has also tried to provide the reader with some practical considerations for future practice or research. We have, however, encouraged author autonomy, and you will notice that each chapter may have a slightly different tone, format, and structure.

We have brought together some of the leading experts in the field of sport coaching, both from a UK and global platform. Our experts come from both academia and the applied world, and as a result we hope that this book can give you, the reader, practical takeaway messages or actions, which you can apply to your own coaching practice.

If you are a coach, some of this content may cause you to raise your eyebrows and challenge your own ideals and beliefs within your own coaching. You may disagree with some of the messages within these chapters, and that's OK! However, please consider reading these chapters with an open mind and be prepared to consider different perspectives to some of these contemporary issues within coaching.

For those interested in developing research within coaching, we hope that this book sparks new ideas that can advance these current debates within the field.

As both academics and applied practitioners, we (Amy and Jen) have enjoyed creating a book that can potentially challenge existing assumptions within the discipline and may inspire new avenues of thought. Happy reading!

1 Myths about Deliberate Practice

Edward Coughlan

The following chapter is a whistle-stop tour through the brief and illustrious history of deliberate practice. Following a general introduction, there is discussion on the origins and definition of the terms. Next, a summary of the research that followed, including the implications and limitations of this work. Then, a look at the misunderstandings and misinterpretations of the evidence that lead to myths about deliberate practice finding their way into the public domain. We conclude with information for the effective practical application of deliberate practice for the development of expertise in your sport of choice.

General introduction

Since 1993 there has been one phrase synonymous with the development of expertise in every domain, be that medicine, art, business, military, engineering, and many others – and that phrase is *deliberate practice*. Deliberate practice has had the most discussion, debate, and even controversy, within the sport domain and what it takes to become a world-class athlete, even though the original research that sparked this revival of interest in expertise was focused on musicians (Ericsson, Krampe, & Tesch-Römer, 1993). Of course, with any topic that causes widespread discussion between researchers, practitioners, and even the passer-by on the street, there is always a likelihood for misinterpretation, misunderstanding and, in some cases, myth creeping into the narrative.

It is hard to imagine any other topic from the areas of sport science of physiology, biomechanics, and psychology garnering as much attention around the globe as deliberate practice has, since the beginning of the twenty-first century. It has appeared on news bulletins, radio shows, newspapers, magazines, podcasts, webinars, blogs, chat forums, public discourse, and selected book chapters, and it has even inspired television documentaries. One individual went so far as to give up his day job in the pursuit of greatness by only following the tenets of deliberate practice (see www.thedanplan.com for more on this remarkable, yet unfortunate story). It has also been the catalyst for entire books to be written just on the topic of expertise, in the popular psychology book market, with titles such as *The Talent Code: Greatness Isn't Born. It's Grown. Here's How* (Coyle, 2009), *Talent is Overrated: What Really Separates World-Class Performers from Everybody Else* (Colvin, 2008), *Outliers: The Story of Success* (Gladwell, 2008), *The Sports Gene: Inside the Science of Extraordinary Athletic Performance* (Epstein, 2014), and many more. More recently, the academics that provided the evidence others have been inspired by have joined the popular psychology book market with more evidence-based offerings, such as Anders Ericsson's *Peak: Secrets from the New Science of Expertise* (Ericsson & Poole, 2016) and Mark Williams's *The Best: How Elite Athletes are Made* (Williams & Wigmore, 2020).

The Ericsson, Krampe, and Tesch-Römer (1993) paper brought a renewed energy to the nature versus nurture debate by introducing objective data to the discourse and adding evidence to support the nurture argument for the development of expertise across domains. Before this, discussions were more theoretical and philosophical rather than empirical (Ward, Belling, Petushek, & Ehrlinger, 2017). Nature protagonists will continue to contribute their research as it progresses, but there appears to be a greater appreciation these days of the impact of items such as deliberate practice to the acquisition of skills. The infancy of the study of genomics may still have a significant say in this longstanding debate (Pitsiladis et al., 2013).

The Origins of Deliberate Practice

Our fascination about the limits of human potential has been a topic of conversation for centuries. Why are some better than others? Where previously we believed that such gifts of excellence were passed on from one generation to the next by virtue of your status in the community (Galton, 1869), we now know that there is a lot more to the acquisition of expertise than privilege and the impact of your environment and significant others, in that environments are instrumental to a person's development (Howe, Davidson, & Sloboda, 1998). Therefore, it is no surprise that when Anders Ericsson, Ralph Krampe, and Clemens Tesch-Römer attempted to quantify the variables that may contribute to the development of expertise, their findings were met with such an overwhelming response. Over 11,000 citations later, we ask the question, why? In simplest terms, it is likely because for the first time research had uncovered evidence that the limits of human performance may lay solely at the feet of the individual, in other words, if you don't make it, it is more likely your fault than that of the genetics you inherited from your parents. Such a fantastical idea opened people up to the potential that may lie within, if only they had some guidance on how to unlock it.

That original research was a two-study project undertaken across two music academies in Berlin, Germany. The first study was based at the West Berlin Music Academy, a renowned school for developing world-class musicians. In consultation with the staff at the academy, three groups of violinists were recruited as participants based on their ability. A group of 'best' and 'good' violinists from the performance department and a third group of 'music teachers' from the education department. A fourth group of violinists, the 'professionals', were recruited from world-renowned symphonies in Berlin, the Berlin Philharmonic Orchestra and the Radio Symphony Orchestra. The second study was based at the Music Academy of Berlin, and for purposes of comparison to the findings from study one, two groups of pianists were recruited, an 'expert' group of pianists and an 'amateur' group of pianists. The data from these studies was expected to do two things, first, to shed some light on the relationship between the quantity and quality of hours invested into the pursuit of excellence, otherwise known as the monotonic benefits assumption, and second, to identify tangible variables that may suggest a particular form of engagement is more consistent with expertise than others, the latter of which lead to the phrase deliberate practice being first used, and the tenets of deliberate practice defined.

> *Deliberate practice is a highly structured activity, the explicit goal of which is to improve performance. Specific tasks are invented to overcome weaknesses, and performance is carefully monitored to provide cues for ways to improve it further. We claim that deliberate practice requires effort and is not inherently enjoyable. Individuals are motivated to practice because practice improves performance. In addition, engaging in deliberate practice generates no immediate monetary rewards and generates costs associated with access to teachers and training environments. (Ericsson, Krampe, & Tesch-Römer, 1993, p. 368)*

In both studies, first with the violinists, then with the pianists, the participants retrospectively recalled the hours they spent in activities related to their music development through interviews and diary entries from first starting in the domain up to the present day of the study. Next, the dataset was normalized to enable comparison across all groups up to when they were 18 years of age. From this stratification, one form of practice above all others stood out and that was *solitary practice* which was rated as the most relevant to improving overall performance. Further analysis revealed that by 18 years of age, there were notable differences between each of the groups across both studies for their accumulation of hours in this solitary practice and remarkable similarities between the best musicians in each study. The 'best' and 'professional' violinists and the 'expert' pianists had accumulated 7,410, 7,336, and 7,606 hours in solitary practice activities, respectively. In comparison to 5,301, 3,420, and 1,606 accumulated hours for the 'good' and 'music teacher' violinists and 'amateur' pianists, respectively (see Figure 1.1).

When this solitary practice was compared to other musical activities, such as practicing with others, as well as everyday activities, such as household chores, for *effort* to engage, *relevance* to overall performance improvement and *enjoyment* during engagement, the importance of this type of practice was further magnified. When asked to rate such activities on a scale of 1 to 10, initial analysis showed no between-group differences; however, when the scores were collapsed across groups and compared to the grand mean for all activities, more distinct differences emerged. It was at this juncture of the research that the potency of this solitary practice was redefined as deliberate practice in line with the definition provided earlier.

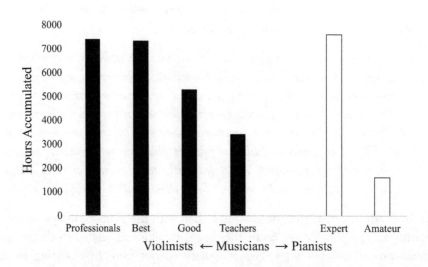

Figure 1.1 Hours accumulated in solitary practice by 18 years of age for professional, best, good, and music teacher violinists and expert and amateur pianists (adapted from Ericsson, Krampe, & Tesch-Römer, 1993).

Another finding that stood out was how sleep was rated high for relevance to overall performance improvement, which speaks to the intensity of deliberate practice. In practical terms, working on a weakness is more taxing than working on an aspect of performance that you are already sufficiently proficient (Eccles, Balk, Gretton, & Harris, 2020). The attention required is intense and is not sustainable over long periods of time, hence why sleep was found to be such an important factor in the biographies of the best and professional violinists and expert pianists, because it enabled them to engage and reengage in repeated bouts of deliberate practice. It is this repeated cycle of identifying rate-limiting factors of performance and committing hours of deliberate practice to overcoming such deficits that appears to separate the best from the rest (Eccles, Leone, & Williams, 2020; Ericsson, 2007).

What happened next?

Following on from the seminal paper in 1993, there was an immediate interest from researchers all over the world to determine whether deliberate practice as defined by Ericsson, Krampe, and Tesch-Römer (1993) was applicable to their respective domains. The first research to replicate the work of Ericsson et al. came from Canada in wrestling (Starkes & Hodges, 1996), followed by football and field hockey in Belgium (Helsen, Starkes, & Hodges, 1998). From there, many other researchers examined the potential impact of deliberate practice for the development of their experts in sports and other domains (for a review, see Baker & Young, 2014). The results from those first replication studies supported the relationship between the accumulated hours of deliberate practice and the level of expertise attained by their athlete participants. For the wrestlers, there was clear distinction between all levels from club to Olympic-standard athletes and the same for the footballers and field-hockey players from provincial, national, and international honours, thereby supporting the monotonic benefits assumption, albeit with less hours than the musicians had reported in 1993. In the years that followed, many other domains also showed support for this relationship with deliberate practice engagement (for other reviews, see Ericsson, 2018; Macnamara, Moreau, & Hambrick, 2016).

Other aspects of the original work did not receive the same immediate support. As far as the definition was concerned, both the enjoyment and effort tenets seemed to change to fit with the difference between practicing a musical instrument and practicing in a sporting environment. For example, one can practice the violin alone; however, it is all but impossible to practice wrestling alone, and the same can be said about a lot of other sports, bringing into question the solitary practice aspect of the definition. In addition, because of social contact with others during practice, especially in team sports, the enjoyment scores also appeared to be higher (Ericsson, 2003). However, it has been suggested that this inflation of enjoyment scores is the result of participants rating all practice activities and not just the specific deliberate practice elements of the session. The interference of time on the recall of what actually happened at the time of practice, especially if some manner of success was experienced in the interim period, has also been suggested as a reason for such differences (Coughlan, Williams, McRobert, & Ford, 2014).

Furthermore, the effort in some sports, such as football or hockey, appeared to benefit from adding a physical effort rating in the data collection process, in addition to the initial cognitive effort suggested by Ericsson et al. However, researchers appeared to agree with the general concept of what deliberate practice proposed and its relationship with the development of expertise (Ford, Hodges, & Williams, 2013). As more researchers attempted to replicate the 1993 study in their respective sports, the original definition became diluted and misapplied to suit each particular setting. Unfortunately, review papers that followed failed to identify that these subsequent studies deviated from the tenets and methodology and were not consistent with the definition of deliberate practice, and they themselves then surmised that deliberate practice was not all what it was suggested to be (Tucker, & Collins, 2013; Hambrick et al, 2014). Such misunderstandings are to be expected when a topic becomes so popular, almost a victim of its own success. But such interaction is welcome in academia, and those papers resulted in important responses from Anders Ericsson himself to ensure the narrative around deliberate practice didn't begin to suggest that it was a silver bullet for success and the only important factor for the development of expertise (Ericsson, 2013, 2014). Subsequent research that remained faithful to the original definition continued to show support for the tenets of deliberate practice as suggested by Ericsson et al. (Coughlan, Williams, & Ford, 2019). In fact, Ericsson (2020) has recently thought it necessary to explicitly delineate deliberate practice from other forms of practice, such as purposeful practice and naïve practice, which share very little, if any of the tenets of deliberate practice, though they are oftentimes included in datasets for research into what is required in becoming an expert (see Hambrick, et al., 2014; Macnamara, Moreau, & Hambrick, 2016).

Inevitably, as more research was conducted across domains and, in particular, across sports, the potential that the engagement in deliberate practice earlier in the development of young athletes might reap even greater rewards became a worrying trend (Ford, Ward, Hodges, & Williams, 2009). This led to some important push back from researchers in favour of a more age-appropriate approach to athletic development and gave rise to the on-going debate of early specialization versus diversification (for reviews, see Côté, Baker, & Abernethy, 2003, 2007). The suggestion to intensify children's practice to accelerate their competency and proficiency in the hope of developing more mature skills earlier, because of the expectation that it would lead to a more successful adult career in their sport of choice, appears to be a fallacy (Boccia, Cardinale, & Brustio, 2020; Kearney & Hayes, 2018).

Misunderstandings and misinterpretations of deliberate practice

10,000 hours quickly became synonymous with speaking about expertise and, in particular, deliberate practice. Coaches could be heard encouraging their players to rack up their hours of (deliberate) practice to get closer to attaining this magical number, after which expertise would be theirs to enjoy. Even as recently as 2013, *Nature Neuroscience* published an article titled: '10,000 hours to perfection with an opening line': 'It is widely accepted that expertise takes practice – hence the "10,000-hour rule" – that intense practice for up to 10 years distinguishes expert performers from merely good' (Miall, 2013, p. 1168). The first time anyone ever mentioned 'The 10,000-Hour Rule' was the author and journalist Malcolm Gladwell when he titled the second chapter in his best-selling popular science book *Outliers: The Story of Success* (Gladwell, 2008, p. 35). Gladwell goes on to write: 'In fact, researchers have settled on what they believe is the magic number for true expertise: ten thousand hours' (p. 40). In fact, they did not. He could not have predicted the fallout that followed, and to his credit, years later admitted the error of reducing deliberate practice to a quantifiable number and apologized to Anders Ericsson during a symposium.

This unfortunate misinterpretation of the work immediately quantified deliberate practice in a manner that was never stated in the research and, in fact, it took attention away from the quality-based aspects of deliberate practice and further lead to a misunderstanding about what constituted deliberate practice (Ericsson, 2016). The incredible momentum from Gladwell's book led Ericsson himself to suggest that journalists should leave research to the researchers (Ericsson, 2012), which, not surprisingly, sparked some backlash from within that community. There are still articles written announcing that deliberate practice is not the only answer to becoming an expert (Hambrick, Burgoyne, Macnamara,

& Ullén, 2018), even though Ericsson himself never said it was. Throughout the years, as he engaged with all-comers through commentary responses in journals (Ericsson, 2005, 2014) and staged debates with journalists and academics, he consistently reminded people that he never specified a number of required hours of deliberate practice, and as people continued to embellish his research, he repeated the simplicity of the original definition, but emphasized that it should not misguide people into thinking that deliberate practice was easy.

More recently, others have begun to outline the recurring mistruths and myths surrounding deliberate practice in the hope that when people engage in deliberate practice, they do so properly (Eccles et al., 2020). Some of these common misunderstandings are that deliberate practice is just practice, and that it is about out-practicing or out-working others (Eccles et al., 2020). Hopefully, with time, the benefits of deliberate practice in conjunction with other forms of practice will be understood and applied for the benefit of coaches and athletes (Ericsson, 2020; Ford, Coughlan, Hodges, & Williams, 2016; Ford & Coughlan, 2019).

The application of deliberate practice

There have been several studies that have directly applied the principles of deliberate practice (e.g. Coughlan, Williams, McRobert, & Ford, 2014; Coughlan, Williams, & Ford, 2019; Hyllegard & Yamamoto, 2005), and the findings have led to the development of some guiding frameworks for the application of deliberate practice to increase the likelihood of one's effort resulting in an overall performance improvement. One such guide is the ASPIRE framework which stands for Analyse, Select, Practice, Include feedback, Repetition, Evaluate (Ford & Coughlan, 2019 – see Table 1.1 for a working example in golf).

Another guide is the EXPERTS framework, which was proposed by Eccles et al. (2020) to outline the key principles of deliberate practice to those interested in applying them in their respective domain (see Table 1.2).

Both the ASPIRE and EXPERTS frameworks provide coaches, practitioners, and athletes with guiding principles to ensure that should they want to engage in deliberate practice, they actually do so. Oftentimes, athletes and coaches get transfixed by the rush of the practice effect of repetition without repetition and begin to chase perfection of execution as it acutely appears in the practice environment (Ranganathan, Lee, & Newell, 2020). Sport is highly variable in what it presents to an athlete in the heat of competition, and this variability should be reflected in practice (Araújo & Davids, 2011). Deliberate practice is effortful,

Table 1.1 Example of ASPIRE for improving the accuracy of a golfer's bunker play (adapted from Ford & Coughlan, 2019).

Step	Activity
1. Analyse	Performance analysis between coach and athlete identifies bunker shots as a rate-limiting variable for overall scores in competition, both personally and in comparison to other competitors.
2. Select	Select bunker shots, techniques, and tactics, as well as goals for a session in relation to what was identified in Step 1.
3. Practice	Design and do practice sessions for bunker shots on the golf course, with increasing variability and increasing representativeness of what may occur in a competitive setting, staying true to the sequencing of the game (i.e. finish out the hole).
4. Include feedback	Track practice and engage in feedback to determine how effective the effort invested is in leading to attaining the goals set in Step 2.
5. Repetition	Repetition of the task by repeating the process of finding a solution from different starting positions, for example, varying lies, in different bunkers, on different holes.
6. Evaluate	Performance analysis of bunker shots in competition relative to previous statistics and other competitors to provide feedback on how practice should be continued, progressed, and integrated.

not immediately rewarding, not inherently enjoyable and needs to be relevant to overall performance improvement (Ericsson, Krampe, & Tesch-Römer, 1993); this simple definition should serve as a constant checklist to athletes and coaches as to whether they are engaging in deliberate practice or not. The bespoke nature of deliberate practice is what makes it difficult to see how a group of people can engage in the same practice activity and be justified in thinking that each are engaging in deliberate practice. This is not to suggest that group practice is not important for them, it is just that it is unlikely to be deliberate practice (Ericsson, 2020).

To conclude this chapter on deliberate practice, it is worth noting that long before Ericsson, Krampe, and Tesch-Römer (1993) identified this potent type of practice, people had been engaging in it for decades, maybe even centuries, without the need for it ever to be defined. It is impossible to think that anyone has achieved expertise in any domain without engaging in many hours of deliberate practice. It is not a panacea for acquiring expertise, no one thing is, but without it, expertise will not be acquired. It is not for the faint-hearted, as it will test you

Table 1.2 The EXPERTS framework for the application of the principles of deliberate practice (adapted from Eccles, Leone, & Williams, 2020).

Principles of Deliberate Practice	Principle Description
Established training techniques	Deliberate practice gets the most out of established and proven methods of development
eXisting skills as building blocks	Deliberate practice enables incremental improvement to emerge through the modification of existing skills
Pushing the envelope	Deliberate practice encourages athletes to attempt tasks just outside of their current ability (Guadagnoli & Lee, 2004)
Enhancing mental representations	As skills improve, more sophisticated mental representations may develop
Responding to feedback	As skills improve, engaging in feedback is needed to avoid arrested development
Total application and focus	Deliberate practice demands intensity of application and focus unlike any other form of practice
Specific goals	Deliberate practice is relevant to overall performance improvement which benefits from clear and specific goal-setting

to the very limits of your motivation to stay involved in your sport of choice. The development of expertise is not a linear process, and there is little or no evidence to suggest that anybody has figured out a perfect approach for everyone. However, an understanding of the inter-relationship between all facets of performance and a holistic approach to connecting across the disciplines is a good place to start (Henriksen, Stambulova, & Roessler, 2010). One thing is for sure, deliberate practice never needed embellishing, sensationalizing, or mythologizing, because it is powerful and enriching just as it was, is, and will continue to be.

References

Araújo, D., & Davids, K. (2011). What is exactly acquired during skill acquisition. *Journal of Consciousness Studies, 18*, 7–23.

Baker, J., & Young, B. (2014). 20 years later: Deliberate practice and the development of expertise in sport. *International Review of Sport and Exercise Psychology, 7*, 135–157.

Boccia, G., Cardinale, M., & Brustio, P. R. (2020). Performance progression of elite jumpers: Early performances do not predict later success. *Scandinavian Journal of Medicine & Science in Sports, 31*, 132–139.

Colvin, G. (2008). *Talent is Overrated: What Really Separates World-Class Performers from Everybody Else*. London: Nicholas Brealey Publishing.

Côté, J., Baker, J., & Abernethy, B. (2003). From play to practice: A developmental framework for the acquisition of expertise in team sports. In J. Starkes & K. A. Ericsson (Eds.), *Expert Performance in Sports: Advances in Research on Sport Expertise* (pp. 89–110). Champaign, IL: Human Kinetics.

Côté, J., Baker, J., & Abernethy, B. (2007). Play and practice in the development of sport expertise. In G. Tenenbaum & R. C. Eklund (Eds.), *Handbook of Sport Psychology* (3rd ed., pp. 184–202). New York: Wiley.

Coughlan, E. K., Williams, A. M., & Ford, P. R. (2019). Lessons from the experts: The effect of a cognitive processing intervention during deliberate practice of a complex task. *Journal of Sport & Exercise Psychology, 41*, 298–308.

Coughlan, E. K., Williams, A. M., McRobert, A. P., & Ford, P. R. (2014). How experts practice: A novel test of deliberate practice theory. *Journal of Experimental Psychology: Learning, Memory, and Cognition, 40*, 449–458.

Coyle, D. (2009). *The Talent Code: Greatness Isn't Born. It's Grown. Here's How*. London: Bantam.

Eccles, D. W., Balk, Y., Gretton, T., & Harris, N. (2020a). 'The forgotten session': Advancing research and practice concerning the psychology of rest in athletes. *Journal of Applied Sport Psychology*, 1–22.

Eccles, D. W., Leone, E. J., & Williams, A. M. (2020b). Deliberate practice: What is it and how can I use it? *Journal of Sport Psychology in Action*, 1–11.

Epstein, D. (2014). *The Sports Gene: Inside the Science of Extraordinary Athletic Performance*. New York: Portfolio.

Ericsson, K. A. (2003). The development of elite performance and deliberate practice: An update from the perspective of the expert-performance approach. In J. Starkes & K. A. Ericsson (Eds.), *Expert Performance in Sport: Recent advances in Research on Sport Expertise* (pp. 49–81). Champaign, IL: Human Kinetics.

Ericsson, K. A. (2005). Recent advances in expertise research: A commentary on the responses to the special issue. *Applied Cognitive Psychology, 19*, 233–241.

Ericsson, K. A. (2007). Deliberate practice and the modifiability of body and mind: Toward a science of the structure and acquisition of expert and elite performance. *International Journal of Sport Psychology, 38*, 4–34.

Ericsson, K. A. (2012). The danger of delegating education to journalists: Why the APS Observer needs peer review when summarizing new scientific developments. Unpublished manuscript. Retrieved from http://www.psy.fsu.edu/faculty/ericsson

Ericsson, K. A. (2013). Training history, deliberate practice and elite sports performance: An analysis in response to Tucker and Collins review: What makes champions? *British Journal of Sports Medicine, 47*, 533–535.

Ericsson, K. A. (2014). Why expert performance is special and cannot be extrapolated from studies of performance in the general population: A response to criticisms. *Intelligence, 45*, 81–103.

Ericsson, K. A. (2016). Summing up hours of any type of practice versus identifying optimal practice activities: Commentary on Macnamara, Moreau, & Hambrick (2016). *Perspectives on Psychological Science, 11*, 351–354.

Ericsson, K. A. (2018). The differential influence of experience, practice, and deliberate practice on the development of superior individual performance of experts. In K. A. Ericsson, R. R. Hoffman, A. Kozbelt, & A. M. Williams, (Eds.), *The Cambridge Handbook of Expertise and Expert Performance* (pp. 745–769). Cambridge: Cambridge University Press.

Ericsson, K. A. (2020). Towards a science of the acquisition of expert performance in sports: Clarifying the differences between deliberate practice and other types of practice. *Journal of Sports Sciences*, *38*, 159–176.

Ericsson, A., & Pool, R. (2016). *Peak: Secrets from the New Science of Expertise*. London: The Bodley Head.

Ericsson, K. A., Krampe, R. T., & Tesch-Römer, C. (1993). The role of deliberate practice in the acquisition of expert performance. *Psychological Review*, *100*, 363–406.

Ford, P. R., & Coughlan, E. K. (2019). Operationalizing deliberate practice for performance improvement in sport. In N. J. Hodges & A. M. Williams (Eds.), *Skill Acquisition in Sport: Research, Theory and Practice*, 3rd Edition (pp. 183–199). London: Routledge.

Ford, P. R., Coughlan, E. K., Hodges, N. J., & Williams, A. M. (2015). Deliberate practice in sport. In J. Baker & D. Farrow (Eds.), *Routledge Handbook of Sport Expertise* (pp. 347–362). London: Routledge.

Ford, P. R., Hodges, N. J., & Williams, A. M. (2013). Creating champions: The development of expertise in sports. In S. B. Kaufman (Ed.), *Beyond Talent: The Complexity of Greatness* (pp. 391–314). Oxford: Oxford University Press.

Ford, P. R., Ward, P., Hodges, N. J., & Williams, A. M. (2009). The role of deliberate practice and play in career progression in sport: The early engagement hypothesis. *High Ability Studies*, *20*, 65–75.

Galton, F. (1869). *Hereditary Genius: An Inquiry into its Laws and Consequences*. London: Macmillan Publishers.

Gladwell, M. (2008). *Outliers: The Story of Success*. Boston, MA: Little, Brown and Company.

Guadagnoli, M. A., & Lee, T. D. (2004). Challenge point: Framework for conceptualizing the effects of various practice conditions in motor learning. *Journal of Motor Behavior*, *36*, 212–224.

Hambrick, D. Z., Burgoyne, A. P., Macnamara, B. N., & Ullén, F. (2018). Toward a multifactorial model of expertise: Beyond born versus made. *Annals of the New York Academy of Sciences*, *1423*, 284–295.

Hambrick, D. Z., Oswald, F. L., Altmann, E. M., Meinz, E. J., Gobet, F. & Campitelli, G. (2014). Deliberate practice: Is that all it takes to become an expert? *Intelligence*, *45*, 34–45.

Henriksen, K., Stambulova, N., & Roessler, K. K. (2010). Holistic approach to athletic development environments: A successful sailing milieu. *Psychology of Sport & Exercise*, *11*, 212–222.

Hyllegard, R., & Yamamoto, M. (2005). Testing assumptions of deliberate practice theory, relevance, effort, and inherent enjoyment of practice on a novel task. *Perceptual Motor Skills*, *101*, 283–294.

Kearney, P. E., & Hayes, P. R. (2018). Excelling at youth level in competitive track and field athletics is not a prerequisite for later success. *Journal of Sports Sciences*, *36*, 2502–2509.

Kearney, P. E., Comyns, T. M., & Hayes, P. R. (2020). Coaches and parents hold contrasting perceptions of optimal youth development activities in track and field athletics. *International Journal of Sports Science & Coaching*, *15*, 157–169.

Macnamara, B. N., Moreau, D., & Hambrick, D. Z. (2016). The relationship between deliberate practice and performance in sports: A meta-analysis. *Perspectives on Psychological Science*, *11*, 333–350.

Miall, C. (2013). 10,000 hours to perfection. *Nature Neuroscience*, *16*, 1168–1169.

Pitsiladis, Y., Wang, G., Wolfarth, B., Scott, R., Fuku, N, Mikami, E., He, Z., Fiuza-Luces, C., Eynon, N., & Lucia, A. (2013). Genomics of elite sporting performance: What little we know and necessary advances. *British Journal of Sports Medicine*, *47*, 550–555.

Ranganathan, R., Lee, M. H., & Newell, K. M. (2020). Repetition without repetition: Challenges in understanding behavioral flexibility in motor skill. *Frontiers in Psychology, 11,* 2018.

Tucker, R., & Collins, M. (2012). What makes champions? A review of the relative contribution of genes and training to sporting success. *British Journal of Sports Medicine, 46,* 555–561.

Ward, P., Belling, P., Petushek, E., & Ehrlinger, J. (2017). Does talent exist: A re-evaluation of the nature-nurture debate. In J. Baker, S. Cobley, J. Schorer, & N. Wattie (Eds.), *Routledge Handbook of Talent Identification and Development in Sport* (pp. 19–34). London: Routledge.

Williams, M., & Wigmore, T. (2020). *The Best: How Elite Athletes are Made.* London: Nicholas Brealey Publishing.

2 The Science of Fun in Sport

Fact over Fiction

Amanda J. Visek and Anna Feiler

Fun. This three-letter word carries an array of beliefs about its place in sport. Among many youth sport organizations and leagues, fun is believed to be central to the sport experience and a top priority in the delivery of programming early in children's motor development and athletic skill acquisition, thus the charge to 'make it fun'. Yet, when youth athletes mature and grow in their athleticism, thereby matriculating to higher levels of competitive play, fun as a focal point and an integral part of the sporting experience drops from the foreground to the background. Once intricately tied at younger ages and earlier stages of participation, fun and athletic development are increasingly regarded as mutually exclusive at both later ages and more advanced participation stages. What is more, regardless of an athlete's age, or their athletic prowess, very often they are subjected to sweeping generalities of what is believed to make playing sport fun for them, based none other than on their biological sex and gender identity. The binary expectations of what is fun for girls and women in sport, and what is fun for boys and men in sport, are as categorically different as the meaning attached to pink versus blue. These are just some of the many (mis) conceptions about fun.

This chapter is dedicated to dispelling these and other misunderstandings of fun. It draws on a developing body of research unpacking what it really means for athletes to have fun and the place it holds for them over the lifecycle of their athletic participation (i.e. the fun ethos). Herein, we first describe the fun ethos and the foundational research (i.e. the fun integration theory's FUN MAPS) on which it was established. Second, we forward a set of evidence-informed fun tenets, whilst dispelling prevailing misconceptions of fun. Third and finally, we provide practical recommendations, based on the current state of the scientific literature, to facilitate righting the errors of our thinking, believing, and coaching in sport.

The Fun Ethos

Fun is an immediate hedonic experience marked by positive affective states described as joy, pleasure, and satisfaction. In sport, it is such a critical experience, in part, because its allure is what draws many of us to participating for the first of times and it is the defining experience that has been key to maintaining the longevity of our involvement in sport over time (see Carpenter et al., 1993; Fraser-Thomas, Côté, & Deakin, 2008; Gardner, Magee, & Vella, 2016, 2017; Gould & Petlichkoff, 1988; Macdonald, Côté, Eys, & Deakin, 2011; Petlichkoff, 1992; Scanlan, Carpenter, Lobel, & Simons, 1993; Synder, 2014; Tuffey, Medbery, & Gould, 2006; Weinberg et al., 2000; Yungblut, Schinke, & McGannon, 2012). Thus, at its core, fun is a powerful experience that can drive the most sustaining form of motivation, that is, intrinsic motivation (see Deci & Ryan, 1987 and Ryan & Deci, 2017).

As we unveil later in the chapter, fun can be a pivotal component to motivating athletes to pursue the highest levels of sport. What, then, makes playing sport fun and how do we create and sustain these experiences? For years, a commonly held contention in sport has been that what makes playing fun for one athlete is nearly guaranteed to be different than what drives fun for another athlete. In other words, what is fun for one person has been regarded as distinctively unique as their psychological makeup and independent lived experiences. As individuals, by definition, we are considered discrete idiosyncratic persons separate from one another. This begs the question: is what makes playing sport fun for you all that different than what makes playing sport fun for us? Could there be universal tenets for what makes playing sport fun for all of us?

An emergent area of sport science research, the FUN MAPS, which have given rise to the data-informed fun integration theory and fun ethos, engaged youth athletes as expert informants to answer these very questions (e.g. Visek et al., 2015, 2020a, b). Based on the science conducted so far, among the most key findings has been the discovery that what makes playing sport fun may be far more universally similar among athletes (i.e. the fun ethos) than it is fundamentally different. Thus, the belief that fun is highly variable from athlete to athlete appears to be more fiction rather than fact.

Foundationally, fun, in sport, is an experience demarcated by 11 fun-factors (i.e. *Trying Hard* [e.g. trying your best, working hard, staying active, competing], *Positive Team Dynamics* [e.g. playing well together, supporting teammates], *Positive Coaching* [e.g. having knowledge of the sport, being encouraging, allowing mistakes while staying positive, giving clear consistent communication], *Learning and Improving* [e.g. being challenged, learning from mistakes, improving skills to play at the next level], *Games* [e.g. getting playing time, playing against an evenly matched team], *Practice* [e.g. having well-organized sessions, getting water breaks, including a variety of activities], *Team Friendships* [e.g. getting along with teammates, being part of team year after year], *Mental Bonuses* [e.g. keeping a positive attitude, winning], *Game Time Support* [e.g. having a referee that makes consistent calls, parents showing good sportsmanship], *Team Rituals* [e.g. showing team spirit; high-fiving, fist-bumping], and *Swag* [e.g. having quality gear and equipment, earning medals, wearing a cool uniform]), collectively comprised of 81 fun-determinants; select determinants are provided above in brackets for illustrative purposes – see Visek et al., 2015 for a full review of the fun integration theory's FUN MAPS and complete list of fun-determinants within each fun-factor. The fun ethos include a set of tenets that have evolved based on the developing research that has informed our current understanding of fun in sport, and amid doing so, dispels common misconceptions that have held permanence in sport, namely, that: (a) what is fun for female athletes is different than male athletes, (b) what is fun for older athletes is categorically different from younger athletes, and (c) the fun priorities of competitive sport athletes are radically different from recreational sport athletes. Next, we present the three evidence-informed tenets that have the potential to shift coaching in ways that optimize fun for all athletes.

Fun Tenets

The Fun Priorities of Athletes are Uniformly Similar, Regardless of Sex/Gender

Most recently, when investigating the fun priorities of athletes, a secondary-analysis study of the FUN MAPS by Visek et al. (2020b) found that girls and boys responded in remarkably similar ways. Among the top fun-factors for boys was *Trying Hard*, *Positive Team Dynamics*, and *Positive Coaching*, followed secondarily by *Learning and Improving*, *Games*, *Practice*, *Team Friendships*, *Mental Bonuses*, and *Game Time Support*. Of lesser importance were *Team Rituals* and *Swag*. For girls, the findings were the same. The results of this study, along with a large and established body of evidence in developmental psychology, neuroscience, and even behavioural neuroendocrinology continue to challenge sex- and gender-based binary beliefs and expectations (see Hyde et al., 2019 for further reading). The idea that females and males, or girls and boys, are so different from one another, and that these differences transcend most spheres of life (see Jones, 1990), including sport, is what has been termed the *gender differences hypothesis*. Overwhelmingly though, research has and continues to support the *gender similarities hypothesis* that posits females and males are comparably more similar than they are different. Despite an abundance of scientific support for the gender similarities hypothesis, what triumphs mainstream thinking, believing, and being, is the gender differences hypothesis.

For example, females are, and have been historically, characterized by gender stereotypes and sociocultural milieus which define them, in large, by their need for social relatedness. Thus, in sport, beliefs about what makes playing sport fun for them tends to centre around the quality of the relationships they have formed and the nature of their interpersonal dynamics with teammates. This is easily seen through internet search engines. Enter the terms *girls* or *women* or *female* with *sport* and *fun* and the images yielded are primarily of them huddled together, giggling, hugging one another, sitting arm-in-arm on the bench smiling, or celebrating together jumping up and down in unison. Conduct the same internet image search using the terms *boys* or *men* or *male* followed by *sport* and *fun* and the results are remarkably different. Boys and men are seen racing to the ball, battling for the puck, colliding, kicking hard, and challenging their opponents – images which exemplify beliefs that what makes playing sport fun for boys and men are related to being competitive, mastering skills, and achieving. More recently, we have begun to see images of girls and women that capture their athleticism; however, the images that define girls and women in sport (e.g. bonding with one another on the side-line), compared to boys and men in sport (e.g. competing), are still more disparate than they are similar.

When it comes to understanding how we are more similar than different, self-determination theory (Deci & Ryan, 1985, 2017), one of the most comprehensive and scientifically supported theories of motivation, posits there are three basic, universal psychological needs among all of us: (a) the need for autonomy (i.e. self-determination), (b) competence (i.e. mastery), and (c) social relatedness (i.e. interactions and relationships with others). Thus, if what drives motivation is more common than it is different, perhaps what makes playing sport fun is also more commonplace than it is different. In an empirical attempt to unveil the priorities of athletes when it comes to fun, Visek et al.'s (2020b) study observed *Trying Hard*, *Positive Team Dynamics*, and *Positive Coaching* were of top priority for both girls and boys; and in parallel with self-determination theory, close examination of the determinants that define the three aforementioned fun-factors exemplify our psychological need for autonomy, competence, and relatedness, respectively.

Further comparative analysis by Visek et al. also indicated girls and boys rated the importance of approximately 93% of the 81 fun-determinants similarly.

Meaning, they did not vary in how they rated the importance of determinants such as *trying your best, working hard, being active, getting playing time, being challenged, getting touches on the ball, learning from mistakes,* and *playing well* (see Visek et al., 2020b for full comparison review). Yet, despite the mounted evidence across numerous disciplines of science that support the gender similarities hypothesis, including sport science, the gender differences hypothesis – that is more fiction than it is fact – continues to be the generally accepted 'truth'. This, in turn, perpetuates the sociocultural and gender stereotypes that reinforce errors in our thinking that lead to false ideas and disparate ways in which girls and boys, and women and men, are coached.

The Fun Priorities of Athletes are Consistently the Same Across Age

The same study that refuted long-held ideas of what is most fun for girls versus boys (e.g. Visek et al., 2020b), also found the fun priorities of older athletes (i.e. U14–U19) to be extraordinarily like those of younger athletes (i.e. U9–U13). Moreover, the relative order by which older athletes and younger athletes rated, and thus ranked, the importance of the fun-factors mirrored the results observed between girls and boys; that is, *Trying Hard, Positive Team Dynamics,* and *Positive Coaching* were among the factors of primary importance, followed by *Learning and Improving, Games, Practice, Team Friendships, Mental Bonuses,* and *Game Time Support* which observed slight variances in rank order but were statistically found to be insignificant, and lastly *Team Rituals* and *Swag* holding importance, though less in comparison to the other nine fun-factors. When thoughtfully considering and calibrating what is fun for child athletes earlier in their sport participation years, evidence would suggest the same holds true for adolescent athletes. Additional research is needed to corroborate these findings to definitively conclude that fun is not implicated by biological age. Yet, the lack of age-related effects observed in the research, so far, aligns with the findings previously discussed regarding sex biology (i.e. females compared to males) and gender identity (i.e. girls compared to boys).

The Fun Priorities of Elite Athletes Mirror those of Recreational Athletes

When discussing fun in the context of the available sport options for young athletes, the word 'fun' finds itself holding multiple meanings entangled within one another. On the one hand, fun is regarded as a vital component of any athlete's experience because it maintains their involvement in sport (e.g. Fraser-Thomas, Côté, & Deakin, 2008; Gardner, Magee, & Vella, 2016, 2017; Gould & Petlichkoff, 1988; Snyder, 2014) and its absence is commonly known and empirically supported as the leading reason why athletes leave sport (e.g. Armentrout & Kamphoff, 2011; Durant et al., 1991; Fraser-Thomas, Côté, & Deakin, 2008; Gardner, Magee, & Vella, 2017; Petlichkoff, 1992; Weiss & Williams, 2004). Despite the essentialness of sport being a fun experience, the word takes on new, and at times, not so welcomed meaning, particularly in the context of discussions regarding its place in sport relative to athletes' level of play. For example, recreational sport is often touted 'for fun', whereas competitive sport is seen as 'for advancement'. Thus, the grassroots rec or house leagues are where athletes go to 'have fun' and the select travel and Olympic development programs are where they go to 'get to the next level'. The selection of one inherently implies an absence of the other (Martin, 2015) and this is especially apparent in organized sport (Visek et al., 2020b) where fun is not consistently viewed in our work-oriented and economics-based society as congruent with performance and higher-level sport (Bengoechea, Strean, & Williams, 2004; Henderson, Glancy, & Little, 1999; Visek et al., 2018, 2020b). Instead, fun can hold a negative connotation, and thus it is something to be feared and avoided (West, 2018) or only bestowed upon athletes as a reward at the end of practice for working hard or as a break from intense training when coaches let the athletes, finally, 'have some fun' (Bengoechea, Strean, & Williams, 2004).

In these contexts, fun is seen as a carefreeness (Ryan & Huta, 2009) akin to child's play defined by goofing off and fooling around, not paying attention or being on task, and generally slacking off and not playing hard. As such, it is associated with undermining athletic development (Bengoechea, Strean, & Williams, 2004; Visek et al., 2018; West, 2018), whereas the research conducted by Visek et al. (2015, 2020a, b) who engaged youth athletes in identifying all that is fun when playing organized sport tells a different story – that at the heart of fun is athletic development. A retrospective study of Olympians from across two quadrennia investigated (a) what motivated Olympians to get involved in sport early in their development and (b) what drove them to pursue the pinnacle of their sport. Findings indicated fun was a consistent factor in both the initiation and continued persistence to achieve the highest level possible (Snyder, 2014). Indeed, the results from this study underscore the significance of fun across the lifecycle of Olympians' participation, development, and performance in sport, and the findings from Visek et al. work highlight its role in the development of youth. Together, evidence suggests fun is a critical component at all stages of athletic development and can be considered a requisite element in developing elite and even Olympic athletes (Lundqvist & Sandin, 2014).

Additionally, in the same study that Visek et al. (2020) conducted a comparative analysis of the fun priorities of girls and boys, and younger and older athletes; they also compared recreational sport athletes and travel sport athletes. Based on the research shared herein, so far, it comes as no surprise that the fun priorities of travel sport athletes were remarkably like those of recreational youth athletes with no defining significant differences apart from 5 of the 81 fun-determinants that would be expected to play a more important role in the fun experiences of elite youth travel athletes. These included *practicing with specialty trainers/coaches, going to sports camps, staying in hotels for games and tournaments, traveling to new places to play*, and *playing in tournaments*. In fact, recreational athletes and travel athletes rated 94% of the 81 fun-determinants similarly regarding their degree of importance. Like the sex and age comparisons conducted, *Trying Hard, Positive Team Dynamics*, and *Positive Coaching* were of primary importance among both recreational and travel athletes, followed by *Learning and Improving, Practice, Games, Team Friendships, Game Time Support*, and *Mental Bonuses* of secondary importance and, finally, *Team Rituals* and *Swag* rounded out the factors of tertiary importance.

What Predisposes Misconceptions of Fun in Sport?

Unbeknownst to us on a conscious level, the sheer structure by which sport is organized leads us to errors in our thinking, which are the result of the ways in which we classify athletes into what are most often a binary sport classification system (e.g. sex [female or male], age [younger or older; U9–U19], level of play [recreational or select/elite]). Based on categorizing people on an identified trait, ideas about them based on that trait are preserved, including prejudices and stereotypes (Bigler & Liben, 2006, 2007) – and sport is wrought with categorization. Early in their participation, young athletes are sorted by their most salient biological traits (i.e. sex, age) and soon thereafter they are further sorted by their athletic traits (i.e. skill, playing level), and this carries on throughout their sporting years. Sorting them into binary 'this' versus 'that' implies both the presence and absence of one thing versus the other. According to Kahneman (2011), this is a result of the intuitively fast ways in which we think, which are based on existing schemas and biases we hold that can result in errors in our thinking. Indeed, sport's binary categorization system, and the ways in which the meaning of fun morphs and inverts depending on the context in which it is used (e.g. fun = goofing off, fun = key to athletic development), has contributed to misunderstanding of its meaning, and the misconceptions we hold about it for athletes based on traits such as sex/gender, age, and playing level.

Coaching Recommendations

Below are recommendations that align coaching practices with what it really means for athletes to have fun playing sport congruent with the state of the science:

- Make fun a focal point for all athletes' development in sport; it is critical to maintaining long-term participation as well as furthering athletic advancement.
- Remember that fun is not happenstance or coincidental, it must be fostered with intent to evoke the experience athletes describe as fun.
- Become familiar with the fun integration theory's 11 fun-factors and the 81 fun-determinants that define the factors; integrate them into practices/training sessions and competitive games.
- Shift binary-based coaching (e.g. sex/gender, age, playing level) that creates bias towards emphasizing differences to coaching approaches that recognize and appreciate the universality of athletes' fun-determinants and priority needs.
- For further reading on integrating fun in coaching practices, see Visek et al. (2018) and Arvinen-Barrow, Visek, & Barrow (2020).

References

Armentrout, S. M., & Kamphoff, C. S. (2011). Organizational barriers and factors that contribute to youth hockey attrition. *Journal of Sport Behavior, 34*(2), 121–136.

Arvinen-Barrow, M., Visek, A. J., & Barrow, A. (2020). Pidä hauskaa: Have fun! In M. L. Sachs, L. Tashman, & S. Razon (Eds.), *Performance Excellence: Stories of success from the Real World of Sport and Exercise Psychology*. Lanham, MD: Rowman & Littlefield.

Bengoechea, E. G., Strean, W., & Williams, D. J. (2004). Understanding and promoting fun in youth sport: Coaches' perspectives. *Physical Education and Sport Pedagogy, 9*, 197–214. https://doi.org/10.1080/1740898042000294994

Bigler, R. S., & Liben, L. S. (2006). A developmental intergroup theory of social stereotypes and prejudice. In R. V. Kail (Ed.), *Advances in Child Development and Behavior* (Vol. 34, pp. 39–89). San Diego, CA: Elsevier. https://doi.org/10.1016/S0065-2407(06)80004-2

Bigler, R. S., & Liben, L. S. (2007). Developmental intergroup theory: Explaining and reducing children's social stereotyping and prejudice. *Current Directions in Psychological Science, 16*, 162–166. https://doi.org/10.1111%2Fj.1467-8721.2007.00496.x

Carpenter, P. J., Scanlan, T. K., Simons, J. P., Lobel, M., & Brook, S. (1993). A test of the sport commitment model using structural equation modeling. *Journal of Sport and Exercise Psychology, 22*, 119–134. https://doi.org/10.1123/jsep.15.2.119

Deci, E. L., & Ryan, R. M. (1985). *Intrinsic Motivation and Self-determination in Human Behavior*. New York: Plenum.

Durant, R. H., Pendergrast, R. A., Donner, J., Seymore, C., & Gaillard G. (1991). Adolescents' attrition from school-sponsored sports. *The American Journal of Diseases of Children, 145*, 119–123. https://doi:10.1001/archpedi.1991.02160100051022

Fraser-Thomas, J., Côté, J., & Deakin, J. (2008). Examining adolescent sport dropout and prolonged engagement from a developmental perspective. *Journal of Applied Sport Psychology, 20*(3), 318–333. https://doi:10.1080/10413200802163549

Gardner, L. A., Magee, C. A., & Vella, S. A. (2016). Social climate profiles in adolescent sports: Associations with enjoyment and intention to continue. *Journal of Adolescent Psychology, 52*,112–123. https://doi:10.1016/j.adolescence.2016.08.003

Gardner, L. A., Magee, C. A., & Vella, S. A. (2017). Enjoyment and behavioral intention predict organized youth sport participation and dropout. *Journal of Physical Activity and Health, 14*(11), 861–865. https://doi:10.1123/jpah.2016-0572

Gould, D., & Petlichkoff, L. (1988). Participation motivation and attrition in young athletes. In F. Smoll, R. Magill, & M. Ash (Eds.), *Children in Sport* (3rd ed., pp. 161–178). Human Kinetics.

Henderson, K., Glancy, M., & Little, S. (1999). Putting the fun into physical activity. *Journal of Physical Education, Recreation & Dance, 70*(8), 43–45. https://doi.org/10.1080/07303084.19 99.10605706

Hyde, J. S., Bigler, R. S., Joel, D., Tate, C. C., & Van Anders, S. M. (2019). The future of sex and gender in psychology: Five challenges to the gender binary. *American Psychologist, 74*, 171–193. https://doi.org/10.1037/amp0000307

Jones, K. (1990). The gender differences hypothesis: A synthesis of research findings. *Educational Administration Quarterly, 26*, 5–37. https://doi.org/10.1177/0013161X90026001002

Kahneman, D. (2011). *Thinking, Fast and Slow*. New York: Farrar, Straus, and Girous.

Lundqvist, C., & Sandin, F. (2014). Well-being in elite sport: Dimensions of hedonic and eudaimonic well-being among elite orienteers. *The Sport Psychologist, 28*(3), 245–254. https://doi.org/10.1123/tsp.2013-0024

MacDonald, D. J., Côté, J., Eys, M., & Deakin, J. (2011). The role of enjoyment and motivational climate in relation to the personal development of team sport athletes. *The Sport Psychologist, 25*(1), 32–46. https://doi.org/10.1123/tsp.25.1.32

Martin, M. (2015). Assessing the sociology of sport: On gender identities in motion and how to de-essentialize difference(s). *International Review for the Sociology of Sport, 50*(4–5), 542–546. https://doi.org/10.1177%2F1012690214555165

Petlitchkoff, L. M. (1992). Youth sport participation and withdrawal: Is it simply a matter of fun? *Pediatric Exercise Science, 4*, 105–110. https://doi.org/10.1123/pes.4.2.105

Ryan, R. M., & Deci, E. L. (2017). *Self-determination Theory: Basic Psychological Needs in Motivation, Development, and Wellness*. New York: Guilford Press.

Ryan, R. M., & Huta, V. (2009). Wellness as healthy functioning or wellness as happiness: The importance of eudemonic thinking. *Journal of Positive Psychology, 4*, 202–204. https://doi.org /10.1080/17439760902844285

Scanlan, T. K., Carpenter, P. J., Lobel, M., & Simons, J. P. (1993). Sources of enjoyment for youth
sport athletes. *Pediatric Exercise Science, 5*, 275–285. https://doi.org/10.1123/pes.5.3.275

Synder, C. (2014). The path to excellence: A view on the athletic development of U.S. Olympians who competed from 2000-2012. In S. Riewald (Ed.), *Initial Report of the Talent Identification and Development Questionnaire to U.S. Olympians*. USOC Sport Performance and Coaching Education Divisions.

Tuffey, S., Medbery, R., & Gould, D. (2006). *Complete Report: Kids Tell Us What Is Fun*. Greensboro, NC: USA Swimming and the U.S. Ski and Snowboard Association. https://www.teamunify.com/akkkw/UserFiles/Image/Links/kids_tell_us_what_fun.pdf

Visek, A. J., Achrati, S. M., Mannix, H., McDonnell, K., Harris, B. S., & DiPietro, L. (2015). The fun integration theory: Toward sustaining children and adolescents sport participation. *Journal of Physical Activity & Health, 12*, 424–433. https://doi.org/10.1123/jpah.2013-0180

Visek, A. J., Ivarsson, A., Mannix, H., Lind, J., Altéus, C., Berktan, O., Werner, A., Borg, E., Enoksson, M. Stenling, A., & Learner, J. (2020a). *Toward Development of Sweden's Own FUN MAPS: A Cross-cultural Application to Inform Youth Sport Programming*. Presented at the Association for Applied Sport Psychology Annual Conference, Orlando, FL.

Visek, A. J., Mannix, H., Chandran, A., Cleary, S., McDonnell, K., & DiPietro, L. (2020b). Toward understanding youth athletes' fun priorities: An investigation of sex, age, and levels of play. *Women in Sport & Physical Activity Journal, 28*, 34–49. https://doi.org/10.1123/wspaj.2018-0004

Visek, A. J., Mannix, H., Mann, D., & Jones, C. (2018). Integrating fun in young athletes' sport experiences. In Knight, C. J., Harwood, C. G., & Gould, D. (Eds.), *Sport Psychology for Young Athletes* (pp. 7–13). Routledge. https://doi.org/10.4324/9781315545202

Weinberg, R., Tenenbaum, G., Mckenzie, A., Jackson, S., Anshel, M., Grove, R., & Fogarty, G. (2000). Motivation for youth participation in sport and physical activity: Relationships to culture, self-reported activity levels, and gender. *International Journal of Sport Psychology, 31*, 321–346.

Weiss, M. R., & Williams, L. (2004). The why of youth sport involvement: A developmental perspective on motivational processes: A lifespan perspective. In M. R. Weiss (Ed.), *Developmental Sport and Exercise Psychology: A Lifespan Perspective* (pp. 223–268). Morgantown, WV: Fitness Information Technology.

West, E. (2018). 10U Q&A: What's wrong with fun? American Development Model. USA Hockey. https://www.admkids.com/news_article/show/908348

Yungblut, H. E., Schinke, R. J., & McGannon, K. R. (2012). Views of adolescent female youth on physical activity during early adolescence. *Journal of Sports Science and Medicine, 11*, 39–50.

3 Communities of Practice

Common Misconceptions

Diane M. Culver, Tiago Duarte, and Don Vinson

The term 'Community of Practice' (CoP) is one of the most influential learning theories of recent times – and also one of the most misunderstood. In this chapter, we will delve into some of the myths surrounding CoPs in order to help you, the reader, better understand the nature and value of social learning. The University of Ottawa Research Group for Coach Development (see Bertram, Paquette, Duarte, & Culver, 2014) has been considered a hotbed for coach development research (Rangeon, Gilbert, & Bruner, 2012) – and could itself be described as a CoP. I (Diane) joined the group 25 years ago, and Tiago 11 years ago, both initially as graduate students. Over the years, our group has periodically welcomed researchers from other groups interested in social learning theory, and Don is one such person. When I initially joined the group, I was starting to explore Wenger's (1998) book for my doctoral research. I was part of this CoP of graduate students and professors who cared to make a difference for coach development. Once I became a professor in this group, I strived to continue this by bringing my knowledge of social learning theory to our meetings. During my time within the group, it has not been uncommon to hear the same misconceptions of CoPs we will discuss from graduate and undergraduate students who join our community. The following chapter presents some of these common misconceptions which serve to reinforce certain myths about CoPs. We will explore the extent to which the myths we have so commonly heard have a solid foundation. The chapter takes the form of a series of our recollections of discussions we have experienced over the last 25 years, with Tiago and Don voicing the perspectives of newer group members. The conversations are part historical and part current. In this manner, we will walk you through the major concepts related to CoPs and our developing understanding of these over the years since the publication of Wenger's (1998) seminal work *Communities of*

Practice: Learning, Meaning, and Identity. We begin by telling you something of the story of Tiago's first Ottawa research group meeting, with Diane giving her answer to the question 'are CoPs innovative?'

Diane: It is not fair to call a group of people who meet to reflect on a subject a *pedagogical innovation.* The ancient Greek philosophers were doing exactly that five centuries B.C., and even named it education. Of course, this form of education has influenced tremendously modern civilization, as witnessed by the spread of higher education organizations around the world. Then, as now, education is not just a matter of knowing but also of becoming – of better understanding the kind of person we want to be; education shapes our identities. Research has found coaches' lifelong experiences outside of the realm of coach education programmes have an important impact on who they are and what they have become (Taylor, Werthner & Culver, 2014). In particular, we started using constructivist theorists, such as Peter Jarvis, Jennifer Moon, and Etienne Wenger, to help us understand that as an individual learns, their identity changes, and they become a different person.

Tiago: (reflecting): When Diane mentioned these authors, I got excited. I knew a few of these names as she had sent me a list of articles and books before the beginning of classes. Among the recommended resources, I had started reading Wenger's book on CoPs (1998; today he is named WengerTrayner). I mentioned a quotation from the beginning of the book: 'CoPs are everywhere. We all belong to CoPs. At home, at work, at school, in our hobbies ... In laboratories, scientists correspond with colleagues, near and far, in order to advance their inquiries' (Wenger, 1998, p. 6). I could not wait to partake in as many CoPs as I could, such as the research group, the different courses I was enrolled in, the gym, and the university cycling club.

Diane (smiling as she took-in Tiago's enthusiasm): While I appreciate your excitement Tiago, you are falling into a common trap: That is, believing everything is a CoP.

Myth 1: Everything is a CoP

Diane: What Wenger meant by the quotation you referred to is that we all are involved in different CoPs in our daily lives, even if most of these are 'so informal and pervasive that they rarely come into explicit focus' (Wenger, 1998, p.7). Given the assumptions of social learning theory – that humans are fundamentally social beings, and that learning is at the core of our existence – it is understandable that this myth has become widespread. For many individuals, the concept is entirely intuitive, causing confusion. Indeed, most of the CoPs that we are involved in are organic, having not been purposefully nurtured. Misconceptions of what a CoP is have misled people; first, to assume that everything that brings people together is a CoP; and second, to underestimate what it takes to build and sustain a healthy CoP around a specific practice. Pertaining to the first of these misconceptions, for example, in our chapter about clarifying the concept of CoPs (Culver & Trudel, 2008), we mentioned that a sport team as a whole, including athletes and coaches, is not a CoP. Why? Because, despite the athletes and coaches having a common goal, such as winning the league, the practice of the athletes is not that of the coaches. For instance, athletes do not need to understand how to teach a certain sport skill; they only need to execute it. It is the coach's role to create the environment for this to happen. However, athletes also learn a lot from each other and can have norms that are different than those promoted by the coach. This is important for coaches to realize so that they do not deprive athletes of the opportunity to fully engage in the practice of becoming an athlete (Galipeau & Trudel, 2005).

Tiago: Okay. So now that we know a little of what is not a CoP, what exactly is a CoP?

Diane: To answer this, I will give you a reflection on the evolution of the concept. To start with, CoPs were not clearly defined. The seminal book by Wenger (1998) lacked a precise definition. Instead, the author listed 14 indicators that a CoP might be present. These included: a shared way of talking about the way 'things are done', members knowing what others know, shared jargon, quick set-up of problems to be addressed, and such. The existence of such indicators points to a certain extent to the presence of the three key dimensions of a CoP (i.e. mutual engagement, joint enterprise, and shared repertoire)[1]. Only a few years after the 1998 text, a broadly used definition appeared in a practical book for organizations: 'Communities of practice are groups of people who share a concern, a set of problems, or a passion about a topic, and who deepen their knowledge and expertise in this area by interacting on and ongoing basis' (Wenger, McDermott, & Snyder, 2002, p. 12).

Tiago: Okay, so now we have a clear definition of a CoP?

Diane: Yes, and no. I believe it will help to continue talking about the evolution of the theory. CoP has been the main concept of the social learning theory, but it is only part of it. In fact, CoPs can encompass one or more social learning spaces. These might include various personal networks, mentor–mentee pairs, task teams, and so on. For example, within an athlete CoP, a senior player may mentor a junior player, or the forwards may comprise a small CoP within the larger CoP (Christensen, Laursen, & Sorensen, 2011). The latest developments clarify the conditions making a CoP and those associated with the simpler, more pervasive concept of a social learning space (Wenger-Trayner & Wenger-Trayner, 2020). The main conditions shared by a CoP and a social learning space involve people engaging together concerning something they care to make a difference about, driving the learning agenda around that caring by paying attention to everything that happens, and engaging their uncertainty, as well as the centrality of meaning and identity. A CoP, however, requires that identity is associated with a shared practice, whereas in a social learning space, the common concern to make a difference is not tightly connected to a shared practice. For example, coach developer learning programmes frequently bring together practitioners for a specified period of time (e.g. 18 months) to engage with a series of workshops, debate ideas collaboratively, and draw on the support of designated mentors. Such programmes would probably most accurately be described as social learning spaces, rather than CoPs, because the practitioners are not usually engaged in a common practice (see Vinson, Huckle, & Cale, 2020). Furthermore, over time a social learning space may become a CoP, although this is not necessarily the objective of a social learning space.

Don: Why does this distinction matter?

Diane: The term CoP has become so well-used around the world in so many different disciplines that, like many influential learning theories, it has become over-simplified to the extent that it is not generating the value that it should and could. For example, members of CoPs do not have to agree with each other all the time – CoPs do not have to be harmonious!

Myth 2: CoPs often become echo chambers

Diane: In their most recent book, Etienne and Beverley Wenger-Trayner (2020) make a distinction, not evident in their earlier writing, between two different uses of the term CoP. They refer to the earlier conceptualization of CoPs (i.e. Lave & Wenger, 1991) as being **part of Phase 1** of the theory. Here, learning is shown as the trajectory into a CoP. Therefore, newcomers who are at the periphery of a community will learn and become core members as they engage with more experienced others and start their learning journey by doing simpler, minimal risk tasks involved with the practice (e.g. for apprentice tailors this might be sewing on buttons, and not cutting the cloth for a garment). Our research on CoPs for coach development has taught us that even all the coaches in a club do not always make a generative CoP, that is, one in which knowledge is negotiated and co-created by members. Some sport contexts, such as karate, where leadership is very hierarchical, are not conducive to a coach CoP (Culver & Trudel, 2008). The sensei is all powerful, therefore there is no possibility of coaches' co-creating knowledge as this would be challenging the status quo. This is the type of community described earlier in the chapter (see also Lave & Wenger, 1991), where apprentices participate in community as they gradually learn to become competent in a trade. A trade in which competence is usually proscribed by a master or set of masters. In this type of community, knowledge can become ossified. It is, therefore, *not a myth* that certain types of CoPs can result in the reproduction of existing practices, 'a history of social learning over time' (Wenger–Trayner & Wenger–Trayner, 2020, p. 31), without going beyond these in the creation of new knowledge (Cushion, 2008).

Don: So we need to look beyond Phase 1 to better understand the value of CoPs? What does this entail?

Diane: **Phase 2** of the theory refers to learning partnerships to develop a practice, and thus focuses on the CoP as a fertile space for learning and the development of practices. During the 2010s, Wenger-Trayner et al. realized that many of the challenges faced by a globalized world require the complicity of people from different areas of competence, thereby involving many CoPs and other social learning spaces, that is, a landscape of practice. Thus, **Phase 3** refers to the cross-boundary learning that occurs when different social learning spaces intersect in landscapes of practice. Such cross-boundary learning helps to address the following issue: 'It is difficult for CoPs to be deeply reflective unless they engage with the perspective of other practices' (Wenger-Trayner & Wenger-Trayner, 2015, p. 19).

Diane: With all that said, when some organizations come to us to create a CoP, we first must identify what their needs are, then decide if a CoP approach is suitable or if another approach, such as a landscape of practice perspective, might work better. For instance, we were involved recently in a project to promote gender equity and leadership development for women in sport (Culver, Kraft, Din, & Cayer, 2019). In this project, we took a landscape perspective with the aim of affecting change at different levels of the sport system. Funded federally, this project involved developing social learning leaders (one level), who facilitated a CoP for 12 sport leaders (a second level), each of whom was implementing a gender equity/leadership project within their respective organizations (a third level). A landscape approach afforded multiple instances of boundary crossing between the three levels. For instance, CoP members from two sports joined forces to create a new 'women in sport' conference for the coaches of the two sports. In so doing, they used the skills and connections made in the sport leaders CoP to create a new social learning space for their coaches. With a landscape approach, we sought to change the experiences of women and girls at the national, provincial, and regional levels.

Don: So, what you are saying is that sometimes to really create change, using social learning principles on multiple levels is easier.

Diane: This actually leads to another myth.

Myth 3: CoPs can be established overnight and are an easy solution

Tiago: I went to a coaching conference last week and the organizers had put a 'CoP' block in the programme from 5.30 to 6.30 pm each evening. Is there a problem with that?

Diane: I've seen those kinds of sessions too – they are really well-intended and are also evidence that people believe in the power of social learning, but ultimately this approach is too simplistic. This misconception stems from CoPs becoming a fad. Many people, and not just in sport, jumped (and are still jumping) on this seemingly simple, intuitive idea: that learning and change would happen if you assembled people with a common interest. However, as implied above, there is an art involved in framing and sustaining a CoP over time. Callary (2013) found that an ice skating club established a CoP without ever having heard of the concept. Although what Callary found was not easy, it sounded organic, but required deliberate work from the leadership to nurture a space for learning. Moreover, Culver, Trudel, and Werthner (2009) described a sport leader who was able to promote many changes to a sport organization from defying the rules and the status quo, to put athlete development at the core of coaching. However, Culver, Trudel, and Werthner's (2009) study revealed that, due to a lack of quality social learning leadership, the CoP lost its focus and was never able to really re-capture the initial vision. Vinson et al. (in press) found that it took many months for most members of the social learning space they investigated to really align to the group – and that some practitioners never moved beyond a rather superficial engagement. Facilitating social learning is not easy and takes a considerable investment in time.

Tiago: So as a social learning leader, I have to accept that some of my group might engage more than others?

Diane: Of course – these people are human beings! We have found that lots of social learning leaders focus immense energy and time in encouraging everyone to engage with the group. This mistake relates to the idea that members of a CoP are similar in characteristics and ways of thinking. While historically, as in the times of the medieval craft guilds, practice was relatively unchanging, the twenty-first century world is a global one. Virtually all CoPs are permeable and require a high degree of openness and agility to respond to the demands of the times. Therefore, this is a very important misconception, because it is directly tied to learning and the production of knowledge. If a CoP is to thrive, there needs to be a healthy amount of debate around meaning and the application of knowledge to practice. And, as noted above, injections of different perspectives are essential. It is the cycles of collective and individual critical reflection and action that lead to the co-creation of new ways of doing things (see Kraft, Culver, & Cayer, 2020).

Tiago: When I was leading a CoP with Canadian wheelchair coaches who were in competition with one another, one of coaches said, 'So, you are saying that we should share our secrets with the people we are trying to beat? That will never work!'. Can social learning be valuable in competitive situations?

Diane: When winning is what counts, it is not hard to see how a learning situation that relies on sharing and openness might be a challenge. Stories of successful coaches guarding the secrets of their success are very believable (Lemyre, Trudel, & Durand-Bush, 2007). In the world of professional and high performance sport, where keeping one's job is more often than not dependent on a winning record, one can imagine that a CoP of such coaches might be a real challenge. This myth is, therefore, partly true. Research has demonstrated that some highly competitive coaches do belong to CoPs; however, this is usually when the coaches are not directly competing against each other. An exception is the baseball league from Culver, Trudel, and Werthner's (2009) study mentioned above, where the technical director took a very strong role to structure the whole league and facilitate the co-operation between the coaches to develop all the athletes. Vinson, Huckle, and Cale (2020) reported that international sports coaches felt they were able to learn more by engaging in a social learning space with coaches from sports other than their own because they felt they were not going to be judged in relation to their technical competence. Moreover, Duarte, Culver, and Paquette (2021) reported that after 12 months together, despite initial concerns, competitive coaches reported they were impressed to see how much the members of the community were willing to share. NCCA women coaches would meet with coaches from other sports at their same university (Bertram, Culver, & Gilbert, 2016), which rendered considerable value for them and their university sport programmes.

Don: I am getting the idea that each social learning space has its own characteristics which influence how they should be managed. Right?

Diane: Right! The formulation and facilitation of each CoP is unique. No two CoPs will be the same, which is actually easy to understand when one recognizes that it is the individuals who make up the space, and the difference they want to make is not uniform. For instance, one of the very innovative ways that the concept of social learning has been used for coach development are the learning tours organized for Cricket Australia high-performance coaches. These tours involved coaches who did compete against each other, travelling together for about a week. The driving theme of these tours was how to create a culture of excellence, a topic of mutual interest (Culver, Holder, & Rynne, 2020).

Tiago: It appears that understanding all of this complexity is going to require considerable expertise on the behalf of the social learning leader?

Myth 4: CoPs require a 'master' practitioner as leader

Diane: The response to this myth provides some tips for sustaining a CoP or social learning space. While you need to do your homework about the CoP context and who will be its members, you do not need to be a content expert to facilitate a CoP. That is, if you are facilitating a CoP of para-athletics coaches, for example, you do not need to be an expert coach of para-athletics, but you need to understand the lay of the land and who the key individuals involved are. A good general understanding of work of a para-athletics coach is very helpful. You absolutely do need to understand how to support social learning. For a start, as with any group, it is good to establish some ground rules. The most important of these is to be sure that the CoP is a safe space for all members to express themselves. As a head coach said at the end of a six-month CoP initiative, 'One thing is for sure, you have to leave your ego at the door!' (Culver, 2004). This is very important, especially if you have power imbalances in your CoP (i.e. a head coach with assistants and other coaches supervised by this head coach). If CoP members do not feel they can be vulnerable (e.g. sharing what they do not know), learning will be hindered (Wenger-Trayner & Wenger-Trayner, 2015). Social learning, as intuitive and innate as it may be for humans, is not the learning paradigm that most people are accustomed to; think of the traditional education most of us have experienced that is teacher-driven.

Don: What are some of the ways to make participating in a CoP worthwhile for coaches?

Diane: There are many other things to consider but the most important is to create value for the members. To start, it is often worthwhile to explore with the participants their learning theory, especially given what we said above about traditional education being how most people perceive learning. In social learning spaces, the curriculum is a learning versus teaching one, driven by the needs of the group. In our experience, coaches are giving their time to participate in a CoP, because they are passionate about their practice, but coaches have a lot on their plates. Whether they are paid professionals or volunteers, coaches are busy people. The best way to be ensure value is created for your CoP members is to keep the focus of the CoP activities centred on their learning. Often, we will start our CoP activities with an exercise to brainstorm such learning needs by dividing members into small groups and having them agree on their needs, writing these on post-it notes, and bringing the notes back to the large group to put on a wall to be voted on by all (Kraft, Culver, & Cayer, 2020). If you are meeting online, there are multiple tools that you can use for such activities. Whatever you decide, it is imperative to create a shared learning space online, even when meeting in person. We use Google docs or the whiteboard functions in Zoom or Microsoft Teams for shared reflections that members contribute to during and between meetings. As a facilitator, you need to be sure that the group pays attention to these reflections and loops back to check on the effects of this shared learning. This is an essential part of creating value in social learning spaces.

Tiago: So in other words, a critical role for the social learning facilitator is to help the participants carry the group reflections to their practice and bring the effects back to the group.

Don: Let's reflect on our list of the important myths and their practical repercussions.

Summary and Conclusion

Myth 1: Everything is a CoP. Myth busted! CoPs have become an often-misunderstood fad. Although we have no interest in 'policing' what is and what isn't a CoP, we have discussed that the most valuable social learning spaces and CoPs feature several powerful constructs: (a) practitioners who come together because they care to make a difference, (b) pay attention to everything that happens, and (c) engage their uncertainty. Only certain groups feature such constructs, and these are elements which underpin the group's capacity to thrive. It is also worth noting that the Wenger-Trayners have never suggested that social learning spaces and CoPs are the only way of helping practitioners learn but rather might be a helpful lens to better understand professional development in certain contexts and conditions.

Myth 2: CoPs often become echo chambers. A partial myth. CoPs might become echo chambers or feature-ossified practice without careful nurturing. Social learning leaders need to ensure the CoP is an environment that welcomes different perspectives. Social learning leaders should plan for criticality and recognize that the space needs to be safe but progressive. The social learning theory is continually evolving – so being a social learning leader requires a specialized, and agile, skillset.

Myth 3: CoPs can be established overnight and are an easy solution. Myth busted! Social learning leadership requires substantial investment on a number of levels. Framing and planning group interactions is a complex and challenging task which requires careful thought on a continuous basis. Furthermore, social learning takes considerable time, and so social learning leaders need to be committed to the task for the long-term. In order for each group to thrive, social learning leaders should also appreciate that every group requires bespoke consideration.

Myth 4: CoPs require a 'master' practitioner as leader. A partial myth. A healthy CoP can benefit from a social learning facilitator; however, that role does not require an experienced person within the field. That said, the facilitator must be prepared to manage power imbalances within the social learning space to be sure that every voice is heard. Social learning leadership remains something that is challenging and which requires considerable investment of time, thought, and energy.

Diane, Don, and Tiago: We believe social learning theory has enabled us to better understand the professional learning of so many coaches and coach developers over the last 25 years. The concepts underpinning the theory are complex, but extremely powerful, and we will continue to wrestle with them as we care to make a difference in coach development. Our hope is that you will also care to make a difference in your communities and will be able to lean on the profound insights to be found in social learning theory to enhance your practice.

Note

1 Mutual engagement refers to the interactions of CoP members while negotiating the meaning of their joint enterprise. A shared repertoire comprises the tools, stories, routines, and general ways of doing things that are developed over time by the CoP, and that members must know to be full members of the CoP.

References

Bertram, R., Gilbert, W., & Culver, D. (2016). Using appreciative inquiry to create high-impact coach learning: Insights from a decade of applied research. *Practitioner, 18*(2), 59–65. doi: 10.12781/978-1-907549-27-4-9

Bertram, R., Paquette, K., Duarte, T., & Culver, D. (2014). Assessing the value created through participating in a graduate studies community of practice. *Transformative Dialogues: Teaching & Learning Journal, 7*(1), 1–14.

Callary, B. (2013). Coaches create and sustain a community of practice. *PHEnex Journal, 4*(3), 1–13.

Christensen, M. K., Laursen, D. N., & Sørensen, J. K. (2011). Situated learning in youth elite football: A Danish case study among talented male under-18 football players. *Physical Education and Sport Pedagogy, 16*(2), 163–178.

Culver, D. M. (2004). *Enriching Knowledge: A Collaborative Approach between Sport Coches and a Consultant/Facilitator*. Doctoral dissertation, University of Ottawa, Canada.

Culver, D. M., & Trudel, P. (2008). Clarifying the concept of communities of practice in sport. *International Journal of Sports Science and Coaching, 3*(1), 29–32.

Culver, D. M., Holder, D., & Rynne, S. R. (2020). Travel-based learning: Study tours for high-performance coaches. In B. Callary, & B. Gearity (Eds.), *Coach Education and Development in Sport: Instructional Strategies* (pp. 129–140). New York: Routledge.

Culver, D. M., Kraft, E., Din, C., & Cayer, I. (2019). The Alberta women in sport leadership project: A social learning intervention for gender equity and leadership development. *Women in Sport and Physical Activity Journal, 27*(2), 110–117. doi: 10.1123/wspaj.2018-0059

Culver, D. M., Trudel, P., & Werthner, P. (2009). A sport leader's attempt to foster a community of practice. *International Journal of Sports Science & Coaching, 4*(3), 365–383. doi: 10.1260/174795409789623900

Cushion, C. (2008). Clarifying the concept of communities of practice in sport: A commentary. *International Journal of Sports Science & Coaching, 3*(1), 15–17.

Duarte, T., Culver, D. M., & Paquette, K. (2021). Assessing the value created in a social learning space intervention: Four vignettes of parasport coaches. *International Sport Coaching Journal, 1*(aop), 1–14. doi: 10.1123/iscj.2020-0006

Galipeau, J., & Trudel, P. (2005). The role of athletics, academic, and social development of student-athletes in two varsity sport teams. *Applied Research in Coaching and Athletics, 20*, 1–14.

Kraft, E., Culver, D. M., & Cayer, I. (2020). Communities of practice: A how-to model for building social learning spaces. Retrieved from https://coach.ca/sites/default/files/2020-10/CoP%20FINAL-EN.pdf

Lave, J., & Wenger, E. (1991). *Situated Learning: Legitimate Peripheral Participation*. New York: Cambridge University Press. doi: 10.1017/CBO9780511815355

Lemyre, F., Trudel, P., & Durand-Bush, N. (2007). How youth-sport coaches learn to coach. *The Sport Psychologist, 21*(2), 191–209. doi: 10.1123/tsp.21.2.191

Rangeon, S., Gilbert, W., & Bruner, M. (2012). Mapping the world of coaching science: A citation network analysis. *Journal of Coaching Education, 5*(1), 83–113. doi: 10.1123/jce.5.1.83

Taylor, S., Werthner, P., & Culver, D. M. (2014), A case study of a parasport coach and a life of learning. *International Sport Coaching Journal, 1*, 127–138. doi.org/10.1123/iscj.2013-0005

Vinson, D., Huckle, V., & Cale, A. (2020). "I've had a magical journey": Understanding how international sports coaches learn through cross-sport boundary encounters. *Sports Coaching Review*, 1–26.

Vinson, D., Simpson, H.-J. & Cale, A. (in press) "I felt I'd lost myself as a coach and not really knowing who I was": Coach Developer learning as negotiating identity through engagement, imagination and alignment, *Educational Review*.

Wenger, E. (1998). *Communities of Practice: Learning Meaning and Identity*. New York: Cambridge University Press.

Wenger, E., McDermott, R. A., & Snyder, W. (2002). *Cultivating Communities of Practice: A guide to Managing Knowledge*. Boston, MA: Harvard Business School Press.

Wenger-Trayner, E., & Wenger-Trayner, B. (2015). Learning in a landscape of practice: A framework. In E. Wenger-Trayner, M. Fenton-O'Creevy, S. Hutchinson, C. Kubiak, & B. Wenger-Trayner (Eds.), *Learning in Landscapes of Practice: Boundaries, Identity, and Knowledgeability in Practice-based Learning* (pp. 13–29). New York: Routledge.

Wenger-Trayner, E., & Wenger-Trayner, B. (2020). *Learning to Make a Difference: Value Creation in Social Learning Spaces*. Cambridge: Cambridge University Press. doi:10.1017/9781108677431

4 A 'Fundamental' Myth of Movement with a 'Functional' Solution

James R Rudd, Jonathan D Foulkes, Mark O'Sullivan, and Carl T. Woods

Over the last two centuries, there has been a belief that coaching and physical education should be informed by a blend of experiential and empirical knowledge (Bailey et al., 2018). The challenge we face, though, is that whilst these forms of knowledge coexist and entangle to inform an individual's pedagogical practices, they operate on very different timescales. For example, stage-based models of movement skill that prioritize the acquisition of idealized, *fundamental* 'techniques' are still common to many national sporting policy documents. This manifests in many coaches and teachers, often having been coached themselves by such linearized approaches, to continue to draw on such experiential knowledge to instil the *fundamentals* into the youth athletes of today. Thus, the challenge is in overcoming these 'myths of yesterday' to progress into the 'truths of today'. Namely, the movement science literature stage-based models were contemporary in academic texts books in the early to mid-twentieth century. The myths of 'fundamentals' emerged from mid-to-end twentieth-century motor learning literature, grounded in the idea that practitioners must reduce the amount of information in an environment to assist the learners' brains in processing information. At the end of this chapter, we provide a contemporary understanding of movement learning, calling for a shift in coaching practice that moves from 'fundamental' to *functional*. That is, we call for a shift from reductionist applications to facilitating emergent functional relationships between the performer and the constraints of their environment (Renshaw & Chow, 2018).

Fundamental Movement Skills

Fundamental movement (motor) skills are considered to be the foundational skills that enable the acquisition and development of more complex skills, often required for participation in many organized and non-organized physical activities for children and adolescents (Seefeldt, 1980). In the simplest terms, they are the foundational stones from which all movement is to be built upon. The premise is that achieving mastery of a group or set of fundamental movement skills means a performer will become both a versatile and highly skilled mover across a wide range of physical activity and performance environments. It is a widely held assumption across the sporting community that once a child or adult has 'mastered' the fundamentals of a given sport or activity, they will then be able to advance to competitive game play, where they can be taught complexities of the game, such as tactics and strategy.

Despite these long-held assumptions, the concept of fundamental movement skills has, in recent years, been critiqued for its – ironically – lack of theoretical foundation (Almond, 2014). Moreover, its ontological basis is dualistic, viewing movements as separate to or detached from the context in which they emerge, thereby neglecting the essential embodied–embedded nature of learning. To that end, the aim of this chapter is to explore the conceptual and theoretical roots of fundamental movement skills, and by doing so, begin to appreciate how traditional approaches to motor learning have tacitly reinforced traditional sport coaching pedagogical practice. The second part of this chapter will explore how the contemporary motor learning theory of ecological dynamics moves us to appreciate the *functional* nature of movement skills, leading to the reconceptualization of fundamental movement skills to *functional movement solutions*. Finally, we explore the wider ramifications of an ecological approach to how we conceptualize learning and sport coaching practice.

'The Roots of The Tree': Where it originated

For much of the twentieth century, the dominant theories of skill learning were stage or stepped theories of learning, and the information processing theory. Thus, we start with a brief insight into both of these theoretical constructs.

Maturational stage perspective of motor development (1925–1960s)

Movement scientists of the early twentieth century believed that the development and learning of movement skills were first driven by genetics (nature) and that once a rudimentary form was developed further learning was driven by the environment (nurture). The maturational stage perspective categorizes movement skills as being in one of two stages: either phylogenetic or orthogenetic movement patterns. Phylogenetic movement patterns, such as walking, develop without assistance as they are integral for interaction with our surroundings and essential for the survival of the human species. Orthogenetic motor skills, on the other hand, reflect socially driven motor skills which are not required in order to function in normal everyday activity and, as a result, are more affected by the practice of complex movements, for example skills such as an overarm throw or tennis serve (Magill, 2011). However, as pointed out by Wickstrom (1977), it becomes hard to distinguish between phylogenetic and orthogenetic skills once a child has mastered walking. For example, throwing has been categorized as phylogenetic, as a rudimentary form which will develop without practice and instruction (e.g. Espenschade & Eckert, 1967).[1] A possible reason for this confusion, as pointed out by Langendorfer and Roberton (2002), is that phylogenetic skills are driven by genetics, and as such, a rudimentary throwing technique would be regarded as predominantly phylogenetic, while a masterful throwing pattern would be considered orthogenetic. This perspective could be applied to all movement skills, as argued by Gallahue, Ozmun, and Goodway (2012). In summary, the maturational stage perspective sets out that fundamental movement skills are driven by genetics until children possess a rudimentary motor pattern (orthogenetic), and that they will only progress to mastery (orthogenetic) with opportunity for practice, instruction, and modelling (McKenzie, Alcaraz, Sallis, & Faucette, 1998).

Information-processing theory (1960s–2000s)

The information-processing theory moves away from a maturational world view of movement skills towards a more cognitive-oriented theoretical explanation as to *where* and *how* children learn movement skills. Specifically, this theoretical stance moves away from the stage approach (as seen in the maturational stage perspective), as it does not view early learning as being driven by genetics, but rather by the processing power of our brains (Summers & Anson, 2009). It can be said that the information-processing theory was a more useful theory for coaches and practitioners as it provides a pedagogical template for how a practitioner could support the learning of movement skills. Despite critiques of the theory, which we will go onto unpack shortly, it is still the dominant foundational theory for teaching and coaching in sport at all levels.

Information-processing theory postulates that information enters an individual through the sensory system (e.g. visual, auditory, proprioceptive) and, like a computer, is encoded and stored in either short- or long-term memory, depending upon the importance of the information. The central nervous system acts as the 'hardware' whose function is to order, monitor, select, and organize the information, which dictates an internalized prescription of movement, coded as symbolic knowledge structures (Anson, Elliot, & Davids, 2005). Information-processing theory, thus, drives a top-down approach to movement with a construct located inside the brain, such as a schema or a mental representation (Schmidt, 1975). This representation is consolidated as a result of the learning process so that a plan of action can occur before a movement emerges. This approach holds with the premise that learning is reflective of the maturation of a mental model and is a gradual linear process (Wulf & Lewthwaite, 2016; Wulf, Shea, & Lewthwaite, 2010; Wolpert & Flanagan, 2010). This theory posits that children become skilled movers through consistent repetition of a skill, progressing through three observable stages of learning: cognitive, associative, and autonomous, as they consolidate a mental representation. In the cognitive stage, the child is overwhelmed by a wealth of information. The child's full attention is focused on trying to understand the 'fundamentals' – in other words, the demands of the goal-directed movement and the elaboration of a plan of action (i.e. the movement response). This cognitive stage is characterized by high attentional/cognitive load, whilst execution is effortful, erratic, and full of errors. In the associative stage, the child understands the 'basics' and tries to gradually reduce the discrepancy between the intended and the actual performance (i.e. reduce variability in the movement) by means of repeated practice, leading to a reduction in attentional demands meaning the brain has more processing power for more tactical and technical information. In the final stage of learning – the autonomous stage – the execution of the goal-directed movement or skill typically involves a minimal number of conscious thought processes, whereby accurate and coordinated movements are performed autonomously. The child is now understood as possessing a great deal of cognitive capacity to take on more challenging aspects of the game.

A 'Well-Trodden Path': The rise of the traditional approach to sport coaching and physical education

The traditional approach to the motor learning process has led to the belief that to teach movement skills, a qualified supervisor/teacher/coach is needed to prescribe a putative, 'ideal' movement pattern to speed up the learning process by reducing any deviations from these technical templates. This model of learning is still dominant and has manifested itself in sports programmes across the globe. Traditionally, it takes the guise of being structured through the division of a task into an introductory activity, followed by a skill/drill practice phase where the focus is on the rote repetition of a technique or aspects of it (see example linear lesson plan in Figure 4.1). In ideal conditions when children have mastered the skill, they finish with a game or performance routine.

The aim of this linear pedagogy is to teach 'technical proficiency', as it emphasizes a technique first orientation, wherein optimal techniques are learned 'before the introduction of rules and game play' (Blomqvist et al., 2001). The teaching and learning experience for the child includes both prescriptive actions

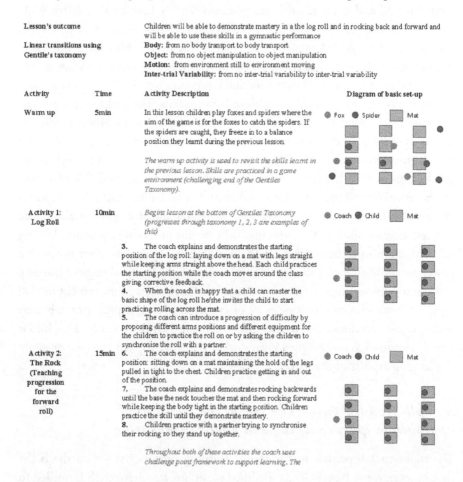

Figure 4.1 Example of linear gymnastics lesson plan, common practice in physical education, and teacher training.

(following technical demonstrations and instructions from the teacher/coach) and repetitive actions to try to replicate the 'optimal' technique, where variability is reduced until a performer can execute a motor skill efficiently and reliably (Schmidt et al., 2018). Verbal feedback is often a one-way, 'top-down' process, with the teacher *telling* the child what they are doing incorrectly and proposing a different (and presumed to be better or 'correct') way of skill development (see Box 4.1 for pedagogical principles). From the learners' perspective, the experience can be highly prescriptive, as they receive constant instructions/corrective feedback for reproducing different forms of movement or patterns of play (Davids et al., 2012; Chen, Martin, Ennis, & Sun, 2008). Meaning, the coach/teacher seeks to transmit knowledge about how something 'should' be done into the minds of the child to be consolidated, stored, and rolled out when the timing is 'right'. Thus, it is arguable that the rigidity and one-size-fits-all nature of this approach leaves little room for emotionally engaged and motivated children.

Box 4.1 Four common pedagogical principles of information-processing theory.

(1) There is a correct optimal movement pattern for each fundamental movement skill.

(2) Movement skills are broken down or simplified into key components of a skill for learning, as performing an optimal movement pattern is often beyond the reach of children who are in the early stage of learning a skill.

(3) Movement variability (or error) is viewed as noise in the system, which the child must reduce in their quest towards mastery of a skill.

(4) Focus of attention when performing a movement skill can be implicit or explicit and is dependent on what stage of learning a child is currently at.

'Fitting the Jigsaw': Coaching as a compartmentalized practice

The information-processing theory is ontologically dualist, as factors which may influence the development of fundamental movement skills, such as strength, flexibility, reaction time, are viewed as independent to the cognitive development of schema. Fleishman (1975), for example, stated that there are a finite set of human abilities that underlie all performances of a task. The 9 motor abilities are largely physical abilities and comprise static strength, static flexibility, dynamic strength, explosive strength, trunk strength, dynamic flexibility, gross body coordination, gross body equilibrium, and stamina (Fleishman, 1975). Schema theory and the work by Fleishman (1975) are considered independent but complementary to one another, in that if you can develop strength, it will likely be complementary, but not necessarily essential for skill execution. This understanding about the relationship between abilities and perceptual motor programmes has been questioned by Esther Thelen (1989) and other dynamical system theorists (e.g. Scott Kelso, 1995). Specifically, Thelen found that an infant's walking gait is constrained by overall body mass and leg strength, with these factors directly implicating walking ability. This suggested that motor abilities are not underlying, innate, or separate from perceptual skill development, but rather are entangled in the learning process.

Box 4.2 Further limitations of information-processing theory.

Another major limitation of the information-processing theory is the lack of clarity around the principle of changes in the hypothetical cognitive structure (trace, schema), wherein correlated changes in performance as a result of practice can only be inferred (Kelso et al., 1995; Whiting & Vereijken, 1993). This is known as the 'black box' approach, where we see information go into the system and the resultant movement outcome(s), but we cannot be sure what has happened in the interim within the 'black box', failing to identify wherein the brain particular skills are stored and updated. This limitation has been addressed partially by recent advancements in neural imaging technologies which have indicated that both sensory and motor areas of the brain reveal a high degree of plasticity and are capable of sending signalling to the central nervous system to undertake complex skills (Blake, Byl, & Merzenich, 2002; Mogilner et al., 1993). An additional limitation of the information-processing approach is that these theories are based on highly controlled experiments and manipulation of individual variables which are not representative of the real-world setting (Vilar, Araújo, Davids, & Renshaw, 2012). There is an alternative approach to motor learning that

---

> focuses on how these underlying mechanisms interact and change during the course of learning – Ecological Dynamics (Davids, 1994).

'Toward a Different Path': Contemporizing fundamental

Dynamical systems theory and ecological psychology (1990–present)

Dynamical systems theory moves the premise of fundamental movement skills to *functional movement solutions*. This is because it views human movement as a highly intricate network of co-dependent sub-systems (e.g. respiratory, circulatory, nervous, and perceptual) that are comprised of a large number of interacting complex components (e.g. blood cells, oxygen molecules, bone) (Button et al., 2020). The dynamical systems approach deemphasizes the top-down approach skill learning (Ribeiro et al., 2019). This means that motor learning becomes a continual process of shifting the balance between ecological information (omnipresent within our environment) and intrinsic dynamics of the individual (e.g. the capacity that exists at the time a new task is to be learned), as the system becomes attracted towards an emergent, stable pattern (Kugler & Turvey, 1987).

Ecological psychology postulates a constant, cyclical use of information to regulate an animal's behaviour (Gibson, 1979). For example, as human animals move about their econiches (e.g. playscapes, schoolyards, football pitches, basketball courts, aquatic environments), they detect structure in 'information' (visual, acoustic, haptic, and proprioceptive) specifying different surfaces, objects, mediums, and events that invite or repel action (Gibson, 1966, 1979). The detection of this information (specifically, its structure by way of surface contour, texture, and colour) is an exploratory process grown through *direct* engagement and interaction (Gibson, 1979).

Coupled, dynamic systems theory and ecological psychology help us explain self-organized behaviour, common to all physical and neurobiological systems. It is the passage from one organized state of the system to another (Kelso et al., 1995). Observed changes in movement skill behaviour, in this respect, are a function of the system itself (self-organization), with no prior authority controlling or prescribing the behaviour. Once the learning has taken place, this becomes an attractor state, a stable state for the overall dynamic system. Learning does not just stabilize the control and coordination of movements but changes the whole system – promoting a constant, *functional* shift between stability and flexibility (Kelso et al., 1995).

Towards functional *movement solutions*

To support how sport scientists, coaches, and teachers utilize these theories in practice, they have been operationalized under the umbrella of ecological dynamics. Ecological dynamics approach views movement as emerging from a self-organizing relationship formed between an individual, the task being performed, and the environment in which it occurs (Davids, Handford, & Williams, 1994; Warren, 2006). Intentional actions are understood as dynamic functional movement solutions that emerge as each learner continuously interacts with an array of constraints related to the task and environment (Davids et al., 1994; Seifert et al., 2018; Button et al., 2020). Through an ecological dynamics conceptualization of how movement emerges, there is a necessity to reconceptualize fundamental movement skills as functional movement solutions. Functional movement solutions refer to the repertoire (cognition, perception, and actions) of behaviours which allow an individual to navigate the environment, interact with others, and negotiate tasks to achieve intended goals (Chow et al., 2020). For example, as children interact with their surroundings, new functional movement solutions will emerge, with these solutions revealing new information and with it, opportunities for action, referred to as *affordances* (Gibson, 1979) (see Box 4.3). This is a continuous cyclical process of exploration and revelation.

Box 4.3 What are affordances?

The affordances of the environment are what it offers the animal, what it provides or furnishes, either for good or ill. The verb to afford is found in the dictionary, but the noun affordance is not. I have made it up. I mean by it something that refers to both the environment and the animal in a way that no existing term does. It implies the complementarity of the animal and the environment.

Gibson (1979)

In other words, affordances are properties of an animal-environment system, scaled to action capabilities (e.g. speed, strength), and body

---

dimensions (height, weight) (Davids et al., 2013) that provide different opportunities or invitations for (inter)actions (Rietveld & Kiverstein, 2014; Withagen et al., 2012). Indeed, humans perceive the environment in relation to its functionality and its meaningfulness detected in affordances, which provides insights into what they learn and how they decide to act (O'Sullivan et al., 2020; Reed, 1996).

A child who has the opportunity to explore many rich and varied movement environments will experience continual synergy (re)formation, leading to a greater breadth of stable coordination patterns (known as *attractors* in dynamical systems theory) to support movement functionality (Hanford et al., 1997). The re-shaped repertoire of coordinated movement patterns that emerges through learning and development will increase the likelihood that the child will become proficient and confident in their own ability to function and perform successfully, across multiple sporting and physical activity environments (Rudd et al, 2021). By embracing the term 'functional movement solution' as practitioners, we open ourselves up to a constraints-led approach to the acquisition of movement skills (Renshaw & Chow, 2019).

'Simple Rules; Complex Patterns': The constraints-led approach to coaching and teaching

The constraints-led approach (CLA) is an important coaching methodology built upon the foundations of dynamical systems theory and ecological psychology. Using this methodology, coaches can support performers in adapting their movements to the tasks and environments in which they are performing (Davids et al., 1994, 2008; Handford et al., 1997; Button et al., 2020). It is based on Newell's (1986) model of interacting constraints, which he defined as boundaries that shape the coordination and control of an animal's behaviour, from a practical perspective. Two important points from Newell's (1986) model of interacting constraints are worth briefly highlighting: (i) practice is a *search* for task solutions and (ii), the main goal of a performer is to satisfy the immediate constraints acting on them. The key here is that constraints do not cause behaviour, but continually perturb it (Davids, Hanford & Williams, 1994). As the performer moves through an environment, the continual coupling between perception and action leads to self-organization of our internal biological systems (cardiovascular system, muscular system nervous system, etc.) to satisfy impinging constraints this is key to the functionality of an individual, with functionality implying the ability to find functional solutions in a particular performance environment (Rudd et al., 2020, Woods et al., 2020). That is why this approach calls for a shift in perspectives, from 'fundamental' to 'functional' (O'Sullivan et al., 2020, Rudd et al., 2020). Given constraints do not cause behaviour but perturb it, they concurrently reduce the number of configurations available to a complex, dynamical system at any instance (Juarrero, 2000). There are many classes of constraints which can shape the behaviours of a complex dynamical system, and it has been well-documented that Newell (1986) considered *organismic*, *task*, and *environmental* constraints to be the most influential (see Figure 4.2). Organismic constraints refer to the characteristics of each individual, such as genes, height, weight, muscle–fat ratio, cognitions, and emotions. These constraints need to be considered carefully by teachers and coaches since such organismic constraints vary between, and within, each individual over different timescales. They can be influenced by factors operating over timescales of learning (hours, days, weeks) and maturation, ageing, and development (months and years). Environmental constraints are more global and can consist of physical variables in nature, such as ambient light, temperature, and altitude, or social features such as historical, cultural and societal values, beliefs, and customs. Task constraints are more specific to

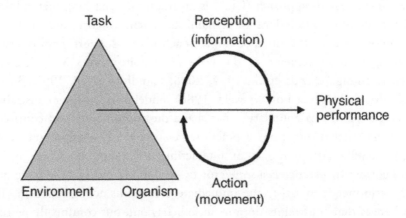

Figure 4.2 Newell's model of interacting constraints, illustrating the cyclical process of perception and action.

performance contexts than environmental constraints and include task goals, specific rules associated with an activity, use of activity-related implements or tools, and particular surfaces or objects involved in performance (Davids et al., 2008). A broad range of varied movement and play experiences, not only during childhood and youth but also into adulthood, can help an individual maintain and enhance physical activity to support their skilled adaptation to the environment (Button et al., 2020; Chow et al., 2020).

Fundamentally, a CLA highlights the non-linear interactions between performer (individual), task, and environment (Handford et al., 1997; Davids et al., 2008). In the CLA, more skilful performance emerges through self-organization under constraints as individuals become perceptually attuned to the key information sources which can regulate their actions in specific performance environments (when performing or learning) (Chow, 2013). A distinguishing feature of the CLA is that its practice design and delivery is informed by the principles of a non-linear pedagogy (see Box 4.4 and Figure 4.3 in addition to Rudd et al., 2020a, b).

Box 4.4 Principles of non-linear pedagogy.

(1) *A Representative learning design* highlights the importance of skill transfer between multiple settings. Informational constraints sampled from competition (i.e. opponents, ground surfaces, time of day) are carefully designed in to practice tasks to support learning transfer.

(2) *Movement-perception coupling* must be maintained when performing skills. This means that skills are practiced in their entirety rather than broken down into component parts or in decontextualized fashion.

(3) *An external focus of attention* allows for self-organization of movement patterns to meet the goal of the task.

(4) *The manipulation of constraints* through careful manipulation of task constraints will lead to self-organization and the emergence of a new functional movement pattern.

(5) *Infusing perturbations within the learning process.* This means that we see variability as exploration of the taskscape and not as error in the system as would be the case with traditional pedagogies. This means as long as the skill is functional and achieves the intended outcome, then it is to be accepted as a solution.

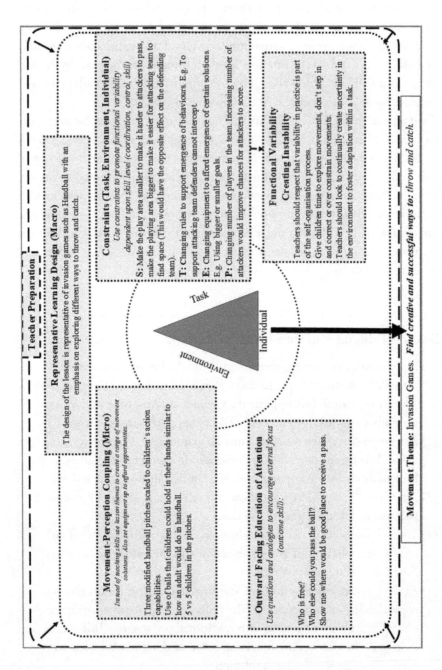

Figure 4.3 SAMPLE-PE research project example: Non-linear invasion games lesson plan for young children.

Manipulation of task constraints to support the emergence of functional movement solutions

Manipulating task constraints can be a powerful pedagogical tool to support the exploratory activity of learners at all levels of skill and experience. A key and often overwhelming challenge for inexperienced practitioners is identifying which task constraints to be manipulated to encourage an individual to explore their environment – developing their functional movement skills. The STEP framework (Youth Sport Trust, 2018) suggests how parents, teachers, and coaches could facilitate learning by attending to four major task constraints: space, task, equipment, and people. Manipulating one or more of these constraints can help to influence learners' intentions to explore different affordances in a performance environment. For example, learning can be encouraged by changing the equipment in a learning task and the number of people taking part in an activity or game. Manipulating these task constraints could lead learners to explore an abundance of affordances (opportunities for action). Let us consider a child who tends to repeat the same movement solution, whilst being challenged by the teacher to explore different ways of negotiating a particular play space. The child could be moved out of their comfort zone and challenged to adapt their actions, not by directions in the form of specific, prescriptive instructions but rather by teachers introducing very simple rule changes to change intentions and guide exploration, for an example, see Box 4.5.

Box 4.5 Example of a coach manipulating task constraints.

A soccer coach observing a small-sided game might want to educate players on the possibilities of exploiting gaps and space (by dribbling, passing, or shooting) just after they have won back possession. The coach may add a task constraint such as if a team intercepts a pass and scores a goal, then that goal counts as double. This task constraint places a risk on passing but does not exclude its utility. When in possession, this risk could invite players both with and without the ball to self-organize their individual and collective behaviours to support the player in possession. While the targeted intention with the task constraint is to shine a light on opportunities to exploit opponent's defensive disorganization just as they lose possession, it also invites opportunities for teammates and opponents to continuously adapt their positions to local information (e.g. player in possession and positioning of nearest opponents).

Conclusion

The aim of this chapter was to explore the conceptual and theoretical roots of fundamental movement skills, starting from the maturational stage perspective and its subsequent effects on pedagogical practices in sports coaching. In contrast, it is hoped that the contemporary learning theories around ecological dynamics, highlighted in the second part of this chapter, have emphasized the progress that has been made in this field in recent years. In particular, it is hoped that the shift towards the idea of movement skills now being seen as *functional movement solutions* restores the balance between the performer and their environment when seeking to explain and understand movement skill. We encourage coaches at all levels to explore the contemporary ideas introduced in this chapter, broadening their experiential knowledge guided by contemporary empirical insights.

Note

1 Interestingly, though, in the second edition of this text, the authors labelled such an action as an orthogenetic skill – perhaps highlighting the paradoxical nature of categorising movement in a dichotomised way.

References

Almond, L. (2014). Serious flaws in an FMS interpretation of physical literacy. *Science & Sports*, v.29, S60.

Anson, G., & Elliot, D. (2005) Information processing and constraints-based views of skill acquisition: Divergent or complementary? *Motor Control*, v.9(3), 217–241.

Bailey, R. P., Madigan, D. J., Cope, E. and Nicholls, A. R. (2018) The prevalence of pseudoscientific ideas and neuromyths among sports coaches. *Frontiers in Psychology*, v.9, pp.641.

Blake, D. T., Byl, N. N. and Merzenich, M. M. (2002) Representation of the hand in the cerebral cortex. *Behavioural Brain Research*, v.135 (1–2), pp.179–184.

Blomqvist, M., Luhtanen, P., & Laakso 1, L. (2001). Comparison of two types of instruction in badminton. *European Journal of Physical Education*, v.6(2), pp.139–155.

Button, C., Seifert, L., Chow, J. Y., Davids, K. and Araujo, D. (2020) *Dynamics of skill acquisition: An Ecological Dynamics Approach.* Champaign, IL: Human Kinetics Publishers.

Chen, A., Martin, R., Ennis, C. D., and Sun, H. (2008) Content specificity of expectancy beliefs and task values in elementary physical education. *Research Quarterly for Exercise and Sport*, v.79, pp.195–208.

Chow, J. Y. (2013) Nonlinear learning underpinning pedagogy: Evidence, challenges and implications. *Quest*, v.65, pp.469–484.

Chow, J. Y., Davids, K., Shuttleworth, R. and Araújo, D. (2020) Ecological Dynamics and Transfer from Practice to Performance in Sport. In *Skill Acquisition in Sport: Research, Theory and Practice*, edited by A. M. Williams and N. Hodges. London: Routledge.

Davids, K., Araújo, D., Hristovski, R., Passos, P. and Chow, J. Y. (2012) Ecological dynamics and motor learning design in sport. *Skill Acquisition in Sport: Research, Theory and Practice*, pp.112–130.

Davids, K., Araújo, D., Vilar, L., Renshaw, I. and Pinder, R. (2013) An ecological dynamics approach to skill acquisition: Implications for development of talent in sport. *Talent Development and Excellence*, v.5 (1), pp.21–34.

Davids, K., C. Handford, and Williams, M. (1994) The Natural Physical Alternative to Cognitive Theories of Motor Behaviour: An Invitation for Interdisciplinary Research in Sports Science? *Journal of Sports Sciences*, v.12 (6), pp.495–528.

Davids, K. W., Button, C. & Bennett, S. J. (2008) *Dynamics of Skill Acquisition: A Constraints-led Approach*. Champaign, IL: Human Kinetics.

Espenschade, A. S. and Eckert., H. M. (1967) *Motor Development*. Columbus, OH: Charles E. Merril Inc.

Fleishman, E. A. (1975) Toward a taxonomy of human performance. *American Psychologist*, v.30 (12), p.1127.

Gibson, J. J. (1966) The senses considered as perceptual systems.

Gibson, J. J. (1979) *The Ecological Approach to Visual Perception*. Boston, MA: Houghton, Mifflin and Company.

Goodway, J. D., Ozmun, J. C. and Gallahue, D. L. (2019) *Understanding Motor Development: Infants, Children, Adolescents, Adults*. Jones & Bartlett Learning.

Handford, C., Davids, K., Bennett, S. and Button, C. (1997) Skill acquisition in sport: Some applications of an evolving practice ecology. *Journal of Sports Sciences*, v.15, pp.621–640.

Juarrrero, A. (2000). Dynamics in action: Intentional behavior as a complex system. *Emergence*, v.2 (2), pp.24–57.

Kelso, J. A. S. (1995) *Dynamic Patterns: The Self-organization of Brain and Behavior*. Cambridge, MA: MIT Press.

Kelso, J. A. S., Case, P., Holroyd, T., Horvath, E., Rączaszek, J., Tuller, B. and Ding, M. (1995) Multistability and metastability in perceptual and brain dynamics. In: (ed.) *Ambiguity in Mind and Nature*. New York: Springer. pp.159–184.

Kugler, P. N. and Turvey, M. T. (1987) *Information, Natural Law, and Self-assembly of Rhythmic Movement: Theoretical*. Hillside, NJ: Lawrence Erlbaum Associates.

Langendorfer, S. J. and Roberton, M. A. (2002) Individual pathways in the development of forceful throwing. *Research Quarterly for Exercise and Sport*, v.73 (3), pp.245–256.

Magill, R. A. and Anderson, D. (2010) *Motor Learning and Control*. New York: McGraw-Hill Publishing.

McKenzie, T. L., Alcaraz, J. E., Sallis, J. F. and Faucette, F. N. (1998) Effects of a physical education program on children's manipulative skills. *Journal of Teaching in Physical Education*, v.17 (3), pp.327–341.

Mogilner, A., Grossman, J. A., Ribary, U., Joliot, M., Volkmann, J., Rapaport, D., Beasley, R. W. and Llinas, R. R. (1993) Somatosensory cortical plasticity in adult humans revealed by magnetoencephalography. *Proceedings of the National Academy of Sciences*, v.90 (8), pp.3593–3597.

Newell, K. (1986) Constraints on the development of coordination. *Motor Development in Children: Aspects of Coordination and Control*.

O'Sullivan, M., Davids, K., Woods, C. T., Rothwell, M., and Rudd, J. (2020) Conceptualizing physical literacy within an ecological dynamics framework. *Quest*.

Reed, E. S. (1996). *Encountering the World: Toward an Ecological Psychology*. New York: Oxford University Press.

Renshaw, I. and Chow, J. Y. (2019) A constraint-led approach to sport and physical education pedagogy. *Physical Education and Sport Pedagogy*, v.24, pp.103–116.

Ribeiro, J. F., Davids, K., Araújo, D., Guilherme, J., Silva, P. and Garganta, J. (2019) Exploiting bi-directional self-organising tendencies in team sports: the role of the game model and tactical principles of play. *Frontiers in Psychology*, v.10, p.2213.

Rietveld, E. and Kiverstein, J. (2014) A rich landscape of affordances. *Ecological Psychology*, v.26 (4), pp.325–352.

Rudd, J., Renshaw, I., Savelsbergh, G., Chow, J. Y., Roberts, W., Newcombe, D., & Davids, K. (2021). *Nonlinear Pedagogy and the Athletic Skills Model: The Importance of Play in Supporting Physical Literacy*. London: Routledge.

Rudd, J. R., Crotti, M., Fitton-Davies, K., O'Callaghan, L., Bardid, F., Utesch, T., Roberts, S., Boddy, L. M., Cronin, C. J. and Knowles, Z. (2020a) Skill acquisition methods fostering physical literacy in early-physical education (SAMPLE-PE): Rationale and study protocol for a cluster randomized controlled trial in 5–6-year-old children from deprived areas of North West England. *Frontiers in Psychology*, v.11, p.1228.

Rudd, J. R., Pesce, C., Strafford, B. W. and Davids, K. (2020b) Physical literacy-A journey of individual enrichment: An ecological dynamics rationale for enhancing performance and physical activity in all. *Frontiers in Psychology*, v.11, p.1904.

Schmidt, R. A. (1975) A schema theory of discrete motor skill learning. *Psychological Review*, v.82 (4), p.225.

Schmidt, R. A., Lee, T. D., Winstein, C., Wulf, G. and Zelaznik, H. N. (2018) *Motor Control and Learning: A Behavioral Emphasis*. Champaign, IL: Human Kinetics.

Seefeldt, V. and Gould, D. (1980) Physical and psychological effects of athletic competition on children and youth.

Summers, J. J. and Anson, J. G. (2009) Current status of the motor program: Revisited. *Human Movement Science*, v.28 (5), pp.566–577.

Thelen, E. (1989) The (re) discovery of motor development: Learning new things from an old field. *Developmental Psychology*, v.25 (6), p.946.

Vilar, L., Araújo, D., Davids, K. and Renshaw, I. (2012) The need for 'representative task design'in evaluating efficacy of skills tests in sport: A comment on Russell, Benton and Kingsley (2010). *Journal of sports Sciences*, v.30 (16), pp.1727–1730.

Whiting, H. T. A. and Vereijken, B. (1993) The acquisition of coordination in skill learning. *International Journal of Sport Psychology*.

Wickstrom, R. L. (1977). Fundamental motor patterns. Philadelphia, PA: Lea & Febiger.

Withagen, R., de Poel, H. J., Araújo, D., & Pepping, G. J. (2012). Affordances can invite behaviour: reconsidering the relationship between affordances and agency. *New Ideas in Psychology*, 30(2), 250–258. https://doi.org/10.1016/j.newideapsych.2011.12.003

Wolpert, D. M., and Flanagan, J. R. (2010) Motor learning. *Curriculum Biology*, v.20 (11), pp.467–472.

Woods, C. T., Rudd, J., Robertson, S. and Davids, K. (2020) Wayfinding: how ecological perspectives of navigating dynamic environments can enrich our understanding of the learner and the learning process in sport. *Sports Medicine-Open*, v.6 (1), pp.1–11.

Wulf, G. and Lewthwaite, R. (2016) Optimizing performance through intrinsic motivation and attention for learning: The OPTIMAL theory of motor learning. *Psychonomic Bulletin & Review*, v.23 (5), pp.1382–1414.

Wulf, G., Shea, C. and Lewthwaite, R. (2010) Motor skill learning and performance: A review of influential factors. *Medical Education*, v.44 (1), pp.75–84.

Youth Sport Trust (2018). *TOP PE [Online]*. Loughborough: Youth Sport Trust.

5 The Stepping Stone?

Challenging the Myth that Women's Sport is Less Significant than Men's Sport

Ali Bowes

Introduction

It would appear that there has never been a better time to be a woman in sport or working in women's sport. Despite a persistent gender gap, Sport England reported that, at a recreational level, in 2019, there had been year-on-year increases in the numbers of women that are regularly active, and millions of women that want to get involved in more sport (Sport England, 2020). Buoyed by the ever-increasing numbers of girls taking part in sport, a phenomenon not restricted just to England (e.g. Cooky and Messner, 2018), now more than ever women are claiming their space in sport at the highest level. Women's sport has subsequently seen increases in equitable media coverage (e.g. Petty and Pope, 2019), female-specific sport science research and support (e.g. Mountjoy, 2014), and growths in financial reimbursement in a range of sports. Clearly, the world of women's sport, and women's involvement in sport, is shifting and progressing. However, women's sports are often discussed as a poor relation to 'real' sport, that is men's sport, especially as the elite aspect of women's sport start to enter processes of professionalization (Bowes and Culvin, 2021).

In line with the increasing number of women competing in sport, however, there has been a decline in the number of women coaching women's sport, with men dominating the profession (Pastore, 1991; Clarkson et al., 2018). It is thought the increasing professionalization of women's sport, bringing with it paid coaching opportunities, has increased the number of men working in women's sport. Clarkson et al. (2018) note that women coaches are thus a marginalized group, which does little to change the perception that most sports are fiercely masculine domains. Following this trend, 2018 saw one of the most high-profile appointments in women's football in recent years, when Phil Neville accepted the position of Head Coach of England's women's national team on a three-year contract.

Neville's appointment – deemed 'controversial' by some (Evening Standard, 25 January 2018) – prompted discussions around the role of men working in the women's game, with some openly questioning his commitment to the role. Former national team player Rachel Yankey was quoted:

'Is he looking to get into the men's game and manage there? Yeah, I'm sure he is', Yankey said. 'For him it probably will be used for progression, but what I'd love to see is for him to help female coaches'. (Evening Standard, 25 January 2018)

Fast forward two years, and Neville's 'progression' from the women's national role was confirmed, when he announced he would step down at the end of his contract:

England Women's job was always three-year project before club football, says Phil Neville. (Whyatt, 2020)

It prompted widespread discussion about the sentiment of Neville's statements and dismay from those within the women's game:

England's record appearance-maker Fara Williams says Phil Neville demonstrated a 'lack of respect' towards the women's game after the national coach described the role as a stepping stone to club management. (Sky Sports, 2 June 2020)

In the article, Williams was quoted as saying:

'I was hurt by those comments. I am no longer with that squad but I certainly know what it means to me to play for England. I know what it means for the girls there currently, staff that are there currently [and] that were there before. Comments like that are not needed in my opinion. I think he could have probably handled that, or the comments could have been made a little bit better. I just think it shows a little lack of respect for our game and, as I say, where it was and where we are trying to get it to'. (Sky Sports, 2 June 2020)

Drawing upon some of these ideas, this chapter aims to challenge the myth that women's sport is a 'stepping stone' for (often male) coaches. The chapter starts with an historical and socio-cultural discussion of women's involvement in the masculine cultures of sport, followed by a discussion of the implications surrounding the progression of some women's sports towards professionalization. By then questioning why women's sport is considered to have a lower value than men's sport, it will provide sport coaches with the tools to challenge dominant narratives about girls' and women's sport.

A socio-cultural history of women in sport

Feminist commentators on the history of sport have highlighted two concurrent ideologies around sport that have contributed to the marginalization and discrimination of women: the masculinist origins of sport and restrictive gender norms for women (Messner, 1988). This opening section will explain how these two strands of thought have problematized women's involvement in sport. According to Guttmann (1991), there has never been a time in history when women have been as involved in sports as men. Sport was a space that enabled boys to turn into men, seemingly teaching them important life lessons about manhood and hegemonic forms of masculinity, such as strength, power, aggression, bravery, stoicism, and competitiveness. As Messner and Sabo (1990: 9) state, sport is 'an institution created by and for men'. It is this reality which ultimately led to sport being identified as being a 'male domain' or a 'masculine preserve', and the cultural, physical, and symbolic exclusion of women from sport has given sport a masculinist bias.

The history of women in sport in the Western world is one that has also been constrained by gender norms and medical myths (Gregg and Taylor, 2019). Hargreaves (1994) designates the history of women's involvement in sport as restricted by nineteenth-century medical opinions on the frailty of women, which symbolically rendered them unsuitable for participation in sport. The common belief that physical activity could damage women's unique anatomy and hinder their child-bearing abilities disqualified them from vigorous activity. Doctors and exercise specialists warned against strenuous activity for women because of their perceived instability due to menstruation, and these notions acted as a controlling measure on the activities women could participate in.

Towards the end of the nineteenth century, there was a breakthrough as physicians began to recognize the positive health effects of gentle exercise for women. However, the frailty myth contributed to the systematic subordination of women in sports for 'years to come' (Hargreaves, 1994: 43). When this notion was dismissed – though not entirely forgotten, even to this day – women were then constrained by the 'dictates of fashion' (which only served to confirm the old medical stereotype of a frail, weak, delicate women) and often took part in little or no physical activity (Hargreaves, 1994). Both women and men believed that women were the weaker sex, and this offered apparent proof. The myths had become self-fulfilling prophecies, which presented women with limited opportunities for physical activity and confirmed the idea of sport as, in general, an unattainable pursuit for women.

The late nineteenth century also saw the development of a number of boarding schools for girls throughout the United Kingdom, and there followed the emergence of women's team games. For the most part, these team games were different from the sports played by the boys in their separate schools, due to the assumptions about the capabilities of women and the clothes they were expected to wear. Hargreaves (1994) notes that during the 1890s, competitive games for females included lacrosse, rounders, netball, and cricket. The emergence of these Victorian sportswomen challenged the system that had restricted opportunities in sport to men (Guttmann, 1991). However, Hargreaves (1994: 63) explains, 'although physical education was becoming an integral feature of the curriculum, conventional ideas that competitive games enhanced masculinity and were incompatible with essential feminine characteristics prevailed'. Despite these gendered constraints, some women *were* taking part in 'men's' sports, with Jean Williams (2003) claiming that the first recorded game of women's football was in 1888.

The interwar years in the first half of the twentieth century saw women taking up different sports and challenging common perceptions about the capabilities of women's bodies. In 1920, there were approximately 150 women's football teams in operation throughout the United Kingdom, with Williamson (1991: 15) describing the feeling at the time: 'it was as if the country had been gripped by ladies football fever'. However, when the FA proclaimed that 'the game of football is quite unsuitable for females and should not be encouraged' (The FA, 1921, cited in Williamson, 1991, p. 17), the organization enforced a pitch ban on women's football in 1921. This move epitomized the feeling that women's involvement in sport was a threat to men's sport. Not lifted until 1971, the ban effectively halted the growth of the sport in the United Kingdom for 50 years. It was around this time that radical feminist movements were developing in Western nations, with calls by women for greater access to society in general. These shifting perceptions and expectations of women were also mirrored in sport, as more women started to take part in traditionally male activities.

As Messner and Sabo (1990: 9) state, 'women's movement into sport (as athletes and spectators) has challenged the naturalization of gender difference and inequality, which has been a basic aspect of the institution of sport'. The naturalization of gender difference – an understanding that men and women have inherently different physical capabilities – helps us to understand the problems associated with women's continued participation in sport, even as women contest these notions through their involvement. Hartmann-Tews and Pfister (2003: 7) confirm that the doing of gender in sport involves 'the presentation of the body and the demonstration of the physical', and this 'appears to provide convincing evidence ... of the "natural" hierarchy of the sexes'. What they meant by this is that the segregation of sport by sex categories, and the subsequent disparities in performance between male and female athletes, helps to perpetuate ideas that men's sport is superior. And so, when men's world records are faster, higher, or further than women's records, this is used as evidence to perpetuate the myths that men are biologically better suited to sport, and possibly that women should not be playing or trying to compete. Whilst this belief is less common than before, especially in most Western countries, it is now being reconstituted into other discussions about women's position in sport. The next section on the professionalization of women's sport will outline some of these issues.

The professionalization of women's sport

UN Women (2020) noted that in 2019, women's sport gained 'unprecedented attention', reporting positive shifts in women's participation and leadership, alongside developments in equal pay, safeguarding policies, and media coverage. In the absence of any major men's football tournaments, the FIFA Women's World Cup rightfully took centre stage for the month of June, with the organization reporting viewing figures of the official broadcast across all platforms at 1.12 billion, a record audience for the competition (FIFA, 2019). Alongside the staging of the Netball World Cup, the Wimbledon tennis championships, and later the Solheim Cup, sports media organization's in the United Kingdom and beyond started to make space for women's sport coverage. Despite consistently being underrepresented in the sport media (Bruce, 2016), a six-week period between June 7 and July 14 found near parity in the coverage of women's sport compared to men's sport (Women's Sport Trust, 2019). However, as the Women's Sport Trust (2019) noted, the challenge is now sustaining coverage of women's sport outside of these landmark, major events, with academic research long highlighting inequalities in quantity and quality of media coverage (Bruce, 2016).

Growing, although sporadic, media coverage has come alongside an increasing professionalization of women's sport, with both often seen as evidence of positive changes for women in sport. Although progress narratives around women's sport have been critiqued (e.g. MacLachlan, 2019), there has been definite changes in women's sport as moves are made towards professional settings (Bowes and Culvin, 2021). Despite the Ladies Professional Golf Association (LPGA) being the longest running professional sports organization for women, the formation of the Women's Tennis Association (WTA) in 1973 is often considered one of the most significant advancements in professional women's sport. Shortly after the WTA was formed, Billie Jean King's victory in the notorious 'battle of the sexes' tennis match against Bobby Riggs (Gregg & Taylor, 2019) arguably shifted public expectations of what women can achieve in sport. Currently, the most profitable sport for women, tennis is celebrated for its equal pay in the four major tournaments, although research has highlighted that women's earnings are considerably lower in less publicized middle- and low-tier competitions (Flake et al., 2013), with some male players (controversially) supportive of the disparity (Djokovic, 2016).

There have been numerous attempts around the world – with mixed success – in establishing professional women's team sport leagues. The All-American Girls Professional Baseball League ran for 11 years from 1942 (Weiller and Higgs, 1994), with other examples across different sports including basketball and ice hockey. However, the turn of the twenty-first century saw an expansion of professional women's sports leagues across the globe (Taylor et al., 2019), of which perhaps the most significant development has been in professional women's football (soccer). The first professional soccer league for women was launched in 2001 in America and, as with women's basketball in the United States, there has been three iterations of the league, with the first two attempts dogged by failures. The current version, the National Women's Soccer League (NWSL), has been in operation since 2012, and there are multiple semi-professional and professional women's football leagues around the world, with England's Women's Super League fully professional since the 2018–19 season.

Following the professionalization of the top tier of women's football, there have been increasing moves to professionalize other women's sports in the United Kingdom. England's international netballers achieved full-time professional status in 2016, although the domestic Netball Super League (NSL) retains semi-professional status. It's a similar story in rugby and cricket: Since 2019, 28 of England's female rugby players receive central contracts from the Rugby Football Union (RFU), but the elite Premier 15s league remains a mixture of amateurs and semi-professionals. In cricket, England's best players first received fulltime centralized contracts in 2014. At a domestic level, in 2020, the England and Wales Cricket Board (ECB) announced that both the men's and women's versions of the new 'Hundred' competition – a 100-ball format of the game –

would feature paid contracts and equal prize money. Upon closer inspection, the average salaries were reported at £8,000 for the women, compared to £66,600 for the men (Martin, 2020).

As women continue to transition into paid opportunities in sport, equal (or equitable) pay debates are starting to become more prominent. In most competitive sports, and especially those dominated by men and rooted in masculine origins, women are paid less than men for the same job. Women's experiences as paid athletes are notably different from men's, often receiving much less pay and shorter contracts with issues around benefits and conditions including maternity (Clarkson et al., 2020). Reports into the conditions and experiences of women footballers have found that the development of the professional game has not been without its problems. Written and detailed contracts were rare, half of all players were not remunerated by their clubs, and there were further issues including childcare, contract length, and post-career playing options (FIFPRO, 2017). An updated 2020 report, titled 'Raising Our Game', highlighted a continued call from elite women footballers for fair treatment, decent work, equal opportunities, and the right to viable career paths as professionals in the industry (FIFPRO, 2020).

For many sportswomen, this acts as evidence that they are valued less than men. The following section will unpick, however, some of the *socio-cultural conditions* around women's involvement in sport that have led to these disparities, focusing on perceptions of ability and the commercialization of women's sport.

Why are women valued less in sport?

There are multiple arguments that are used when we consider the question of why women are valued less in sport. Having considered both the historical background to women's involvement in sport, and the contemporary move towards professional women's sport, the following discussion will focus on two points that are pertinent to understand:

1. Perceptions of physical ability
2. Mediatization and commercialization

Perceptions of physical ability

We know that men and women generally operate in separate spaces in the sporting world, with sport being one of the few social institutions that segregates the two sexes. This separation is naturalized through the notion of physical difference (Anderson, 2008), a long- standing notion rooted in the medical myths of the past. Socio-cultural norms dictated that, due to the supposed natural capability of men – and thus the supposed natural incapability of women – male and female athletes could not compete with or against each other (Pieper, 2016). Due to the gendered structure of elite sport, there are often comparisons of performances made across gender categories, which are then used to justify the continued segregation. This process ultimately acts as evidence of a hierarchy that places men as faster, higher, and stronger, and thus more important than women.

Channon et al. (2016) explain that one of the most problematic aspects of sex segregation is the reinforcement of the notion that, in sport and athletic performance, *all* men and women are categorically different from each other. This isn't to say men and women *haven't* competed against each other – the aforementioned 'battle of the sexes' being a prime example. There have also been notable examples of women competing against (and also beating) men in professional golf (e.g. Bowes and Kitching, 2020). Whilst the success of female athletes here can challenge inherent beliefs about the superiority of men, women athletes often draw on these biological arguments to reduce their success. Allison (2020) highlights how professional women football players in America recognized the role of biological essentialism (the belief that men's bodies are different to, and more capable than, women's bodies) in devaluing women's athletic abilities. Despite an overlapping of athletic ability between the sexes, this belief in a biological gender difference was then used to justify unequal value and reward in sport, yet simultaneously to critique patterns of resource inequality (Allison, 2020).

Whilst debates around the abilities of men and women persist, as coaches working in women's sport, it is important you have an awareness of issues around biological essentialism and the discussion around ability. After all, men and women often play by the same sets of rules and with the same equipment in sport (Allison, 2020), yet generally the number and quality of resources are unequal. The comparative lack of resources for women's sport further entrenches 'the supposed inferiority of women's sport to men's, part of a vicious cycle of mutually reinforcing gender ideology and material resources' (Allison, 2020: 4). Through understanding the consequences of history on women's involvement in sport today, and using that knowledge to understand how we might talk about the capabilities of women's bodies, we can contribute to altering the 'stepping stone' narrative.

Mediatization and commercialization

For some, the close relationship between media coverage and elite levels of sport are obvious, and at its simplest level: less television coverage = less advertising money = less money in the sport = less money for athlete salaries. However, to understand this argument, we need to pay attention to the histories of commercialized, televised sport. As noted, women were excluded (either practically via pitch bans, or symbolically, due to medical myths of frailty and socio-cultural expectations of femininity) from taking part in a range of sports. This enabled men's sports – including players, teams, and leagues – to thrive. In the 1960s, as television transitioned into colour screening and live footage, sport became favourable content for broadcasters (Johnsen and Solvoll, 2008). However, at this stage, women were still banned from playing football and were only taking formative steps into widespread, organized sport. Coupled with the fact that most decision-makers in both sport (Burton, 2015) and the media are men (Hardin, 2013), as television became more mainstream in people's homes, it is unsurprising that it was men's sport they were watching.

Unsurprisingly then, research has been found to demonstrate a mis-match in coverage of men's and women's sports. The vision of sport as a male space and women as outsiders is one that has been perpetuated by the mass media, in terms of both quantity and quality of coverage. Bruce (2008: 57) notes that the sports media 'can simultaneously challenge and reinforce dominant assumptions that sport is primarily a male domain'. She identifies four commonplace and persistent 'rules' of media coverage that reinforce this notion, the first being the symbolic annihilation of women's sport through perpetual low rates of reporting (Bruce, 2016). When women are covered, they are often sexualized or feminized, or journalists even display ambivalence (Bruce, 2016). More recently, and as noted above, there has been *some* evidence of positive change, with Biscomb and Griggs (2013) documenting a shift towards a greater awareness of, and coverage of, women athletes in traditional sports media.

The sport–media relationship is seen as central to promote commercial interest in women's sport (Mansfield and Killick, 2011). This relationship is seen as vital to the sustainability of women's sport, and the move towards the professionalization of all aspects of sport, including both playing and coaching. However, the slower commercialization of women's sport has meant that women's experiences as paid athletes are notably different to men's in most sports. Writing about the WNBA basketball league in America, Agha and Berri (2021) highlight disparities in the amount of estimated revenue that is committed to female players (25%)

compared to male players in the NBA (50%). Further disparities are seen in golf (Bowes and Kitching, 2020), tennis (Flake et al., 2013), and football. In considering the 2016 'equal pay for equal play' movement by the USWNT, Archer and Prange (2019) draw on a labour rights perspective, an expressive power argument – that equal pay would send a valuable message about the value of women's sport – and a historical injustice approach, to justify gender equality in pay. They highlight how the historical inequalities in sport manifest in pay disparities and sports organizations have a moral responsibility to redress this imbalance.

As coaches working in women's sport, it is important that you are able to recognize the disparities in media coverage, the impact on commercialization, and the subsequent detriment to the business of women's sport. In considering the *value* of women's sport, as demonstrated by the quantity of media coverage, financial investments or player wages, an awareness of historical inequalities is essential in changing the 'stepping stone' narrative.

Concluding thoughts: Challenging the stepping stone myth?

As you have seen throughout this chapter, sport is a 'fundamentally sexist institution that is male dominated and masculine in orientation' (Theberge, 1981: 342). Despite this, women have continued to engage with sport as both athletes and spectators. Women's continued presence in sport, and their increasing positioning as professionals, has the potential to challenge myths about the capabilities of women (Bowes and Kitching, 2020). As coaches working in the world of sport, it is essential that you have the knowledge and understanding of the myths of sport – in this case, about gender – to enable you to be able to contribute to creating an environment in sport that is an inclusive, positive space for all people. In understanding the ways in which women's sport can be *seen as* less valuable, less exciting, less dramatic than men's sport, you can challenge these very notions and lay the foundations for more nuanced, informed discussions about the impact of history on women's involvement in sport at all levels today. Only when women's sport is *valued on a more equal footing*, and this means overcoming the constraints of history, can the notion of the 'stepping stone' be seriously removed.

References

Agha, N., & Berri, D. (2021). Gender differences in the pay of professional basketball players. In A. Bowes & A. Culvin (Eds.), *The Professionalisation of Women's Sport: Issues and Debates*. Bingley: Emerald.

Allison, R. (2020). Privileging difference: Negotiating gender essentialism in US women's professional soccer. *Sociology of Sport Journal*, 1–9.

Anderson, E. (2008). "I Used to Think Women Were Weak": Orthodox masculinity, gender segregation, and sport. *Sociological Forum, 23*(2), 257–280.

Archer, A., & Prange, M. (2019). 'Equal play, equal pay': Moral grounds for equal pay in football. *Journal of the Philosophy of Sport, 46*(3), 416–436.

Biscomb, K., & Griggs, G. (2013). "A splendid effort!" Print media reporting of England's women's performance in the 2009 Cricket World Cup. *International Review for the Sociology of Sport, 48*(1), 99–111.

Bowes, A., & Culvin, A. (2021). *The Professionalisation of Women's Sport: Issues and Debates*. Bingley: Emerald

Bowes, A., & Kitching, N. (2020). 'Wow these girls can play': Sex integration in professional golf. *Qualitative Research in Sport, Exercise and Health*, 1–18.

Bruce, T. (2008). Women, sport and the media: A complex terrain. In C. Obel, T. Bruce, & S. Thompson (Eds.), *Outstanding: Research about Women and Sport in New Zealand* (pp. 51–71). Hamilton, NZ: University of Waikato, Malcolm Institute for Educational Research.

Bruce, T. (2016). New rules for new times: Sportswomen and media representation in the third wave. *Sex Roles, 74*(7–8), 361–376.

Burton, L. J. (2015). Underrepresentation of women in sport leadership: A review of research. *Sport Management Review, 18*(2), 155–165.

Channon, A., Dashper, K., Fletcher, T., & Lake, R. J. (2016). The promises and pitfalls of sex integration in sport and physical culture. *Sport in Society, 19*(8–9), 1111–1124.

Clarkson, B. G., Cox, E., & Thelwell, R. C. (2019). Negotiating gender in the English football workplace: Composite vignettes of women head coaches' experiences. *Women in Sport and Physical Activity Journal, 27*(2), 73–84.

Clarkson, B. G., Culvin, A., Pope, S., & Parry, K. D. (2020). Covid-19: Reflections on threat and uncertainty for the future of elite women's football in England. *Managing Sport and Leisure*.

Cooky, C., & Messner, M. A. (2018). *No Slam Dunk: Gender, Sport and the Unevenness of Social Change*. New Brunswick: Rutgers University Press.

Djokovic, N. (21 Mar 2016). Novak Djokovic: men's tennis should fight for more prize money than women. *The Guardian*. https://www.theguardian.com/sport/2016/mar/21/novak-djo kovic-indian-wells-equal-prize-money-tennis

Evening Standard (25 January 2018) Phil Neville will use England women's role as a stepping stone, claims Rachel Yankey. https://www.standard.co.uk/sport/football/phil-neville-will-use -england-womens-role-as-stepping-stone-claims-rachel-yankey-a3749971.html

FIFA (2019, October 18). FIFA Women's World Cup 2019 watched by more than 1 billion. https://www.fifa.com/womensworldcup/news/fifa-women-s-world-cup-2019tm-watched-b y-more-than-1-billion#:~:text=A%20combined%201.12%20billion%20viewers,record% 20audience%20for%20the%20competition.

FIFPro World Players' Union (2017). *Global Employment Report: Working Conditions in Professional Women's Football*. FIFPro.

FIFPro World Players' Union (2020). *Raising Our Game Report*. FIFPro.

Flake, C. R., Dufur, M. J., & Moore, E. L. (2013). Advantage men: The sex pay gap in professional tennis. *International Review for the Sociology of Sport, 48*(3), 366–376.

Forster, J. (2006). Global sports organisations and their governance. *Corporate Governance, 6*(1), 72–83.

Gregg, E. A., & Taylor, E. (2019). History and evolution of women's sport. In N. Lough & A. Geurin (Eds.), *Routledge Handbook of the Business of Women's Sport* (pp. 11–22). London: Routledge.

Guttmann, A. (1991). *Women's Sports: A History*. New York: Columbia University Press.

Hardin, M. (2013). Want changes in content?: Change the decision makers. *Communication & Sport*, *1*(3), 241–245.

Hargreaves, J. (1994). *Sporting Females: Critical Issues*. New York: Psychology Press.

Hartmann-Tews, I., & Pfister, G. (2003) *Sport and Women: Social Issues in International Perspective*. London: Routledge

Johnsen, H., & Solvoll, M. (2007). The demand for televised football. *European Sport Management Quarterly*, *7*(4), 311–335.

Mansfield, L. & Killick, L. (2012): The UK netball superleague: A case study of franchising in elite women's sport organisations. *European Sport Management Quarterly*, *12*(5), 545–567.

Martin, A. (4 March 2020). Men's and women's competitions in the hundred to have equal prize money. *The Telegraph*. https://www.theguardian.com/sport/2020/mar/04/mens-and-womens -competitions-in-the-hundred-to-have-equal-prize-money

McLachlan, F. (2019). It's boom time!(again): Progress narratives and women's sport in Australia. *Journal of Australian Studies*, *43*(1), 7–21.

Messner, M. A. (1988). Sports and male domination: The female athlete as contested ideological terrain. *Sociology of Sport Journal*, *5*(3), 197–211.

Messner, M. A., & Sabo, D. F. (1990). *Sport, Men, and the Gender Order: Critical Feminist Perspectives*. Champaign, IL: Human Kinetics Books.

Mountjoy, M. L. (2014). Handbook of sports medicine and science: The female athlete. Hoboken, NJ: Wiley Blackwell.

Pastore, D. L. (1991). Male and female coaches of women's athletic teams: Reasons for entering and leaving the profession. *Journal of Sport Management*, *5*(2), 128–143.

Petty, K., & Pope, S. (2019). A new age for media coverage of women's sport? An analysis of English media coverage of the 2015 FIFA Women's World Cup. *Sociology*, *53*(3), 486–502.

Pieper, L. P. (2016). 'Preserving la différence': The elusiveness of sex-segregated sport. *Sport in Society*, *19*(8–9), 1138–1155.

Sky Sports (2 June 2020) Phil Neville showed a 'lack of respect' with England head coach comments, says Fara Williams. https://www.skysports.com/football/news/11095/11999044/ phil-neville-showed-a-lack-of-respect-with-england-head-coach-comments-says-fara-williams

Sport England (2020) Active Lives Adult Survey November 2018/19 Report. https://sporten gland-production-files.s3.eu-west-2.amazonaws.com/s3fs-public/2020-04/Active%20Lives% 20Adult%20November%2018-19%20Report..pdf?BhkAy2K28pd9bDEz_NuisHl2ppuqJ tpZ

Taylor, T., O'Connor, D., & Hanlon, C. (2020) Contestation, disruption and legitimization in women's rugby league. *Sport in Society*, *23*(2), 315–334.

Theberge, N. (1981). A critique of critiques: Radical and feminist writings on sport. *Social Forces*, *60*(2), 341.

UN Women (2020). COVID-19, women, girls and sport: Build back better. https://www.unw omen.org/-/media/headquarters/attachments/sections/library/publications/2020/brief-covid -19-women-girls-and-sport-en.pdf?la=en&vs=2629

Weiller, K. H., & Higgs, C. T. (1994). The all american girls professional baseball league, 1943–1954: Gender conflict in sport? *Sociology of Sport Journal*, *11*(3), 289–297.

Whyatt, K. (28 May 2020) England women's job was always a three-year project before club football, says Phil Neville. *The Telegraph*. https://www.telegraph.co.uk/football/2020/05/28/england-womens-job-always-three-year-stepping-stone-club-football/

Williams, J. (2003). The fastest growing sport? women's football in England. *Soccer & Society*, *4*(2–3), 112–127.

Williamson, D. J. (1991). *Belles of the Ball: [The Early History of Women Football]*. R&D Associates.

Women's Sport Trust (2019, September 4). Has the media changed the game for women's sports coverage? https://www.womenssporttrust.com/has-the-media-changed-the-game-for-womens-sports-coverage/

6 Myths about Learning Styles in Sport Coach Education

Anna Stodter

Learning is a central concern in sport coaching, an emerging profession that relies on developing an appropriately qualified workforce for its success. Effective coach education, learning, and development is crucial to this professionalization. However, the effectiveness and theoretical underpinnings of formal coach education and non-formal continuing professional development (CPD) opportunities have for several years been called into question by practitioners and researchers alike. Alongside a perceived lack of relevance to practice and alignment with how coaches learn, myths around learning and education are rife both in the way that coaches are taught, and in the theories about athletes' learning that they are expected to implement. From experiences on professional development courses within sport coaching, many will be familiar with the visual, auditory, reading/writing, and kinaesthetic (VARK) learning styles inventory (Fleming & Mills, 1992), well-known for depicting the ways different types of learners prefer to receive information. Although generally well-intentioned and intuitively appealing, the problem with relying on such models is their lack of robust underpinning evidence and the potential for missing out on the benefits that could be gained from using 'proven' or more effective ways to encourage learning. This chapter sets out to explain one of the commonly held beliefs that permeate coach learning contexts and explore some of the surrounding evidence and practitioner's experiences. In doing so, it will challenge potential myths surrounding learning styles and make evidence-informed suggestions for enhancing educational opportunities in sport coaching.

Learning styles theory

'Learning styles' refers to the idea that individuals differ in how they learn and in the mode of instruction most effective for them. These differences in learning preferences are classified according to particular 'styles', which, according to the prevalent *meshing hypothesis,* should be matched to particular formats of learning activities (Pashler, McDaniel, Rohrer & Bjork, 2009). There are over 70 different classification systems or taxonomies of learning styles including 'activists' versus 'theorists' and 'left brainers' versus 'right brainers' (Coffield, Moseley, Hall & Ecclestone, 2004), but probably the most common is the VARK inventory (Fleming & Mills, 1992). This theory claims that some people will learn best by seeing or watching (visual learning), some by hearing or listening (auditory learning), some by reading or writing (read/write), and others by doing and practicing (kinaesthetic learning). Applied to a sport coaching context, VARK learning styles theory predicts that some athletes would best learn a new tactical approach by watching others executing it perhaps on video, whereas other athletes would learn best by listening to a description from the coach of how to do it. A third set of athletes would learn the tactical approach most effectively by reading printed information in a playbook, while a final type of athlete would need to take part in a practical session themselves to learn it best.

The intellectual history of learning styles can be traced back to 1960's efforts to reach African American youth that certain educators deemed 'culturally deficient' (Fallace, 2019, p. 349). By the 1970s, with deficit and race-specific language removed, educators diverged from these problematic ethnocentric origins, and the idea moved beyond its application to specific racial, ethnic, and cultural groups to gain wider popularity. Learning styles have since acquired huge influence and sustained worldwide acceptance within education (Howard-Jones, 2014; Newton & Salvi, 2020; Pashler et al., 2009). Alongside several thousand published articles and dozens of influential textbooks on the topic, there is a thriving commercial industry devoted to learning styles assessment tools and professional development workshops for educators. The idea has gained dogmatic status with acceptance amongst professional educators at all levels and contexts, as well as the general public. Given sport coaching's bio-psychological origins and educational aspirations (Jones, 2006), it is no surprise that learning styles have also gained traction on the sports field and in the education of coaches.

Learning styles in sport coaching

Practitioners in charge of developing and educating athletes will likely recognize the varying speed and manner with which individuals will pick up new ideas or skills. There is strong intuitive appeal in the idea that sport coaches should pay close attention to learning styles by 'diagnosing' and designing learning interventions around them (Braakhuis, 2015). Indeed, an understanding of athlete learning styles is promoted as a 'must-have for your coaching toolbox' (Hanson, 2020), as knowing who is which type of learner 'will help you coach or teach effectively' (Dunn, 2009, p. 30). An athletic version of the VARK inventory was developed to allow coaches and athletes to identify their own learning style and in turn aid the coach in tailoring their communication to cater to individuals' preferences (Dunn & Fleming, 2013). On completing this online inventory, the coach or athlete can access help sheets detailing strategies that apply to their learning preference, with the opportunity to pay for full information in an academic or business profile. Examples include instructions on how to work with other learners, how to take in information (e.g. field trips, trial and error, and real-life examples for those with a strong preference for kinaesthetic learning), how to perform well in examinations (e.g. draw things for those with a strong preference for visual learning), and how to best engage with online learning (Dunn & Fleming, 2013). It is argued that if a coach can understand these learning preferences and adjust how they deliver to suit each individual athlete, they will be much more effective and efficient in developing athletes' skills and knowledge (Dunn, 2009; Hanson, 2020).

The simple allure of learning styles has helped it become a standard discourse in coaching and coach education (Mulvenna, Moran & Leslie-Walker, 2019). In the United Kingdom, those involved in sport are brought up with the idea through school and college education systems. The current syllabus for Business and Technology Education Council (BTEC) national qualifications in sport, 'widely recognised by industry and higher education as the signature vocational qualification' features the characteristics of VARK learning styles and how learning 'should be presented' to each type of learner (Pearson Education Limited, 2019, p. 193). Meanwhile, a recent study investigating introductory national governing body formal coach education demonstrated how the VARK inventory was presented as *the* way athletes obtain new sporting skills, creating a single and continuing belief in the idea (Mulvenna et al., 2019). In order to develop athletes' technical and tactical skills and bring about learning, coaches were urged to discover each individual's preferred style and adapt their method of communication accordingly, for example through using a whiteboard for a visual learner or verbal instructions for an auditory learner. The presentation of learning styles as 'gospel' was supported by coach educators' use of varied visual media to support visual learners on the course, modelling the approach and reinforcing the surrounding rhetoric through their own coach development methods.

In line with the idea that coaches particularly value learning from others (e.g. Nash & Sproule, 2012; Stozkowski & Collins, 2015), course participants modelled their coaching behaviour on the practices showcased by the coach educators, almost unquestionably retaining and continuing to implement the notion of learning styles two years after attending the course (Mulvenna et al., 2019). A similar example of the pervasiveness of learning styles in coach education comes from a theory-informed programme for development rugby coaches in New Zealand, which involved coaches completing a VARK questionnaire to identify their learning preferences then discussing the merits of accommodating the learning preferences of their athletes (Cassidy, Potrac & McKenzie, 2006). These activities provoked enthusiastic buy-in from coaches as a 'real revelation' (p.150) and a worthwhile tool to re-interpret their own learning experiences and change their practice. For instance, after the course the participant coaches reported using 'whiteboard presentation' (p.151) and playbooks to express information in line with the different learning preferences of their players (Cassidy et al., 2006). Even the minimal evidence available on the impact of formal education on coaching behaviour suggests that adjusting instruction to match learning styles of individual athletes is a rare concept that 'sticks' particularly well with coaches, accounting for the only consistent change from pre-course to post-course behaviours in one Canadian evaluation case study (Gilbert & Trudel, 1999).

This pervasiveness through the layers of learning from coach educators to coaches is evidenced by a recent survey which found that 89% of coaches in the United Kingdom and Ireland have come across the ideas or practice of learning styles, and 62% believed that individuals learn better when they receive information in their preferred learning style (Bailey, Madigan, Cope, & Nicholls, 2018). Coaches reported using learning styles frequently in their practice, with the majority (57%) coming across the idea on core coaching courses delivered by their sports organization. Significant directions of transfer of these ideas are therefore likely to be from coach educators to trainee coaches, through teaching materials and practices endorsed by national governing bodies for sport. Indeed, research into sport governing bodies' training for coach educators, who deliver coaching courses and assess coaches' competency, uncovers a further layer of endorsement for similar popular learning models (Stodter & Cushion, 2019). The reproduction of such compelling messages down the levels of sporting authority is most likely to lead to 'buy-in' from well-meaning coaches with an interest in learning and general knowledge about neuroscience (Bailey et al., 2018). The modern-day sport coach is often portrayed as aiming to facilitate learning, guiding, and empowering the athlete to self-manage their own development as part of an 'athlete-centred' approach (Braakhuis, 2015; Pill, 2018). Learning styles can be positioned as relevant to and feeding into these ideals, enabling the individualized tailoring of instruction to bring about 'better learning'. They offer a simple, intuitive, 'quick-fix' model to more easily integrate psychological science in navigating the dynamic complexities of individual skill development and communication central to sport coaching. In combination, these factors can make coaches feel 'terrible' for not incorporating learning styles into their practice (Seaman, 2012, p. 1).

Are learning styles a myth, and is this a problem?

Based on rigorous reviews of the literature (e.g. Pashler et al., 2009; Newton & Salvi, 2020), the answer is a resounding *yes* (Kirschner, 2017). The widespread and well-intentioned enthusiasm for the idea and implementation of learning styles in sport coaching has become quite concerning when we look more carefully at the evidence base. Despite a mass of supporting literature, very few studies have used experimental methodologies capable of testing the validity of learning styles, particularly in sport and coaching (Fuelscher, Ball & MacMahon, 2012). Of those that have done so in education, several have found evidence directly contradicting the meshing hypothesis whereby learners are predicted to benefit from instruction matched to their preferred learning style (Pashler et al., 2009). Based on their review of the evidence for learning styles, Pashler et al. (2009) produced essential research design principles which can be applied in the sporting context to determine scientific validity. First, learners – such as athletes or coaches – should be divided into groups based on their learning styles (e.g. visual and kinaesthetic learners). Participants from each group must then be randomly assigned to receive one of multiple methods of instruction (e.g. using visual and kinaesthetic learning methods). After the instructional intervention, all participants should be tested in the same way. To provide acceptable evidence for learning styles, the results would need to show that the instructional method most effective for those with one learning style (e.g. visual instruction leads to optimal test performance for the visual learning style group) is not the most effective method for those with a different learning style (e.g. visual instruction does not lead to the best test outcomes for the kinaesthetic learning style group). There remain no tests of learning styles that follow Pashler's design principles and none that relate to technical skill development, meaning there is no adequate empirical support for the use of learning styles in sport, coaching, or coach education (Fuelscher et al., 2012).

Research in sport and motor skill learning has used the VARK-athlete inventory to test and inform learning preferences, but this sport-specific test remains based on classroom content learning (Fuelscher et al., 2012). A sample item asks athletes to choose how they would give a new athlete directions to the training complex: by drawing a map (visual), telling them the directions (auditory), writing them down (read/write), or by going with them to the destination (Kinaesthetic) (Dunn & Fleming, 2013). Anyone with involvement in sport as an athlete or coach will recognize the limited 'face validity' of this and other inventory items to the processes of learning it claims to assess. More recent updates from the wider educational field back up the claim that learning styles instruments lack validity and reliability, and that pedagogical interventions should not rely on them (Alvarez-Montero, Leyva-Cruz, & Moreno-Alcaraz, 2018). In fact, research repeatedly and consistently suggests that while learners do have preferences for the format in which information is presented to them, matching instruction to specific styles has limited impact on subsequent learning (Pashler et al., 2009).

Using learning styles in coaching and coach education then is ill-advised as it may not help learning and could even be restrictive and harmful. Learners may internalize their labelled style and limit themselves to only activities aligned with that modality, and coaches or coach educators may 'pigeon-hole' and guide learners away from their non-preferred modalities (Bailey, 2017). Proponents of VARK suggest educators working in sport should move away from visual means of information presentation and instead cater to athletic populations' stronger preference for Kinaesthetic and multi-modal learning than non-athletic populations (Braakhuis, 2015). Notwithstanding the issues with 'diagnosing' learning styles, teaching within the preferred instructional method in this way may actually 'kill' learning (De Bruyckere, Kirschner, & Hulshof, 2015). There is even evidence to support the idea that learning can be promoted by taking learners out of their comfort zones, not keeping them within it (Coffield et al., 2004). There is therefore an important difference between the way someone thinks they prefer to learn and what actually leads to better learning (De Bruyckere et al., 2015). To use an illustrative metaphor, while one may prefer to eat cake as their favourite food, consuming only cake is not the most effective diet for bringing about healthy outcomes (Kirschner, 2017).

Instead, the learner should remain at the centre of the education process, with the task itself guiding learning activities and methods of communication (Mulvenna et al., 2019). While the idea of learning styles is a simple but powerful way to bring learning, the process of learning, and a focus on varying methods of instruction to coaches' attention (Cassidy et al., 2006), the limited available resources would be better devoted to adopting the increasing number of educational practices that are supported by a strong evidence base (Pashler et al., 2009). This is particularly the case within the developing, largely grassroots-focused profession of sport coaching where resources are scarce.

Evidence-informed suggestions for coach education

It is important to model appropriate approaches to learning in coach education (McCullick, Belcher, & Schempp, 2005), yet research on the formal education of coaches and coach developers suggests there is a lack of concern for evidence-informed processes of learning (Lyle & Cushion, 2017; Stodter & Cushion, 2019). While coach education seems to be a considerable part of the problem in fostering flawed pseudoscientific beliefs and practices in coaching, it can also be part of the solution. Learning styles was the most prevalent in a collection of various myths about learning and the brain espoused by British and Irish sport coaches in Bailey et al.'s (2018) survey, evidently propagated through core coach education and related CPD. These authors suggest that formal coach education opportunities could be strengthened by further research into effective educational practices in sport, enhancing interdisciplinary scientist-practitioner partnerships and cultivating a healthy scepticism in coaches to protect against fallible ideas (Bailey et al., 2018). Evidence suggests that coaching practitioners 'cherry pick' information that fits in to their existing biography in a tacit, unreflective process focused on 'what works' in context (Stodter & Cushion, 2017). This can unwittingly reinforce and reproduce problematic ideas and practices without concern for their origins and underpinning meanings. A more beneficial use of resources in coach education would therefore be to incorporate a deliberately evidence-informed focus on learning about learning, and how to learn as a practitioner (Lyle & Cushion, 2017; Pacquette & Trudel, 2018). This approach would set up better subsequent learning by helping coaches to navigate the abundance of information available, developing lifelong learners who can evaluate the source and quality of new ideas and use evidence to reason amongst alternatives. Moving coaches from simplistic 'dualist' or right/wrong ways of thinking, with knowledge provided by authorities, towards more sophisticated relativist conceptions of knowledge (Entwistle & Peterson, 2004) would better enable them to understand what has been learned and adapt it for effective experimentation and practice in context. In this vein, a recent review of research in coach learning and education recommended helping coaches to recognize their own views of learning and reducing the unthinking acceptance or rejection of information that could be of little worth, or indeed highly valuable (Pacquette & Trudel, 2018; Stodter & Cushion, 2017).

For example, coaches could be encouraged to examine their own understanding of learning styles through facilitating application of research evidence to reflective practice. What follows is an examination of the experiences of one coach who underwent a shift in perspective through this process. Sam Birtwistle is a UEFA 'B' Licence qualified coach with 10 years' experience of coaching elite level football and teaching primary physical education. Sam currently works in the youth development phase at a professional football club academy. As part of a final year university placement module, Sam was required to identify a concept to explore in more depth through applying evidence to reflective practice via experimentation and evaluation in context. Here are his reflections on the process.

Practitioner box: Exploring learning styles in practice

Throughout my 10 years of involvement within sport coaching and education environments, I had been told by other coaches and mentors that learning styles played an important role in how children took on information, and therefore how they learned. I took the opportunity of a placement module during my time at university to observe how information given to children is geared towards learning styles in classroom and football coaching environments, comparing the two and investigating the implications for learning and development.

Initially, I perceived learning styles as an important 'tick box' to enable learning. I believe these preconceived ideas originated from my formal coach education on the English Football Association (FA) coaching pathway from level one to level three. On these courses, VARK learning styles were advocated as a fundamental tool for giving information, with the use of multiple modalities in each coaching session insisted upon, despite being disputed by academics. During the first half of my placement module, I worked in line with the idea that each individual's capacity for learning was dependant on their particular learning style. However, on beginning to look deeper into the research and evidence on the effect of 'matching' learning styles to instruction (e.g. Pashler et al., 2009), I have changed how I perceive learning styles and their value within education and coaching.

Engaging with this research and collating some of my own evidence in practice helped me to question my beliefs. I asked 44 children in classroom and football academy settings to complete a VARK questionnaire (Dunn & Fleming, 2013). The results helped me identify each child's preference, yet there seemed to be no useful pattern or common way of learning in each group or setting. This highlighted the fact that the choice of learning style might be dependent on the situation and/or previous knowledge and was not fixed as an internal preference. My thoughts shifted from placing importance on meeting the preferences of those with different learning styles in each coaching session to the value of clear communication and creating environments where learning can take place. Pashler et al. (2009) support this, stating that learning styles should not be confused with methods of communication and that the standard of communication outweighs the importance of specific learning styles or preferences. While individuals will prefer different ways to learn, it does not mean their learning is isolated to their particular preference. This is where I feel effective communication plays an important role in the transfer, understanding, and recall of information between educator and learner.

Now effective communication for me is to get the athletes to achieve the desired goals, where the goals can be applying or transferring knowledge, correcting skills, explaining concepts, or enhancing motivation. This ties in with Côté and Gilbert's (2009) definition of effective coaching as positively influencing competence, confidence, connection, and character/caring through interactions with athletes. In applying what I read about learning styles, the specific style or method of delivery became less important to me than the message itself. There is still however a place for coaches to use the VARK inventory as a tool for exploiting multi-modal delivery methods. For example, dual coding, which involves combining words (audio or read/write) with visuals, is a method shown to help people effectively retrieve information and learn better (Weinstein & Sumeracki, 2019). During a coaching session, I might now explain the learning outcome and demonstrate it as part of the same process. This helps *all* athletes regardless of their preferences to receive the information, integrate it, and learn better, providing two different ways of remembering it later on.

Given that research evidence has discredited learning styles, coaches that continue to focus purely on using this approach could have a negative effect on their athletes by failing to provide instruction in an appropriate way (Pashler et al., 2009). Through engaging with this research evidence and applying it to my coaching practice, I have come to agree that learning is a process that occurs as a result of experience, constructed from multiple types of information and not a single method of instruction. Now, the *meaning* of the information received takes on much more importance than the mode of delivery (Newton, 2015). By developing a greater understanding around VARK learning styles and how differ-ent modes of instruction can be used in my coaching, I have been able to re-assess my beliefs and become a better coach in the process. There are far more useful and evidence-informed methods than learning styles to facilitate learning, and it is around effective communication that I will aim to continue my own learning.

Recommendations for practice

- There is no adequate empirical support for the use of learning styles in sport, coaching, or coach education, so relying on them in practice is not only ill-advised but may even be restrictive and harmful (Fuelscher et al., 2012).
- The learner should remain at the centre of the education process, with the task itself guiding learning activities and methods of communication. The quality of communication itself, and the meaning attached to it, is more important than the modality in which information is put across (Mulvenna et al., 2019; Pashler et al., 2009).
- Use deliberately evidence-informed approaches to help coaches to recognize their own views of learning. For example, Stodter and Cushion's (2017) process of coaches' professional learning is grounded in data from soccer coaches and could be used as a thinking tool to improve professionals' learning (Lindley, 2020).
- Aim through coach education to develop lifelong coach learners who can use evidence to reason amongst alternative ideas and adapt them for practical application and experimentation in context (Pacquette & Trudel, 2018).

It is clear that despite an intuitive appeal and welcome foregrounding of learning, the idea of learning styles has deeply concerning foundations and has been repeatedly discredited in science and applied educational practice. The worrying propagation of learning styles as well as other oversimplified and flawed pseudoscientific theories in sport through coach education jeopardizes the quality of learning opportunities and the wider credibility of coaching as a legitimate profession (De Bruyckere et al., 2015; Stodter & Cushion, 2019). Adjusting the focus of formal education and CPD for sport coaches and coach educators to build in evidence-informed ideas in learning about learning would better enable practitioners to judge the quality of content and sources of information they come across and adapt new ideas for effective practice in context.

References

Alvarez-Montero, F., Leyva-Cruz, M. G., & Moreno-Alcaraz, F. (2018). Learning styles inventories: And update of Coffield, Moseley, Happ & Ecclestone's reliability and validity matrix. *Electronic Journal of Research in Educational Psychology, 16(3)*, 597–629.

Bailey, R. (2017). Science, pseudoscience and exercise neuroscience: Untangling the good, the bad, and the ugly. In R. Meussen, S. Schaeffer, P. Tomporoski, & R. Bailey (Eds.), *Physical Activity and Educational Achievement: Insights from Exercise Neuroscience*. London: Routledge.

Bailey, R., Madigan, D. J., Cope, E. C., & Nicholls, A. R. (2018). The prevalence of pseudoscientific ideas and neuromyths among sports coaches. *Frontiers in Psychology, 9*, 641.

Braakhuis, A. J. (2015). Learning styles of elite and sub-elite athletes. *Journal of Human Sport and Exercise, 10(4)*, 927–935.

Cassidy, T., Potrac, P., & McKenzie, A. (2006). Evaluating and reflecting upon a coach education initiative: The Code of rugby. *The Sport Psychologist, 20*, 145–161.

Coffield, F., Moseley, D., Hall, E., & Ecclestone, K. (2004). *Learning Styles and Pedagogy in Post-16 Learning: A Systematic and Critical Review*. London: Learning and Skills Research Centre.

Côté, J. and Gilbert, W. (2009). An Integrative Definition of Coaching Effectiveness and Expertise. *International Journal of Sports Science & Coaching, 4(3)*, 307–323.

De Bruyckere, P., Kirschner, P., & Hulshof, C. D. (2015). *Urban Myths about Learning and Education*. Oxford: Elsevier.

Dunn, J. (2009). Using learning preferences to improve coaching and athletic performance. *Journal of Physical Education, Recreation and Dance, 80(3)*, 30–37.

Dunn, J. L., & Fleming, N. (2013). *The VARK Questionnaire for Athletes*. Online accessed 11/11/2020 http://vark-learn.com/the-varkquestionnaire/the-vark-questionnaire-for-athletes/

Entwistle, N. J., & Peterson, E. R. (2004). Conceptions of learning and knowledge in higher education: Relationships with study behaviour and influences of learning environments. *International Journal of Educational Research, 41*, 407–428.

Fallace, T. (2019). The ethnocentric origins of the learning style idea. *Educational Researcher, 48(6)*, 349–355.

Fleming, N. D., & Mills, C. (1992). Not another inventory, rather a catalyst for reflection. *To Improve the Academy, 11*, 137–144.

Forrest, C. (2018). The Myth of Dale's Cone of Experience. Online accessed 03/06/2020 https://www.getmygrades.co.uk/the-myth-of-dales-cone-of-experience/

Fuelscher, I. T., Ball, K., & MacMahon, C. (2012). Perspectives on learning styles in motor and sport skills. *Frontiers in Psychology*, DOI: 10.3389/fpsyg.2012.00069

Gilbert, W., & Trudel, P. (1999). An evaluation strategy for coach education programs. *Journal of Sport Behavior, 22(2)*, 234–251.

Hanson, B. (2020). *Athlete Assessments*. Online accessed 12/11/2020. https://www.athleteassessments.com/athlete-learning-styles-must-have-coaching-toolbox/

Howard-Jones, P. A. (2014). Neuroscience and education: Myths and messages. *Nature Reviews Neuroscience, 15*, 817–824.

Jones, R. L. (2006). *The Sports Coach as Educator: Re-conceptualising Sports Coaching*. London: Routledge.

Kirschner, P. A. (2017). Stop propagating the learning styles myth. *Computers & Education, 106*, 166–171.

Letrud, K., Hernes, S., & Boylan, M. (2018). Excavating the origins of the learning pyramid myths. *Cogent Education, 5(1)*, 1–17.

Lindley, K. (2020). A thinking tool to improve learning: Why do we pick up certain things and ditch the rest? Online accessed 01/12/2020 at [https://medium.com/@CoachDeveloper/a-th inking-tool-to-improve-learning-f32fc9e3375e]

Lyle, J., & Cushion, C. J. (2017). *Sport Coaching Concepts: A Framework for Coaching Practice.* Abingdon: Routledge.

McCullick, B. A., Belcher, D., & Schempp, P. G. 2005. What works in coaching and sport instructor certification programs? The participants view. *Physical Education & Sport Pedagogy,* *10*(2), 121–137.

Mulvenna, C., Moran, M., & Leslie-Walker, A. (2019). Investigating the way soccer coach education discusses player learning styles. *The International Journal of Sport and Society, 11.*

Nash, C., & Sproule, J. (2012). Coaches perceptions of their coach education experiences. *International Journal of Sport Psychology, 43,* 33–52

Newton, P. (2015). The learning style myth is thriving in higher education. *Frontiers in Psychology, 6,* 1908.

Newton, P., & Salvi, A. (2020). How common is belief in the learning styles neuromyth, and does it matter? A pragmatic systematic review. *Frontiers in Education, 5,* 602451. DOI: 10.3389/feduc.2020.602451

Pacquette, K., & Trudel, P. (2018). Learner-centred coach education: Practical recommendations for coach development administrators. *International Sport Coaching Journal, 5,* 169–175.

Pashler, H., McDaniel, M., Rohrer, D., & Bjork, R. (2009). Learning styles: Concepts and evidence. *Psychological Science in the Public Interest, 9*(3), 105–119. DOI: 10.1111/j.1539-6053.2009.01038.x

Pearson Education Limited (2019). *Pearson BTEC Level 3 National Diploma in Sport Specification (Issue 6).* Online accessed 19/11/2020 at [https://qualifications.pearson.com/content/dam/pdf/BTEC-Nationals/Sport/20161/specification-and-sample-assessments/9781446939482-BTEC-nationals_L3_diploma-sport-spec.pdf]

Pill, S. (2018). *Perspectives on Athlete-Centred Coaching.* Abingdon: Routledge

Seaman, J. (2012). Learning styles as a basis for paddlesports instruction: A review of the literature and some alternatives to add to the conversation. *Journal of Paddlesports Education.* Online accessed 10/02/2021 at [https://cdn.ymaws.com/www.americancanoe.org/resource/re smgr/sei-focus/learning_styles_as_a_basis_f.pdf]

Stodter, A., & Cushion, C. J. (2017). What works in coach learning, how, and for whom? A grounded process of soccer coaches' professional learning. *Qualitative Research in Sport, Exercise and Health, 9*(3), 321–338.

Stodter, A., & Cushion, C. J. (2019). Layers of learning in coach developers' practice-theories, preparation and delivery. *International Sport Coaching Journal, 6*(3), 307–316.

Stozkowski, J., & Collins, D. (2015). Sources, topics and use of knowledge by coaches. *Journal of Sports Sciences.* DOI: 0.1080/02640414.2015.1072279

Weinstein, Y., & Sumeracki, M. (2019). *Understanding How We Learn: A Visual Guide.* Abingdon: Routledge.

7 Common Misconceptions about Parental Involvement in Youth Sport

Insights for Coaches

Sam Elliott

Introduction

I recently delivered a workshop to a group of youth sport coaches who worked with elite (national and state level), sub-elite (regional and representative), community (local), and school (private programs) sporting athletes. The workshop was organized in response to a collective call for advice about 'dealing' with parents involved in their sports programmes. At the beginning of the workshop, I asked the coaches to participate in an interactive live poll using Slido™. The poll simply asked coaches to describe their experiences with parents in sport using less than five words. The activity was designed to gauge their general feelings of, dispositions toward, and perceptions about parents' involvement in organized sport. At the outset, it was clear that these coaches had cultivated a dichotomous understanding about parental involvement as a matter of being 'good' or 'bad' rather than what is recognized in the literature as a complex and 'intricate social experience' (Knight, Berrow, & Harwood, 2017, p. 96). Consequently, the point of departure for the workshop began with the identification of coaches deeply seeded beliefs that parents are problematic, and thus in need of repair. Notwithstanding the potential for parents to exhibit confrontation, abusive, and even aggressive behaviour in youth sport (e.g. see Elliott & Drummond, 2015; Shields, Bredemeier, LaVoi, & Power, 2005; Shields, LaVoi, Bredemeier, & Power, 2007), the aim of this chapter is to challenge the way in which coaches think about parents involvement in youth sport by drawing on the current evidence to illuminate some common misconceptions.

To begin, it is worthwhile considering how and why so many coaches view parents in a negative light. Individual experiences certainly play an influential role

Flinders University study on 'ugly parents syndrome' impact on falling sport interest

PARENTS' aggressive behaviour on the sidelines is embarrassing junior footballers, making them lose confidence and even quit the sport, research shows.

Figure 7.1 A headline example of how the media tend to report scholarly investigations about parental involvement in youth sport.

but notions about parental involvement in youth sport are deeply engrained in broader society and culture (Elliott & Drummond, 2013). Popular culture (e.g. movies such as *Friday Night Lights* and television series such as 'One Tree Hill') can reinforce, maintain, and perpetuate the notion that parents' involvement in their child's sport can be one of pressure, impossible expectations placed on children, and vicarious parenting behaviour (Elliott & Drummond, 2017a). It is further reinforced in how the media sensationalizes the negative, yet newsworthy stories about parenting in sport. A prominent tool of persuasion lies in the construction of headlines (e.g. see Figure 7.1) that include phrases such as 'ugly parent syndrome', 'helicopter parents', and 'pressuring parents' which ultimately shapes broader conversations in society and culture about parenting discourses in sport. The problem with sensationalizing stories about negative parental behaviour in youth sport is that it parsimoniously illuminates one aspect of a broader scientific literature that offers a rich understanding about the role of parents, the influence they exert on youth sport, and the factors that impact on parents' involvement (see Knight, 2019). Consequently, the way in which coaches tend to discuss parental involvement in youth sport is devoid of parents' enormous and largely positive involvement, without which, most children would not have access or opportunities to participate in organized sport (Holt & Knight, 2014).

The objective of this chapter is to highlight a series of commonly held views in practice about parental involvement in youth sport and present counter perspectives to these myths and misconceptions in an effort to enhance, expand, and extend coaches understanding about, and future interactions with, parents. It is hoped that by addressing these misconceptions, coaches will be better prepared to positively influence the way in which parent–coach interactions manifest in practice.

Misconception 1: 'The problem with parents is that they live vicariously through their child's sport'.

One deeply seeded idea is that pressuring, overzealous, highly invested, and highly competitive forms of parental involvement manifest from parents' vicarious desires for their children to achieve something parents themselves were unable to do (Holt & Knight, 2014). Indeed, popular press frequently attributes parents' inappropriate behaviours in youth sport to the notion of their own unfulfilled sporting ambitions (Dorsch, Smith, Wilson, & McDonough, 2015). This perspective is grounded in the 'reverse-dependency' literature in which it is posited that the underlying basis of parent-induced stress is a result of parents' identity with their children and desire for them to do well (Smoll, Cumming, & Smith, 2011).

Parents typically express a desire for their child to learn and experience fun and enjoyment in sport but tend to adapt goals over time based on their child's early successes and failures in sport (Dorsch et al., 2015). Consequently, parents can exhibit high social and emotional investment in their child's sport, even if their original intentions emphasized fun and learning through sport (Dorsch et al., 2015). However, the idea that vicarious forms of parental involvement can serve to fully explain why parents engage in youth sport in the manner that they do is limited because it fails to consider the range of additional and complex stressors – many of which involve interactions between parents and the surrounding youth sport climate – which can additionally influence the nature of parental involvement. For instance, several studies have shed light on the complex range of competitive, developmental, and organizational stressors parents encounter in youth sport (Harwood & Knight, 2009a, 2009b; Hayward, Knight, & Mellalieu, 2016; Wiersma & Fifer, 2008). Parents can experience varying degrees of competitive stress from pre-competition anxiety, child deselected or team omission, and the types of competitive behaviour their child displays during competition (Neely, McHugh, Dunn, & Holt, 2017). They can also encounter a range of organizational stressors including financial and time demands, governing organizational systems and processes, and concerns about coaching practices (Lienhart, Nicaise, Knight, & Guillet-Descas, 2020). Furthermore, it can be difficult for parents to manage developmental stressors associated with supporting their child's sporting and academic commitments and transition in and out of different pathways (Burgess, Knight, & Mellalieu, 2016).

This body of literature encourages coaches and clubs to move away from simplistic explanations and interpretations about parents in sport toward a more comprehensive understanding and appreciation for the factors that influence how parents behave in youth sport. Parental involvement is complex and can be influenced by other parents and coaches, the youth sport context (e.g. nature and cost of competition), concerns about their own behaviour, and their knowledge and previous experiences in sport (Knight, Dorsch, Osai, Haderlie, & Sellars, 2016). If coaches are to move beyond limiting conceptualizations of parenting in youth sport, they must first consider how parenting can be complex, demanding, and ever-changing.

Misconception 2: The way to address 'bad parents' is by using fines, codes of conduct, and policing measures.

While parents comprise a potential source of conflict and tension for coaches, umpires, and children (Elliott & Drummond, 2015), the literature also recognizes that the vast majority of parents behave in appropriate and supportive ways. For instance, Shields et al. (2005) found that only 13% of parents confessed to demonstrating 'angry criticism toward their child', while a further 14% of parents conceded that they have loudly yelled at or argued with a referee or sport official. Given the small, yet potentially negative risk that parents can pose, it is commonplace for youth sports to adopt a range of what Dorsch, King, Dunn, Osai, and Tulane (2017) describe as 'quick fix solutions' to manage, deter, and punish parental behaviours that undermine children's sport. However, it is possible that coaches and sporting providers overestimate the impact and efficacy of such methods which include fines, codes of conduct, and policing measures.

One of the most common 'quick fixes' are restrictive measures intended to police and/or censor parental side-line verbal behaviour during games (Omli & Wiese-Bjornstal, 2011). The 'Shoosh for kids' (https://sport.nsw.gov.au/ clubs/ryc/fairplay/ShooshforKids) campaign is a recent example of a restrictive approach through which an 'if you can't say anything nice, don't say anything' philosophy is at the heart of the campaign. Other concepts such as 'Silent Saturdays' are hyper-restrictive approaches involving the banning of *all* spectator verbal comments during games. It is arguable, however, that restrictive approaches are fundamentally flawed as a concept, because they have the potential to discourage all forms of parental verbal involvement including encouraging and supporting comments that children enjoy (Omli & Wiese-Bjornstal, 2011). This should not be underestimated given the association between enjoyment and children's continuation behaviour in organized sport.

In the case of the 'Shoosh for kids' campaign, a secondary issue manifests in how parents rationalize verbal comments under the guise of being 'supportive and encouraging'. On the one hand, passionately cheering a child's effort can be perceived as encouraging, while, on the other hand, it has the potential to be perceived as overzealous and a source of embarrassment for the child (Elliott & Drummond, 2017a). This confusion is preserved by a form of interpretation bias inherent in codes of behaviour, which ultimately reinforce and perpetuate inconsistent interpretations and enactment of policy. A final concern is that the restricting parental behaviour during competition may inevitably provoke intensified forms of involvement after the game (e.g. in the car on the way home) – well beyond the remit of clubs and coaches – which can be a precarious and often 'make or break' experience for parent–child relationships (Elliott & Drummond, 2017a, b; Tamminen, Poucher, & Povilaitis, 2017). Consequently, restrictive measures may not necessarily comprise an optimal solution for addressing parental behaviour and conduct in youth sport.

Another 'quick fix' involves the implementation of contractual measures which manifest as codes of behaviour (also known as codes of conduct). Codes of behaviour are generally perceived to be useful in establishing a baseline agreement for conduct in youth sport settings (Brackenridge, Pitchford, & Wilson, 2011). However, the historical and sociocultural context in which competition takes place can impact the effectiveness of codes of behaviour (Elliott & Drummond, 2015). For example, in the context of Australian football, it is commonplace for parents to read and sign a code of behaviour at the commencement of the season. However, as the season culminates in season-ending finals and awards, the effectiveness of the code of behaviour on parents' involvement is, according to parents, coaches, and child participants, questionable (Elliott & Drummond, 2015). The other inherent problem with codes of behaviour relates to interpretation bias. For instance, a typical code of behaviour may promote rules or codes such as 'be supportive and encouraging towards children' and 'do not shout instructions or criticisms to the child' (Smoll et al., 2011). This type reflects dichotomous classifications of parenting as either good or bad, supportive or pressuring, and positive or negative (Knight, 2019). Notwithstanding the fact that the research has consistently demonstrated that parenting in sport is a complex phenomenon, an overreliance on codes of behaviour is problematic because the meaning and enactment of support, encouragement, instruction, and criticism, for instance, may differ from person to person and context to context. For example, it is socially acceptable for parents and spectators to be quiet during service in a tennis match and equally acceptable to make noise from the side-line toward a player during an Australian football game (Elliott & Drummond, 2015). Similarly, the provision of specific, honest, and critical feedback may be inappropriate in some settings, especially if children perceive enhanced feelings of anxiety and reduced feelings of enjoyment and motivation. Yet, in other settings like talent pathways, specific and even 'harsh' feedback from parents may be seen as entirely appropriate and sought after in the eyes of child participants (Elliott, Drummond, & Knight, 2018). This perspective debunks the notion of a universal and shared understanding about what constitutes support and encouragement in youth sport, and thus reiterates why codes of behaviour cannot be solely relied upon to arrest issues surrounding inappropriate parental behaviour in youth sport.

A final approach, though less understood in the literature, involves the distribution of fines and other punitive measures to deter and punish negative parenting behaviours. Although this approach is not, to our knowledge, theorized or evaluated in the sport parenting literature, it can involve the banning of players and parents in response to unruly and inappropriate displays of negative parental involvement (Omli & Wiese-Bjornstal, 2011). For clubs and organizations that do employ a fines-based system, there are some unanswered questions that need addressing. For instance, who interprets what behaviours contravene acceptable and appropriate standards and what form of expertise and judgement do they possess? It is likely that this type of role is undertaken by a volunteer, which could provoke further disagreement and tension in such a role. Another issue relates to the nature of the punitive measure. How is the size of the fine, or the amount of games one is banned from, decided? The weight of punishment is particularly problematic because parents may positively assess a net benefit of actively engaging in unruly behaviour towards coaches, players, and officials, especially if the anticipated indiscretion (e.g. yelling at a coach or umpire) is deemed 'worth it'. To this end, an unintended consequence of employing punitive measures is the preservation, rather than discouragement, of problematic parenting behaviours. A final concern is that punitive measures, like restrictive and contractual measures, are relatively understudied in the field of sport parenting. Consequently, adopting such methods may not be best practice given that they present as reactive, atheoretical strategies for dealing with theoretically complex issues. Furthermore, the weight of evidence in the current stock of knowledge advocates for more interpersonal and educative approaches premised on working 'with' as opposed to 'against' and 'on top of' parents (Kwon, Elliott, & Velardo, 2020; Thrower, Harwood, & Spray, 2019).

Misconception 3: Parents should step back because coaches have the predominant influence on child-athlete development in sport

According to the literature, the dynamic relationship between parent, child, and coach shifts during the specializing years (children aged approximately 12–15 years) whereby parents tend to take a 'back seat' as the coach–athlete relationship rapidly develops (Côté, 1999). Many coaches prefer this because they perceive that parents can thwart their child's athletic development through the display of anger and complaints (Ross, Mallett, & Parkes, 2015) and failure to respect the role of the coach (Knight & Harwood, 2009). Within this backdrop, coaches can be forgiven for thinking that they exert the predominant influence of child–athlete outcomes in sport, especially as children begin to solidify their involvement in a chosen sport. However, current research perspectives indicate that the role of parents remains crucial throughout all stages of a young athlete's career (Wuerth, Lee, & Alfermann, 2004). This is reflected in a recently developed heuristic detailing the integrated and dynamic interactions between family, team, and environmental systems in youth sport (Dorsch et al., 2020). The 'youth sport system' as theorized by Dorsch et al. recognizes the influential role of the family unit, and parents specifically, on children's attitudes, behaviours, experiences, and outcomes across the entire sporting journey. Therefore, a more impactful and evidence-based position is the recognition that parents should not reduce their involvement (e.g. take a 'step' back) but rather adapt the nature of their involvement along the journey (Harwood & Knight, 2015; Wuerth et al., 2004).

If parents are to successfully adapt their involvement to different stages of their child's sporting development, one important consideration is their responsiveness to their child's preferences, needs, and changing goal orientations. For instance, parents can promote children's enjoyment in sport during the sampling years (e.g. 6–12 years) by showing care, listening, and participating in engaged and informed conversations, understanding children's pre, during, and post competition preferences and recognizing children as more than child-athletes (Furusa, Knight, & Hill, 2020). Yet in the specializing years (e.g. 12–15 years), some research suggests that athletes prefer parents to help them prepare for competition, provide support and encouragement during competition, and offer constructive feedback after competition (Knight, Neely, & Holt, 2011). Similarly, for parents who have children involved in high performance or talent pathways, especially during the specializing years (e.g. 12–15 years), research suggests that children's changing expectations, motivations, and dual-career opportunities require tailored and responsive forms of parental involvement (Elliott et al., 2018). Therefore, parents' ability to 'lean in to and out of' different roles and responsibilities across their child's sporting years is necessary for parents to optimize their involvement. What the research tells us is that there is not necessarily a net reduction of parents' involvement in youth sport but rather a modification to the roles and responsibilities they assume. Coaches should therefore temper expectations that parental involvement will decrease as children begin to solidify their involvement in sport. More aptly, coaches are encouraged to support parents to modify and respond to children's changing preferences and emotional needs as opposed to the gradual withdrawal of their involvement as coach–athlete relationships mature. The vital message here is that while coaches are clearly pivotal for the physical and psychosocial development of youth sport participants, so too are parents.

Misconception 4: To work with parents this season, it's just a matter of working out what 'types' of parents I will encounter.

A number of guidelines for communicating with parents in youth sport have been proposed in the literature (e.g. see Smoll et al., 2011; Van Mullem & Cole, 2015). The guidelines provide specific ideas and advice for coaches depending on the different 'types' of parents they might encounter. In a commentary by Van Mullem and Cole (2015), seven types of parents were described including performance-focused, emotionally driven, seasoned veteran, financial influencer, verbal abuser, submissive bystander, and clock watcher parents. Similarly, Smoll et al. (2011) contended that parents can be commonly classified as one of either disinterested, overly critical, scream from the bench, side-line coach, or overly protective. They suggest that pre-season meetings are an important feature of the youth sporting season for improving parent and coach communication, but the nature of interactions can be modified depending on the type of parents they encounter. Therefore, the guidelines perpetuate the idea that coaches merely need to decipher the kind of parents they will encounter each season to tailor their communication and interactions. I argue that this is a problematic scenario, because it ignores the underlying influences on parents' behaviour and involvement. To make this point a useful analogy is to imagine water running from a tap into a bucket with holes in it. Coaches who subscribe to a typology-oriented approach for communicating with parents are merely seeking to plug the most exposed holes to prevent leakage (which might manifest as the parenting behaviours which coaches find difficult). In this case, parental stress provoked, for instance, by coaching styles or a lack of feedback, if not address, will continue to pose a 'leakage' risk for coaches. Instead, coaches may be able to slow or stop the water flow altogether by understanding the difficulties parents are experiencing or anticipating and seeking ways to address them together rather than pigeonholing parents from the outset. In this way, any guidelines which encourage coaches to typecast parents may not necessarily be an optimal, particularly if coaches lack the training, skills, and experience to effectively implement such advice (O'Connor, 2011).

Summary

This chapter sought to expand coaches understanding about the complexity of being a parent in youth sport. By disrupting the dominant discourses surrounding parents in sport maintained and perpetuated by many coaches, it is hoped that readers will work to develop an empathetic and understanding approach if (and when) challenging situations occur with parents. Although it is beyond the scope of the chapter, it is worthwhile pointing out that more work is needed to progress theoretically informed discussions about parent–coach relationships in youth sport (Holt & Knight, 2014). However, in the meantime, the misconceptions presented here will hopefully provide a point of reflection for coaches to challenge their own assumptions about parenting behaviours and attitudes displayed in the context of youth sport. This is critical, perhaps now more so than ever, as sports seek to return in the wake of the global pandemic. Given the adverse impact of the pandemic on youth participants and parents physical and mental health (Elliott et al., 2021), the manner in which parents involve themselves in youth sport should be supported from an understanding perspective.

References

Brackenridge, C., Pitchford, A., & Wilson, M. (2011). Respect: Results of a pilot project designed to improve behaviour in English football. *Managing Leisure, 16*(3), 175–191.

Burgess, N. S., Knight, C., & Mellalieu, S. D. (2016). Parental stress and coping in elite youth gymnastics: An interpretative phenomenological analysis. *Qualitative Research in Sport, Exercise and Health, 8*(3), 237–256.

Côté, J. (1999). The influence of the family in the development of talent in sport. *The Sport Psychologist, 13*(4), 395–417.

Dorsch, T. E., King, M. Q., Dunn, C. R., Osai, K. V., & Tulane, S. (2017). The impact of evidence-based parent education in organized youth sport: A pilot study. *Journal of Applied Sport Psychology, 29*(2), 199–214.

Dorsch, T. E., Smith, A. L., Blazo, J. A., Coakley, J., Côté, J., Wagstaff, C. R., . . . King, M. Q. (2020). Toward an integrated understanding of the youth sport system. *Research Quarterly for Exercise and Sport*, 1–15.

Dorsch, T. E., Smith, A. L., Wilson, S. R., & McDonough, M. H. (2015). Parent goals and verbal sideline behavior in organized youth sport. *Sport, Exercise, and Performance Psychology, 4*(1), 19.

Elliott, S., & Drummond, M. (2013). A socio-cultural exploration of parental involvement in junior Australian Rules football. *Asia-Pacific Journal of Health, Sport and Physical Education, 4*(1), 35–48.

Elliott, S., & Drummond, M. (2015). The (limited) impact of sport policy on parental behaviour in youth sport: A qualitative inquiry in junior Australian football. *International Journal of Sport Policy and Politics, 7*(4), 519–530.

Elliott, S., & Drummond, M. (2017a). During play, the break, and the drive home: The meaning of parental verbal behaviour in youth sport. *Leisure Studies, 36*(5), 645–656.

Elliott, S., & Drummond, M. (2017b). Parents in youth sport: What happens after the game? *Sport, Education and Society, 22*(3), 391–406.

Elliott, S., Drummond, M., & Knight, C. (2018). The experiences of being a talented youth athlete: Lessons for parents. *Journal of Applied Sport Psychology, 30*(4), 437–455.

Elliott, S., Drummond, M., Prichard, I., Eime, R., Drummond, C., & Mason, R. (2021). Understanding the impact of COVID-19 on youth sport in Australia and consequences for future participation and retention. *BMC public health, 21*(1), 1–16.

Furusa, M. G., Knight, C., & Hill, D. M. (2020). Parental involvement and children's enjoyment in sport. *Qualitative Research in Sport, Exercise and Health*, 1–19.

Harwood, C., & Knight, C. (2015). Parenting in youth sport: A position paper on parenting expertise. *Psychology of Sport and Exercise, 16*, 24–35.

Harwood, C., & Knight, C. (2009a). Stress in youth sport: A developmental investigation of tennis parents. *Psychology of Sport and Exercise, 10*(4), 447–456. doi:10.1016/j.psychsport.2009.01.005

Harwood, C., & Knight, C. (2009b). Understanding parental stressors: An investigation of British tennis-parents. *Journal of Sports Sciences, 27*(4), 339–351.

Hayward, F., Knight, C., & Mellalieu, S. (2016). A longitudinal examination of stressors, appraisals, and coping in youth swimming. *Psychology of Sport and Exercise.*

Holt, N. L., & Knight, C. (2014). *Parenting in Youth Sport: From Research to Practice.* Routledge.

Knight, C. (2019). Revealing findings in youth sport parenting research. *Kinesiology Review, 8*(3), 252–259.

Knight, C., & Harwood, C. G. (2009). Exploring parent-related coaching stressors in British tennis: A developmental investigation. *International Journal of Sports Science & Coaching, 4*(4), 545–565.

Knight, C., Berrow, S. R., & Harwood, C. G. (2017). Parenting in sport. *Current Opinion in Psychology, 16*, 93–97.

Knight, C., Dorsch, T. E., Osai, K. V., Haderlie, K. L., & Sellars, P. A. (2016). Influences on parental involvement in youth sport. *Sport, Exercise, and Performance Psychology, 5*(2), 161.

Knight, C., Neely, K. C., & Holt, N. L. (2011). Parental behaviors in team sports: How do female athletes want parents to behave? *Journal of Applied Sport Psychology, 23*(1), 76–92.

Kwon, J., Elliott, S., & Velardo, S. (2020). Exploring perceptions about the feasibility of educational video resources as a strategy to support parental involvement in youth soccer. *Psychology of Sport and Exercise, 50*, 101730.

Lienhart, N., Nicaise, V., Knight, C., & Guillet-Descas, E. (2020). Understanding parent stressors and coping experiences in elite sports contexts. *Sport, Exercise, and Performance Psychology, 9*(3), 390.

Neely, K. C., McHugh, T.-L. F., Dunn, J. G., & Holt, N. L. (2017). Athletes and parents coping with deselection in competitive youth sport: A communal coping perspective. *Psychology of Sport and Exercise, 30*, 1–9.

O'Connor, D. (2011). Enhancing coach-parent relationships in youth sports: Increasing harmony and minimising hassle: A commentary. *International Journal of Sports Science & Coaching, 6*(1), 49–52.

Omli, J., & Wiese-Bjornstal, D. M. (2011). Kids speak: Preferred parental behavior at youth sport events. *Research Quarterly for Exercise and Sport, 82*(4), 702–711.

Ross, A. J., Mallett, C. J., & Parkes, J. F. (2015). The influence of parent sport behaviours on children's development: Youth coach and administrator perspectives. *International Journal of Sports Science & Coaching, 10*(4), 605–621.

Shields, D., Bredemeier, B., LaVoi, N., & Power, F. (2005). The sport behaviour of youth, parents and coaches. *Journal of Research in Character Education, 3*(1), 43–59.

Shields, D., LaVoi, N., Bredemeier, B., & Power, F. (2007). Predictors of poor sportspersonship in youth sports: Personal attitudes and social influences. *Journal of Sport and Exercise Psychology, 29*(6), 747–762.

Smoll, F. L., Cumming, S. P., & Smith, R. E. (2011). Enhancing coach–parent relationships in youth sports: Increasing harmony and minimizing hassle. *International Journal of Sports Science & Coaching, 6*(1), 13–26.

Tamminen, K. A., Poucher, Z. A., & Povilaitis, V. (2017). The car ride home: An interpretive examination of parent–athlete sport conversations. *Sport, Exercise, and Performance Psychology, 6*(4), 325.

Thrower, S. N., Harwood, C. G., & Spray, C. M. (2019). Educating and supporting tennis parents using web-based delivery methods: A novel online education program. *Journal of Applied Sport Psychology, 31*(3), 303–323.

Van Mullem, P., & Cole, M. (2015). Effective strategies for communicating with parents in sport. *Strategies, 28*(1), 13–17.

Wiersma, L. D., & Fifer, A. M. (2008). "The schedule has been tough but we think it's worth it": The joys, challenges, and recommendations of youth sport parents. *Journal of Leisure Research, 40*(4), 505–530.

Wuerth, S., Lee, M. J., & Alfermann, D. (2004). Parental involvement and athletes' career in youth sport. *Psychology of Sport and Exercise, 5*(1), 21–33.

8   Coaching is a 24-hour-a-day job

Brendan Cropley, Sheldon Hanton, and Lee Baldock

> My life in athletics never ends. There is never a moment that I can be out of touch with my job. It is truly a 24/7 job ... there simply isn't enough time to do what is required. Handling my work commitments with my commitments at home with personal time is impossible, and I always feel I am letting one part go to work on another.
>
> (ANONYMOUS NCAA ATHLETICS COACH IN LANGE, 2008).

It has become increasingly accepted that while sport coaching can be a potentially fulfilling vocation, it is also inherently contested and stressful (Cropley et al., 2020c). Researchers have detailed how coaches encounter a range of organizational, performance, and personal stressors due to the complex multiplicity of their role (e.g. Baldock et al., in press 2021; Olusoga et al., 2012). These demands, which are manifested in various ways depending on the context in which coaching occurs (e.g. participation; performance), are thought to place considerable internal and external pressure on individuals as they strive to ensure success through enacting an ever-expanding number of tasks and operating under idealistic expectations (Cropley et al., 2020b; McCarthy & Giges, 2017). This pressure is potentially magnified given the public evaluation of coaches' work, which is often measured by outcome parameters (e.g. win/loss record) that are determined by the performance of their athletes over which they have little control (Altfeld et al., 2018).

Perhaps as a result, there has been an underlying perception amongst many coaches that in order to fulfil their role requirements, they should dedicate increasing amounts of time and effort to the job. Indeed, engagement in coaching has been described as a consuming experience that encompasses long working hours (Olusoga & Thelwell, 2017). Such views are perhaps exacerbated by accounts of the *qualities of great sport coaching* by leading organizations, such as the International Olympic Committee (IOC), that detail, 'Coaching in many ways is a 24/7 365-days-a-year job as top coaches live and sleep the art of coaching' (IOC, nd). It is unsurprising, therefore, that more coaches, particularly those who occupy paid and full-time positions, have adopted the understanding that there is a requirement to commit themselves physically and mentally to coaching 24 hours-a-day (cf. Joncheray et al., 2019).

While some coaches may argue that their motivation, persistence, and passion for the job result in extended working hours (cf. Bentzen et al., 2017), we contend that this is potentially both counterproductive and irresponsible. It has become commonly accepted, for example, that coaches should be considered as *performers* in the sporting environment, and consequently they need to ensure that they are appropriately prepared and positioned to be able to *perform* (Rynne et al., 2017). It is unlikely, however, that adopting an attitude to practice that requires coaches to apply themselves and/or be available for their athletes and other stakeholders 24 hours-a-day will allow them to perform effectively over a sustained period of time – this is the crux of the *24-hour-a-day* myth. Specifically, such working practices are likely to increase feelings of depletion, cynicism, and devaluation (McNeill et al., 2017). Carson et al. (2019) also reported that coaches with less ability to manage their workload are more susceptible to experiencing ill-being (e.g. exhaustion, reduced sense of accomplishment). Consequently, it has been reported in a growing number of anecdotal accounts and empirical research studies that coaches who inappropriately over-extend themselves are more likely to experience decreased professional functioning and effectiveness, which can result in the psychological syndrome of *burnout* (e.g. Baldock et al., in press 2021; Cropley et al., 2020a; Olusoga et al., 2019).

We appreciate that the evolving pressure to succeed (whatever success may 'look like' across the different contexts in which coaches work) has resulted in a perceived need for coaches to go above and beyond what might be traditionally expected of them. Coaches often work irregular and long hours, regularly taking time out of their personal lives to complete work-related tasks as a result (Altfeld et al., 2018). In this chapter, however, we challenge the perception that coaching should be viewed and/or performed as a 24-hour-a-day job. We discuss the potential consequences associated with this *myth* through the perspectives of coach stress, coping, and mental well-being. In doing so, we consider how the notion of the *coach as a performer* should be expressed and highlight the importance of personal effectiveness and self-care strategies that can help coaches to better manage themselves, their workload, and their ability to perform. While our discussion predominantly focuses on those formally employed in coaching, who perhaps operate at the *performance level* (see Rynne et al., 2017), many of our arguments extend to other levels of sport, and thus all coaches should consider how the issues and implications presented translate to the context of their own work.

The demanding nature of coaching

> It (coaching) takes a toll on you … You're trying to be committed like the athlete, or they don't feel like you're putting in the same work they are. A lot of the time, you fear losing kids (athletes), ones that you have worked with for a long time. There are many parents that see their child as the next champion and, if you're not there, they may go elsewhere if they believe they aren't getting enough attention.

> (Nick Pedrazzini, Head Coach, Redlands Swim Club, Brisbane Australia; Sydney Morning Herald, 16/10/2019).

The nature of sport coaching is considered as inherently uncertain (e.g. sport is contested), ambiguous (e.g. coaches never know for certain what stakeholders are thinking), and complex (e.g. dynamic and micro-politically laden environments; Thompson et al., 2015).

Combine this with the range of roles and tasks that coaches are expected to carry out, and it is easy to understand why coaching is reported to be intrinsically demanding and why individuals may become consumed by the vocation (Cropley et al., 2020b; Olusoga & Thelwell, 2017). For example, researchers have reported that coaches can be responsible for, amongst other things, a variety of: (a) direct task behaviours (e.g. coaching and performance management, pastoral care); (b) indirect task behaviours (e.g. programming and scheduling, managing a team of athletes and support staff; recruitment and talent identification); (c) organizational and administrative behaviours (e.g. budgeting, reporting, record keeping); and (d) public relations behaviours (e.g. liaising with stakeholders, representing the organization; sharing with other coaches; Rynne et al., 2017).

In attempts to fulfil their role effectively, coaches need to build and sustain relationships with a range of stakeholders (e.g. athletes, parents, board members, sponsors) whose agendas are often in conflict (McCarthy & Giges, 2017; Thelwell et al., 2010). Indeed, coaching is, in essence, a social endeavour, underpinned by human-to-human interaction and the need to develop effective interpersonal relationships (Olusoga et al., 2019). Researchers have argued that occupations in which job roles are built on these relational principles often increase the risk of workers becoming frustrated, overwhelmed, and over-burdened (Schutte et al., 2000). This is perhaps particularly relevant to sport coaching as 'a coach and an athlete are mutually and causally interdependent and thus how one feels, thinks and behaves affects and is affected by how the other feels, thinks and behaves' (Jowett, 2017, p. 155).

High quality coach–athlete relationships take time to develop and require an on-going commitment to invest time, effort, and energy in order to maintain the strength of the relationship. It is likely, that in striving to build and maintain high-quality relationships, coaches dedicate more and more time to the individuals with whom they work in an attempt to demonstrate responsibility and care in the relationship and to be accountable for helping athletes gain a competitive edge (Davis et al., 2019). This is perhaps augmented as coaches are frequently primarily judged by the performance of their athletes and are consequently more likely to intensify their efforts to support athletes' goal striving and to help build their own professional standing (Altfeld et al., 2018). Certainly, the quality of the coach-athlete relationship is reported to be associated with important performance-related (e.g. motivation; efficacy) and mental well-being (e.g. positive affect) athlete outcomes and is considered to be an indicator of coach effectiveness (Jowett, 2017). The more athletes expect, therefore, the more the coach will perhaps give themselves to the role to satisfy such expectations irrespective of the personal investment this may require.

While managing relationships in the context in which the coach works is core to the coaching process, to operate effectively within their role coaches need to maintain their own psychological and emotional states by managing, coping, and adapting to the plethora of demands that are associated with their positions (Cropley et al., 2020a). As a result, considerable attention has been afforded to understanding the nature of the demands that coaches experience, particularly at the more elite levels of sport (see Baldock et al., 2020; Norris et al., 2017 for reviews). For example, coaches have indicated the experience of demands related to: performance factors (e.g. opposition, athlete performance, preparation, competition issues, pressure to succeed); organizational factors (e.g. finance, organizational stability, travel, administration, leadership, managing relationships); and personal factors (e.g. work–life balance, social life, personal relationships, well-being) (see e.g. Baldock et al., in press 2021; Potts et al., 2018; Thelwell et al., 2008). While such demands have been reported for some time, the emergent professional status of the field of sport coaching has arguably intensified the challenges that coaches experience. Indeed, researchers have recently highlighted: the growing internal and external pressures placed on coaches to perform due to augmented financial incentives (McNeill et al., 2018), the increasingly volatile nature of the professional sport environment (Hill & Sotiriadou, 2016), enhanced scrutiny (Cropley et al., 2020a), greater prevalence of short-term contracts linked to competition cycles (Altfeld et al., 2015), and high levels of job insecurity caused by high turnover rates, and the subsequent financial implications associated with job loss (Carson et al., 2019).

Demands are inevitable but coping efforts determine responses and outcomes

Coping, defined as 'constantly changing cognitive and behavioural efforts to manage specific external and/or internal demands that are appraised as taxing or exceeding the resources of the person' (Lazarus & Folkman, 1984, p. 141), is deemed as vital if coaches are to perform under pressure (Potts et al., 2018). Specifically, researchers have indicated that an inability to cope with stressors can hinder the level and direction of coaches' focus, increase the experience of negative affect, and impede their decision-making ability (Thelwell et al., 2017). Furthermore, a growing body of research has reported that failing to cope with the demands of sport coaching can potentially decrease professional functioning and detrimentally impact on physical health and mental well-being outcomes (e.g. low satisfaction, depression, burnout; see e.g. Bentzen et al., 2017; Olusoga et al., 2019). Conversely, coaches who are able to cope with the number and intensity of stressors they experience are able to demonstrate adaptive response patterns and even thrive in the high-pressure coaching environment (Brown et al., 2017; Cropley et al., 2020a). Individuals who are able to cope effectively, therefore, are likely to 'stay vital and engaged in their jobs over an extended period of time' (Bentzen et al., 2017, p. 143). Given the rapid development of the professional status of the field, however, Cropley et al. (2020b) asserted that a gap has emerged between how coaches are educated and developed and the skills required to cope with the demands associated with *modern-day* coaching. In support of this, researchers have recently reported that although coaches employ a multitude of coping strategies, coping efforts are often only moderately effective, and in some cases, ineffective (Baldock et al., in press 2021; Olsen et al., 2020).

The links between coping with stressful demands and perceptions of the *time intense* nature of coaching (and thus the understanding that coaching requires a 24-hours-a-day commitment) are perhaps twofold. First, to deal with the level of pressure placed on them to perform and the related level of insecurity that coaches experience in their jobs, it has been reported that coaches tend to extensively adopt *problem-focused* (e.g. approaches to dealing with the environmental demand) coping strategies (Olsen et al., 2020). In doing so, coaches may be attempting to exert a level of control over their role by engaging in different forms of preventive behaviours (e.g. planning; increasing effort). Such strategies could be associated with a *more is better* attitude, however, which over time is unlikely to be efficient or effective. Through longitudinal studies, researchers have supported this contention, asserting that by increasing engagement in the role to balance demands and coping efforts, coaches undertake longer yet less effective working hours (Altfeld et al., 2015; Bentzen et al., 2017).

Second, researchers have acknowledged the importance of coaches utilizing dyadic and social support mechanisms for effective coping (e.g. Norris et al., 2020; Thelwell et al., 2010). Nevertheless, in performance environments, which are characterized by high job turnover, where replacements for a coach's position are discussed in the media while the individual is still in-post, and where certain jobs are envied by many, coaches are less likely to utilize coping mechanisms that involve working with others (Baldock et al., in press 2021). The lack of trust that coaches may have in using such resources, possibly due to the lack of perceived job security which reduces their willingness to share their stress experiences, results in individuals bearing the full burden of the demands they encounter (Altfeld et al., 2018). Thus, coaches frequently use self-reliance strategies that require considerable personal investment.

In sum, coaches may feel that by increasing the amount of time they give to their role and coping attempts, they will be in a better position to enhance the level of control they have over the demands that they experience (e.g. 'If I put extra time into scheduling training my athlete is more likely to feel as though I am committed and so we can form a better relationship'). Coping, however, requires considerable effort (Lazarus & Folkman, 1984). Coaches need to ensure that they have the physical and mental capacities to make appropriate decisions when making sense of the demands they are experiencing and subsequently selecting and implementing coping mechanisms in a way that successfully deals with stressors in an efficient manner. Despite this, it has been detailed that coaches often forget to take time for themselves to rest and recover from the demands of their job, and thus reduce the likelihood that they will be able to sustain their performance (Olusoga et al., 2019). Increasing workload and devoting large amounts of time to meet the challenging demands of the job at the expense of coaches' own health and well-being, therefore, appears counterproductive. Indeed, inadequate coping skills, and insufficient recovery and time away from the job could lead to 'critical health situations that might contribute to emotional exhaustion and potentially burnout' (Altfeld et al., 2015, p. 138). The consequences of this also go beyond the coach, with researchers acknowledging that an imbalance between performance (e.g. managing demands) and recovery in coaches can directly influence athlete outcomes (e.g. performance, engagement, winning) and the coach–athlete relationship (Olusoga et al., 2010; Stebbings & Taylor, 2017). As a result, it appears imperative that coaches pay explicit attention to their psychological functioning in order to perform optimally in their role (McNeill et al., 2018).

Coach burnout: Key to dispelling the 24-hour myth

In light of the numerous and complex demands that coaches experience, and the seemingly limited ability to exert effective coping efforts, it has been posited that burnout, a negative work-related syndrome, is highly prevalent in the lives of coaches (Altfeld et al., 2018; McNeill et al., 2018). Burnout is defined as a multidimensional psychological syndrome with three central characteristics: (a) *emotional exhaustion* (e.g. feeling overwhelmed, emotional and/or physical depletion); (b) *depersonalisation* (e.g. a negative or detached attitude towards the personal relationships at work); and (c) *reduced personal accomplishment* (e.g. a sense of inefficiency, low self-esteem, inadequacy, see Olusoga et al., 2019). Burnout is widely considered to be an indicator of ill-being and is consequently linked to decreased performance at work, a reduction in coach–athlete relationship quality, and emotional (e.g. depressed mood) and cognitive (e.g. diminished decision-making) issues (Altfeld et al., 2018; Bentzen et al., 2017). Furthermore, athletes whose coaches report elevated levels of burnout have indicated that their coaches withdraw from coach–athlete interactions, become more autocratic in their coaching style, and are less empathetic (Kellmann et al., 2016).

There is a lack of consensus in the literature concerning the causes of burnout in coaches, perhaps because burnout is considered to be an 'individualised experience' (McNeill et al., 2017, p. 181). Researchers have suggested, however, that burnout is caused by, amongst other things, excessive workload, a lack of support, a lack of opportunity for personal and professional growth, limited control (e.g. over athlete performance; over work-based decisions), and a lack of balance between perceived effort and reward (Alfeld et al., 2018; Kellmann et al., 2016). Furthermore, it is thought that burnout results from individuals being exposed to chronic stressors over an extended period, during which they perceive that their personal resources (e.g. coping strategies) are outweighed by the level of the demands experienced (McNeill et al., 2017). Despite the lack of agreement, given that many causes relate to workload and being overburdened, it is permissible to argue that coaches who believe that the job requires extended personal investment and a 24-hour-a-day commitment are more likely to experience burnout. Consequently, it is imperative that coaches who adopt this attitude (and approach) redress the balance between the investment they make to the job (e.g. time) and the investment they make to themselves (e.g. recovery). We are not suggesting that coaches should relinquish responsibility in their role, but instead they need to improve their accountability to the concept of being a *performer* by developing work practices, recovery strategies, and personal resources that minimize the risk of burnout. Indeed, coaches widely advocate physical and psychological recovery strategies for their athletes to facilitate their adaptation to training and preparation for competition, yet rarely accept that the same principles relate to their own circumstances (Altfeld et al., 2018).

To summarize, we propose that coaches are not fulfilling their responsibility as a *performer* in the sporting environment, and their commitment to their athletes and employers, if they: (a) undertake excessive workloads that engulf their personal life; (b) do not undertake the necessary recovery strategies, including rest and rejuvenation, to balance themselves and restore personal resources; (c) do not develop personal and dyadic coping strategies that allow them to effectively adapt to the demands they experience; and (d) fail to proactively manage their ability to function in the different elements of their lives and thus position themselves to perform on a consistent basis. The potential severity of the personal and professional consequences of burnout offers a stark warning to coaches to thoroughly examine their working practices and the nature of their motivation (e.g. are behaviours initiated because they are satisfying, valued, and interesting or because the coach aims to avoid guilt, to enhance ego, or to satisfy external demand) that orientates them to commit themselves physically and mentally to the vocation 24 hours-a-day. In doing so, we argue that coaches need to locate their own mental well-being at the centre of their efforts to perform effectively in their role.

Mental well-being: Key to coach performance

Putting in more hours would be counterproductive to my well-being. It's (work–life balance) the most difficult part of the job. You need a supportive wife who is willing to make sacrifices in order for me to do my job properly … It's important that when you

do see the children, that you're totally there with them, which I'm going to be honest and
say I'm not, because I'm still thinking about other things (the job).

(Eddie Howe, former Bournemouth FC Head Coach,
England; *The Guardian* 06/11/2015)

The notion that mental well-being may be a key determinant of coach performance has gained momentum in recent literature, particularly as well-being has been classified as important for human *thriving* (e.g. the experience of personal development and success; Brown et al., 2017). Specifically, mental well-being is associated with an individual's level of psychological functioning, and researchers have argued that if a high-level of functioning is achieved, superior performance is likely to be experienced that 'orientates an individual to achieve success' (Brown et al., 2017, p. 168). This contention is supported by definitions of mental well-being that consider it to be a state of internal equilibrium, in which individuals are able to moderate their emotions, demonstrate flexibility in their ability to cope with adverse life events, and function in social and professional roles (Galderisi et al., 2015). Certainly, if coaches are able to experience high levels of happiness, satisfaction, and positive affect (e.g. *hedonic* well-being outcomes) through actualizing individual growth, leading a meaningful life, and realizing their own potential (e.g. *eudaimonic* well-being processes), it is likely that they will adopt adaptive approaches to managing the demands associated with their role and be better positioned to perform effectively (Cropley et al., 2020b).

Researchers have recently indicated that a number of work-related variables can have a negative impact on a coaches' experiences of mental well-being. These include spending more hours per week coaching, workload manageability, poor work–life balance, reduced perceptions of autonomy, lack of trust from their organization, and having few social networks in the sector (Carson et al., 2019; Norman & Rankin-Wright, 2018). Given that such variables have been consistently linked to emotional exhaustion, depersonalization, reduced personal accomplishment, and thus the onset of burnout, it appears imperative that coaches adopt an approach to practice that prioritizes their mental well-being. In relation to the purposes of this chapter, this means that coaches need to consider enhancing their *personal effectiveness* by learning to function productively with a sense of control, developing the personal characteristics that can mediate the stress experience (e.g. hardiness), and improving their ability to cope with demands while accomplishing the activities associated with their role (Mazerolle et al., 2011). Additionally, to counteract the demanding nature of their role and support their mental well-being, coaches should engage in self-care practices (e.g. time away from work, personal growth activities, reflective practice). Such practices have been purported to result in enhanced self-awareness and self-regulation (e.g. the capacity to manage and adapt cognitive and affective states to facilitate goal-directed behaviours), both of which can reduce the likelihood of burnout and enhance well-being (McNeill et al., 2018; Quartiroli et al., 2019).

Supporting the improvement of coach well-being is both an individual and organizational responsibility. For example, while it may be difficult to negotiate expanding workloads and irregular working hours, it is important that coaches commit to approaches that improve the balance between the different aspects of their lives, and thus give them the necessary time for recovery and rejuvenation (Olsen et al., 2020). Ensuring that coaches physically and mentally 'clock off', leaving work for work hours, and engaging in regular *mind-set cleanses* (e.g. identifying what coaches need to do more/less of and what they need to start/stop doing) would help to manage the balance (Altfeld, 2018). Sport organizations should also be proactive in tracking coach workload and work–life balance as well as staff satisfaction to identify potential issues before well-being is affected. In doing so, it is likely that individuals will be able to maintain a positive level of professional and social functioning/performance. Indeed, researchers have called for sport organizations to create specific policies that encourage the management of work hours to prevent potential employee burnout (Carson et al., 2019).

Individuals also need to develop strategies that allow them to be productive by *prioritizing the right things*. This may require coaches to really question their habitual routines and to be open-minded to the notion that even with a seemingly endless list of tasks to complete, they can still function productively by focusing on actions that matter most in a particular moment and then attending to those actions with full concentration, psychological space, and energy (Allen, 2015). The aim is to focus on those activities that can (to some extent) be controlled that are directly linked to the individual's sense of purpose, which helps to enhance perceptions of autonomy and competence (Stebbings & Taylor, 2017).

Coaches should dedicate time to their own personal and professional development, perhaps emphasizing growth in their coping repertoires and ability to self-regulate. Researchers have argued that coaches should emphasize the development and use of a wider range of emotion-focused coping strategies (e.g. attempts to manage the emotional response to demands) to mitigate the potentially negative impact of stressors (Olsen et al., 2020; Olusoga et al., 2012). Emotion-focused strategies can include the use of psychological skills (e.g. relaxation and activation strategies, self-talk, imagery) that can, if used effectively, re-focus individuals on intrinsic sources of enjoyment, support the maintenance of a sense of competence and purpose, enhance the experience of positive affect, and support psychological detachment from work (McNeill et al., 2018; Olsen et al., 2020). Finally, one mechanism that has recently been advocated as an approach that supports the development of the personal characteristics (e.g. hardiness) required to elicit adaptive responses to stressors, is that of *reflective practice* (Cropley et al., 2020a). Coaches are encouraged, therefore, to adopt an approach to work that emphasizes time and space for reflective practice to occur as a method of learning from their experiences, building on their strengths, and making better sense of their work and the environment in which it occurs (see Cropley et al., 2018 for a review). Sport organizations have a key role to play in providing coaches with the opportunities (e.g. provision of stress management training, advocating continual professional development) and resources (e.g. access to networks, dedicated time) to help coaches in their pursuit to improve use and effectiveness of coping strategies. By highlighting their commitment to supporting coach development, it is likely that coaches can feel more valued by their employers, which will potentially improve coach retention, enhance perceptions of relatedness, and facilitate mental well-being (Carson et al., 2019).

Concluding thoughts

I tell our guys here (coaching staff at the Baltimore Ravens) all the time: 'We're not punching the clock here'. You're going to be evaluated on how well your guys play. That's it. How well you're doing the job, not how long you're doing the job. But sometimes to do it well does take some time. There's a lot that goes into it.

(John Harbaugh, Baltimore Ravens NFL Coach;
Washington Post 18/05/2020)

Coaches are clearly highly passionate, persistent, and motivated individuals who strive to improve performance while working in demanding environments (Bentzen et al., 2017). As a result, we understand that coaches dedicate a considerable amount of time to the job in an attempt to fulfil the requirements of the multitude of activities they may be tasked with and in the quest to be successful. We also accept that to do this, coaches encounter numerous demands with which they must effectively cope to protect themselves from the adverse effects of stressors (e.g. strain; exhaustion) and to demonstrate the adaptive behaviours that allow them to survive and thrive in the complex situations in which they work (Cropley et al., 2020a). Given these circumstances, it is widely accepted that coaches should be considered as performers in their own right and must, therefore, exhibit the qualities (e.g.

personal effectiveness, personal characteristics, self-care, recovery mechanisms) that protect them from burnout, enhance their mental well-being, and position them to consistently perform in their role (Baldock et al., 2020). It is counterintuitive, therefore, to consider coaching as a 24-hour-a-day job. Specifically, individuals who operate in highly demanding environments and invest considerable amounts of time and effort to satisfy internal and external expectations are not likely, over a sustained period, to be able to maintain the psychological, emotional, and physical states required to perform effectively (Altfeld et al., 2018). We appreciate that there are many complex, interrelated factors associated with the notion of coaching being considered as a 24-hour-a-day job. Coaches who engage in extended working hours, taking time out of their personal lives to fulfil tasks associated with their role, often do so with good intentions. As we have argued in this chapter, however, coaches have a responsibility to their athletes, the field of coaching and to themselves to optimize their workloads and manage personal- and work-related variables to improve mental well-being, which is directly linked to human performance (cf. Brown et al., 2017). We challenge individuals and organizations, therefore, to alter their understanding of how success in sport can be achieved, swapping a *more is better* (24-hour-a-day) approach with one that embraces *performance through productivity*. To do this, focus should be placed on creating facilitative workplace conditions (e.g. collaborative working; recovery; autonomy), supporting individuals to develop a range of personal resources that can be used effectively to enable adaptive outcomes to demanding situations, and embracing the importance of mental well-being as a mechanism that supports thriving.

'You've got to work smart, not hard, but it's got to be effective … If you get an equal amount of stimulation, which is learning and fun, then you are going to perform better. It's no different for the coach; if I'm all learning and no fun then I'm going to perform only half as well as I possibly can. Enjoy the moment and understand now it's work time and now it's down time. If you get that balance right, you don't burn out you keep performing to a high level'.

(Steve Hansen, former New Zealand Rugby Union Head Coach;
ESPN 15/09/2015)

References

Allen, D. (2015). *Getting Things Done* (2nd ed.). Pitakus.

Altfeld, S., Mallett, C., & Kellmann, M. (2015). Coaches' burnout, stress, and recovery over a season: A longitudinal study. *International Sport Coaching Journal, 2,* 137–151. http://dx.doi.org/10.1123/iscj.2014-0113

Altfeld, S., Schaffran, P., Kleinert, J., & Kellmann, M. (2018). Minimising the risk of coach burnout: From research to practice. *International Sport Coaching Journal, 5,* 71–78. https://doi.org/10.1123/iscj.2017-0033

Baldock, L., Cropley, B., Mellalieu, S. D., & Neil, R. (2020). Stress and well-being of those operating in groups. In R. Schinke & D. Hackfort (Eds.), *The Routledge International Encyclopaedia of Sport and Exercise Psychology* (pp. 620–634). Routledge.

Baldock, L., Cropley, B., Neil, R., & Mellalieu, S. D. (in press, 2021). Stress and mental well-being experiences of professional football coaches. *The Sport Psychologist.*

Bentzen, M., Lemyre, N., & Kenttä, G. (2017). A comparison of high-performance football coaches experiencing high- versus low-burnout symptoms across a season of play: Quality of motivation and recovery matters. *International Sport Coaching Journal, 4,* 133–146. https://doi.org/10.1123/iscj.2016-0045

Brown, D., Arnold, R., Fletcher, D., & Standage, M. (2017). Human thriving. A conceptual debate and literature review. *European Psychologist, 22,* 167–179. https://doi.org/10.1027/1016-9040/a000294

Carson, F., Malakellis, M., Walsh, J., Main, L., & Kremer, P. (2019). Examining the mental well-being of Australian sport coaches. *International Journal of Environmental Research and Public Health, 16,* 1–12. https://doi.org/10.3390/ijerph16234601

Cropley, B., Baldock, L., Hanton, S., Gucciardi, D., McKay, A., Neil, R., & Williams, T. (2020a). A multi-study exploration of factors that optimize hardiness in sport coaches and the role of reflective practice in facilitating hardy attitudes. *Frontiers in Psychology.* https://doi.org/10.3389/fpsyg.2020.01823

Cropley, B., Miles, A., & Knowles, Z. (2018). Making reflective practice beneficial. In R. Thelwell & M. Dicks (Eds.), *Professional Advances in Sports Coaching: Research and Practice* (pp. 377–396). Routledge.

Cropley, B., Thelwell, R., Mallett, C., & Dieffenbach, K. (2020b). A commentary and reflection on sport psychology in the discipline of sports coaching. *Journal of Applied Sport Psychology, 32,* 121–128. https://doi.org/10.1080/10413200.2019.1695690

Cropley, B., Thelwell, R., Mallett, C., & Dieffenbach, K. (2020c). Editorial: Exploring sport psychology in the discipline of sports coaching. *Journal of Applied Sport Psychology, 32,* 1–4. https://doi.org/10.1080/10413200.2019.1695295

Davis, L., Jowett, S., & Tafvelin, S. (2019). Communication strategies: The fuel for quality coach-athlete relationships and athlete satisfaction. *Frontiers in Psychology.* https://doi.org/10.3389/fpsyg.2019.02156

Galderisi, S., Heinz, A., Kastrup, M., Beezhod, J., & Sartorius, N. (2015). Toward a new definition of mental health. *World Psychiatry, 14,* 231–233. https://doi.org/10.1002/wps.20231

Hill, B., & Sotiriadou, P. (2016). Coach decision-making and the relative age effect on talent selection in football. *European Sport Management Quarterly, 16,* 292–315. https://doi.org/10.1080/16184742.2015.1131730

International Olympic Committee (n.d.). *Qualities of a Great Sports Coach.* https://stillmed.olympic.org/media/Document%20Library/OlympicOrg/IOC/What-We-Do/Protecting-Clean-Athletes/Athletes-Space/Athletes-Entourage/Coaches/EN-Qualities-of-a-coach.pdf - accessed on 12/12/2020.

Joncheray, H., Burlot, F., & Julla-Marcy, M. (2019). Is the game lost in advance? Being a high-performance coach and preserving family life. *International Journal of Sports Science & Coaching, 14,* 453–462. https://doi.org/10.1177/1747954119860223

Jowett, S. (2017). Coaching effectiveness: The coach-athlete relationship at its heart. *Current Opinion in Psychology, 16,* 154–158. http://dx.doi.org/10.1016/j.copsyc.2017.05.006

Kellmann, M., Altfeld, S., & Mallett, C. (2016). Recovery-stress imbalance in Australian football league coaches: A pilot longitudinal study. *International Journal of Sport and Exercise Psychology, 14,* 240–249. https://doi.org/10.1080/1612197X.2015.1020662

Kobasa, S. (1979). Stressful life events, personality, and health: an inquiry into hardiness. *Journal of Personal and Social Psychology, 37,* 1–11. https://doi.org/10.1037//0022-3514

Lange, C. (2008). *A Matter of Balance: Work and Life in Intercollegiate Athletics.* NCAA.

Lazarus, R., & Folkman, S. (1984). *Stress, Appraisal, and Coping.* Springer.

Mazerolle, S., Pitney, W., Casa, D., & Pagnotta, K. (2011). Assessing strategies to manage work and life balance of athletic trainers working in the NCAA Division I setting. *Journal of Athletic Training, 46,* 194–205. https://doi.org/10.4085/1062-6050-46.2.194

McCarthy, P., & Giges, B. (2017). Helping coaches meet their psychological needs. In R. Thelwell, C. Harwood, & I. Greenlees (Eds.), *The Psychology of Sports Coaching. Research and Practice* (pp. 101–113). Routledge.

McNeill, K., Durand-Bush, N., & Lemyre, N. (2017). Understanding coach burnout and underlying emotions: A narrative approach. *Sports Coaching Review, 6,* 179–196. http://dx.doi.org/10.1080/21640629.2016.1163008

Norman, L., & Rankin-Wright, A. (2018). Surviving rather than thriving: Understanding the experiences of women coaches using a theory of gendered social well-being. *International Review of the Sociology of Sport, 53,* 424–450. https://doi.org/10.1177%2F1012690216660283

Norris, L., Didymus, F. F., & Kaiseler, M. (2017). Stressors, coping, and well-being among sports coaches: A systematic review. *Psychology of Sport and Exercise, 33,* 93–112. https://doi.org/10.1016/j.psychsport.2017.08.005

Norris, L., Didymus, F. F., & Kaiseler, M. (2020). Understanding social networks and social support resources with sports coaches. *Psychology of Sport and Exercise.* Ahead of print: https://doi.org/10.1016/j.psychsport.2020.101665

Olsen, M., Haugan, J., Hrozanova, M., & Moen, F. (2020). Coping amongst elite-level sports coaches: A systematic review. *International Sport Coaching Journal.* https://doi.org/10.1123/iscj.2019-0051

Olusoga, P., Bentzen, M., & Kenttä, G. (2019). Coach burnout: A scoping review. *International Sport Coaching Journal, 6,* 42–62. https://doi.org/10.1123/iscj.2017-0094

Olusoga, P., Maynard, I., Hays, K., and Butt, J. (2012). Coaching under pressure: A study of Olympic coaches. *Journal of Sports Sciences, 30,* 229–239. https://doi.org/10.1080/02640414.2011.639384

Olusoga, P., & Thelwell, R. (2017). Coach stress and associated implications. In R. Thelwell, C. Harwood, & I. Greenlees (Eds.), *The Psychology of Sports Coaching. Research and Practice* (pp. 128–141). Routledge.

Potts, A., Didymus, F. F., & Kaiseler, M. (2018). Exploring stressors and coping among volunteer, part-time and full-time sports coaches. *Qualitative Research in Sport, Exercise & Health, 11,* 46–68. https://doi.org/10.1080/2159676X.2018.1457562

Quartiroli, A., Etzel, E., Knight, S., & Zakrajsek, R. (2019). Self-care as key to others' care: The perspectives of globally situated experienced senior-level sport psychology practitioners. *Journal of Applied Sport Psychology, 31,* 147–167. https://doi.org/10.1080/10413200.2018.1460420

Rynne, S. B., Mallett, C., & Rabjohns, M. (2017). High performance coaching: Demands and development. In R. Thelwell, C. Harwood, & I. Greenlees (Eds.), *The Psychology of Sports Coaching. Research and Practice* (pp. 114–126). Routledge.

Schutte, N., Toppinen, S., Kalimo, R., & Schaufeli, W. (2000). The factorial validity of the Maslach Burnout Inventory-General Survey across occupational groups and nations. *Journal of Occupational and Organizational Psychology, 73*, 53–66. https://psycnet.apa.org/doi/10.1348/096317900166877

Stebbings, J., & Taylor, I. (2017). Definitions and correlations of coach psychological well- and ill-being. In R. Thelwell, C. Harwood, & I. Greenless (Eds.), *The Psychology of Sports Coaching: Research and Practice* (pp. 170–184). Routledge.

Thelwell, R., Wagstaff, C., Rayner, A., Chapman, M., and Barker, J. (2017). Exploring athletes' perceptions of coach stress in elite sport environments. *Journal of Sports Sciences, 35*, 44–55. https://doi.org/10.1080/02640414.2016.1154979

Thelwell, R., Weston, N., & Greenlees, I. (2010). Coping with stressors in elite sport: A coach perspective. *European Journal of Sport Science, 10*, 243–253. https://doi.org/10.1080/17461390903353390

Thelwell, R., Weston, N., Greenlees, I., & Hutchings, N. (2008). Stressors in elite sport: A coach perspective. *Journal of Sport Sciences, 26*, 905–918. https://doi.org/10.1080/02640410801885933

Thompson, A., Potrac, P., & Jones, R. (2015). 'I found out the hard way': Micro-political workings in professional football. *Sport, Education and Society, 20*, 976–994. https://doi.org/10.1080/13573322.2013.862786

9   10,000 hours and Early Specialization

Short-term Gains or Long-term Pain?

Jody McGowan, Simon Walters, and Chris Whatman

Introduction

10,000 hours of practice is often cited as the magic number required to become an expert. As outlined in chapter 1, this 'myth' became conversationally popular after Malcolm Gladwell, in his 2008 book *Outliers: The story of success* devoted an entire section to it (Gladwell, 2008). However, it is a concept that has been mis-used in a sporting context for a lot longer (Ford, Ward, Hodges, & Mark Williams, 2009). The 10,000 hours concept emerged in 1993 following research on elite violinists titled 'the role of deliberate practice in the acquisition of elite performance' (Ericsson, Krampe, & Tesch-Roemer, 1993). This retrospective study compared 10 of the best violin students from a world-renowned music academy to 10 potential career violinists who were simply 'good' and 10 performers who were likely to become nothing more than music teachers. Following individual interviews, and based on retrospective reporting of practice hours, they estimated that the violinists in the top group would have on average amassed 10,000 hours of practice by the age of 20, most of this being deliberate practice (organized and structured activities in which the main aim is skill development and enhancing performance). This contrasted with the merely 'good' group, who they estimated at around 8,000 hours and the 'teachers' group at just 5,000. The authors concluded that deliberate practice was an important factor in differentiating the expert from the merely good in this group of musicians. They did not, however, state that 10,000 hours should be treated as a rule or target, nor that by applying this number of hours to other aspects of life would ensure expertise. Additionally, little attention was given to individual variability in each group. For example, some in the 'good' group amassed over 10,000 hours and some in the expert group less. Despite this number being a theory based on estimation, this research suggested that deliberate practice had a big effect on reaching expert or elite status. In the sporting context, this research simply added momentum to a practice that was largely witnessed already in eastern bloc countries. This involved a process of talent identification based on physical characteristics followed by intensive specific training from a young age. The aim was to produce world-class athletes, which in some cases did occur, albeit at a massive cost to many who did not make it (Popkin, Bayomy, & Ahmad, 2019).

10,000 hours was a concept that was easily understood, easily reported in popular media and nicely simplistic for a lay audience. The myth quickly became embedded in the world of coaching and athlete development and the "10,000-hour rule" became one of the major drivers for earlier intensive sport-specific training in children in Western societies. This concept is now recognized in the youth sport literature as early specialization.

Sport specialization has been defined as intensive participation in one sport, year round, at the exclusion of other sports (Jayanthi, Labella, Fischer, Pasulka, & Dugas, 2015). Early specialization refers to this practice occurring before the onset of puberty (Downing, Redelius, & Nordin-Bates, 2020). Several expert sport medicine groups have discouraged early specialization and it has been shown in many disciplines to have several potentially negative consequences. Psychological; athletes burn out (Brenner, 2007; DiFiori et al., 2014; Donald-son & Ronan, 2006; Myer et al., 2015) and have a sense of identity predominantly based around themselves as athletes (Ryba, Aunola, Kalaja, Selanne, & Ronkainen, 2016), physical; athletes get injured (Jayanthi et al., 2015; McGuine et al., 2017; Pasulka, Jayanthi, McCann, Dugas, & LaBella, 2017; Post et al., 2017), and sociological; athletes may become socially isolated by intense training regimes (Malina, 2010; Popkin et al., 2019). Also, the main driver for youth specializing early, deliberately, and intensively practicing skills to get a 'head start' in the competitive world of that sport has also been debunked recently (Matzkin & Garvey, 2019; Roetert, Woods, & Jayanthi, 2018). In most sports, early specialization does not appear to result in an increased likelihood of achieving elite success as an adult (Bridge & Toms, 2013; Buckley et al., 2017; Moesch, Elbe, Hauge, & Wikman, 2011; Wilhelm, Choi, & Deitch, 2017). In a sample of 148 elite and 95 near elite Danish athletes, results clearly demonstrated that the elite athletes had specialized at an older age, they had trained less when they were children and they had intensified their training more than their near elite peers in late adolescence (Moesch et al., 2011). On the pro-early specialization side of the argument, we hear many anecdotes of elite success (Tiger Woods, the Williams sisters) as a result of intensive, deliberate practice from a young age (Smith, 2015). So, although the literature seems to expose some fundamental flaws in the message to specialize early, many athletes, parents, and coaches continue to buy into the magical 10,000 hours of practice notion as a probable pathway to elite success. The purpose of this chapter is to explore the negative effects to a young person's health from specializing too early, specifically the physiological effects of intensive participation in specialized training programmes during the vulnerable adolescent growth period. We will look at the international injury data emerging from these practices and will then address the important question: how much is too much? Finally, we will present some international best practice athlete development examples.

Early adolescent physiological vulnerability in sport: Are we creating long-term pain?

The musculoskeletal system of children is physiologically vulnerable during peak periods of growth (Jackowski et al., 2009; Zwick & Kocher, 2014). In an immature skeleton, the presence of epiphyseal growth plates results in vulnerable sections in the long bones of the skeleton that are prone to both acute shearing forces and repeated traction from attached tendons and muscles (Caine & Purcell, 2016). During the adolescent growth spurt, the various layers in the growth plate in long bones undergo rapid proliferation and render these regions weaker than that of mature bone (Zwick & Kocher, 2014). It has also been shown that bone mineral density is lowest during and just after the adolescent growth spurt (Jackowski et al., 2009; Zwick & Kocher, 2014), making bone injury more likely. An immature skeleton also has apophyses, which are secondary ossification centres in bones and attachments for tendons (Rosendahl & Strouse, 2016). These apophyses are a source of physiological vulnerability to loading. Sudden acute forces can result in acute avulsion fractures, or gradual overloading from repetitive tasks can result in stress-related conditions such as severs disease (heel pain) (Caine & Purcell, 2016). Skeletal maturation and growth occur in response to hormonal changes that occur during puberty. There is a significant variation in the chronological age at the onset of puberty. Race (Burrows, Baxter-Jones, Mirwald, Macdonald, & McKay, 2009), gender (Sheehan & Lienhard, 2019), nutrition (Johnson et al., 2013), environment (Santos et al., 2019), and genetics (Huang, Biro, & Dorn, 2009) can all influence individual timing as well as the rate of growth and maturation changes. Peak height velocity refers to the period in which a child experiences the fastest increase in their long bone growth during adolescence. Girls typically reach peak height velocity earlier than boys (11.3 ± 0.4 years versus 13.4 ± 0.3 years) (Sheehan & Lienhard, 2019). These intrinsic vulnerabilities expose children to an injury risk that mature adults no longer carry.

Sport carries an inherent risk of injury, however, certain training behaviours and competition environments during the adolescent growth spurt have been shown to increase the risk of injury to the growing athlete (Hartwig et al., 2019; Jayanthi et al., 2015; Luke et al., 2011; Post et al., 2017; Roos, Taube, Zuest, Clénin, & Wyss, 2015; Theisen et al., 2013; Walters, Read, & Estes, 2017). Both the number of sports injuries and the type of injury appears to differ from the adult population (Wik et al., 2020). It is estimated that between 44–74% of children younger than 15 years sustain a sport- related injury every year (McGowan, Whatman, & Walters, 2020; Street & Jacobsen, 2017). In par- ticular, overuse injuries are an increasing concern worldwide. By definition, an overuse injury is one that occurs gradually due to submaximal loading of tissue (DiFiori et al., 2014). As mentioned earlier, the relative weakness of the growth plate during the pubertal growth spurt and the presence of apophyses means repeated high loading can result in localized inflammatory pain, often termed as traction aphophysitis. Conditions such as Osgood Schlatter's disease and sev- ers disease are common examples of this phenomenon and have been noted to be presenting in increasing numbers in clinical practice over the past 10 years (DiFiori, 2010). The phenomenon of early specialization has seen a significant increase in pre-pubescent children attending multiple training sessions every week for the same sport. These sessions are often heavily focussed on the deliber- ate practice model, where adult-directed drills result in children repeating similar tasks many times over. Several studies have demonstrated an association between training hours and overuse injury. In our study of NZ children aged 10–13 years who attended a sport tournament, we found for every additional hour of train- ing per week, children increased their odds of sustaining an overuse injury by 9%. When sports start demanding multiple training sessions, the odds for injury simply start to increase for the child. There is also evidence that participating in a single organized sport year-round increases the risk of sustaining an overuse injury (Cuff, Loud, & O'Riordan, 2010). Early specialization practices often see sports which have traditionally been seasonal, spanning multiple seasons due to elite skill camps, training academies, and off-season competitions. All of these 'add-ons' are touted as offering advantages to the young athlete, a chance to get ahead of the bunch, but with the associated increased injury risk, it is likely to have the opposite effect. Injuries can cause significant pain and disability to the young athlete, and consequently a decline in performance or even dropout. In order to minimize injury risk, sport organizations and coaches should be aware of the age of the adolescent growth spurt and look out for its identifiable signs, such as rapid growth in stature (height) and leg length (Wik et al., 2020).

Winning at all cost? Important considerations for coaches when working with early adolescent children in sport

With the pressure to succeed in sport, we are seeing many children partake in intensive sport-specific training from increasingly young ages. In a study we conducted on New Zealand children (mean age 12.6 ± 0.5 years) attending a national sporting competition in 2017, we found 25% were highly specialized and a further 43% were moderately specialized (on a path to specialization). Seventy-seven per cent of children we surveyed stated they participated in a single sport year-round. This is despite the evidence of the risk of injury increasing with these practices. In a survey of 117 coaches and 226 players (mean age 15.4 ±1.4 years) from netball, football and basketball teams in New Zealand, 87% of players reported hiding an injury to continue playing, and 87% of coaches had witnessed an injured player play on when they clearly should not have (Whatman, Walters, & Schluter, 2018). For clinicians in New Zealand, this is supported by what we are seeing in our practice – young athletes feeling pressured to return early from injury. The culture of win at all costs that has crept its way into children's sport is a real concern. Who is going to remember the 12-year-old local club rugby champions from 2020 when selecting the All Blacks in 2030? Children who play when injured are not only risking long-term pain or disability but also risk having to deal with poor performance and a sense of failure.

This has been demonstrated multiple times in clinical practice. A clinical example of this was that of two 12-year-old boys who were referred to physiotherapy. They had both sustained a sport-related knee injury, resulting in surgery to reconstruct the anterior cruciate ligament. One had been playing a team sport since he was 5. He had played for his club team, and each year from age 8, had been selected in the 'club representative team' for his age group. This year, he had also been selected in the provincial team. He was training for these teams every night except Friday and played two to three games each weekend. The other boy was an academy player in another popular team sport, 'a real talent' according to his mother. He was playing for the club side, the representative side, and attended academy trainings three times weekly, with intensive training camps for an entire week over the school holidays. Both boys had sustained what can only be termed as catastrophic injuries, which 10 years earlier would have been a completely unusual occurrence in the physiotherapy clinic. Both rehabilitated well, but neither returned to their previous sport. They felt left behind. Maybe coincidently, but in the 14–16 months of rehabilitating, many of their peers had grown and excelled in their sport. These two boys' training schedules resembled that of an elite athlete at ages 10–11 and 12. Unfortunately, these types of injuries, with similar background training stories, are presenting in increasing frequency to sport medicine clinics (McGowan, Reid, & Caldwell, 2017).

There is a growing body of evidence suggesting an association between training volume and injury in children participating in intensive organized sport (Cuff et al., 2010; Jayanthi et al., 2015; McGowan et al., 2020; Olsen, Fleisig, Dun, Loftice, & Andrews, 2006; Post et al., 2017). The pressure to perform, and the pressure to win in sports involving players this young is perceived in New Zealand by many as damaging our young athletes and has led to a 'Balance is Better' campaign initiated by Sport New Zealand (our government agency for sport) and five of our biggest sports (Football, rugby, netball, hockey, and cricket). The campaign has arisen due to concerns over increasing youth dropout rates from sport, a corresponding increase in youth sport injuries over the last decade, and concerns about burnout and a lack of age-appropriate developmental opportunities (Accident Compensation Corporation, 2017; Zealand, 2020).

So how much is too much? How do we know when to push and when to back off? And what is being done to elicit change?

The volume of weekly sport participation may be the most important factor in analysing injury risk in youth athletes (McGowan et al., 2020). Single sport specialization may be a stand-alone risk factor to increased injury in some youth sports (Bell et al., 2016; Hall, Barber Foss, Hewett, & Myer, 2015; Jayanthi et al., 2015; McGuine et al., 2017; Pasulka et al., 2017; Post et al., 2017). However, it may be more correct to discuss how specializing *early* (remember this is defined as before the onset of puberty) leads to large volumes of intense training, and how this increases injury risk. Seventy five per cent of children in the 10–13 year old age group we investigated were still playing multiple sports, but for many of them (48%), at least one of their sports involved an intensive training pathway

(McGowan et al., 2020). In that 48%, we found a significant association with injury, with these multi-sport athletes having 1.72 times the odds of sustaining an overuse injury when compared to the single sport (specialized) group. Therefore, despite these children sampling a range of sports as recommended in youth sport guidelines (Brenner et al., 2016; LaPrade et al., 2016; Lloyd et al., 2016; McLeod et al., 2011), they were also engaging in significant weekly volumes of organized sport and sustaining more overuse injuries. This intensive sport participation also leaves no time for rest or to participate in unstructured play. So what does the research tell us regarding how much is too much in youth sport?

Participating in structured sport practice and competition for more hours per week than chronological age (in years) has been shown in several studies to increase the risk of any injury (Jayanthi et al., 2015; Post et al., 2017; Purnell, Shirley, Nicholson, & Adams, 2010) and overuse injury (Jayanthi et al., 2015; McGowan et al., 2020) in youth athletes. While this is possibly still too much for many children (McGowan et al., 2020; Purnell et al., 2010), and in particular those going through their adolescent growth spurt (Wik et al., 2020), it is a clear, easy-to-remember guide for organizations, coaches and parents to manage volume.

Participating in a single sport continuously for more than 8 months of the year was also shown to increase the risk of any injury (McGowan et al., 2020; Post et al., 2017) and overuse injury (Cuff et al., 2010; McGowan et al., 2020; Olsen et al., 2006; Post et al., 2017) in youth athletes. It appears important to make sure sports have an off season as used to be the norm. Simple changes like avoiding training through school holidays will go a long way to reducing injury risk whilst at the same time encouraging young people to participate in less adult-controlled structured activities and engage in more free-play (Coutinho, Mesquita, Davids, Fonseca, & Côté, 2016; McGowan et al., 2020; Memmert, Baker, & Bertsch, 2010).

Children who engage in more than twice as many hours per week in organized sport compared with hours spent being active in free-play (unstructured adult free activity) have been found to be 1.52 times more likely to sustain an overuse injury, irrespective of the total number of hours per week of activity (McGowan et al., 2020). Quite simply, encourage more free play.

There is no magic number defining success. No number of hours on its own, no magic age when there will be the ability to tolerate intensive specialized training, no magic way to prevent all sport injuries. The old saying 'practice makes perfect' has seen multiple re-incarcerations, most recently from Popkin et al.:

'perfect practice at the right time, in an intrinsically driven athlete, makes perfect' (Popkin et al., 2019). What we can be sure of, is that 10,000 hours is not going to guarantee success, and for the majority will result in either injury, burnout, and subsequently drop out with implications for wellbeing. Making sport fun and safe for children who have yet to reach skeletal maturity is essential for the long-term health of our population. Sports organizations, coaches, parents, teachers, health professionals, and sport administrators all need to do their part in protecting the future of the early adolescent participant in sport.

There are some positive changes taking place. In New Zealand, the major sport governing body rolled out the 'Balance is Better' campaign (Zealand, 2020). This evidence-based framework promotes an approach to youth sport aimed at maximizing participation rates, enjoyment, and skill development in a safe environment. Their website has resources for coaches, parents, and administrators to understand the rationale for not pushing early specialization, as well as practical ideas, case studies, and methods to evoke change. https://balanceisbetter.org.nz/.

In Norway, the national governing body for sport (NIF) legislated rules for children which included the removal of published competition tables in sport for children under the age of 12 (Skirstad, Waddington, & Safvenbom, 2012). The focus on ensuring the child's rights were met has resulted in increased participation numbers in youth sport (Green, Roberts, Thurston, & Vaage, 2015), as well as their most successful Winter Olympics medal haul in 2018 (Mather, 2018). In Sweden, the United Nations Convention on the Rights of the Child was incorporated into Swedish sport (Eliasson, 2017), being formally written into Swedish law in January 2020 (Government Offices of Sweden, 2020). A recent law was also introduced in Puerto Rico that supports the development of policies protecting minors in sport including the removal of competition tables before age 9 and no more than 3 games per week until age 16 (Farrey, 2020). Violation of any of these countries' rules sees coaches and clubs facing fines or suspension (Ellingsen & Danielsen, 2017; Farrey, 2020).

The significance of coaches to a young person's sporting experiences and development cannot be overestimated. In a recent U.S. study examining what children enjoy about their sporting experience, 81 determinants of fun were identified (Visek et al., 2018). Five of the top ten reasons related to the influence of coaches or the environment created by coaches. Coaches therefore can have a major influence on parents' decisions to specialize their children early. However, coaching behaviour does not appear in a vacuum, and the onus falls on organizations to create competition structures that do not encourage early specialization, and to educate their coaches and parents about what constitutes a positive sporting experience for a young person. Possibly success in youth sport should be defined by the number of children that return to that sport each year, rather than the number of wins, trophies, and championship points achieved.

Conclusion

Adolescent sport practices have changed worldwide over the last 20 years (Bergeron, 2010). The trend towards more frequent, intensive, and structured sport from a young age has been an outcome of a range of economic and societal changes within sport (Mostafavifar, Best, & Myer, 2013). There is a burgeoning youth sport industry that has emerged creating opportunities for the growth of specialized training centres, specialized training sessions, and academy programmes in and out of schools. Structured sport programmes often fit better into the modern world where parents both work and unsupervised play is less common and perceived as less acceptable by many in society. The biggest driver to change, however, is probably the fact that sport now offers a legitimate career pathway for an athlete. The frequently mis-interpreted 10,000-hour rule sees many children, parents, coaches, and sport codes encouraging intense sport programmes from increasingly younger ages. Unfortunately for many of our children, starting intensive specialized training early has detrimental effects on their growing bodies as well as on their lifelong love of sport. Whilst there will always be the success stories of some high-profile early specializers, these will be the exception rather than the rule. There is now substantial evidence demonstrating that the costs for the vast majority of young people specializing in sport too early outweigh the gains.

References

Accident Compensation Corporation. (2017). Accident Compensation Corporation Injury Statistics Database. Retrieved July 26, 2017 https://www.acc.co.nz/about-us/statistics/#injury-stats-nav

Bell, D. R., Post, E. G., Trigsted, S. M., Hetzel, S., McGuine, T. A., & Brooks, M. A. (2016). Prevalence of sport specialization in high school athletics: A 1-year observational study. *American Journal of Sports Medicine, 44*(6), 1469–1474. doi:10.1177/0363546516629943

Bergeron, M. F. (2010). The young athlete: Challenges of growth, development, and society. *Current Sports Medicine Reports, 9*(6), 356–358. doi:10.1249/JSR.0b013e3181fc70f3

Brenner, J. S. (2007). Overuse injuries, overtraining, and burnout in child and adolescent athletes. *Pediatrics, 119*(6), 1242–1245. Retrieved from http://pediatrics.aappublications.org/content/pediatrics/119/6/1242.full.pdf

Brenner, J. S., LaBella, C. R., Brooks, M. A., Diamond, A., Hennrikus, W., Weiss Kelly, A. K., . . . Emanuel, A. (2016). Sports specialization and intensive training in young athletes. *Pediatrics, 138*(3). doi:10.1542/peds.2016-2148

Bridge, M. W., & Toms, M. R. (2013). The specialising or sampling debate: A retrospective analysis of adolescent sports participation in the UK. *Journal of Sports Sciences, 31*(1), 87–96. doi:10.1080/02640414.2012.721560

Buckley, P. S., Bishop, M., Kane, P., Ciccotti, M. C., Selverian, S., Exume, D., . . . Ciccotti, M. G. (2017). Early single-sport specialization: A survey of 3090 high school, collegiate, and professional athletes. *Orthopaedic Journal of Sports Medicine, 5*(7), 1–7. doi:10.1177/2325967117703944

Burrows, M., Baxter-Jones, A., Mirwald, R., Macdonald, H., & McKay, H. (2009). Bone mineral accrual across growth in a mixed-ethnic group of children: are Asian children disadvantaged from an early age? *Calcified Tissue International, 84*(5), 366–378. doi:10.1007/s00223-009-9236-8

Caine, D., & Purcell, L. (2016). The exceptionality of the young athlete. In D. Caine & L. Purcell (Eds.), *Injury in Pediatric and Adolescent Sports*. Heidelberg, Switzerland: Springer.

Coutinho, P., Mesquita, I., Davids, K., Fonseca, A. M., & Côté, J. (2016). How structured and unstructured sport activities aid the development of expertise in volleyball players. *Psychology of Sport and Exercise, 25*, 51–59. doi:10.1016/j.psychsport.2016.04.004

Cuff, S., Loud, K., & O'Riordan, M. A. (2010). Overuse injuries in high school athletes. *Clinical Pediatrics, 49*(8), 731–736. doi:10.1177/0009922810363154

DiFiori, J. (2010). Overuse injury of the physis: A "growing" problem. *Clinical Journal of Sport Medicine, 20*(5), 336–337. doi:10.1097/JSM.0b013e3181ebb55d

DiFiori, J., Benjamin, H. J., Brenner, J., Gregory, A., Jayanthi, N., Landry, G. L., & Luke, A. (2014). Overuse injuries and burnout in youth sports: A position statement from the American medical society for sports medicine. *Clinical Journal of Sport Medicine, 24*(1), 3–20. Retrieved from www.cjsportmed.com

Donaldson, S. J., & Ronan, K. R. (2006). The effects of sports participation on young adolescents' emotional well-being. *Adolescence, 41*(162), 369–389.

Downing, C., Redelius, K., & Nordin-Bates, S. M. (2020). An Index Approach to Early Specialization Measurement: An Exploratory Study. *Frontiers in Psychology, 11*, 999. doi:10.3389/fpsyg.2020.00999

Eliasson, I. (2017). The gap between formalised children's rights and children's real lives in sport. *international Review for the Sociology of Sport, 52*(4), 470–496. doi:10.1177/1012690215608516

Ellingsen, J. E., & Danielsen, A. G. (2017). Norwegian Children's Rights in Sport and Coaches' Understanding of Talent [Article]. *International Journal of Children's Rights, 25*(2), 412–437. doi:10.1163/15718182-02502006

Ericsson, K. A., Krampe, R. T., & Tesch-Roemer, C. (1993). The role of deliberate practice in the acquisition of expert performance. *Psychological Review, 100*(3), 363–406. Retrieved from http://articles.sirc.ca/search.cfm?id=340121

Farrey, T. (2020). The government is reining in youth sports. The adults are worried. *New York Times*. Retrieved from https://www.nytimes.com/2020/01/07/sports/youth-sports-rules-us.html

Ford, P. R., Ward, P., Hodges, N. J., & Mark Williams, A. (2009). The role of deliberate practice and play in career progression in sport: The early engagement hypothesis. *High Ability Studies, 20*(1), 65–75. doi:10.1080/13598130902860721

Gladwell, M. (2008). *Outliers. The Story of Success*. New York: Little, Brown and Company.

Government Offices of Sweden. (2020). *Children's rights*. Retrieved 3rd September, 2020, from https://www.government.se/government-policy/childrens-rights/

Green, K., Roberts, K., Thurston, M., & Vaage, O. (2015). '[We're on the right track, baby], we were born this way'! Exploring sports participation in Norway [Article]. *Sport, Education and Society, 20*(3), 285–303. doi:10.1080/13573322.2013.769947

Hall, R., Barber Foss, K., Hewett, T. E., & Myer, G. D. (2015). Sport specialization's association with an increased risk of developing anterior knee pain in adolescent female athletes. *Journal of Sport Rehabilitation, 24*(1), 31–35. doi:10.1123/jsr.2013-0101

Hartwig, T. B., Gabbett, T. J., Naughton, G., Duncan, C., Harries, S., & Perry, N. (2019). Training and match volume and injury in adolescents playing multiple contact team sports: A prospective cohort study. *Scandinavian Journal of Medicine and Science in Sports, 29*(3), 469–475.

Huang, B., Biro, F. M., & Dorn, L. D. (2009). Determination of relative timing of pubertal maturation through ordinal logistic modeling: evaluation of growth and timing parameters. *Journal of Adolescent Health, 45*(4), 383–388. doi:10.1016/j.jadohealth.2009.02.013

Jackowski, S. A., Faulkner, R. A., Farthing, J. P., Kontulainen, S. A., Beck, T. J., & Baxter-Jones, A. D. G. (2009). Peak lean tissue mass accrual precedes changes in bone strength indices at the proximal femur during the pubertal growth spurt [Article]. *Bone, 44*(6), 1186–1190. doi:10.1016/j.bone.2009.02.008

Jayanthi, N., Labella, C., Fischer, D., Pasulka, J., & Dugas, L. R. (2015). Sports-specialized intensive training and the risk of injury in young athletes: A clinical case-control study. *American Journal of Sports Medicine, 43*(4), 794–801. doi:10.1177/0363546514567298

Johnson, W., Choh, A. C., Curran, J. E., Czerwinski, S. A., Bellis, C., Dyer, T. D., . . . Demerath, E. W. (2013). Genetic risk for earlier menarche also influences peripubertal body mass index. *American Journal of Physical Anthropology, 150*(1), 10–20. doi:10.1002/ajpa.22121

LaPrade, R. F., Agel, J., Baker, J., Brenner, J. S., Cordasco, F. A., Côté, J., . . . Provencher, M. T. (2016). AOSSM early sport specialization consensus statement. *Orthopaedic Journal of Sports Medicine, 4*(4). doi:10.1177/2325967116644241

Lloyd, R. S., Cronin, J. B., Faigenbaum, A. D., Haff, G. G., Howard, R., Kraemer, W. J., . . . Oliver, J. L. (2016). National strength and conditioning association position statement on long-term athletic development [Article]. *Journal of Strength and Conditioning Research, 30*(6), 1491–1509. doi:10.1519/JSC.0000000000001387

Luke, A., Lazaro, R. M., Bergeron, M. F., Keyser, L., Benjamin, H., Brenner, J., . . . Smith, A. (2011). Sports-related injuries in youth athletes: Is overscheduling a risk factor? *Clinical Journal of Sport Medicine, 21*(4), 307–314. doi:10.1097/JSM.0b013e3182218f71

Malina, R. M. (2010). Early sport specialization: Roots, effectiveness, risks. *Current Sports Medicine Reports, 9*(6), 364–371. doi:10.1249/JSR.0b013e3181fe3166

Mather, V. (2018). Olympics 2018 results. *New York Times*. Retrieved from https://www.nytimes.com/interactive/2018/sports/olympics/medal-count-results-schedule.html

Matzkin, E., & Garvey, K. (2019). Youth Sports Specialization: Does Practice Make Perfect? *NASN School Nurse, 34*(2), 100–103. doi:10.1177/1942602X18814619

McGowan, J., Reid, D. A., & Caldwell, J. (2017). Post-operative rehabilitation of anterior cruciate ligament reconstruction in the skeletally immature child: A systematic review of the literature. *Physical Therapy Reviews*, 1–16. doi:10.1080/10833196.2017.1364541

McGowan, J., Whatman, C., & Walters, S. (2020). The associations of early specialisation and sport volume with musculoskeletal injury in New Zealand children. *Journal of Science and Medicine in Sport, 23*(2), 139–144. doi:https://doi.org/10.1016/j.jsams.2019.09.002

McGuine, T. A., Post, E. G., Hetzel, S. J., Brooks, M. A., Trigsted, S., & Bell, D. R. (2017). A prospective study on the effect of sport specialization on lower extremity injury rates in high school athletes. *The American Journal of Sports Medicine*, 0363546517710213. doi:10.1177/0363546517710213

McLeod, T. C. V., Decoster, L. C., Loud, K. J., Micheli, L. J., Parker, J. T., Sandrey, M. A., & White, C. (2011). National athletic trainers' association position statement: prevention of pediatric overuse injuries. *Journal of Athletic Training (National Athletic Trainers' Association)*, *46*(2), 206–220. Retrieved from www.nata.org/jat

Memmert, D., Baker, J., & Bertsch, C. (2010). Play and practice in the development of sport-specific creativity in team ball sports. *High Ability Studies*, *21*(1), 3–18. doi:10.1080/135981 39.2010.488083

Moesch, K., Elbe, A. M., Hauge, M. L. T., & Wikman, J. M. (2011). Late specialization: the key to success in centimeters, grams, or seconds (cgs) sports. *Scandinavian Journal of Medicine and Science in Sports*, *21*(6), e282–e290. doi:10.1111/j.1600-0838.2010.01280.x

Mostafavifar, A. M., Best, T. M., & Myer, G. D. (2013). Early sport specialisation, does it lead to long-term problems? *British Journal of Sports Medicine*, *47*(17), 1060–1061. doi:10.1136/ bjsports-2012-092005

Myer, G. D., Jayanthi, N., Difiori, J. P., Faigenbaum, A. D., Kiefer, A. W., Logerstedt, D., & Micheli, L. J. (2015). Sport specialization, part I: Does early sports specialization increase negative outcomes and reduce the opportunity for success in young athletes? *Sports Health*, *7*(5), 437–442. doi:10.1177/1941738115598747

Olsen, S. J., II, Fleisig, G. S., Dun, S., Loftice, J., & Andrews, J. R. (2006). Risk factors for shoulder and elbow injuries in adolescent baseball pitchers. *American Journal of Sports Medicine*, *34*(6), 905–912. doi:10.1177/0363546505284188

Pasulka, J., Jayanthi, N., McCann, A., Dugas, L. R., & LaBella, C. (2017). Specialization patterns across various youth sports and relationship to injury risk. *The Physician and Sports Medicine*, 1–9. doi:10.1080/00913847.2017.1313077

Popkin, C. A., Bayomy, A. F., & Ahmad, C. S. (2019). Early sport specialization. *The Journal of the American Academy of Orthopaedic Surgeons*, *27*(22), e995–e1000. doi:10.5435/ JAAOS-D-18-00187

Post, E. G., Trigsted, S. M., Riekena, J. W., Hetzel, S., McGuine, T. A., Brooks, M. A., & Bell, D. R. (2017). The association of sport specialization and training volume with injury history in youth athletes. *The American Journal of Sports Medicine*, 1–8. doi:10.1177/0363546517690848

Purnell, M., Shirley, D., Nicholson, L., & Adams, R. (2010). Acrobatic gymnastics injury: Occurrence, site and training risk factors. *Physical Therapy in Sport 11*(2), 40–46. doi:10.1016/j.ptsp.2010.01.002

Roetert, E. P., Woods, R. B., & Jayanthi, N. A. (2018). The benefits of multi-sport participation for youth tennis players. *Coaching & Sport Science Review*, *75*, 14–17.

Roos, L., Taube, W., Zuest, P., Clénin, G., & Wyss, T. (2015). Musculoskeletal injuries and training patterns in junior elite orienteering athletes. *BioMed Research International*, *2015*, 1–8. doi:10.1155/2015/259531

Rosendahl, K., & Strouse, P. J. (2016). Sports injury of the pediatric musculoskeletal system. *La Radiologia Medica*, *121*(5), 431–441. doi:10.1007/s11547-015-0615-0

Ryba, T. V., Aunola, K., Kalaja, S., Selanne, H., & Ronkainen, N. J. (2016). A new perspective on adolescent athletes' transition into upper secondary school: a longitudinal mixed methods study protocol. *Cogent Psychol*, *3*(1), 1–15.

Santos, C., Bustamante, A., Katzmarzyk, P. T., Vasconcelos, O., Garganta, R., Freitas, D., . . . Maia, J. (2019). Growth velocity curves and pubertal spurt parameters of Peruvian children and adolescents living at different altitudes. The Peruvian health and optimist growth study. *American journal of human biology: the official journal of the Human Biology Council, 31*(6), e23301. doi:10.1002/ajhb.23301

Sheehan, D. P., & Lienhard, K. (2019). Gross motor competence and peak height velocity in 10- to 14-year-old Canadian youth: A longitudinal study. *Measurement in Physical Education & Exercise Science, 23*(1), 89–98.

Skirstad, B., Waddington, I., & Safvenbom, R. (2012). Issues and problems in the organization of children's sport: A case study of Norway. *European Physical Education Review, 18*(3), 309–321.

Smith, M. (2015). Early sport specialization: A historical perspective. *Kinesiology Review, 4*(3), 220–229. doi:10.1123/kr.2015-0024

Street, E., & Jacobsen, K. (2017). Prevalence of sports injuries among 13- to 15-year-old students in 25 low- and middle-income Countries. *Journal of Community Health, 42*(2), 295–302. doi:10.1007/s10900-016-0255-x

Theisen, D., Frisch, A., Malisoux, L., Urhausen, A., Croisier, J.-L., & Seil, R. (2013). Injury risk is different in team and individual youth sport. *Journal of Science and Medicine in Sport, 16*(3), 200–204. doi:10.1016/j.jsams.2012.07.007

Visek, A. J., Mannix, H., Chandran, A., Cleary, S. D., McDonnell, K., & DiPietro, L. (2018). Perceived importance of the fun integration theory's factors and determinants: A comparison among players, parents, and coaches. *International Journal of Sports Science & Coaching, 13*(6), 849–862.

Walters, B. K., Read, C. R., & Estes, A. R. (2017). Effects of resistance training, overtraining, and early specialization on youth athletes. *The Journal of Sports Medicine And Physical Fitness.* doi:10.23736/S0022-4707.17.07409-6

Whatman, C., Walters, S., & Schluter, P. (2018). Coach and player attitudes to injury in youth sport. *Physical Therapy in Sport 32*, 1–6. doi:10.1016/j.ptsp.2018.01.011

Wik, E. H., Martínez-Silván, D., Farooq, A., Cardinale, M., Johnson, A., & Bahr, R. (2020). Skeletal maturation and growth rates are related to bone and growth plate injuries in adolescent athletics. *Scandinavian Journal of Medicine and Science in Sports, 30*(5), 894–903.

Wilhelm, A., Choi, C., & Deitch, J. (2017). Early sport specialization: Effectiveness and risk of injury in professional baseball players. *Orthopaedic Journal of Sports Medicine, 5*(9), 1–5. doi:10.1177/2325967117728922

Zealand, S. N. (2020). *Balance is Better.* Retrieved from https://sportnz.org.nz/resources/balance-is-better-philosophy/

Zwick, E. B., & Kocher, R. (2014). Growth dynamics in the context of pediatric sports injuries and overuse. *Seminars in Musculoskeletal Radiology, 18*(5), 465–468. doi:10.1055/s-0034-1389263

10 They Really Are 'a Different Kettle of Fish'

Myths Surrounding the 'Effective Coaching' of the Female Athlete

Luke Jones and Zoë Avner

Introduction

In this chapter, we consider the origins of the embedded myth that there is a 'special formula' or 'different set of rules' for 'solving the puzzle' of how to coach female athletes. And, in so doing, we review the implications of this myth for female athletes and move to suggest a theoretically informed alternative approach for those who coach/supervise/develop them. To make these suggestions, we build upon our on-going socio-cultural analysis of the dominant coaching knowledge and conditioning practices typical to the production of elite female athletes (Jones, Mills, & Avner, 2020; Jones, Avner, Mills, & Magill, in press/forthcoming).

We begin by explaining our myth. For emphasis, we present a short narrative 'a different kettle of fish' that depicts how this myth manifests itself in a fictional coaching context. Next, we move on to discuss where the myth originated from and why certain common-sense assumptions regarding female athletes continue to flourish. We conclude by highlighting the value of a Foucauldian awareness of power-knowledge to consider the effects and implications of the identified myth and its truth claims. In doing so, we present some suggestions for coaches who are seeking to engage in 'gender effective coaching' (Jones et al., 2020) in an elite sports context where this myth holds considerable currency.

In this chapter, we refer to an established body of post-structuralist informed coach education research (much of which has been informed by the thoughts of French philosopher Michel Foucault) that encourages on-going reflection, problematization, and re-imagination of the dominant 'truths' that inform and guide everyday sports coaching practices (Denison, 2019; Denison & Avner, 2011;

Denison, Mills & Jones, 2019; Jones et al., 2020). Accordingly, and crucially, the discussion and suggestions in this chapter should not be read as a sweeping dismissal of attempts to coach in 'gender or minority-responsive' ways — far from it. The normative construct of sport and sport coaching has routinely been identified as a straight, white, able-bodied male preserve (Rankin-Wright & Norman, 2017). Consequently, the numerous ways in which this construct is unproblematically reproduced and normalized through overt and more subtle sexist, ableist, homophobic, and racist coaching practices needs to be challenged and changed (for further reading around the problematic manifestation of these intersections in sport and coaching, see Gearity and Metzger, 2017). We firmly believe that coaches have an important role to play as agents of change and social inclusion within their respective coaching contexts (Shogan, 1999). Our aim in this chapter is to challenge readers to consider the power-knowledge implications of current efforts to coach in 'gender and diversity responsive' ways — efforts which are largely informed by reductionist and problematic assumptions around these populations.

The myth

In our recent contribution in a well-respected sports coaching textbook, the sub-section within which our chapter on 'gender effective coaching' (Jones et al., 2020) was entitled 'A guide to coaching *different* populations'. This innocent allocation is a telling and significant indication that within discussions surrounding sports coaching, a 'myth' or 'normalized truth' presides. The myth is as follows: to work successfully with female athletes, there is a 'different set of rules' or a 'special formula' that must be determined. The basis of this myth is the understanding that sportswomen are an inherently, biologically, psychologically, and emotionally 'different population' from their male peers. As Steward (2016, p. 417) identified from his longitudinal empirical research, female athletes are 'different in many ways from their male counterparts' making coaching them 'a challenge'.

The common assumption about the 'different' and 'challenging' nature of coaching female athletes (in comparison to the default and apparently more manageable responsibility of coaching male athletes) is customarily present in discussions regarding 'best practice' for coaching women (Steward, 2016). Accepted wisdom therefore dictates that to be an 'effective coach of female athletes' one needs to possess an in depth understanding of these 'natural differences' and how to manage them. Moreover, if one is to competently choreograph one's relationships and practices when coaching females, one needs to be aware how to best 'treat female athletes' by becoming intimately familiar with their 'unique' needs.

For example, coaches need to be aware of the physical differences between male and female athletes. Bryan and Sims (2014, p. 15) explained that 'Coaches of female athletes need to be especially mindful of and understand the differences between female and male physiological processes'. Furthermore, as Steward (2016) identified, the aspiring coach also needs to understand that women have different psychologies and therefore ways of communicating. Indeed, Steward also mentioned how researchers have traditionally emphasized women's communication styles as seeking feelings more than solutions, and being based around conversations that are often an end in themselves, and that for female athletes, expressing emotions is more important than seeking solutions. Research and conventional wisdom therefore suggest that there are certain 'rules' or 'guidelines' for best managing female athletes' bodies, minds, and emotions.

A certain picture has been painted — specifically that time spent attempting to coach female athletes is akin to completing a Rubik's cube, as a puzzle, that due to women's' inherent differences, is 'as rewarding as it is challenging' (Steward, 2016, p. 417). It is unsurprising therefore that in an attempt to 'solve the riddle' of how to 'best coach' females, coaches 'tend to rely on firmly established truths about what supposedly "naturally" drives and motivates athletes of different genders' (Jones, et al., 2020, p. 141).

So, what does the belief in this myth surrounding the difference in female athletes look like in practice? To give a deeper insight into the applied implications of this myth, we return to the fictional characters we used to emphasize our observations regarding 'gender effective coaching' in Jones et al. (2020) – Assistant Coach Anton, and his older male colleague, Head Coach Mike, both coaching staff from the North American female varsity soccer programme – 'The Falcons'.

'A different kettle of fish'

We join Anton and the Falcons on a sweltering early summer's evening during pre-season. Head Coach Mike is at a faculty meeting for the first part of the session; therefore, it is Anton's first time leading a session solo with the group. Thus far, the team has been working on small-sided possession games in a designated area. As the session unfolds, it seems to be running smoothly, so Anton retreats up the natural grass embankment adjacent to the field to get a better perspective on the game. From his elevated position, despite his shades, he squints against the setting sun and reflects upon his initial observations of coaching an elite female squad.

I am seriously impressed with the standard and ability of these players. Some of the first touches of Elise in particular, are ridiculous. Both feet too. But its so quiet! Where is the intensity? Where is the demanding the ball and the competitive edge?! It is like watching a silent film. The men's game is so loud in comparison!

Down below, the session moves into a drinks break, and the players take advantage of the halt in play to hydrate and come together in their familiar groups. As Anton observes playful splashing from water bottles, the re-adjustment of hair bands, laughter, and vibrant hand gestures, it dawns upon him that, left to sort the teams out for themselves at the start of the session, the players have almost exclusively been playing together in their respective year groups. He identifies a consequence of this; smaller groups of tentative younger players – likely first years/rookies – have ended up making up the numbers on the periphery of things.

Right – we cannot have this. Let's mix things up. Its pre-season after all. These players are going to be playing together all year, so it's time to integrate the group and see how we get on.

Striding purposefully down the bank, Anton summons the players together and asks them to take off their drenched and sweaty bibs (pinnies). He then proceeds to lecture the players about team cohesion and in doing so reallocates the bibs in a random fashion. Anton requests that the same session continue with the same parameters before turning to head back up to his crow's nest position. As he starts to walk away from the space, he senses that something has gone awry. Something in the timbre of the air has changed, and with this realization he feels the prickly heat of embarrassment and trespass rising within. A gnawing sensation tells him that the carefree, happy go lucky faces that were everywhere a minute ago have now been replaced by anxious looks. The session resumes, and is it him, or does the standard and fluidity drop and do more passes go astray?

Mercifully, Mike arrives soon after, and Anton's segment of the evening's session winds down. As is routine, Mike next organizes the players into their daily shuttles (funnily enough Anton notices this too is organized according to the year group) as the players' times are recorded on an iPad by the dutiful trainer hovering on the touchline. While the players perform the exhausting and lung-busting runs, Mike saddles up to Anton, and asks 'How did it go'? After confessing what he elected to do with his mini pep-talk and by intentionally re-arranging the teams, Mike responds with a shrug of the shoulders and a knowing head tilt and smile.

> *Ah. You will get used to it. It's just not the same as the men's game. Coaching women is a 'different kettle of fish'. I've been doing it for years now, and you get a feel for the nuances and the small things. Trust me, they are as good as men in many many ways, but some of the things you would do coaching men just don't fly here – the 'make up' of female players just means you need to try your best to figure out what it is that they need, and over time you do get a feel for it. And more often than not, especially with the group dynamics stuff, I find it's just easier to stay out of it and let them sort it out themselves!*

Making sense of Anton's story: Where does the myth come from?

As we have previously identified, informed discussion about how to coach any population needs to recognize that the experiences of athletes of any gender do not occur in a vacuum, but within the broader historical-social-cultural contexts of society that have been shaped over time by dominant discourses (ways of knowing) and power relations (Jones et al., 2020). In this section, we consider more closely certain dominant discourses and how the resultant 'truths' about female athletes that they sustain (for example those that are held by 'experts' like Head Coach Mike) have come to gain such authority. In doing so, we can begin to answer the questions: Where does this myth come from? Why does this myth continue to be promoted as 'the way things are' in sports contexts? And, why does this myth about how to coach women remain unquestioned?

Established research that has focused on the social context of women's sport has explored how the 'different nature of women' continues to be reinforced in sports settings (Hargreaves, 1994). Given the scope of the current chapter, in what follows, we briefly identify what we see as three of the main reasons why the notion that 'women are different' and requiring of 'specialist attention' is so pervasive and has such authority in sport. First, we elaborate on the socio-cul-tural-historic *gender norms* that position the female body as weaker and less capa-ble than the male body – and how these roles have consistently been perpetuated and exaggerated by sport. Second, we move on to consider how the increased application of *sports science support* has served to frame female athletes as physiologically inferior to males. Third, we consider how enduring and contemporary *media depictions of the female athlete* have sustained certain truths about women's essential characteristics.

Gender norms in sport

The realm of sport has long been critiqued for sustaining the traditional gender order and perpetuating problematic gender norms. Indeed, critical theorists have repeatedly advised that sport functions as a hegemonic space that marginalizes certain groups. Specifically, it marginalizes those individuals who do not conform with a narrow, socially constructed normative masculinity which largely privileges white, able, heterosexual bodies while naturalizing sport as the display of traditionally masculine traits such as speed, strength, hyper-competitiveness, and bravery (Anderson, 2008; Connell, 2005).

Historically 'masculine' forms of sport (e.g. Rugby, Soccer, American Football) have been identified as particularly instrumental in the reproduction of 'hegemonic masculinity' (Connell, 2005) and of orthodox views of female athletes and coaches as weaker and less capable (Fielding-Lloyd & Meân, 2011). It is important to acknowledge that times do change, and that contemporary sport does often afford a site of contestation of traditional gender norms (Cox & Thompson, 2000; Heinecken, 2015) and identities (Buzuvis, 2010). However, it is also clear that on the whole, despite signs that women may be experiencing greater freedoms across certain sports settings (Burke, 2019), the notion that women are the 'weaker or fairer sex' has, throughout the years, been ably and consistently abetted by what some have called the 'misogynistic gender regime of institutionalised sport' (Anderson, 2008).

While these problematic views of female athletes and leaders are arguably less openly and overtly expressed nowadays, their continued traction is still evident. For instance, research into women-only or separatist coach education or skills courses – a common and privileged strategy to address gender imbalance in traditionally male domains such as coaching (e.g. Fielding-Lloyd & Meân, 2008; 2011) – has demonstrated the problematic discursive production of these courses as 'scaling back' or 'pandering to' underconfident/less competent female participants and/or coaches. As a result of framing these courses as 'lesser' or as designed for women who are lacking the competence or confidence to succeed in mixed environments, women's peripheral role in historically male dominated environments is further justified, while masculine ways of doing are simultaneously reproduced as the 'default' unproblematic standard to ascribe to and strive for.

It is important to note that many of these problematic traditional social norms and gendered understandings and sporting practices have historically been reproduced and abetted through a complex power–knowledge nexus. In particular, bio-scientific knowledge has a long history of being produced and recruited to support and uphold myths around female frailty and women's unsuitability to sport and physical activity, thereby further naturalizing the traditional gender order (Dunning, 1986; Theberge, 1993). And it is to this enduring connection between bio-scientific knowledge production about the female sporting body and the reproduction of unequal gendered power relations, which we next turn our attention.

Sports science support

One side effect of the increasing professionalization of women's sport is that more attention than ever is now paid to the identification, development, and conditioning of elite-level female athletes. Correspondingly, numerous approaches now circulate to examine female athletes' physiological capabilities and conditioning. This is unsurprising given the dominance of what Denison, Mills, and Konoval (2017) have called the 'disciplinary logic of sport', where a 'prevailing belief exists that a coach-driven, bio-scientific, and systematically structured training programme, in concert with a highly disciplined work ethic is necessary for athletes to win' (Mills, Denison, & Gearity, 2020, p. 245).

That elite female athletes now have access to sports science support is of course not an entirely bad thing. It is an important step towards gender equity as well as being an essential shield for the health of female athletes as they compete, like their male counterparts, at increasingly higher intensities. However, let us for a moment play devil's advocate and take a closer look at what might be happening as a result of the increased infiltration of sports science support into the realm of elite women's sport. For example, let us consider how this shift acts to sustain the myth under discussion. As we have identified previously,

> *According to the logic instilled by sports physiology and medicine, female bodies are less able to withstand the physiological demands of certain bodily practices. Therefore, that a female athlete ... needs nurturing rather than challenging appears to follow as an unquestioned correlated 'truth'. A problematic binary understanding of what it means to be female athlete is legitimised, and this legitimised logic guides and governs the practices and attitudes that make up the fabric of the contemporary coaching of females. (Jones et al., 2020, p. 141)*

Therefore, since sport scientists frequently advise that the female body and mind works differently to that of a male, it is likely that coaches (like Head Coach Mike) continue to assume that female athletes need to be 'worked out' and treated with extra care. What is key to the discussion here is that the increased proliferation of 'oven-ready' findings from sports science legitimizes the prescription of alternative management in the coaching of the female sportsperson (read adopting a special formula different to that required for males). Moreover, as a result of sports science support becoming more and more routine in elite female sport settings, the constraining 'truth' that while male athletes need to be 'trained', because their bodies are different, female athletes need to be 'cared for' using a special approach, continues to flourish (Jones, et al., in press/forthcoming). The third important connection which we next turn to is the connection between media coverage and representations of female athletes and the reproduction of unequal gendered power relations in sport and wider society.

Media depictions of the female athlete

Feminist media studies have successfully brought our attention to the underrepresentation and misrepresentation of women in sport media through common strategies, such as trivializing women's sporting accomplishments, objectifying/sexualizing their bodies, and perpetuating the myth of female frailty (Bruce, 2016; Kane, LaVoi, & Fink, 2013). As such, they have drawn attention to the key role of sporting media in upholding and perpetuating a problematic binary understanding of sex/gender (Cooky & Dworkin, 2013) and perpetuating problematic gender norms and stereotypes surrounding female athletes.

While it is perhaps fair to say that from a gender equity and diversity stand-point, sporting media have, by and large, been on the 'wrong side' of sporting history, media coverage of female athletes has started to evolve recently under popular pressure. This has largely coincided with the gradual professionaliza-tion of women's sport and the rising popularity of social media in the sporting mediascape (Vann, 2014).

Interestingly, the rising importance of social media has, with some exceptions (e.g. Toffoletti & Thorpe, 2018), largely been construed as a positive develop-ment and empowerment tool for female athletes who, theoretically, are now able to take control of how they are represented in the media (Heinecken, 2015). However, as Toffoletti and Thorpe (2018) have argued, this is not necessarily the case. In fact, social media can serve to further disempower female athletes,

as they become increasingly subjected to a neoliberal logic of market commodi-
fication and experience increasing pressures to strictly adhere to wider accepted
social norms and values. As the authors suggest, the intersection of social media
and a neoliberal market economy may have done more to restrict rather than
expand the range of subjectivities that female athletes can endorse and practice.

To summarize, historically, the production of bio-scientific knowledge and
of media representations of female athletes has played a key role in normalizing
traditional gender norms and upholding the gender order. While the progressive
investment of sport science in elite female sport and increase in media coverage
and representation sounds promising and progressive 'on paper', as we go on
to argue in the next section, in order to determine whether we are witnessing
a genuine change in tide rather than a freedom fallacy (Jones, et al., forthcoming), it is necessary to consider the total power effects of these developments in
women's elite sporting contexts.

'Thinking with Foucault' to manage the myth

The key point that we would like to re-emphasize by examining this myth is
that all sporting knowledges and coaching 'truths' are both useful and dangerous
– that is, they have benefits *and* problematic (un)intended consequences. As
Foucault (1991, p. 343) infamously put it, 'not everything is bad, but that
everything is dangerous, which is not exactly the same as bad. If everything is
dangerous, then we always have something to do'. As such, our task is to adopt
an active but critical 'pessimistic activism' (p. 343) to consider the total effects
and (un)intended consequences of taken-for-granted 'truths' and normalized
'best' practices in sports coaching. In particular, Foucault was highly critical
and concerned with the effects of *individualizing* scientific knowledges (e.g.
medicine; psychiatry) – that is, of knowledges which seek to produce and promote
a universal/singular truth and an essential and fixed descriptor of categories of
the population (see for example *Abnormal* (2003) for a more detailed critique).

Fast-forward and transpose to our sporting context, the matter of this chapter and Anton's position. Foucault would perhaps urge us and Anton to problematize the coaching 'truths' and 'best' coaching practices produced through all
types of knowledges, but particularly those which promote a singular or fixed
truth – for example, about what a female athlete needs or quintessentially is.
Foucault would also urge us to consider *all* of what these established gendered
'truths' and 'best' practices that are derived from this myth do, including their
(un)intended consequences. For example, (a) the ways in which they support

the reproduction of an unhelpful and highly problematic binary understanding of gender in sport; (b) the ways in which they normalize a problematic understanding of the female athlete as requiring 'extra work' or 'extra care and support' (Jones et al., 2020); and (c) how they continue to reproduce masculine ways of knowing and doing in sport and sport coaching as the 'default' unproblematic standard to ascribe to and strive for.

Of course, we are not calling for sport coaches to simply dismiss sport science or sport psychology knowledge or the coaching truths and best practices produced through these bio-scientific knowledges; that would simply be ridiculous. For example, it would be completely counterproductive for coaches to dismiss the potential positive impact of knowing more about the physiological effects of menstruation on female athletes' threshold loading in training and ability to perform in competitions. However, in the same vein, we would argue that to *not* consider the total effects of framing coaching female athletes as 'rewarding and challenging' (Steward, 2016) or female athletes as 'more emotional' and 'seeking feelings more than solutions' is equally problematic. In other words, we argue that for coaches to not consider both the intended and unintended effects of dominant coaching 'truths' and 'best' practices on (a) their female athletes' sense of self, performance, and wellbeing, (b) their own ability to form meaningful and positive relationships with their athletes, and (c) their ability to effectively and ethically solve a host of coaching dilemmas is short sighted.

Accordingly, the question becomes less whether a myth is *true* or *false* and more about considering the total effects of established 'truths' and 'best' practices on athletes' and coaches' sense of self, wellbeing, and performance and on coaching effectiveness and innovation at large (Denison & Avner, 2011). We propose that a coach's aim and energies should not necessarily be channelled towards seeking to discover if assumptions regarding the female athlete are *true* or not, but rather that the important issue is to know how to coach effectively and ethically in a context where the 'power' of these assumptions or this 'myth' manifests. To be able to do so, a coach must be comfortable being able to problematize (Denison, 2019) and to constantly reflect on the notion that 'coaching female athletes effectively' in line with dominant prescriptions from the world of sports science is a 'modernist foundation' (Denison et al., 2013), that borrows from largely problematic socio-historic gender norms, and as such can and should be 're-imagined' (Denison et al., 2019). We urge coaches responsible for the development of female athletes to show more 'dexterity' in their application of gendered coaching 'truths' and 'best' practices. This means understanding that they are not unquestionable, fixed, permanent, and inherently positive, but rather that they are political, contextual, fluid, and consequently are both useful and dangerous. We see such dexterity and critical awareness as an essential step towards

- reactivating marginalized knowledges in sports coaching and
- the subsequent development of more ethical and effective gender and diversity responsive coaching practices.

Conclusion

In this chapter, in another effort to develop more effective and ethical approach to coaching women in sport (LaVoi, 2016), we have once more encouraged readers to consider the advantages of 'Coaching with Foucault' (Denison, 2019). Specifically, we have promoted how Foucault provides a toolkit with which to interrogate taken-for-granted assumptions and practices that percolate surrounding the coaching and development of elite female athletes. In doing so, we have argued that a 'gender effective coach' understands the necessity to not rely on, but rather to routinely question the existing practices and assumptions that dominate sport. We purport that in order to act as a competent and compassionate coach of an individual of any gender, rather than being a slave (read docile coach) to any coaching myth, instead a coach 'must engage in the on-going process of observation, reflection, and refinement of practice' (Denison & Jones, 2011, p. 148). What is more, we are confident that should a coach embrace this process of 'thinking with Foucault' they may be inspired to re-imagine new, more ethical, and effective gender and diversity responsive coaching and sporting practices (Denison et al., 2019).

References

Anderson, E. (2008). "I used to think women were weak": Orthodox masculinity, gender segregation, and sport. *Sociological Forum, 23*(2), 257–280.

Bruce, T. (2016). New rules for new times: Sportswomen and media representation in the third wave. *Sex Roles, 74*(7–8), 361–376.

Bryan, C., & Sims, S. (2014). Appropriate and inappropriate practices for coaching female athletes, *Strategies, 27*, 13–17.

Burke, M. (2019). Is football now feminist? A critique of the use of McCaughey's physical feminism to explain women's participation in separate leagues in masculine sports. *Sport in Society, 22*, 499–513.

Buzuvis, E. (2010). Caster Semenya and the myth of a level playing field. *The Modern American, 6*, 36–42.

Connell, R. W. (2005). *Masculinities*. Cambridge, UK: Polity Press.

Cooky, C., & Dworkin, S. L. (2013). Policing the boundaries of sex: A critical examination of gender verification and the Caster Semenya controversy. *Journal of Sex Research, 50*(2), 103–111.

Cox, B., & Thompson, S. (2000). Multiple bodies: Sportswomen, soccer and sexuality. *International Review for the Sociology of Sport, 35,* 5–20.

Denison, J. (2019). What it really means to 'think outside the box': Why Foucault matters for coach development. *International Sport Coaching Journal, 6,* 354–358.

Denison, J., & Avner, Z. (2011). Positive coaching: Ethical practices for athlete development, *Quest, 63,* 209–227.

Denison, J., & Jones, L. (2011). Accreditation of PGA master coaches: A commentary. *Annual Review of Golf Coaching, 5,* 147–149.

Denison, J., Mills, J., & Jones, L. (2013). Effective coaching as a modernist formation: A Foucauldian critique. In P. Potrac, W. Gilbert, & J. Denison (Eds.), *The Routledge Handbook of Sports Coaching* (pp. 388–399). London: Routledge.

Denison, J., Jones, L., & Mills, J. (2019). Becoming a good enough coach. *Sports Coaching Review, 8*(1), 1–6.

Dunning, E. (1986). Sport as a male preserve: Notes on the social sources of masculine identity and its transformations. *Theory, Culture & Society, 3*(1), 79–90.

Fielding-Lloyd, B., & Meân, L. J. (2008). Standards and separatism: The discursive construction of gender in English soccer coach education. *Sex Roles, 58*(1-2), 24–39.

Fielding-Lloyd, B., & Meân, L. (2011). 'I don't think I can catch it': women, confidence and responsibility in football coach education. *Soccer & Society, 12*(3), 345–364.

Foucault, M. (1991). 'On the Genealogy of Ethics: An Overview of Work in Progress', interview with Michel Foucault. In P. Rabinow (Ed.), *The Foucault Reader* (pp. 340–372). London: Penguin.

Foucault, M. (2003). *Abnormal: Lectures at the Collège de France, 1974-1975* (Vol. 2). New York: Macmillan.

Gearity, B., & Metzger, L. (2017). Intersectionality, microaggressions, and microaffirmations: towards a cultural praxis of sports coaching. *Sociology of Sport Journal, 34,* 160–175.

Heinecken, D. (2015). 'So tight in the thighs, so loose in the waist': Embodying the female athlete online. *Feminist Media Studies, 15,* 1053–1052.

Jones, L., Mills, J., & Avner, Z. (2020). Gender effective coaching with Foucault. In E. Cope & M. Partington (Eds.), *Sports Coaching: A Theoretical and Practical Guide* (pp. 135–145). London: Routledge

Jones, L., Avner, Z., Mills, J., & Magill, S. (forthcoming). Changing tides or freedom fallacy? A Foucauldian cautionary reading of Women's professional football's evolving contexts. In A. Bowes & A. Culvin (Eds.), *Women's Football in a Global, Professional Era.*

Kane, M. J., LaVoi, N. M., & Fink, J. S. (2013). Exploring elite female athletes' interpretations of sport media images: A window into the construction of social identity and "selling sex" in women's sports. *Communication & Sport, 1*(3), 269–298.

LaVoi, N. (2016). *Women in Sports Coaching*. London: Routledge.

Mills, J., Denison, J., & Gearity, B. (2020). Breaking coaching's rules: Transforming the body, sport and performance. *Journal of Sport and Social Issues, 44,* 244–260.

Rankin-Wright, A. J., & Norman, L. (2017). Sport coaching and the inclusion of Black women in the United Kingdom. In A. Ratna & S. F. Samie (Eds), *Race, Gender and Sport: The Politics of Ethnic 'Other' Girls and Women.* London: Routledge.

Shogan, D. (1999). *The Making of High-performance Athletes: Discipline, Diversity, and Ethics.* Canada: University of Toronto Press.

Steward, C. (2016). Female athletes' rankings of coaching behaviour: A longitudinal report. *The Physical Educator, 73,* 417–432.

Theberge, N. (1993). The construction of gender in sport: Women, coaching, and the naturalization of difference. *Social Problems, 40*(3), 301–313.

Toffoletti, K., & Thorpe, H. (2018). Female athletes' self-representation on social media: A feminist analysis of neoliberal marketing strategies in "economies of visibility". *Feminism & Psychology, 28*(1), 11–31.

Vann, P. (2014). Changing the game: The role of social media in overcoming old media's attention deficit toward women's sport. *Journal of Broadcasting & Electronic Media, 58*(3), 438–455.

11 Common Sport and Exercise Nutrition Myths Encountered by Coaches and Athletes

Liz Mahon, Claire Blennerhassett, and Andy Sparks

Introduction

The discipline of sport and exercise nutrition has developed considerably over the past 20 years into a crucial and valuable area of expertise. It now has recognized professional practitioners that sports organizations and individual athletes frequently invest heavily in, to gain performance advantages. The performance advantages that can be obtained by improving the nutritional intake of athletes typically focus on the ability of optimal nutrient intake to drive adaptations to training, and the acute ingestion strategies that can be useful for short-term performance enhancement before, during, or after exercise. However, in many cases, not all athletes and coaches have or can afford direct access to suitably qualified sports nutrition practitioners. Consequently, where expert nutrition advice cannot be directly sought, it is often the coach that is approached for advice with regard to optimal nutrition (Abbey et al., 2017). Whilst the formal training level of coaches has been associated with better nutrition knowledge (Couture et al., 2015), many coaching practitioners are understandably not formally trained in the optimal nutrient strategies for the specific athletes they are working with and are often reliant on researching the best practices for themselves.

In the case of athletes, the most frequently used resource for sports nutrition information is often other athletes (Blennerhassett et al., 2019) or their coach

(Manore et al., 2017), and for the coach, it is the internet that is most likely to be used (Couture et al., 2015). Fortunately, coaches tend to have better nutrition knowledge than their athletes (Heikkilä et al., 2018), but the consensus is that additional knowledge and training is needed and would be beneficial. So, if athlete and coach both need to up skill their nutrition knowledge, it is likely that failure to do so may lead to the adoption of poor or suboptimal nutrient intake practices, which may impact performance and health.

One thing that coaches can do howsoever is obtain a better understanding of the typical nutrient needs and strategies for their athletes and try avoiding common pitfalls in this process. Some of these pitfalls relate to the widespread dogma, inaccurate information, anecdotal 'evidence', and myths that abound in sport and exercise nutrition (Jeukendrup & Killer, 2011). Therefore, the aim of this chapter is to identify some of the most common sport nutrition myths that are encountered by coaches and to provide an evidence-informed and contextual approach to understand their mythical status in order to dispel them. In so doing, the secondary aim is therefore to provide coaches with key considerations and practical recommendations.

Fluid and hydration

In the late 1990s, the American College of Sports Medicine (ACSM) published generic guidelines recommending fluid intakes for athletes (Convertino et al., 1996). These guidelines were originally designed as exactly that – a guide rather than being prescriptive for everyone that exercises. This did little to dispel the myth of generic minimum daily drinking requirements per day, such as the minimum eight glasses for water each day suggestion. Quite obviously this is a vast oversimplification of the actual fluid needs.

Myth: Fluid intake demands are the same for everyone

The key factors that determine fluid requirements are training status (eccrine sweat glands are trainable), exercise duration and intensity (this will determine total fluid loss), sex (determines total number of sweat glands), age (sweat loss is lower in older individuals), environmental conditions (higher temperatures increase core body temperature more rapidly), and the season of the year (warmer months and additional clothing increase sweat losses). It is also important to realize that fluid requirements will change for each individual based on these factors and they are not fixed for a particular daily routine, because each of the key factors is likely to vary, and will need to be considered in determining the pragmatic fluid need estimations (Sawka et al., 2007). The importance of fluid intake prior to exercise is often overlooked, but it is key particularly in preparation for exercise where considerable fluid loss is likely, but also to ensure training sessions are enjoyable. A simple observational study by Peacock et al., (2011) demonstrated that those individuals attending training sessions adequately hydrated, voluntarily completed a larger volume of activity and enjoyed the exercise more than those that were dehydrated to start with. This has potentially important implications for training quality, but also adherence to training sessions.

Myth: Water is the most effective rehydration fluid

Whilst the single most important nutrient for survival may well be the provision of water, it is by no means the most effective fluid with which to rehydrate. Several factors influence the speed of rehydration, and this is mainly determined by the rate of gastric emptying and speed of intestinal absorption (Evans et al., 2016). The speed of gastric emptying is relatively quick for fluids, certainly compared to solids, which require more mechanical and chemical digestion than fluid prior to absorption. However, the speed of fluid replacement can also be influenced by the volume, energy, and electrolyte content, as well as the level of carbonation and the temperature of the fluid. Adding to the complexity of optimum rehydration, drinking behaviour, which may in part alter self-selected or subconscious fluid ingestion rate, is improved with cooler fluids with an enjoyable taste. As a useful guide, Maughan et al., (2016) devised the beverage hydration index which determined and then ranked the speed of rehydration of fluids compared to still water. Of the 13 fluids assessed, the most effective were an oral rehydration solution (Dioralyte™), full fat, and skimmed milk. The most effective fluids contained a blend of water, carbohydrates, and electrolytes. Where exercise is prolonged in nature and considerable fuel has also been used, fluid replacement should also contain carbohydrate, especially if another bout of exercise is likely to take place within 8 hours (Burke et al., 2004), but this may not be required if a meal is consumed in the immediate recovery period. Fluid replacement should however be ~150% of post exercise body weight losses (1 kg lost = 1 litre of sweat losses, so 1.5 litres of fluid replacement would be required), and this should be consumed over a few hours, rather than in a short time period, to encourage absorption rather than water loss via increased urine production.

Dietary fat and carbohydrate intake

The consumption of dietary carbohydrate and fat has been clearly demonstrated to be important for training and performance for both the aerobic and anaerobic pathways (Thomas, Erdman, Burke, 2016). The optimum combination of these macronutrients for athletes' however, has been the subject of considerable debate, leading to myths about the volume and type of carbohydrate and fat needed for performance and to achieve desirable physical attributes (body mass and composition) for the chosen sport.

Myth: Athletes should consume carbohydrate at a set percentage of their energy intake

Historically, a high carbohydrate diet was considered the most important strategy for optimal performance. As such, early nutritional guidelines, regarded as suitable 'for most sports', recommended that carbohydrate should contribute 60–70% of total energy intake (Devlin and Williams, 1991). In addition, carbohydrate loading first described in the 1960s became a common pre-competition strategy to enhance performance in elite athletes. Since then, our understanding of metabolic pathways and the energy demands of exercise have demonstrated that fuel demands differ considerably between sports and training sessions (Burke et al., 2019). Consequently, the percentage targets for carbohydrate have been replaced with the ACSM guidance (published in 2016) to optimize carbohydrate availability for specific exercise loads (Table 11.1). These new targets are expressed relative to body mass but need to be interpreted alongside total energy needs (where deficits required for weight loss may limit total carbohydrate intake), training goals (such as physique, performance, or metabolic adaptation) and feedback from athletes (their tolerance of large volumes of carbohydrate) (Burke and Hawley, 2011). Furthermore, the adoption of some training sessions with low carbohydrate availability (e.g. fasted, training twice a day or short-term high fat-low carbohydrate diet) may provide additional benefits to training adaptations, making generic intake recommendations somewhat redundant (Impey, et al., 2018). Nevertheless, training with low carbohydrate availability should be avoided when the training/competition intensity is high, and dietary intake should ideally be periodized alongside training, to optimize training responses.

Table 11.1 Summary of guidelines for nutrient intake by athletes

Energy and Fuel Availability

Nutrient targets*	Activity	Training Intensity	Guidance on the type and timing of nutrient intake
Carbohydrate 3–5 g kg^{-1} of athlete's body mass per day	Light	Low-intensity or skill-based activities	Timing of intake may be chosen to promote speedy refuelling, or to provide fuel intake around training sessions in the day. Otherwise, so long as total fuel needs are provided, the pattern of intake may simply be guided by convenience and individual choice. Protein- and nutrient-rich carbohydrate foods or meal combinations will allow the athlete to meet other acute or chronic sports nutrition goals
5–7 g/kg^{-1}/day^{1}	Moderate	Moderate exercise programme (i.e. ~1 h–day^{-1})	
6–10 g/kg^{-1}/day^{1}	High	Endurance programme (e.g. moderate-to-high intensity exercise of 1–3 h/day^{1})	
8–12 g/kg^{-1}/day^{1}	Very high	Extreme commitment (i.e. moderate-to-high intensity exercise of 4–5 h/ day^{1})	

Fat

- Total fat intake should be no less than 20% of total energy requirements as fat is essential for absorption of fat-soluble vitamins (Vitamins A, D, E, and K).
- Saturated fat should be no more than 10% of total energy requirements.

Energy

- Energy intake should match energy requirements for normal bodily function and training volume.
- When weight loss is required, energy deficits should be limited to 250–500 kcal·day^{-1} and scheduled outside of periods that place considerable demand on the athlete.

Protein and Protein Supplements

Description	Amount	Guidance
Total daily requirements	1.4–2.0 g/kg⁻¹ of athlete's body mass per day	Protein doses should be regularly distributed, approximately every 3–4 h across the day
Serving size	0.25 g/kg⁻¹/serving⁻¹ or an absolute dose of 20–40 g	Servings of protein should ideally contain high proportions of EAAs and adequate leucine (approx. 700–3000 mg)
Daily requirement during periods of energy restriction when athlete is trying to decrease body fat	2–2.5 g/kg⁻¹/d⁻¹ may be beneficial	Higher levels of protein during energy restriction can help preserve lean body mass
Supplements	May be required during times of heavy training or when consuming sufficient high-quality protein through whole-foods is difficult.	Supplementation is a practical way of ensuring intake of adequate protein quality and quantity. May be required in those following a vegetarian, vegan, or dairy-free diet.

Fluid and Hydration

Timing	Amount	Guidance
Pre-exercise	Ensure adequate hydration prior to the start of exercise	In field setting, use of urine colour charts, urine osmometry, and thirst as a guide to ensure the athlete starts training in a euhydrated state.

(Continued)

135

Table 11.1 (Continued)

During exercise	Where exercise duration is <90 min, a drinking to thirst strategy should be adequate in most cases. Where exercise is >90 min the rate of sweat losses in that environment for the specific athlete needs to be considered in the development of a fluid ingestion plan.	Drinking is also likely to be a key method of achieving CHO intake targets per hour in exercise >45 min in duration. For training sessions <90 min or for strength and conditioning sessions, drinking to thirst is adequate. Using cool and flavoured drinks are likely to enhance intake. Determining fluid losses during exercise >90 min is important to avoid under- or overconsumption of fluids. An athlete-specific plan should be developed that also considers the environmental stress. Consider the inclusion of electrolytes if significant sweat losses are likely, and where providing CHO is needed.
Post-exercise	Intake should be 1.3–1.5 times body weight losses. Where exercise has used considerable amounts of glycogen, 6–10% CHO could also be added.	Estimates of individual fluid losses should be used to determine rehydration volume needs after exercise. Attempting full rehydration following late-evening training may reduce sleep quality.
Supplements**		
Type***	Examples	Guidance
Sports foods	Carbohydrate sports drinks, gels, bars, and confectionary Micronutrients	May supplement intake from food when demands are high or opportunity to refuel is limited, or even for convenience during training. Ingestion strategy must be practiced in training.
Medical supplements	(Iron, Vitamins, etc...)	May be required in specific population groups (e.g. B12/ Λ3 for vegans) or environmental conditions (e.g. vitamin D during winter or for athlete training indoors).

Performance supplements	Sodium bicarbonate/citrate, caffeine, creatine, beta-alanine,	May be suitable for some athletes, but first diet should be assessed to determine if performance enhancements may be gained with adequate nutrition. If need is identified, acute ingestion strategies should be practiced in training. For chronically ingested supplements, continued assessment of athlete health and welfare is key. Ingestion should always be in accordance with evidence-based safety recommendations.

* These general recommendations should be fine-tuned with individual consideration of total energy needs, specific training needs, and feedback from training performance.

** Independently batch tested and listed on the batch tester's webpage. Organizations such as Informed Sport are recommended for this.

*** In all cases, where a supplement is being considered, a cost-benefit analysis must be undertaken to ensure there is an appropriate need and benefit, without likely harm to the athlete. This approach must be evidence-informed. Where coaches and athletes are unable to do this, they are strongly encouraged to approach a suitably qualified performance nutrition practitioner for advice.

Myth: Athletes need to avoid carbohydrate to lose weight

Low carbohydrate diets have been advocated for weight loss for decades and have become increasingly popular amongst athletes. The Atkins diet (established in the 1970s) and the ketogenic diet restrict carbohydrate to as little as <20–50 g/day^{-1}, with the balance of energy from high fat and adequate protein (Bailey and Hennessey, 2020). These diets were proposed to support weight loss, despite *ad-libitum* fat and protein intake by aiding satiety and reducing appetite (Gibson et al, 2015). The few studies that have compared ketogenic diets with standard or low-fat diets for weight loss in athletes have produced equivocal results (Greene, et al., 2018, Rhyu and Cho, 2014) indicating there is insufficient evidence to recommend a ketogenic low carbohydrate diets for weight loss in athletes. In addition, restricting carbohydrate is likely to compromise micronutrient intake (e.g. fibre, vitamins, and minerals found in fruit and starchy vegetables), immune function (Peake et al., 2017), and endurance performance, especially when training and competing at high intensities (Burke et al., 2017).

Common to successful weight loss studies is the need for a negative energy balance, although severe or prolonged energy restriction has adverse consequences for bone health, immune function, hormonal and metabolic function, and growth and development in young athletes (Mountjoy et al., 2018). As such, a practical and conservative energy deficit of 250–500 kcal/day^{-1} (achieved via diet and/or activity) has been proposed for athletes (Thomas et al., 2016). Energy deficit may be easier to achieve with reductions in fat, due to the higher energy density (9 kcal/g^{-1}) compared to carbohydrate (4 kcal/g^{-1}). Achieving an appropriate energy deficit can be challenging for athletes, particularly during periods of high training load, as it can be difficult to quantify energy intake, expenditure, and availability (Burke *et al.*, 2018). Therefore, close monitoring of body composition and signs of fatigue is advisable during periods of energy restriction. To aid weight loss, without compromising health or performance, athletes should be encouraged to consume nutrient-dense foods, high in fibre, vitamins, and minerals and low in fat and sugar (Kerksick et al., 2018). When energy demands are high (>5000 kcal/day^{-1}), nutrient-rich foods may need to be supplemented by refined carbohydrate, high fat, high sugar foods, such as sports drinks and energy gels.

Protein

Proteins are made from amino acids, which are either synthesized or derived from foods. Those that cannot be synthesized are referred to as essential amino acids (EAAs). The nutritional value of a protein is determined by its amino acid profile and proteins containing all essential amino acids are referred to as high biological value proteins. Typically, animal-based proteins (dairy foods, eggs, meat, fish, and poultry) are considered to have high biological value, whereas plant-based proteins usually contain only some of the essential amino acids and therefore have a lower biological value. A particularly important essential amino acids for muscle protein synthesis is the branched chain amino acid (BCAA) leucine. Leucine stimulates the mammalian Target of Rapamycin (mTOR) pathway, which is a molecular pathway that turns on muscle protein synthesis (Phillips & van Loon, 2011), which therefore plays a key role in skeletal muscle adaptations to training.

Myth: More protein is always better

Athletes require more protein than the recommended daily allowance of 0.8 g/kg^{-1}/d^{-1} of body weight (BW) for non-exercising individuals (Thomas *et al.*, 2016). An increase in protein is needed to promote increases in muscle mass, adaptations in the exercising muscle, activation of mitochondrial protein synthesis, and in some cases a substrate for exercise performance (Tipton & Wolfe, 2004). Initially recommendations were provided on a basis of sport performed (endurance athletes: 1.2 to 1.4 g/kg^{-1}/BW^{-1} and strength athletes 1.4 to 1.7 g/kg^{-1}/BW^{-1}). However, it is now recognized as important to adapt intake according to the needs of different training periods, the intensity and duration of the workout, carbohydrate availability, and importantly energy availability. During periods of energy restriction, when athletes are trying to decrease body fat but preserve lean muscle tissue, low-calorie high-protein (2–2.5 g/kg^{-1}/d^{-1}) diets have been shown to be effective at preserving lean mass whilst losing fat (Mettler *et al.*, 2010).

The current guidelines, however, are that 1.4–2.0 g/kg^{-1}/d^{-1} is sufficient for most exercising individuals and focus should be placed on timing and quality of protein intake (Jager *et al.*, 2017). Each time protein is ingested, there is a corresponding spike in muscle protein synthesis. Studies have consistently shown that 20–25 g of high-quality protein produces a maximal response and consuming amounts greater than this at a single feed does not result in bigger gains (Moore *et al.*, 2009; Witard *et al.*, 2014; Symons *et al*, 2009). However, since then, a study by MacNaughton *et al.*, (2016) showed that when larger muscle groups were being trained, 40g of protein resulted in greater muscle protein synthesis than with 20 g. More recently still, Atherton *et al.* (2020) reported that following a 10-week resistance training plan in older males, 40 g of whey protein immediately after exercise provided a significant improvement in some muscle strength assessments in comparison to a 20 g dose. Because of this, recommendations of optimal protein intake are mixed, but general guidance is 0.25 g/kg^{-1} or an absolute dose of 20–40 g per serving, which should ideally contain high proportions of essential amino acids and adequate leucine (approx. 3 g) and be spaced regularly throughout the day (every 3–4 hours) (Jager *et al.*, 2017).

There is a concern amongst some that very high protein diets (>3 g/kg^{-1}/d^{-1}) may be unsafe and lead to harmful effects on kidney and liver function. This belief has persisted despite research on high protein intakes in athletic populations showing no indication of damage to kidney function. A study by Antonio et al. (2016a) showed no harmful effects on kidney and liver function when resistance-trained individuals consumed >3 g/kg^{-1}/d^{-1} for either 8 weeks or 12 months (Antonio *et al.*, 2016b). Concerns over high protein diets have developed from evidence from renal failure patients – extending this to a healthy athletic population is not appropriate (Jager *et al.*, 2017). However, it is important to note that excess protein consumed will not be used for muscle protein synthesis and will potentially lead to unnecessary energy intake. It is also important to avoid ingesting too much protein in place of other macronutrients, in particular carbohydrate, a key fuel for exercise.

Myth: Protein supplements are essential for all athletes

For some, protein supplements may be a helpful addition, however this is dependent on training load, daily energy requirements, and budget, but they are by no means essential for everyone. Only rarely does the typical Western diet not provide enough protein through wholefoods to meet requirements (Ranganathan et al., 2016). Supplementation can however be a useful and practical way to provide high-quality protein after training or in competition, especially when it may not be possible to consume a protein-rich meal. Protein from whey or ⟨-lactalbumin is effective at stimulating muscle protein synthesis as it is rapidly digesting and high in essential amino acids. Branch-chain amino acid supplements are popular due to their role in stimulating muscle protein synthesis, however if consumed alone, they do not provide the full complement of essential amino acids. Whilst the branched-chain amino acids will switch on muscle protein synthesis, other essential amino acids are needed to supply the substrate. A study by Jackman *et al.* (2017) showed that ingestion of branched-chain amino acids increased post-exercise muscle protein synthesis, but by only half that of whey protein.

Supplemental protein might also be useful to vegan athletes, particularly, if achieving sufficient protein through wholefoods proves difficult. At present, there is relatively little research on the effects of plant-based supplements; whilst a few studies show proteins such as rice and soy may perform similarly to dairy in training, recovery, body composition, and performance (Joy *et al.*, 2013), other studies show they are not as effective (Wilkinson *et al.*, 2007). Further research is needed in this area and it is likely that vegan protein powders should contain a mix of complementary proteins to help provide sufficient essential amino acids, especially leucine.

Myth: Sports nutrition supplements are essential for optimal performance

Frequently when people think of the term 'sports nutrition', the first thing that comes to mind is supplements. The sports nutrition supplement industry has of course been in part responsible for providing important financial support to research in this field, but in so doing, it has also done this in order to use that research as a tool for marketing a highly lucrative but competitive business model. This rightly brings with it some questions about conflicts of interest, but without these financial arrangements, much of the high quality and mechanistic work in this field simply would not have been completed. One of the other lasting legacies of this industry is the effect that the marketing strategies have had on public perception. Whilst many would be keen to explore the use of supplements from the outset of a plan to improve athletic performance, what is strongly advocated is a food-first approach. In the majority of cases, getting basic nutrition to an appropriate and optimal level negates the need for the majority of supplements. The number of supplements that have consistently demonstrated improvements in performance are limited, but growing in number (Close *et al.*, 2016), which means that the evidence for each is continually evolving. One of the most important steps when considering the use of supplements is a cost-benefit analysis prior to use (Sport and Exercise Nutrition Register, 2017). Key considerations of this process should be the function that the supplement is being used for (endurance, skeletal muscle size, health), the aspect of training or performance it is intended to help with, and the safety and efficacy of the intended dose and ingestion period. Those considering using supplements must also adhere to the WADA code, keep up to date with the yearly updates to the banned list, and use independently batch-tested products to limit the chance of contamination and a subsequent adverse analytical finding following an anti-doing control.

Summary

In reviewing the evidence associated with common myths surrounding sports and exercise nutrition, this chapter highlights that the typical nutrient needs and strategies for their athletes are dependent on the training goals and demands of the sport. Performance and training adaptations relies on optimizing nutrient availability (carbohydrate and fat for the volume of training) and the consumption of a nutrient-dense diet (rich in vitamins, minerals, and fibre) to prevent micronutrient deficiencies, with optimal protein for muscle protein synthesis and fluid to prevent excessive dehydration. In situations when energy demands are extremely high (e.g. ultra-distance events), opportunities to refuel are limited (e.g. training twice a day) or the athletes dietary intake excludes key nutrients, nutritional supplements (including protein, recovery drinks, vitamins, and minerals) may be required to prevent detriments to performance and ill-health. Table 11.1 summarizes current recommendations associated with optimal sports performance, but coaches should monitor the well-being and performance of the athlete and re-evaluate their nutritional requirements according to how they feel and changes to training load and competition demands.

References

Abbey, E.L., Wright, C.J., Kirkpatrick, C.M. (2017). Nutrition practices and knowledge among NCAA division III football players. *Journal of the International Society of Sports Nutrition*, 19(14):13.

Antonio, J., Ellerbroek, A., Silver, T., Vargas, L. and Peacock, C. (2016a). The effects of a high protein diet on indices of health and body composition: a crossover trial in resistance-trained men. *Journal of the International Society of Sports Nutrition*, 13:3.

Antonio, J., Ellerbroek, A., Silver, T., Vargas, L., Tamayo, A. and Buehn, R. (2016b). A high-protein diet has no harmful effects: a one-year crossover study in resistance-trained males. *Journal of Nutrition & Metabolism*, DOI: 10.1155/2016/9104792.

Atherton, C., McNaughton, L.R., Close, G.L., and Sparks, S.A. (2020). Post-exercise provision of 40 g of protein during whole body resistance training further augments strength adaptations in elderly males. *Research in Sports Medicine* (In Press), DOI: 10.1080/15438627.2020.1770251.

Bailey, C.P., and Hennessy, E. (2020). A review of the ketogenic diet for endurance athletes: performance enhancer or placebo effect? *Journal of the International Society of Sports Nutrition*, 17:33.

Blennerhassett, C., McNaughton, L.R., Cronin, C., and Sparks, S.A. (2019). Development and implementation of a nutrition knowledge questionnaire for ultra-endurance athletes. *International Journal of Sports Nutrition and Exercise Metabolism*, 29(1):39–45.

Burke, L.M., Castell, L.M., Casa, D.J., Close, G.L., Costa, R.S., Desbrow, B., Halson, S.L., Lis, D.M., Melin, A.K., Peeling, P., Saunders, P.U., Slater, G.J., Sygo, J., Witard, O.C., Bermon, S., and Stellingwerff, T. (2019). International association of athletics federations consensus statement 2019: nutrition for athletics. *International Journal of Sport Nutrition and Exercise Metabolism*, 29(2): 73–84.

Burke, L.M., Hawley, J.A., Wong, S.H., and Jeukendrup, A.E. (2011). Carbohydrates for training and competition. *Journal of Sports Sciences*, 29(Suppl 1):S17–S27.

Burke, L.M., Kiens, B., and Ivy, J.L. (2004). Carbohydrates and fat for training and recovery. *Journal of Sports Sciences*, 22(1):15–30.

Burke, L.M., Lundy, B., Fahrenholtz, I.L., and Melin, A.K. (2018b) Pitfalls of conducting and interpreting estimates of energy availability in free-living athletes. *International Journal of Sport Nutrition and Exercise Metabolism*, 1;28(4):350–363.

Burke LM, Ross ML, Garvican-Lewis LA, Welvaert M, Heikura IA, Forbes SG, Mirtschin JG, Cato LE, Strobel N, Sharma AP, Hawley JA. (2017). Low carbohydrate, high fat diet impairs exercise economy and negates the performance benefit from intensified training in elite race walkers. *Journal of Physiology*, 595(9):2785–2807.

Close, G.L., Hamilton, D.L., Philp, A., Burke, L.M., Morton, J.P. (2016). New strategies in sport nutrition to increase exercise performance. *Free Radical Biology and Medicine*, 98:144–158.

Convertino, V.A., Armstrong, L.E., Coyle, E.F., Mack, G.W., Sawka, M.N., Senay Jr, L.C., and Sherman, W.M. (1996). ACSM position stand: exercise and fluid replacement. *Medicine and Science in Sports and Exercise*, 28(1):i–vii.

Couture, S., Lamarche, B., Morissette, E., Provencher, V., Valois, P., Goulet, C., and Drapeau, V. (2015). Evaluation of sports nutrition knowledge and recommendations among high school coaches. *International Journal of Sport Nutrition and Exercise Metabolism*, 25(4):326–334.

Devlin, J.T. and Williams, C. (eds) (1991) Foods, nutrition and sports performance: final consensus statement. *Journal of Sports Sciences*, 9(S1):3, DOI: 10.1080/02640419108729862

Evans, G.H., Watson, P., Shirreffs, S.M., and Maughan, R.J. (2016). Effect of exercise intensity on subsequent gastric emptying rate in humans. *International Journal of Sport Nutrition and Exercise Metabolism*, 26(2):128–134.

Gibson, A.A., Seimon, R.V., Lee, C.M.Y., Ayre, J., Franklin, J., Markovic, T.P., Caterson, I.D. and Sainsbury, A. (2015), Do ketogenic diets really suppress appetite? *Obesity Reviews*, 16:64–76.

Greene, D.A., Varley, B.J., Hartwig, T.B., Chapman, P., Rigney, M. (2018). A low-carbohydrate ketogenic diet reduces body mass without compromising performance in powerlifting and Olympic weightlifting athletes. *Journal of Strength and Conditioning Research*, 32(12):3373–3382.

Impey, S.G., Hearris, M.A., Hammond, K.M., Bartlett, J.D., Louis, J., Close, G.L., and Morton, J.P. (2018). Fuel for the work required: a theoretical framework for carbohydrate periodization and the glycogen threshold hypothesis. *Sports Medicine*, 48(5):1031–1048.

Jackman, S.R., Witard, O.C., Philip, A., Wallis, G.A., Baar, K. and Tipton, K.D. (2017). Branched-chain amino acid ingestion stimulates muscle myofibrillar protein synthesis following resistance exercise in humans. *Frontiers in Physiology*, 7(8):390.

Jager, R., Kerksick, C.M., Campbell, B.I., Cribb, P.J., Wells, S.D., Skwiat, T.M., Purpura, M., Ziegenfuss, T.N., Ferrando, A.A., Arent, S.M., Smith-Ryan, A.E., Stout, J.R., Arciero, P.J., Ormsbee, M.J., Taylor, L.W., Wilborn, C.D., Kalman, D.S., Kreider, R.B., Willoughby, D.S., Hoffman, J.R., Krzykowski, J.L. and Antonio, J. (2017). ISSM position stand: protein and exercise. *Journal of the International Society of Sports Nutrition*, 14:20.

Jeukendrup, A.E., and Killer, S.C. (2010). The myths surrounding pre-exercise carbohydrate feeding. *Annals of Nutrition and Metabolism*, 57(Suppl 2):18–25.

Joy, J.M., Lowery, R.P., Wilson, J.M., Purpura, M., De Souza, E.O., Wilson, S.M., Kalman, D.S., Dudeck, J.E. and Jager, R. (2013). The effects of 8 weeks of whey or rice protein supplementation on body composition and exercise performance. *Nutrition Journal*, 12:86.

Kerksick, C.M., Wilborn, C.D., Roberts, M.D. et al. (2018). ISSN exercise and sports nutrition review update: research and recommendations. *Journal of the International Society of Sports Nutrition*, 15:38.

MacNaughton, L.S., Wardle, S.L., Witard, O.C., McGlory, C., Hamilton, D.L., Jeromsom, S., Lawrence, C.E., Wallis, G.A. and Tipton, K.D. (2016). The response of muscle protein synthesis following whole-body resistance exercise is greater following 40 g than 20 g of ingested whey protein. *Physiological Reports*, 4:15.

Manore, M.M., Patton-Lopez, M.M., Meng, Y., Wong, S.S. (2017). Sport nutrition knowledge, behaviors and beliefs of high school soccer players. *Nutrients*, 9(4):350.

Maughan, R.J., Watson, P., Cordery, P.A., Walsh, N.P., Oliver, S.J., Dolci, A., Rodriguez-Sanchez, N., Galloway, S.D. (2016). A randomized trial to assess the potential of different beverages to affect hydration status: development of a beverage hydration index. *American Journal of Clinical Nutrition*, 103(3):717–723.

Mettler, S., Mitchell, N. and Tipton, K.D. (2010). Increased protein intake reduces lean body mass loss during weight loss in athletes. *Medicine and Science in Sports and Exercise*, 42(2):326–337.

Moore, D.R., Robinson, M.J., Fry, J.L., Tang, J.E., Glover, E.I., Wilkinson, S.B., Prior, T., Tarnopolsky, M.A. and Phillips, S.M. (2009). Ingested protein dose response of muscle and albumin protein synthesis after resistance exercise is young men. *The American Journal of Clinical Nutrition*, 89(1):161–168.

Mountjoy, M., Sundgot-Borgen, J.K., Burke, L.M., et al., (2018). IOC consensus statement on relative energy deficiency in sport (RED-S): 2018 update. *British Journal of Sports Medicine*, 52:687–697.

Peacock, O.J., Stokes, K., and Thompson, D. (2011). Initial hydration status, fluid balance, and psychological affect during recreational exercise in adults, *Journal of Sports Sciences*, 29(9):897–904.

Peake, J.M., Neubauer, O., Walsh, N.P. and Simpson, R.J. (2017) Recovery of the immune system after exercise. *Journal of Applied Physiology*, 122:1077–1087.

Phillips, S.M. and van Loom, L.J. (2011). Dietary protein for athletes: from requirements to optimum intakes, *Journal of Sports Sciences*, 29(suppl 1): S29–S38.

Ranganathan, J., Vennard, D., Waite, R., Dumas, P., Lipinski, B. and Searchinger, T. (2016). *Shifting Diets for a Sustainable Food Future*; Working Document: Creating a Sustainable Food Future, Instalment 11.Washington, DC: World Resources Institute.

Rhyu, H.S., and Cho, S.Y. (2014). The effect of weight loss by ketogenic diet on the body composition, performance-related physical fitness factors and cytokines of Taekwondo athletes. *Journal of Exercise Rehabilitation*. 31;10(5):326–331.

Sawka, M.N., Burke, L.M., Eichner, E.R., Maughan, R.J., Montain, S.J., and Stachenfeld, N.S. (2007). ACSM position stand: exercise and fluid replacement. *Medicine and Science in Sports and Exercise*, 39(2): 377–390.

Sport and Exercise Nutrition Register (2017). Sports and exercise nutrition register (SENr) supplement use in sport: position statement. http://www.senr.org.uk/key-documents/ [Accessed 01/10/2020].

Symons, T.B., Sheffield-Moore, M., Wolfe, R.R. and Paddon-Jones, D. (2009). A moderate serving of high-quality protein maximally stimulates skeletal muscle protein synthesis in young and elderly subjects. *Journal of the American Dietetic Association*, 109(9):1582–1586.

Thomas, D.T., Erdman, K.A., Burke, L.M. (2016). American college of sports medicine joint position statement. Nutrition and athletic performance. *Medicine and Science in Sports and Exercise*, 48(3):543–568.

Tipton, K.D., and Wolfe, R.R. (2004). Protein and amino acids for athletes. *Journal of Sports Sciences*, 22(1):65–79.

Wilkinson, S., Tarnopolsky, M., Macdonald, M. and Macdonald, J. (2007). Consumption of fluid skim milk promotes greater muscle protein accretion after resistance exercise than does consumption of an isonitrogenous and isoenergetic soy-protein beverage. *The American Journal of Clinical Nutrition*, 85:1031.

Witard, O.C., Jackman, S.R., Breen, L., Smith, K., Selby, A. and Tipton, K.D. (2014). Myofibrillar muscle protein synthesis rates subsequent to a meal in response to increasing doses of whey protein at rest and after resistance exercise. *The American Journal of Clinical Nutrition*, 99:86–95.

12 Reflection is 'Wholly Beneficial' for Coaches

Lauren Downham and Chris Cushion

Introduction

An examination of the coaching literature shows that a considerable body of work accepts reflection is an essential part of coach learning, enhancing practice, and developing critical thinking (e.g. Cropley, Miles & Peel, 2012; Cushion, Ford & Williams, 2012; Gilbert & Trudel, 2001; Irwin, Hanton & Kerwin, 2004; Knowles, Gilbourne, Borrie & Nevill, 2001; Knowles, Tyler, Gilbourne & Eubank, 2006; Taylor, Werthner, Culver & Callary, 2015; Cushion, 2016). As a result, research and coach education has focussed on developing and promoting reflection (e.g. Cassidy, Jones & Potrac, 2009; Cushion, 2006; Gilbert & Trudel, 2006). This means that in coaching reflection has become privileged to the extent that the concept has become, what Cotton (2001) described as, a 'hegemonic, natural, indisputable discourse that operates beyond question' (p. 514). Reflection and reflective practice have been presented uncritically and enthusiastically accepted as 'wholly beneficial' for coaches (Fendler, 2003, p. 16) and despite the plethora of written works related to, and favouring, reflection in coaching, few question its 'positive' connotations. Indeed, notions of reflection have shaped what and how coaches think and knitted reflection into the fabric of coaching practice, merging meanings, and promoting a discourse of inseparability – that you 'cannot' coach without reflection (cf. Downham, 2020).

As a consequence, reflection has become ensconced in coaches' vocabulary (Cushion, 2016; Downham & Cushion, 2020) and embedded in the discourse of education providers as part of 'the rhetoric of coaching and coach learning' (Downham, 2020, p. 1). This acceptance has led to an overuse of the term 'reflection' in coach education; as Cushion (2016) argued, reflection has become 'a slogan disguising a range of practices – with divergent understandings and varying approaches'. With no unitary view of reflection, 'practitioners will practice reflection in radically different ways, if at all' (e.g. Cropley et al., 2012; Knowles et al., 2006) (p. 2). Reflection, therefore, is a contested but established concept whose meaning shifts to accommodate the interpretation and interests of those using the terms and is thus an example of 'common rhetoric' (Zeichner & Tabachnick, 1991, p. 1). Rather than explore this, much of the existing research has concentrated on applying 'reflection' to particular practices (e.g. Gilbert & Trudel, 2001; Knowles et al., 2001, 2006; Taylor et al., 2015; Trudel, Culver, & Werthner, 2013) with limited attention paid to problems with its meaning (Cropley et al., 2012) – or actual impact on practice (Cushion et al., 2010). In this chapter, we detail common assumptions underpinning approaches to reflection in coaching – those that may fuel the myth of reflection – before problematizing these assumptions by turning our attention towards what reflection *does* in coaching and through coach education. In doing so, we aim to make explicit the often taken-for-granted aspects of this concept with implications that can support (and challenge) coaches' thinking about reflection.

Reflection in Coaching

Coaches' practice, the design and delivery of coach education, and the work of coach developers, including their use of reflection, will have an approach informed by underpinning and sometimes implicit beliefs about learning (Cushion et al., 2019). One such approach influencing coaching currently is a humanistic approach, based on humanistic psychology (cf. Rogers, 1983; Usher & Edwards, 2005). As Downham and Cushion (2020) explained, the rationale underpinning the educational process in a humanistic approach is 'learner-centred'. That is, where the learner is self-motivated and self-directed, exercising individual agency, and making their own authentic choices about self-development and self-realization (Usher & Edwards, 1994, 2005). Coach developers adopting this approach act as 'guides' who make an 'empowering' contribution encouraging coaches to become autonomous learners to develop their subjectivity and identity (Downham & Cushion, 2020).

Research in coach education contexts (cf. Downham & Cushion, 2020; Downham, 2020), has evidenced how these humanistic ideas (e.g. learner-centeredness, empowerment, and self-direction) underpin reflective practice and foster beliefs that coaches can take control of their own learning through reflection (Downham & Cushion, 2020). To be specific, these ideas have been shown to produce meanings about reflection including the notion that the coach is able to draw out their own learning and be led to a rational understanding of their coaching practice and self through a system of reinforcement or empowerment to achieve their potential (cf. Derbyshire & Fleming, 2008). On the surface then, reflection construed in this positive and learner-centred way can appear to avoid the indoctrination of coaches through coach education (cf. Nelson, Cushion & Potrac, 2006) and sidesteps the exercise of power. Indeed, a key tenet of humanistic approaches (and thus ways of understanding, practicing, and supporting reflection) is that it purports to be 'power free' or attempts to democratize power (Foucault, 1975).

Humanistic approaches to coaches' reflection have been found to retain an individualistic focus on practice, interactions, and ideas to solve problems while broader influences, such as the effects of power relations and culture on subjectivity, remain absent from reflective conversations. Likewise, when adopting this perspective, coach developers have been shown to distance themselves from power relations by maintaining that they hold little or no power over others or choice about how it is exercised (Brookfield, 2009; Downham & Cushion, 2020). Underpinned by these assumptions, it can be argued that reflection is driven by instrumental rationality, with a technical interest focused on professional objectives (e.g. professional development reviews) feedback and 'behaviour change' in a presumed objective world. This means that coaching and coach education is seen as a neutral, benign space where reflection is a desirable activity to develop 'better' coaches who are 'empowered' or made 'autonomous' (Cushion, 2016; Cushion & Jones, 2014; Denison, Mills & Konoval, 2015). However, coaching has dynamic, complex, and diffused networks of power relations where reflection is in fact embedded in a persistent and resilient culture (Cushion, 2016; Cushion & Jones, 2014). This means that power and its effects on subjectivity cannot be ignored during practices of reflection. Instead, it can be considered that reflection operates as a particular activity (e.g. through course material, coach talk, and pedagogical practices) with particular ends throughout coaching and coach education.

What Does Reflection Do?

Reflection has been argued to enhance a number of outcomes such as professional development (e.g. Culver & Trudel, 2006); self-awareness (Cassidy et al., 2009; Gilbert & Côté, 2013); and learning and practice (e.g. Cropley, Miles & Peel, 2012; Cushion, Ford & Williams, 2012; Gilbert & Trudel, 2001; Irwin et al., 2004). In particular, critical thinking has been identified as a key outcome of reflection (e.g. Hall & Gray, 2016; Handcock & Cassidy, 2014; Knowles et al., 2001; Knowles, Borrie & Telfer, 2005; Knowles et al., 2006; Taylor et al., 2015). That is, 'thinking that challenges existing beliefs and assumptions (Brookfield, 2017) to develop knowledge (Cushion, 2016) in light of the broader social context (e.g. discourse and power relations) in which the coach is positioned and constructed' (Fook, 2015; Thompson & Pascal, 2012) (Downham, 2020, p. 3). However, the coaching literature considering reflection has highlighted the limited development of coaches' critical thinking (e.g. Carson, 2008; Cropley, Neil, Wilson & Faull, 2011; Hughes, Lee & Chesterfield, 2009; Knowles et al., 2001, 2006; Stoszkowski & Collins, 2014). 'Rather, the evidence has shown that coaches can complete coach education and accrue experience uncritically, without it impacting meaningfully on how they think and what they do' (Downham, 2020, p. 3). Crucially, this can happen despite coaches believing that change has occurred through reflection (Cushion, Nelson, Armour, Lyle, Jones, Sandford & O'Callaghan, 2010; Gilbert & Trudel, 2001; Stodter & Cushion, 2014).

Limited evidence of critical thought means that although existing rationalistic and neutral interpretations of reflection have been accepted into coaching, reflection is not achieving its intended outcomes in coach education contexts (e.g. challenging coaches' thinking and practice to produce novel and creative ideas). The outcomes of non-reflective reflective practice and the unintended consequences of well-intended (humanistic) approaches to practicing and supporting reflection therefore require further consideration. To explore these questions in greater detail, we provide an example of recent research focused on reflection. We afford this detail because the study was directed specifically at understanding reflection and reflective practice to present a different view of reflection (it's practice and outcomes) to that currently promulgated in the literature (i.e. not simply a 'tool' or a neutral process) which have, by and large, been shaped by psychological approaches (e.g. Irwin et al., 2004; Knowles et al., 2001; Taylor et al., 2015; Trudel et al., 2013; *inter alia*).

Reflection in coaching: An alternative critical perspective

Downham (2020) conducted a 24-month ethnography of a high-performance coach education programme. The programme under study was believed to offer unique experiences and opportunities for coaches from multiple sports at the highest performance level. The programme design emphasized learning from the coaches' own experiences and opportunities through reflection. A key objective of the programme was therefore to support and develop coaches' reflective practice. The methods of the study involved participant observation of education workshops and interviews with coaches and coach developers. The research design enabled prolonged personal engagement with participants and detailed accounts of what happened during the education programme, together this supported an understanding of multiple perspectives, as well as the group culture, beliefs, and behaviours that influenced reflection and reflective practice (Atkinson, 2017). The overall purpose of the research was to understand something of the complexity of reflection in coaching.

Throughout the education programme, reflection and reflective practice were shown to contribute towards the production and regulation of coaches. In other words, reflective practice shaped and normalized coaches to stay within accepted ways of thinking and doing. For example, on completion of workshops, coaches were asked to identify issues in their own practice. However, this seemingly well-intentioned activity became problematic when the issues identified were then judged as either 'good' or 'bad' in light of the workshop content delivered by an external 'expert'. That is, the coaches' beliefs about their practice were organized and shaped based on ideas delivered on the programme that were cast as 'normal', and anything not conforming to this 'normal' was expected to change. From here, the coaches were asked to experiment with their 'new' ideas and subsequently change their practice accordingly. This process triggered reporting mechanisms (reflective journals and reflecting publicly at the next workshop) about any changes made to their practice. Doing reflective practice in this way made the coaches' beliefs about practice public, visible, and available for scrutiny. Each coach and their practice became subject to analysis by both coach developers and fellow coaches. Again, these practices were well intentioned but a consequence of doing it in this way generated content/conversation, interest/disinterest, agreement/disagreement, questioning/challenging framed in ideas according to was considered 'normal' – and these measures of normality, while arbitrary, were decided by coach developers. Indeed, once armed with a normalizing gaze, the coaches used it to regulate themselves and their peers through reflective practice. As a consequence, their beliefs were examined and normalized through reflection. This meant that the coaches' practice and the pressure to conform to a 'new approach' were intertwined with coach surveillance and self-surveillance. Therefore, reflection, as practiced and supported throughout the education programme, required 'self-discipline as self-surveillance and functioned as regulation through self-regulation' (Downham, 2020, p. 172).

This production and regulation of coaches operated through a permanent, but largely silent, network of power relations. Indeed, networks of power can be considered most effective when they go unnoticed, producing effects on subjectivity without the need for external force. Therefore, when practiced in these ways, reflection supported the effectiveness and efficiency of power's exercise because coaches 'watched' themselves to make sure they remained within accepted/normalized ways of coaching (i.e., ways purported in workshops focused on approaches to planning, leadership, critical decision-making, or negotiation skills, etc.). This meant that coaches were not permitted to effect (on their own or with the help of coach developers) certain operations on their own thinking and practice (i.e. relating the self to the self), so as to transform themselves. Crucially, these outcomes were unintended but were in fact amplified through the practices used as part of a humanistic discourse, a discourse that refuted the effects of power. For example, coach developers framed group workshops and their design (e.g. sitting in circles, 'open' discussions, coach presentations) as a 'safe space' to 'share and learn together', but such learning configurations promoted a public sharing and scrutiny of coaches. One-to-one coach developer sessions claimed to be framed as non-judgmental nor leading as they supported coaches to 'find their own answers'. However, the coaches' subjectivities were shaped through the support of behaviour that was 'asking the right questions' and 'being the right kind of learner'. As a result, these humanistic claims and ideas, related to being 'critical' and 'learner-centred' with 'empowering' intent, were problematic, because they acted to disguise and exacerbate rather than ameliorate power's exercise (see also Downham & Cushion, 2020) – the opposite of the programme's intent. Put another way, humanistic discourses influenced disciplinary forces, enhancing the subtlety of power's exercise and reflection's seductive appeal through an enticing rhetoric of opportunity, autonomy, and neutrality. This rhetoric was reinforced when coaches were asked to decide the content of reflective practice conversations at workshops, reassured by coach developers that there was no right and wrong but rather an opportunity to focus on *their* real-life coaching issues. In response, coaches accepted the legitimacy of reflective practice activities and the truth that they invoked – that they were 'empowered' (see also Downham & Cushion, 2020).

These findings mean that although reflection was advocated as an entirely positive endeavour and coaches' reflective practice activities aligned with established reflection practicalities (e.g. identifying issues, asking evaluative questions, considering multiple perspectives, experimenting in practice) (e.g. Gilbert & Trudel, 2001; Irwin et al., 2004; Knowles et al., 2001; *inter alia*), their humanistic construction was troubled. Revealing the political reverberations of reflective practice through a focus on the subtleties of power adds to our understanding of the concept and is meaningful for coaches and their ambitions to coach differently (cf. Avner, Denison, Jones & Boocock, 2020; Denison et al., 2015). This is because coaches in the study 'became active self-governing subjects; disciplining themselves through reflection towards homogeneity (sameness) rather than freedom, choice and emancipation, as humanistic assumptions might suggest' (Downham, 2020, p. 172).

Problematizing what reflection *does* (i.e. its effects and outcomes) when underpinned by humanistic approaches has revealed that the practice can work to limit coaches' thinking. Revealing these unintended consequences challenges coaches and researchers who adopt, promote, and privilege reflection uncritically in coaching.

Conclusion and implications

In this chapter, we have challenged the myth of reflection's accepted status in coaching as an entirely positive activity, with wholly beneficial outcomes for coaches. Of course, we do not argue that coaches should practice without questioning their values, beliefs, and ideas and engage with a process to develop their knowledge and make sense of their experiences. Rather, the purpose of this chapter was to make visible the taken-for-granted reflection in coaching and expose it to critique and challenge. In doing so, we have shown how humanistic approaches to reflection contribute to the concept's application in coaching (i.e., universally good, with assumptions that align with instrumental rationality). Specifically, reflection informed by ideas of 'learner-centred', 'autonomy', and 'empowerment' was connected to relations of power that can operate to produce, constrain, and construct coaches' subjectivity through disciplinary exercises. These humanistic ideas were shown to enhance the subtly of power's exercise, contributing an enticing promise of empowerment through reflective practice that can, in turn, disempower coaches (cf. Denison et al., 2015).

There is scope to propose an alternative way of thinking about reflection, its role and the (unintended) consequences of its practice in coaching. Rather than focusing on reflection as something that is effective or ineffective in terms of coaching practice or other aims, as something which is essentially good or bad, or as something that can free people from constraints, research needs to pose ideas that destabilize those things that coaches might take for granted about reflection in coaching (cf. Nicoll & Fejes, 2008). From a critical sociological perspective, we hope this agenda challenges current conceptions of reflection as a 'tool' or neutral process (i.e. distant from context and devoid of power's effects) unsettling the concept's position as an 'entirely positive activity' for coaches (see also Downham & Cushion, 2020). On contributing an awkwardness into the fabric' of reflection in coaching, implications encourage coaches to consider critically their understanding and 'application' of reflection – a problematic – concept and practice.

References

Atkinson, M. (2017). Ethnography. In Smith, B., & Sparkes, A. (Eds.), *Handbook of Qualitative Research in Sport and Exercise* (pp. 49–61). London: Routledge.

Avner, Z., Denison, J., Jones, L., Boocock, E., & Hall, E. (2020). Beat the game: A Foucauldian exploration of coaching differently in an elite rugby academy. *Sport, Education and Society.* Ahead of Print 7 September 2020.

Braun, V., & Clarke, V. (2019). Reflective on reflexive thematic analysis. *Qualitative Research in Sport, Exercise and Health, 11*(4), 589–597.

Brookfield, S. (2009) The concept of critical reflection: promises and contradictions. *European Journal of Social Work, 12*(3), 293–304.

Brookfield, S. (2017). *Becoming a Critically Reflective Teacher* (2nd ed.). San Francisco, CA: Jossey-Bass.

Carson, F. (2008). Utilizing video to facilitate reflective practice: Developing sports coaches. *International Journal of Sports Science & Coaching, 3*(3), 381–390.

Cassidy, T., Jones, R., & Potrac, P. (2009). *Understanding Sports Coaching: The Social, Cultural and Pedagogical Foundations of Coaching Practice* (2nd ed.). London: Routledge.

Cotton, A. (2001). Private thoughts in public spheres: Issues in reflection and reflective practices in nursing. *Journal of Advanced Nursing, 36*(4), 512–519.

Cropley, B., Miles, A., & Peel, J. (2012). Reflective practice: Value of, issues, and developments within sports coaching. In *Sports Coach UK Original Research Project.* Leeds: Sports Coach UK.

Cushion, C. (2016). Reflection and reflective practice discourses in coaching: A critical analysis. *Sport, Education and Society, 23*(1), 82–94.

Cushion, C., Nelson, L., Lyle, J., Jones, R., Sandford, R., & Callaghan, C. (2010). *Coach Learning and Development: A Review of Literature* (pp. 1–104). UK: Sports Coach.

Cushion, C., Ford, P., & Williams, A. (2012). Coach behaviours and practice structures in youth soccer: Implications for talent development. *Journal of Sports Sciences, 30*(15), 1631–1641.

Denison, J., Mills, J., & Konoval, T. (2015). Sports' disciplinary legacy and the challenge of "coaching differently". *Sport, Education and Society, 22*(6), 772–783.

Derbyshire, C., & Fleming, V. (2008). Mobilizing Foucault: History, subjectivity and autonomous learners in nurse education. *Nursing Inquiry, 15*(4), 263–269.

Downham, L., & Cushion, C. (2020). Reflection in a high-performance sport coach education program: A Foucauldian analysis of coach developers. *International Sport Coaching Journal.* Ahead of print 29 June 2020.

Fendler, L. (2003). Teacher reflection in a hall of mirrors: Historical influences and political reverberations. *Educational Researcher, 32*(3), 16–25.

Fook, J. (2015). Reflective practice and critical reflection. In Lishman, J. (Ed.), *Handbook for Practice Learning in Social Work and Social Care: Knowledge and Theory* (3rd ed., pp. 440–454). London: Kingsley.

Foucault, M. (1975). Prison talk. In Gordon, C. (Ed.), *Power/Knowledge: Selected Interviews and Other Writings 1972–1977: Michel Foucault* (pp. 37–54). Sussex, UK: The Harvester Press.

Gilbert, W., & Côté, J. (2013). Defining coaching effectiveness: A focus on coaches' knowledge. In Potrac, P., Gilbert, W., & Denison, J. (Eds.), *Routledge Handbook of Sports Coaching* (pp. 147–159). London: Routledge.

Gilbert, W., & Trudel, P. (2001). Learning to coach through experience: Reflection in model youth sport coaches. *Journal of Teaching in Physical Education, 21*(1), 16–34.

Gilbert, W., & Trudel, P. (2006). The coach as a reflective practitioner. In Jones, R. (Ed.), *The Sports Coach as Educator: Reconceptualising Sports Coaching* (pp. 113–127). London: Routledge.

Handcock, P., & Cassidy, T. (2014). Reflective practice for rugby union strength and conditioning coaches. *Strength and Conditioning Journal, 36*(1), 41–45.

Irwin, G., Hanton, S., & Kerwin, D. (2004). Reflective practice and the origins of elite coaching knowledge. *Reflective Practice, 5*(3), 425–442.

Knowles, Z., Gilbourne, D., Borrie, A., & Nevill, A. (2001). Developing the reflective sports coach: A study exploring the processes of reflective practice within a higher education coaching programme. *Reflective Practice, 2*(2), 185–207.

Knowles, Z., Borrie, A., & Telfer, H. (2005). Toward the reflective sports coach: Issues of context, education and application. *Ergonomics, 48*(11–14), 1711–1720.

Knowles, Z., Tyler, G., Gilbourne, D., & Eubank, M. (2006). Reflecting on reflection: Exploring the practice of sports coaching graduates. *Reflective Practice, 7*(2), 163–179.

Nelson, L., Cushion, C., & Potrac, P. (2006). Formal, nonformal and informal coach learning: A holistic conceptualisation. *International Journal of Sports Science & Coaching, 1*(3), 247–259.

Nicoll, K., & Fejes, A. (2008). Mobilizing Foucault in studies of lifelong learning. In Fejes, A., & Nicholl, K. (Eds.), *Foucault and Lifelong Learning: Governing the Subject* (pp. 1–18). London: Routledge.

Stodter, A., & Cushion, C. (2014) Coaches' learning and education: A case study of culture in conflict. *Sports Coaching Review, 2*(1), 63–79.

Taylor, S., Werthner, P., Culver, D., & Callary, B. (2015). The importance of reflection for coaches in parasport. *Reflective Practice, 16*(2), 269–284.

Thompson, N., & Pascal, J. (2012). Developing critically reflective practice. *Reflective Practice: International and Multidisciplinary Perspectives, 13*(2), 311–325.

Trudel, P., Culver, D., & Werthner, P. (2013). Looking at coach development from the coach-learner's perspective: Consideration for coach development administrators. In Potrac, P., Gilbert, W., & Denison, J. (Eds.), *Routledge Handbook of Sports Coaching* (pp. 375–387). London: Routledge.

Zeichner, K., & Tabachnick, B. (1991). Reflections on reflective teaching. In Tabachnick, B., & Zeichner, K. (Eds.), *Issues and Practices in Inquiry-oriented Teacher Education* (pp. 1–36). London: Falmer.

13 Do you have to walk it to talk it? The significance of an elite athletic career in becoming a high-performance coach in men's football and rugby union

Alexander D. Blackett

Introduction

Many high-performance sports coaches share a connecting theme with one and another: they each have a previous history as an elite athlete in their respective sport before becoming a coach (Chroni, Pettersen & Dieffenbach, 2020; Ewing, 2019; Mielke, 2007). Focussing on men's football across the United Kingdom for example, after having been elite players, the likes of Pep Guardiola, Ole Gunnar Solskjear, Frank Lampard, Mikel Arteta, Neil Lennon, and Steven Gerrard, to name a few, are all at the time of writing head coaches at some of the best and most prestigious professional teams. Similar trends are seen across men's rugby union within the English men's Premiership: Geordan Murphy, Rob Baxter, Mark McCall, Pat Lam, Stuart Hooper, and others are all head coaches/directors of rugby after serving time as elite athletes. For many of these listed names, their playing careers also include representation at international level.

The trend of elite athlete to high-performance coach is widespread across men's team and individual sports, but also now frequently seen amongst women's sports too. Within tennis, former elite players are becoming coaches of current top players. Individuals such as Lindsay Davenport, Amiele Mauresmo, and Kim Clijsters are matched by esteemed names from within the men's game like

Andre Agassi, Boris Becker, Ivan Lendl, Goran Ivanešević, and John McEnroe in becoming elite-level coaches. Across many sports, there is a deep-rooted history for the athlete to coach pathway, one that has been socially reproduced throughout the twentieth century (Carter, 2006; Pawson, 1973; Taylor, Ward & Thatcher, 1997) and which seems to have come to prominence within the twenty-first century (Blackett, Evans & Piggott, 2017; Rynne, 2014). The pathway has become so established that it now reprises a taken-for-granted assumption, one which has been uncritically accepted without empirical analyses (Ewing, 2019). This has culminated in the 'myth' that it is important to have been an elite athlete in order to be proficient as high-performance coach.

For aspiring coaches then, who do not and will not possess an elite playing career, the misconception of needing to have a competitive-athletic playing career has seemingly created a 'glass ceiling,' one which prevents them from accessing high-performance coaching roles on account of their lack of playing experience at an elite level. Anecdotally, this has become very evident for me as a university lecturer in sports coaching over the past decade. A focal point of my role has been to educate and then support undergraduate students who hold aspirations to become effective and successful coaches at the elite levels of their respective sports. Yet, seldom few students do indeed attain their desired roles, particularly in the sports of men's football and rugby union. I stress the term *yet*, as I sincerely hope after hearing about my students' ambitions and helping them achieve their degrees that they are still pursuing these dreams and that they do indeed one day fulfil them as they continue to work towards these. Nonetheless, no matter how much I try to be as supportive as possible with my current and future students who share the desire to become head coaches of men's Premier League football teams or Premiership rugby union teams, as well as in other sports, based on my experiences, I am becoming ever more dubious that these are realistic ambitions if they have not been elite-level athletes themselves. The myth of needing to have been an elite athlete in order to be a high-performance coach seems to be a steadfast cornerstone of sporting dogma.

When I outline the research on high-performance coach development pathways to my students, emphasizing the seemingly important need to become an elite player in order to successfully transition into elite-level coaching, the names of José Mourinho, Arsène Wenger, Arrigo Sacchi, and André Villas-Boas are readily given as examples that counter the myth. All four are notable anomalies within football (although Mourinho and Wenger were indeed professional players themselves, albeit at a low level), yet unfortunately they are still exceptions to the rule in football and across other sports too. Two quotes are also regularly cited as a base to student rebuttals which have been respectively attributed to Sacchi and Mourinho: (a) 'You do not need to be horse to be a jockey' and; (b) 'You do not need to be a piano to be a pianist'. Both statements seem logical and hard to argue with. Nevertheless, in the world of elite sport, sense and logic seem to be overridden by a mixture of tradition, sentiment, and irrationalism as head coach appointments have been and continue to be largely the 'exclusive preserve of former players' (Kelly, 2008, p. 410).

Fast-tracking: A contradiction to coaching professional standards?

At a time where the role of a coach is being advocated to become fully recognized as a profession, on par with teaching, medicine, and law for example, the actions of national and international governing bodies of sport in accelerating the pathway between elite athlete and high-performance coach seem to go against the desired professional standards these governing bodies themselves have set. On account of their playing histories, current and former professional athletes at present are afforded the opportunity in many sports to circumvent entry-level coaching qualifications. Instead, they can attend condensed higher coaching qualifications which can 'fast-track' their entry into coaching (Blackett et al., 2018; Rynne, 2014). The benefits of doing this are to clearly incentivize athletes to stay in the sport upon their athletic retirement, a particular benefit in mitigating against mental health issues associated with transitions out of sport (Park, Lavallee & Tod, 2013). For coach development scholars, however, the proliferation in accelerating coach education and offering more fast-tracking opportunities has been problematized on the basis for how coaching as whole may struggle to meet the requisite professional standards that it aspires toward.

For example, McMahon, Zehntner, McGannon, and Lang (2020) reported how one former Australian elite-level swimmer was fast-tracked through formal coach education structures three months after their athletic retirement into a state-level coaching post despite 'missing four of the eight modules required for successful completion of the course' (p. 7). Through the research process, the coach reflected upon their experiences as an athlete and revealed how they had received psychological and physical abusive coaching practices. The coach continued to admit how they then went onto recycle these same practices in their own coaching. Through their own athletic career, these poor practices had become entrenched and unquestionably adopted (Benish, Langdon & Culp, 2020); a feature of their coaching which may have been highlighted and reflected upon had they not been fast-tracked through their coach accreditation. Indeed, four out of the eight modules where they were provided the concession of not needing to complete 'all contained content relating to development of ethical coaching practice' (McMahon et al., 2020, p. 8).

Given the recent disclosures made by elite gymnasts in the United Kingdom about abusive coaching practices (Roan, 2020), such potentially recycled toxic coaching practices are therefore not solely applicable to swimming. Furthering the significance of how abusive practices and questionable coaching ideologies are uncritically adopted by all coaches, and not just former athletes who transition into sport, has received growing scholarly attention (see Wilinsky & McCabe, 2020). This emerging body of research has largely been set within post-positivist paradigms that analyse the socio-cultural contexts of sport and coach learning. Such analyses have reported on the significance of how the socio-cultural landscape in which athletes are positioned in prior to their coaching comes to serve as an 'apprenticeship of observation' which shapes their initial coach learning and future coaching practice (Cushion, Armour & Jones, 2003, p.217). As this chapter will continue to explore, this research has indicated how this subconscious learning then implicitly informs future coaching behaviours where questionable coaching practices are sometimes enacted.

At this point I think it necessary to outline that there have been some exceptional coaches that do possess an athletic background who have advanced coaching methods and who are highly regarded as in having changed their sports for the better (e.g. Johnann Cryuff, Pep Guardiola and Jurgen Klopp in football, and others in a variety of sports). Nonetheless, it is important to recognize that this does not always happen and that the transition from elite athlete to high-performance coach is not always a successful one. Irrespective of these failures, the trend of elite athletes fast-tracked into post-athletic high-performance coaching roles does not seem to be abating, rather increasing within senior environments and is also now regularly occurring within youth development contexts also (see Blackett et al., 2019). In turn, this has led onto the reinforcement of the myth being true of having to play to coach, which brings with it several potential concerns and contradictions for professionalizing the role as well as advancing coaching practices for producing better players.

An empirical rationale for fast-tracking

Empirical research on the athlete to coach transition is an emergent one. Chroni et al. (2020) have identified this to arise within Norwegian winter sports, along with McMahon et al. (2020) having reported on the potential negative consequences within Australian swimming. Moreover, Mielke (2007) reported that this pathway is also prevalent in Major League Baseball (MLB), the National Basketball Association (NBA) and to a lesser extent within the National Football League (NFL). Blackett et al. (2017) have also empirically analysed the fast-tracked pathway phenomenon by different means after having sourced the perspectives and beliefs held by senior club board members of professional men's football and rugby union clubs on why they fast-tracked former athletes into head coaching roles of their respective teams. The intention was to extend the coach-centric samples administered by extant research by collecting data from those in positions of power amongst the cultural field of elite sport and who played significant roles in perpetuating the fast-tracked pathway by sanctioning such appointments – offering insight into why the fast-tracking pathway may also exist in other sports.

Blackett et al. (2017) interviewed 8 directors who had been central to the process of coach recruitment for their men's senior teams and had previously appointed 'fast-tracked' coaches. Unsurprisingly, the results indicated club board members prioritize successful on-field performances and an improvement of results when recruiting new coaches. A latent theme underscoring their reasons for appointing fast-tracked coaches though was a desire for the directors to preserve and maintain their own power within the club by selecting coaches who would most likely continue to reproduce the club's culture. Doing this would safeguard the directors' positions within their clubs, as they would receive the approval of the fellow board members, sponsors, staff, players, and spectators. Significantly, there was a perception that appointing a former competitive athlete would better enable the incoming coach to immediately earn the players' respect by socially reproducing the club culture in addition of demonstrating empathy and an overall shared understanding of what the players go through in competition. To illustrate this, one rugby director described being a player as having 'to put your head in some dark places' meaning 'the fact that you've been a player and come through that you then have that knowledge' to be empathetic, but also being attuned to the technical and tactical elements of the game (as cited by Blackett et al., 2017, p. 753). Such sentiments reflected the value assigned by the directors on coaches having previously 'walked in the shoes of their players' and was a valuable resource for the incoming coach to draw upon in legitimizing their authority and earn the players respect.

The significance for coaches earning player respect was central to all directors' views on whether a coach would indeed be successful in achieving the necessary on-field performance outcomes. As cited by Blackett et al. (2017, p. 750), another director explained what guided his recruitment processes:

> *What do I look for? I think that you've got to ask the players how and what they think of the guys, because ultimately they are the assets which you need to sweat. And if a player is not a player or players aren't reactive to the coaches, you can be the best coach in the world but if you can't resonate with that player then you make a choice, you can either get rid of them the player or you get rid of the coach.*

In this regard, the directors articulated a coach's prior competitive athletic background being the bedrock for developing coaching proficiency. Technical and tactical knowledge as well as the more tactile aspects of building cohesive and positive athlete relationships were judged to be best acquired form a competitive athletic history in comparison to formal coach education courses. As such, a recurring theme across the directors' views was the limited value attributed to governing body coaching courses, as illustrated in the following quotes (as cited by Blackett et al., 2017, p. 752):

> *They [qualifications] don't really stack up a lot of the time. There are a lot of guys who have got level three or four coaching certificates that can't coach you know. I employed a bloke who's done RFU (Rugby Football Union) coaching assessor, top of the food chain with all of the qualifications, even got a Welsh RFU senior coaches badge and I put him in front of our forwards because I needed a forwards coach and had to give him the bullet after two months... He just couldn't cope with it and the lads saw through him straight away.*

> *...to me there is a difference between RFU level 27 coach or whatever it is and someone who has just raw personality to do the right thing at the right time, to put an arm around someone when it matters, to kick them up the arse when it matters... I'd far, far look at character... You are far better recruiting a type of character that is going to be a cultural fit to your club.*

Instead of judging coaching candidates on the formal coach accreditation which they had received, the directors prioritized informal coaching knowledge that arose from their everyday experiences as an athlete. That is, there was an assumption that athletes' careers provided them with a coaching apprenticeship to absorb not only the technical and tactical knowledge necessary for coaching efficacy but also the more culturally accepted dispositions for acquiring athlete respect. It is this fundamental belief, along with the ability to quickly earn athlete respect, as to why fast-tracking was preferred over appointing a coach without a competitive playing history. On this basis, there was an evident preference that incoming coaches had indeed been pianos and horses!

Clearly, this is counter to how the previously mentioned professionals within teaching, medicine and law, are assessed, judged, and then appointed based on their accreditation and qualifications to perform in the roles. To put it bluntly, a medical surgeon is not appointed on the amount of time they have spent having been a patient and operated on. Unlike the directors, the assumption that the knowledge a patient has absorbed when introduced and consulted on concerning the operational procedures and underlying theory as to why the surgery is necessary, and how it will be administered, does not supersede the necessary formal qualifications. Patients that have been operated on by the best surgeons many times over cannot be fast-tracked through their surgical qualifications; they must attain the stipulated professional standards in order to be authorized and registered by the prevailing medical councils as surgeons. Indeed, such subjective recruitment processes in men's football and rugby illustrated how senior directors continued to resist the professionalization of coaching by assigning playing experience and the knowledge that arises from the associated socialization process more value over formal coach education (Kelly, 2008).

A conceptualization of fast-tracking

To explain the theoretical and conceptual bases for coach behaviours and practices, Bourdieu's (1989, 1990) sociological framework has been increasingly used. Indeed, Bourdieu's inter-related concepts of *habitus*, *field*, *species of capital*, and *practice* have all produced informative conceptualizations as to why coaches possess certain beliefs and why they implement their coaching in the ways that they do. In this instance, Bourdieu's theoretical framework can shed light onto the underlying reasons as to why these club directors upheld these views and why the myth of needing to have been an athlete to become an effective elite coach persists.

Bourdieu placed significance on how applied actions of individuals (social agents), whether these actions be unconscious or subconscious, ultimately produce an 'output'. For Bourdieu, an 'output' was referred to as the concept of *practice*. All social agents therefore practice within a social world. Society is composed of multiple layered spaces known as *fields*. With Bourdieu emphasizing society to be made of multiple fields means that there is a *delimited* composition to these fields. Social agents may simultaneously be positioned across multiple fields and there are other fields which agents are not associated to. For example, rugby union is a layered social space. A male rugby union player practices within the cultural space of rugby union, but specifically they practice within the men's games and not the women's games. Indeed, the two versions of the game are delimited fields, as although they share cultural similarities, they have their own subcultures that make them distinct from each other (see Barrett, Sherwin & Blackett, 2021). Furthermore, within the delimited field of the men's game, each club creates their own subcultures that form further delimited fields. This becomes evident when considering how each club attempts to define their own individual identities and cultures against other clubs.

As indicated, within these fields, a collective of social agents then produce cultures that are based on accepted and legitimized traditions and values. These values are ingrained into the culture of each field, becoming over time uncritically accepted and which form the basis of an array of myths, such as the importance of having been an elite athlete for becoming an elite coach. The process for how these cultures and myths become logically accepted was conceptualized by Bourdieu (1990) as *doxa*.

When social agents, like athletes practicing within the delimited fields of their sports and clubs, they both consciously and unconsciously assimilate with the specific values of these fields. Over time, this assimilation becomes a subconscious form of 'knowledge' on how the field operates, the culturally accepted norms and expectations concerning the dispositions of how social agents practice within it. This subconscious knowledge becomes the guiding principles of each agent which is embodied to become ingrained in their everyday interactions. The tacit embodiment of these values then leads to the production of an individual's *habitus*, an implicit familiarity of knowing how to engage accordingly within these appropriate social fields. Bourdieu's (1989, p. 43) well-cited explanation of the habitus helps situate how he defines its manifestation: 'when the habitus encounters a social world of which it is the product, it finds itself 'as a fish in water', it does not feel the weight of water and takes the world about itself for granted'. The immediate adherence of the habitus and the continued embodiment in agent's social practice over time was termed as *hexis* by Bourdieu (1990).

When practicing within fields throughout their everyday lives, social agents seek acceptance and legitimacy. In so doing though, they compete for resources of power against other social agents. This process and effectiveness for power is dependent upon the accumulation of a variety of *species of capital*.

Capital was found by Blackett et al. (2017) as being an important concept for how the board members identified, profiled, and then appointed coaches.

Significant for board members were the species of cultural capital and symbolic capital. For example, board members preferred to recruit former athletes, because this indicated that they had greater amounts of what Bourdieu termed as embodied cultural capital – an assumption that through socialization as an athlete the knowledge of the technical and tactical intricacies of playing the game (the 'feel of the game') at an elite level had been acquired and could be transferred into a coaching role. Institutionalized cultural capital, which represents educational qualifications such as NGB coaching certification, was in comparison devalued by the board members in comparison to the embodied cultural capital that was hierarchically valued. Indeed, the quotes cited beforehand clearly indicate this, such as: 'They [qualifications] don't really stack up a lot of the time ...'

Objectified cultural capital in the form of tangible assets such as clothes, cars, and artwork that indicate a coach's taste was not deemed significant in the recruitment process. Institutionalized social capital, however, was highly valued. A former elite athlete having been immersed in the field of elite sport meant there was a presumption that the incoming coach possessed lots of beneficially valuable social networks with important stakeholders like other coaches, players, and their agents to help improve on-field team results. Furthermore, on the basis that former elite athletes could potentially perform sport-specific skills, in contrast to other coaches without an elite athletic background, meant that greater amounts of physical capital were attributed to former elite athletes too. This was seen to be beneficial in helping with coaching proficiency by allowing the coach to perform demonstrations that helped improve athletic performance onto the current players. Moreover, a coach able to perform the skills that they asked and expected their athletes to perform afforded physical capital to be transferred over to symbolic capital. For coaches without an elite athletic playing career then, this coaching attribute and form of capital was not necessarily a resource available to them. Again, the myth of needing to be a piano or a horse is perpetuated here.

Coach development pathways

Club attachment is a seemingly important issue when looking at coach development pathways. The club directors in Blackett et al.'s (2017) work explained how they preferred to 'draw through' current and/or former players of their clubs into coaching roles. They prioritized prospective coaches who had previously represented their club over other candidates who had not. In such a light, this indicates the importance of not only the field's values being embodied by an incoming coach but more significantly that the delimited values of the club's culture would be embodied. To help with this process of developing a future coach's habitus and the subsequently embodiment of this (hexis), athletes who were identified as being prospective coaches of the senior teams were encouraged to gain more coaching experiences within the same club's youth academies alongside their playing careers. This is suggestive of what Cushion and Jones (2014, p. 277) argue as being the 'hidden curriculum' in coach education whereby much of a coach's learning is 'covert and embedded within daily routine and practice', thus becoming part of a 'hidden curriculum'.

Echoing Cushion and Jones' (2014) analysis of the 'hidden curriculum', after Blackett et al (2018, 2020) interviewed individuals who had begun to negotiate the career transition from elite athlete to high-performance coach, they were not able to recall how their respective clubs' values had shaped their coaching practice and importantly their emerging coaching philosophies. Sentiments were frequently recorded from the interviews that explained how going back to clubs they had previously represented as athletes to begin their coaching careers was appealing. As cited by Blackett et al. (2018, p. 222), Roger was one recently retired rugby player who explained his thinking about where he would go to begin his post-athletic coaching career:

> *I'm going back to a team called (current semi-professional rugby football club 1). They are a team I played for when I was a kid and I stayed there until I was twenty four so I know quite a few people down there and I'm intending on going back down there next season because I need to do my level three [coaching qualification] and I think it's a good place to go and work.*

This pathway of returning to a club which novice coaches had previously represented as an athlete is also seen when looking at recent appointments across football and rugby union. Novice coaches with a competitive playing background seldom go to clubs they have not played for when attaining their first post-athletic coaching role. For example, Steven Gerrard returned to Liverpool FC to begin his coaching career within their youth academy, as did Frank Lampard when beginning his post-athletic coaching career at Chelsea FC's youth academy. Within rugby, Nick Evans and Adam Jones both retired from their playing careers at Harlequins FC and were 'drawn through' by the club immediately into coaching roles. There are many more examples, both within and away from football and rugby union, which further emphasize the importance of having some form of club attachment that aids the career transition into a post-athletic coaching role. Yet again, this also indicates the presence of the myth that it is important of needing to have been a former elite player in order to achieve a position as a high-performance head coach.

Practical implications and recommendations

Given the importance placed on the development of a coaching habitus that reflects the values and culture of a high-performance club, in addition to the accumulation of institutionalized social capital, embodied cultural capital, and symbolic capital that form the basis of acceptance, legitimacy, and respect for being seen as effective in the role, then the myth of needing to be an elite athlete prior to becoming a high-performance coach seems largely true. For aspirant coaches to accumulate these species of capital and to develop a coaching habitus that is commensurate with the club's culture so it can be socially reproduced like the directors wished are all acquired from a competitive playing career in these sports. Accessing the 'hidden curriculum' to embody these culturally accepted norms and to be judged a candidate that can and will reproduce the club's culture in future coaching practices seems vital. Unfortunately, however, this imposes what can be considered as the metaphorical glass-ceiling that prevents aspirant coaches in these sports without a competitive playing career accessing high-performance coaching roles at the elite level. The issue is even more concerning for women trying to access elite coaching roles in men's sports. The glass-ceiling can be even be considered as a concrete-ceiling for women on the basis that they are not able to access the valued species of capital and coaching habitus acquired from a playing career in the men's game (Norman, Rankin-Wright & Allison, 2018).

Until more equitable and transparent coach recruitment processes are enacted at a structural level across elite sports, then it is hard for me and others to be less sceptical about the prospects of aspirant coaches without a competitive playing record being able to access these roles. For the time being, however, prospective coaches without a playing background gaining as much experience within elite club environments is important. Although this is easier said than done, accessing the 'hidden curriculum' and portraying a 'feel for the game' as Bourdieu describes, or at least an awareness of how each club's values are embodied in your own coaching habitus is important. This can help acquire the valued species of capital to be considered proficient for the role of high-performance coach within the men's sports of football and rugby union.

References

Barrett, G. M., Sherwin, I., & Blackett, A. D. (2020). Women rugby union coaches' experiences of formal coach education in Ireland and the UK: A qualitative study. Currently under review.

Benish, D., Langdon, D., & Culp, B. (2020). Examination of novice coaches' previous experiences as athletes: Examples of autonomy support and controlling behaviours as influences on future coaching practice. *International Sport Coaching Journal.* Advanced online publication. doi:10.1123/iscj.2019-0031

Blackett, A. D., Evans, A. B., & Piggott, D. (2017). Why 'the best way of learning to coach the game is playing the game': Conceptualising 'fast-tracked' high-performance coaching pathways. *Sport, Education and Society, 22*(6), 744–758. doi:10.1080/13573322.2015.1075494

Blackett, A. D., Evans, A. B., & Piggott, D. (2018). "Active" and "passive" coach pathways: Elite athletes' entry routes into high-performance coaching roles. *International Sport Coaching Journal, 5*(3), 213–226. doi:10.1123/iscj.2017-0053

Blackett, A. D., Evans, A. B., & Piggott, D. (2019). "They have to toe the line": A Foucauldian analysis of the socialisation of former elite athletes into academy coaching roles. *Sports Coaching Review, 8*(1), 83–102. doi:10.1080/21640629.2018.1436502

Blackett, A. D., Evans, A. B., & Piggott, D. (2020). Negotiating a coach identity: A theoretical critique of elite athletes' transitions into post-athletic high-performance coaching roles. *Sport, Education and Society.* Advanced online publication. doi:10.1080/13573322.2020.1787371

Bourdieu, P. (1989). Social space and symbolic power. *Sociological Theory, 7,* 14–25. doi:10.2307/202060

Bourdieu, P. (1990). *The Logic of Practice.* Cambridge, MA: Stanford University Press.

Carter, N. (2006). *The Football Manager: A History.* Abingdon: Routledge.

Chroni, S., Pettersen, S., & Dieffenbach, K. (2020). Going from athlete-to-coach in Norwegian winter sports: Understanding the transition journey. *Sport in Society, 23*(4), 751–773. doi:10.1080/17430437.2019.1631572

Collins, D., Collins, L., & Carson, H. J. (2016). "If it feels right, do it": Intuitive decision making in a sample of high-level sport coaches. *Frontiers in Psychology, 7,* 504. doi:10.3389/fpsyg.2016.00504

Cushion, C. J., & Jones, R. L. (2014). A Bourdieusian analysis of cultural reproduction: Socialisation and the 'hidden curriculum' in professional football. *Sport, Education and Society, 19*(3), 276–298. doi:10.1080/13573322.2012.666966

Cushion, C. J., Armour, K. M., & Jones, R. L. (2003). Coach education and continuing professional development: Experience and learning to coach. *Quest, 55*(3), 215–230. doi:10.1080/00336297.2003.10491800

Ewing, T. (2019). Rethinking head coach credentials: Playing experience, tertiary qualifications and coaching apprenticeships. *International Sports Coaching Journal, 6*(2), 244–249. doi:10.1123/iscj.2018-0092

Kelly, S. (2008). Understanding the role of the football manager in Britain and Ireland: A Weberian approach. *European Sport Management Quarterly, 8*(4), 399–419. doi:10.1080/16184740802461652

McMahon, J., Zehntner, C., McGannon, K.R. & Lang, M. (2020). The fast-tracking of one elite athlete swimmer into a swimming coaching role: A practice contributing to the perpetuation and recycling of abuse in sport? *European Journal for Sport and Society.* Advanced online publication. doi:10.1080/16138171.2020.1792076

Mielke, D. (2007). Coaching experience, playing experience and coaching tenure. *International Journal of Sports Science & Coaching, 2*(2), 105–108. doi:10.1260/174795407781394293

Norman, L., Rankin-Wright, A. J., & Allison, W. (2018). "It's a concrete ceiling; It's not even glass": Understanding tenets of organizational culture that supports the progression of women as coaches and coach developers. *Journal of Sport and Social Issues, 42*(5), 393–414. doi:10.1177/0193723518790086

Park, S., Lavallee, D., & Tod, D. (2013). Athletes' career transition out of sport: A systematic review. *International Review of Sport and Exercise Psychology, 6*(1), 22–53. doi:10.1080/17509 84X.2012.687053

Pawson, T. (1973). *The Football Managers.* London: Eyre Methuen.

Roan, D. (16 July 2020) Gymnastics abuse claims: British Gymnastics steps aside from independent review. Retrieved from https://www.bbc.co.uk/sport/gymnastics/53419739

Rynne, S. (2014). 'Fast track' and 'traditional path' coaches: Affordances, agency and social capital. *Sport, Education and Society, 19*(3), 299–313. doi:10.1080/13573322.2012.670113

Taylor, R., Ward, A., & Thatcher, M. (1997). The people's game. *People Management, 3*, 22–28.

Wilinsky, C. L., & McCabe, A. (2020). A review of emotional and sexual abuse of elite child athletes by their coaches. *Sports Coaching Review.* Advanced online publication. doi:10.1080/21640629.2020.1775378

14 'Questioning in Coaching Leads to Learning'

A Deconstruction of Questioning

Mark Partington

Introduction

This chapter focuses on the coach behaviour of questioning and the popular rise in sports coaching practice (Cope et al., 2016), alongside a shift in ideology,[1] leading to a reduction of direct instruction (Cope & Cushion, 2020). Suggestions are then made on why coach questioning practices[2] (CQPs) have possibly become a traditional pedagogy and are often poorly understood and misused when implemented with learners. With this in mind, three myths associated with CQPs are presented, based on the questioning literature, and some thoughts are then offered on making CQPs more beneficial for learners.

The purposes of this chapter are to (1) highlight myths regarding questioning in coaching practice; (2) review coach questioning practices; (3) suggest some reasons on why questioning has become so popular in sport coaching; and then finally (4) offer some thoughts and recommendations on how to move coach questioning practices forwards. It is hoped by firstly offering three myths identified from the deconstruction of the questioning literature, readers will be able to resonate with their own coaching experiences and possibly reconstruct an understanding that can support their own use of CQPs for the benefits of the learner/s.

The proposed myths and review of questioning

The suggested myths for this chapter, constructed from my reading of the literature, research undertaken and as a coaching practitioner, are the ideological beliefs that:

1) Questions with learners in coaching practice naturally leads to learning.
2) Questions are better than instruction for learning.
3) Questioning leads to an athlete-centred approach to coaching.

Questioning is a coaching behaviour that has the potential to encourage athletes' active learning through problem-solving, discovery, and performance awareness (Chambers & Vickers, 2006), as well as increasing learners' ownership of their learning (Kidman, 2005). Within education, it is suggested that the types of questions asked might be the quintessential activity of an effective teacher (Chambers & Vickers, 2006; Mills, 1995). Notwithstanding the potentially positive effect questioning can ultimately have on learning, past studies investigating the behaviours employed by coaches in a range of sports and learning contexts have consistently found that questioning comprises only a small percentage of their total coaching behaviours (e.g. Becker & Wrisberg, 2008; Isabel et al., 2008; Potrac et al., 2002, 2007). In summary, findings from these past studies revealed that coach questioning typically ranged between 2–5% of the total reported coaching behaviours. However, more recent studies (Harvey & Light, 2015; Cope et al., 2016) have suggested an increase in CQPs. One example being, Cope et al. (2016) when investigating five English youth football CQPs identified 13% of overall time spent on using questions. A trend that seems to be occurring in lots of different sports is this increase in coaches' use of questions with learners.

Some of the dated past research in sports coaching (Potrac et al., 2002, 2007; Smith & Cushion, 2006), using systematic observation, did not split questioning into two different categories. However, questions require an athlete to use different levels of thought processes to answer them. More recently, coach behaviour research has split the different types of questions, mostly using the Coach Analysis Intervention System (CAIS) (see Cushion et al., 2012). CAIS splits questioning into two and defines convergent questions as those that are 'closed' or have limited responses, whereas divergent questions are those that are 'open' and lead to the possibility of the learner/s providing multiple responses and thus encouraging dialogue between the coach and learner/s as well as the learners themselves (Cushion et al., 2012). Studies using CAIS as a data collection tool have found that coaches ask more convergent as opposed to divergent questions. For example, Partington and Cushion (2013) found that English youth football coaches questioning equated to 7.8% of their total behaviours, of which 5.3% were convergent in nature and 2.5% were divergent in nature. In another study, Harvey et al. (2013) investigated the behaviours of three collegiate coaches in the sports of hockey, basketball, and volleyball. Findings showed that the basketball coach used the highest amount of questioning, comprising 13.95% of total behaviours, with 12.94% convergent and 1.01% divergent. 9.67% of the hockey coach's total behaviours were questions, with 8.19% of these convergent and 1.48% divergent. Finally, the volleyball coach's questioning was lowest with only 4.06% of their behaviours comprised of questioning. Of this, 3.21% were convergent and 0.84% divergent. One notable trend in these behavioural studies is the predominant focus on convergent questions, which tend to limit opportunities for the development of dialogue, debate, and reflection (Cope et al., 2016). This is because convergent questions – in contrast with divergent questions, which require the learner to think through a problem or situation and provide an answer – require simply the recall and presentation of information that has been presented to the learner before (Pearson & Webb, 2006). Ultimately, it has been suggested that learning is increased when teachers use effective divergent questioning techniques to help students develop and use critical-thinking abilities (Kissock & Iyortsuun, 1982). So, while we propose that coaches need to ask a greater level of divergent questions in practice, this is not without challenge or difficulty.

As well as identifying the behavioural data of CQPs, Partington and Cushion (2013) wanted to understand the coaches' rationalization for using different types of questions (i.e. convergent and divergent). In the Partington and Cushion (2013) study, 11 participant coaches discussed about giving their learners opportunities to make decisions and think about what they were doing by asking them questions. However, the behavioural analysis clearly showed that the coaches in this study predominately asked convergent questions instead of divergent questions. The 11 coaches' rationalization for using questions clearly pointed to them wanting to ask more divergent questions, but it was clear they did not fully understand how to in an applied setting. The coaches could give examples of divergent questions they had discovered through experience, from watching other coaches, but they found it difficult to think of new effective questions when they coached. So, the coaches used more convergent questions which they found more natural to deliver and which the learners were used to. Fundamentally, for coaches to increase their divergent questioning, coaches' need an understanding of the purpose of it in relation to learning.

Instruction vs. Questioning: The unhelpful dichotomy

In sports coaching, there seem to be a lot of unhelpful dichotomies (e.g. games or drills). One of these dichotomies is instruction and questioning, where "direct instruction has been branded as an approach that coaches should avoid" (Cope & Cushion, 2020: 73). However, positioning one as a better method than the other is problematic when both have a place in supporting learning. Despite this, following a trend that has also occurred in physical education (Cope & Cushion, 2020), questioning seems to have now become a popular behaviour in sports coaching compared to direct instruction. In some way, direct instruction is being replaced with questioning, which practically isn't possible. One reason for this may be the fact that constructivist-informed approaches have become popular in sports coaching. Constructivism rejects the notion of existence being an objective reality and views learning as an interpretative process shaped by prior experience through which we construct our own particular versions of reality (Davis et al., 2000). It is the constructivist-informed approaches, in this case questioning, that seem to have become the new folk pedagogy, becoming every day, often implicit theories on the human mind which direct the actions and behaviours of people (Bruner, 2000). Questioning has then become embedded, and the norm, in coaches' practice (Cope et al., 2016) and 'constructivism' has become embedded in coach education delivery (Dempsy et al., 2020). It is important to note that 'effective' coaching instead of focusing on just constructivism and/or questioning needs to include a range of different behaviours, including instruction and questioning, based on the needs of the learners, the specific topic being undertaken and the environment in which the intervention is situated (Partington & Walton, 2020).

Some thoughts on why questioning has become so popular: debunking the myths

From my academic and practitioner experiences, CQPs seem located within a positivistic paradigm (Yang, 2006), as coaches believe learners giving the 'right' responses to their questions to be an indication of learning. Therefore, instead of CQPs being 'athlete-centred' (Light, 2008), it seems that they are actually coach-led (Cope & Cushion, 2020). Although at times convergent questions are all that is required. This reductionist approach is somewhat superficial and is unlikely to result in learning, given that this type of approach does not compel learners to think about their answers (Leamson, 2000). Reasons for the predominant focus on convergent questioning may be varied, but this may be closely related to the culture that surrounds the coach's participation and practice histories, which have led them to assimilate a deterministic and behavioural view of learning (Nelson et al., 2014). This view of learning is then operationalized in the overuse of instruction, feedback, and convergent questions at the expense of alternative intervention behaviours such as divergent questioning.

Traditional coaching pedagogy assumes the coach is the primary decision maker with learners being passive receivers of such information (Cushion & Jones, 2014). However, the adoption of other coaching approaches is not a simple or straightforward process. Coaches' practices are an enacted manifestation of ideology which is formed through exploitation to social interactions during the course of coaches' lives. As shown in the coach learning literature (e.g. Nelson & Cushion, 2006; Watts & Cushion, 2016) coaches mainly learn from experience in informal settings. Coaches are then persuaded into thinking traditional pedagogy, and the knowledge associated with this discourse to coaching is the 'best way' to coach (Cushion & Jones, 2006). This makes coaching beliefs stable structures that are particularly difficult to change (Strean et al., 1997; Light & Evans, 2011) and leads to coaches valuing certain types of knowledge over others (Cushion et al., 2003). Indeed, the high volume of coach observation studies provides evidence that traditional pedagogy is very much the normality. It is suggested here then that questioning has become a traditional pedagogy.

The traditional pedagogic actions of coaches, like questioning, that at first glance seem like a behaviour coaches implement for the benefits of the learners are sometimes used more because of the value it has in the sport coaching setting (Partington & Campbell, 2020). Questioning seems to be employed not just because coaches want to (e.g. determined or guided by philosophical thinking [see Partington & Campbell, 2020]) but also because other coaches respect and value this behaviour. Furthermore, Harvey and Light (2015) and Cope et al. (2016) found that questioning was reproduced in practice without a clear understanding of *why*, that is, no clear rationale for its use and application. Questioning could be viewed as a clear model of uncritical reproduction of practice which is highly problematic (Cushion & Jones, 2014). This is where coaches do not choose specific coaching methods to address individual learner's needs and they do not seem to have a clear understanding or rationale for their use of questions (Partington & Cushion, 2013). The suggestion here is that questioning could be employed because of the symbolic value it has in sports coaching settings. Striving for status can influence CQPs because coaches want to abide by traditional and current trends driven by coach education and influential people in sport coaching settings.

Thus, the network of power relations in sport coaching settings work to *legitimate* certain ways of coaching (e.g. questioning) that are uncritically accepted and misrecognized by groups with less perceived power. In this sense, questioning is at times reproduced and driven by ideological assumptions, instead of individual beliefs about learning per se (Partington & Campbell, 2020). Similar to Townsend and Cushion's (2015) study, where ex-professional coaches imposed a scale of coaching preference most favourable to their own symbolic goods (i.e. socially distinguished products). Some of these symbolic goods that could also influence CQPs include the higher National Governing Body (NGB) coaching qualifications, social connections with people in senior positions (e.g. managers, coach developers), and experience in professional sport (not just as a player/athlete but as a coach). These organizations and people, who hold the above symbolic goods, influence coaches on the types of behaviours they implement; however, they might not be what is best for their learners. How coaches use of questions are predisposed needs considering, with an increase in awareness needed on themselves (Partington & Cushion, 2013) and the social influences (Cushion & Partington, 2014). Instead, it is suggested that the education literature (suggestions made in the next section) alongside the actual needs of the learners should determine CQPs.

Questioning: Moving forwards

In the teacher education literature, Crowe and Stanford (2010) discuss the need for teachers to 'deliberately plan' their questions before a session. In this way, teachers are able to think about how their questioning will engage learners in thinking about their performance. In order to achieve this, it has been proposed that teachers should ask questions to individuals or smaller groups so that individual needs are catered for (Crowe & Standford, 2010; McNeill et al., 2008). This is also true for coaches, as they need to move beyond simply considering 'content' when they are planning. Within this process of planning, coaches need to allow time for learners to discuss answers amongst themselves rather than wanting immediate responses. It has been suggested that for thinking to happen, it requires the provision of time (Chambers & Vickers, 2006). Moreover, Wiersema and Licklider (2009) highlight the need for teachers to provide occasions for learners to ask questions of themselves and others as this results in greater levels of learning, as learners are required to think and reflect more deeply about their performance. Indeed, Wright and Forrest (2007) suggest that a learner's capability to discuss their performance demonstrates their ability to successfully play the sport. Also, Chambers and Vickers (2006) investigated the effects of bandwidth feedback and questioning on the performance of competitive swimmers. These authors recommended that for athletes to develop thinking skills, coaches need to refrain from giving extrinsic feedback, instead deliberately delaying their feedback by asking questions. Also, for learners to think entails the provision of time so that they are able to consider their answer in relation to the question asked (Daniel & Bergman-Drewe, 1998; Tincani & Crozier, 2007).

Coaches need to be asking more divergent than convergent questions if the purpose is to promote thinking and discussion (Siedentop & Tannehill, 2000), as these require learners to consider a number of possible responses, before selecting the answer they feel to be most appropriate (Daniel & Bergmann-Drewe, 1998; Wright & Forrest, 2007). However, in a physical education context, McNeill et al. (2008) found that student teachers were unable to ask divergent questions that required learners to critically think about their responses. It is possible then that coaches fail to ask divergent questions, because they don't have the knowledge to be able to ask these types of questions, rather than actively resisting the employment of them (Harvey et al., 2010; Light & Evans, 2011).

Calls have been made for formal coach education to be the place where CQPs understanding and transformation needs to occur (Cushion & Nelson, 2012; Partington et al., 2015). Specifically, formal coach education needs to provide an educational platform for coaches to reflect on and confront their beliefs about questioning. One process that would appear attractive in making coaches aware of their beliefs is the utilization of video feedback, given that beliefs are so difficult to articulate through verbalization alone (Carson, 2008; Cushion & Partington, 2014), with reflective conversations (Partington et al., 2015). A further suggestion is that a component of formal coach education models divergent questioning behaviour within the context that the coaching is to be delivered within (Cushion, 2013). The utilization of the education literature on questioning, alongside video reflections and reflective conversations is useful in a development process to support coaches when developing a clear rationale for CQPs and its use in practice (Partington et al. 2015).

As well as the need to support coaches from an agency perspective, it is important to consider the deterministic nature of sport coaching settings (Cushion & Jones, 2014). For the purpose of this chapter, coaches need to be aware and understand *why* they are using questions in their practice, as they can become attuned to their practice settings and influenced by those with symbolic goods. Therefore, identifying the influences, by looking back at past experiences with someone who understands the possible deterministic influence of structure would be a useful part of a developmental process. In addition, providing novice coaches with the understanding of the structural influences early in their education (e.g. first NGB coaching award) could make them more aware of what determines their CQPs when entering a particular sports coaching setting. As described earlier, reflexivity[3] then can provide people [coaches] with a degree of freedom from the social structure (Bourdieu, 2000). When coaches become more aware of possible structural influences, they can then make more informed decisions about their questioning practices based on their learners needs.

Recommendations for coach questioning practices

As already suggested, it is important to highlight that a mixture of coach behaviours, including both instruction and questioning, are important to support learners in coaching practice. As the focus of this chapter was on CQPs this is where the recommendations are focused. If the potential for questioning is to be achieved, coaches need to adopt a different questioning approach to those identified in some of the past coach behaviour studies (Cope et al. 2016). Although coaches need to be aware that asking questions is a skill, which takes time to master, there are some things to consider:

1) Allow *time* for learners to discuss answers amongst themselves rather than expecting immediate responses.
2) For a greater chance of inclusivity, ask questions to individuals or smaller groups.
3) When you ask a question, don't have a particular answer in mind. Let the answers to your questions dictate where the discussion goes next.
4) *Plan* questions to ask your individual learners.
5) Be reflexive of why you are asking questions. Make sure you are asking questions for the benefit of the learner.

Conclusion

This chapter has explored the coach behaviour of questioning and suggested three myths that surround its rise in popularity and determined ideology (Cope et al., 2016). In doing so, the chapter hopefully got people, mainly coaches and coach developers, to think about *why, when,* and *how* they use questions with their learner/s. Possibly moving away from simply asking questions due to tradition or structural influences and to instead put the learner at the centre of the coaching process. Focusing on the needs of the learner and deciding the right pedagogic method for them is an important process for all coaches and coach developers to consider.

Notes

1 For the purpose of this book chapter, an ideology is a system of ideas, beliefs, values, commitments, pattern of thought, held by many, that has a systemised influence on coaches' practice (Cushion & Partington, 2014).

2 Coach questioning practice (CQPs) is the question-response exchange that occurs between coach and learner/s (Cope et al., 2016).

3 It would be useful for coaches to be reflexive of their practice to acknowledge and consider the taken for granted assumptions, which are not automatically identifiable, generated over time and through personal experiences, and the social environment (Partington & Campbell, 2020).

References

Becker, A. J., & Wrisberg, C. A. (2008). Effective coaching in action: Observations of legendary collegiate basketball coach Pat Summitt. *Sport Psychologist, 22*(2), 197–211.

Bourdieu, P. (2000). *Pascalian Meditations.* Cambridge: Polity Press.

Carson, F. (2000). Utilizing video to facilitate reflective practice: Developing sports coaches. *International Journal of Sports Science and Coaching, 3*(3), 381–390.

Cope, E., & Cushion, C. (2020). A move towards reconceptualising direct instruction in sport coaching pedagogy. *Teacher Training and Professional Development. 10,* 70–73.

Cope, E., Partington, M., Cushion, C., & Harvey, S. (2016). An investigation of professional top-level youth football coaches' questioning practice. *Qualitative Research in Sport, Exercise and Health, 8*(4), 380–393.

Crowe, M., & Stanford, P. (2010). Questioning for quality. *Delta Kappa Gamma Bulletin, 76* (4), 36–44.

Cushion, C. J. (2013). Applying game centered approaches in coaching: A critical analysis of the 'dilemmas of practice' impacting change. *Sports Coaching Review, 2*(1), 61–76.

Cushion, C., & Jones, R. L. (2006). Power, discourse, and symbolic violence in professional youth soccer: The case of Albion Football Club. *Sociology of Sport Journal, 23*(2), 142–161.

Cushion, C. J., & Jones, R. L. (2014). A Bourdieusian analysis of cultural reproduction: Socialisation and the 'hidden curriculum' in professional football. *Sport, Education and Society, 19*(3), 276–298.

Cushion, C. J., & Nelson, L. (2012). Coach education and learning: Developing the field. In P. Potrac, W. Gilbert, & J. Denison (Eds.), *The Routledge Handbook of Sports Coaching* (pp. 359–374) London: Routledge.

Cushion, C., & Partington, M. (2014). A critical analysis of the conceptualisation of 'coaching philosophy'. *Sport, Education and Society.* doi: 645 10.1080/13573322.2014.958817

Cushion, C. J., Armour, K. M. & Jones, R. L. (2003). Coach education and continuing professional development: Experience and learning to coach. *Quest, 55*(3), 215–230.

Cushion, C., Harvey, S., Muir, B., & Nelson, L. (2012). Developing the coach analysis and intervention system (CAIS): Establishing validity and reliability of a computerised systematic observation instrument. *Journal of Sports Sciences, 30*(2), 201–216.

Daniel, M.-F., & Bergman-Drewe, S. (1998). Higher-order thinking, philosophy, and teacher education in physical education. *Quest, 50*(1), 33–58.

Davis, B., Sumara, J., & Luce-Kapler (2000). *Engaging Minds: Learning in a Complex World.* Hillsdale, NJ: Lawrence Erlbaum Publishers.

Dempsey, N. M., Richardson, D. J., Cope, E., & Cronin, C. J. (2020). Creating and disseminating coach education policy: A case of formal coach education in grassroots football. *Sport, Education and Society*, 1–14.

Harvey, S., & Light, R. L. (2015). Questioning for learning in game-based approaches to teaching and coaching. *Asia Pacific Journal of Health, Sport and Physical Education*, 6(2), 1–36.

Harvey, S., Cushion, C. J., & Massa-Gonzalez, A.-N. (2010). Learning a new method: Teaching games for understanding in the coaches' eyes. *Physical Education and Sport Pedagogy*, 15(4), 361–382.

Harvey, S., Cushion, C., Cope, E., & Muir, B. (2013). A season long investigation into coaching behaviours as a function of practice state: The case of three collegiate coaches. *Sports Coaching Review*, 2, 13–32.

Isabel, M., Antonio, S., Antonio, R., Rosado, F., & Michel, M. M. (2008). A systematic observation of youth amateur volleyball coaches behavior. *International Journal of Applied Sports Science*, 10(2), 37–59.

Kidman, L. (2005). *Athlete-centred Coaching: Developing Inspired and Inspiring People*. Christchurch, NZ: IPC Print Resources.

Kissock, C., & Iyortsuun, P. (1982). *A Guide to Questioning*. London: Macmillan Press.

Leamnson, R. (1999). *Thinking about Teaching and Learning: Developing Habits of Learning with First Year College and University Students*. Sterling, VA: Stylus.

Light, R. (2008). Complex learning theory in physical education: An examination of its epistemology and assumptions about how we learn. *Journal of Teaching in Physical Education*, 27(1), 21–37.

Light, R. L., & Evans, J. R. (2010). The impact of game sense pedagogy on Australian rugby coaches' practice: A question of pedagogy. *Physical Education and Sport Pedagogy*, 15(2), 103–115.

McNeill, M. C., Fry, J. M., Wright, S. C., Tan, C. W. K., & Rossi, T. (2008). Structuring time and questioning to achieve tactical awareness in games lessons. *Physical Education and Sport Pedagogy*, 13, 231–249.

Nelson, L., Potrac, P. A., Cushion, C., & Groom, R. (2014). Carl Rogers, learning and educational practice: Critical considerations and applications in sports coaching. *Sport, Education and Society*, 19(5), 513.

Partington, M., & Campbell, J. (2020). A guide to understanding coaching philosophy: Moving to a philosophy of coaching. In E. Cope, & M. Partington. *Sports Coaching: A Theoretical and Practical Guide*. London: Routledge.

Partington, M., & Cushion, C. (2013). An investigation of the practice activities and coaching behaviors of professional top-level youth soccer coaches. *Scandinavian Journal of Medicine & Science in Sports*, 23(3), 374–382.

Partington, M., & Walton, J. (2020). A guide to analysing coaching behaviours. In E. Cope & M. Partington. *Sports Coaching: A Theoretical and Practical Guide* (pp. 18–29). London: Routledge.

Partington, M., Cushion, C., Cope, E. & Harvey, S. (2015) The impact of video feedback on professional youth football coaches' reflection and practice behaviour: A longitudinal investigation of behaviour change. *Reflective Practice*, 16(5), 700–716.

Pearson, P., & Webb, P. (2006). Improving the quality of games teaching to promote physical activity. *Journal of Science Medicine and Sport*, 9(6), 9–18.

Potrac, P., Jones, R., & Armour, K. (2002). "It's all about getting respect": The coaching behaviours of a top-level English football coach. *Sport, Education and Society*, 7(2), 183–202.

Potrac, P., Jones, R., & Cushion, C. (2007). Understanding power and the coach's role in professional English soccer: A preliminary investigation of coach behaviour. *Soccer and Society, 8*(1), 33–49.

Smith, M., & Cushion, C. J. (2006). An investigation of the in-game behaviours of professional, top-level youth soccer coaches. *Journal of Sports Sciences, 24*(4), 355–366.

Strean, W. B., Senecal, K. L., Howlett, S. G., & Burgess, J. M. (1997). Xs and Os and what the coach knows: Improving team strategy through critical thinking. *Sport Psychologist, 11*(3), 243–256.

Tincani, M. & Crozier, S. (2007). Comparing brief and extended wait-time during small group instruction for children with challenging behavior. *Journal of Behavioral Education, 16*(4), 355–367.

Townsend, R. C., & Cushion, C. (2015). Elite cricket coach education: A Bourdieusian analysis. *Sport, Education and Society, 22*(4), 528–546.

Wiersema, J. A., & Licklider, B. L. (2009). Intentional mental processing: Student thinking as a habit of mind. *Journal of Ethnographic and Qualitative Research, 3*(2), 117–127.

Wright, J., & Forrest, G. (2007). A social semiotic analysis of knowledge construction and games centred approaches to teaching. *Physical Education and Sport Pedagogy, 12*(3), 273–287.

Yang, M. (2006). A critical review of research on questioning in education: limitations of its positivistic basis. *Asia Pacific Education Review, 7*(2), 195–204.

15 The Evolving Role of the Sport Psychologist and the Myth that their Sole Role is to 'Fix' Athletes

Laura Swettenham, Kristin McGinty-Minister, and Stewart Bicker

Introduction

It is no myth that sport psychology is an 'up-and-coming' addition to the arsenal used by coaches and athletes. Despite its seemingly new appearance, sport psychology has been recognized as an occupation for nearly a century and arguably can be traced back to ancient Greece! While it is not a 'new' discipline in the eyes of the authors, there is still a great deal of suspicion which follows sport psychology (and psychology in general). With this in mind, this chapter hopes to provide the reader with insight into the various roles of sport psychologists by explaining the traditional role of the sport psychologist along with the more recently evolving role whereby the sport psychologist assumes a holistic and organizational approach. Within this chapter, we will unpick the issues related to traditional sport psychology and offer critique about the holistic role of psychology which includes areas, such as mental health, culture, and creating psychologically informed environments. These topics will be brought to life with first-hand examples from the authors. Furthermore, we present practical ideas on how coaches and psychologists can work alongside one another in elite or youth environments to enhance athlete performance and well-being.

The myth

The authors, each of whom work as applied sport psychologists (in training), have often experienced pressure to find 'quick fixes' for performance issues, such as 'sorting out' a player's head which has 'fallen off' in training. While mini-interventions have the potential to provide immediate impact, they often only yield a short-lived alleviation of issues which are rooted deeper than the presenting problem(s). Addressing these presenting issues is crucial, however, more profound work is often required to create sustainable change.

We introduce the prevailing myth: 'The sport psychologist's sole role is to reactively "fix" individual athletes'. In other words, the sport psychologist's role is to reduce or remove issues with individual athletes as they arise. Though we agree that this traditional role of the sport psychologist is vital, recent developments support the notion that a sport psychologist's role should encompass much more. In our experience, one critical role of the sport psychologist is to proactively develop mental health literacy (MHL), culture, the performance system, and the individuals within while also having the ability to react to any problems which arise. Not all sport psychologists will work in this way (and this is OK!), and if they do, they may approach their work in different ways based on their philosophy of practice.

Working *proactively* within a performance system can reduce the reactive, fire fighting role that is often necessary for the sport psychologist and distracts sport psychologists from working in ways which can be valuable to coaches, and more broadly, the performance system. Through working proactively, we can prevent or reduce problems from arising as well as build upon strengths in performance and well-being. The myth that psychologists function only in a reactive role has evolved over time and for valid reasons. For example, determining the source of a 'problem' can be daunting, and failing to address present-moment issues can be dangerous. We will discuss why the myth that sport psychologists provide a reactive or 'quick fix' to problems does have immense value, highlight why as a whole this myth can be false and even damaging, and present practical implications for coaches along the way.

Reactive psychology

We outline in this section why sport psychology and the use of reactive interventions play an important role in performance environments. While this chapter aims to provide insight into the valuable holistic role a sport psychologist can play within a team or organization, it is essential to acknowledge that sport psychologists have traditionally been hired to exclusively promote performance, and many currently work very productively in this role. Like many high-level performance environments, there is an expectation for success, which is ultimately a process of positive change and self-development; the sport psychologist can provide a catalyst for more consistent sporting performance with higher levels of performance satisfaction (Aoyagi et al., 2012).

Throughout the twentieth century, sport psychology was used to increase athletes' ability to perform at a consistent and optimum level. Commonly used practices such as mental-skills training typically provided athletes with the ability to self-regulate and perform at their highest levels despite experiencing anxiety (Vealey, 2001), which can be particularly crucial immediately before important competitions (Kingston et al., 2010). Sport is unpredictable and strenuous, characterized by intense physical activity and psychological strain (Fletcher et al., 2012b). Be it training or competition, athletes are required to perform at their best day in day out. 'Reactive' psychology within sport may be utilized where the sport psychologist can attempt to buffer athletes' presenting stress or lend an understanding ear at critical times. Athletes and coaches may find themselves in situations where immediate intervention is necessary, whereby sport psychologists 'step in' and use their expertise to aid and assist. These interventions can be short due to limited time and resources. Examples from Olympic research (Birrer, 2012) include sport psychologists providing 'crisis management', and McCann's (2008) reflections offer an argument for remaining reflexive for a range of potential issues which may arise, such as performance pressures, distractions, interpersonal conflict, and clinical mental ill-health. During training, the sport psychologist may find meaningful moments of conversation with an athlete or coach that aim to provide immediate reflection or awareness. Giges and Peptipas (2000) provide case examples of 'teachable moments' (Petitpas et al., 1999), which are achieved through brief interventions rooted in the 'here and now' and the 'what' of behaviour, as opposed to the 'why,' and provide rationale for the time- and potentially resource-limited sport psychologist working in the field. Depending on the agreed role (more on this later), sport psychologists 'ringside' or 'pitchside' may find vital moments to gather information and explore an athlete's current mind-set, understand the rationale behind behaviours or decisions, determine the purpose of a particular drill that a coach has given the team, or ask reflective questions to develop self-awareness. Athletes, for the most part, want to perform at their optimum, 'unlock' their potential, make marginal gains in their training, and extract that extra 1% of their abilities. This has often been why sport psychologists are hired. If an athlete, coach, or parent perceives that the athlete needs assistance in achieving sporting success, we might assume that something needs to change, adapt, or improve (such as mental states including motivation, coping with emotions, and dealing with anxiety). These potentially performance-debilitating phenomena, coupled with the expectation for high performance from athletes, understandably result in the search for a 'quick fix' to allow the athlete to get back to scoring goals, making landings, shooting straight, and breaking personal bests.

Given the prevalence of consistent individual and organizational stressors typical of sport performance at all levels, athletes will no doubt encounter moments of extreme stress, requiring the sport psychologist to step in and signpost to relevant services if deemed necessary. For teams in a privileged position, this might involve an internal referral to the clinical psychologist. The consistent expectation to perform under pressure in elite sport has been a significant contributor to many issues with mental ill-health (Schinke et al., 2018) including mental ill-health symptomatology, clinical mental ill-health, suicide attempts, and sadly, successes (Reardon et al., 2019). As a result, mental health in sport has seen a dramatic shift in prioritization with the help of many household names coming forward to share their stories; for example, Michael Phelps has spoken out about his depression, and in a recent BBC feature, Freddie Flintoff detailed his experience living with bulimia for decades. Support staff, coaches, and stakeholders are engaging in Mental Health First Aid to equip themselves with the tools to better handle crisis moments. It seems more important than ever to ensure sport psychologists are on standby to provide support for athletes at all levels of sport – however, 'standing by' is not enough to stem these prevalent mental ill-health issues, which impact at the very least performance, and at most, peoples' lives.

Where the problem lies

Any 'fixing' which must be done at an individual or environmental level is a long-term process. Despite this, sport psychologists are often expected to deliver a few team workshops about mental toughness with the hope that athletes' mind-sets will be 'fixed' as if a magician arrived and rewired brains riddled with lifetimes of individual experiences and beliefs. Unfortunately, we do not have magic wands, and this change can require long-term work within the environment, rather than merely the athletes themselves, to create sustainable change. If a sporting environment is focused on quick fixes, and this is the sole role of the sport psychologist, the performance environment (and the individuals within) will miss the opportunity to grow and flourish.

Researchers have urged sport psychology practitioners to move away from a reactive or quick-fix philosophy and instead engage with approaches which will support athletes throughout their careers and beyond (Nesti, 2004). We will outline examples in line with the philosophies of the authors, indicating why a reactive approach to performance 'issues' is potentially less effective, and how cultivating mental health and psychologically informed environments through a holistic approach to benefit the long-term development of the athlete and performance system can be more impactful.

Proactive psychology

Mental health literacy and flourishing

In this chapter, we understand mental health as 'a state of well-being in which every individual realizes his or her own potential, can cope with the normal stresses of life, can work productively and fruitfully, and is able to make a contribution to her or his community' (WHO, 2003, p. 7). We are beginning to understand the importance of Mental Health Literacy (MHL) or individuals' skills, attitudes, and knowledge which lead to positive mental health behaviours (Gorczynski et al., 2020), in regards to athletes' and stakeholders' mental health and performance. Improved club-wide MHL can prevent and treat mental ill-health symptoms and disorders (Gorczynski et al., 2020), as well as promote positive mental health, also known as flourishing (McGinty-Minister et al., under review).

As most coaches are aware, repairing what is 'wrong' with an individual is insufficient to produce a versatile and capable athlete – it is crucial to identify and build upon their strengths. The model most suited to WHO's definition of mental health includes a distinct continuum of positive mental health, or flourishing, in which the absence of mental ill-health does not equate to mental health (Keyes, 2002). An individual not experiencing mental ill-health while also experiencing high levels of well-being is described as flourishing, and anything less than flourishing indicates impairment (Keyes et al., 2010). You might apply this logic to coaching: if there is nothing *wrong* with an athlete, does this mean they are the most impressive athlete on the pitch? An integral part of a sport psychologist's job should be to implement MHL interventions (often alongside sport psychiatrists or clinical psychologists) which proactively prevent mental ill-health and support those in the performance environment to flourish.

Furthermore, assuming the sport psychologist is in the building to 'fix problems' feeds directly into the deficit model of psychology, which focuses on psychopathy and dysfunction rather than mental health. There is much more to psychology than fixing deficiencies in order to 'break-even'. Human beings are capable of much more than that, and relying on any deficit model of health, whether it be physical or mental, in sport contradicts the levels of achievement we see daily. Furthermore, while the deficit model of psychology contributes to discouraging athletes from engaging with psychologists due to the stigma surrounding something being 'wrong' with the person who interacts with the psychologist, a flourishing model does the opposite: a sport psychologist who is there to help athletes develop as a person and an athlete is much more approachable. Athletes and key stakeholders are more likely to engage with sport psychology when situated in a mental health literate culture which imbues the knowledge that the sport psychologist intends to improve those around them *as well as* for reactive support.

The concept of flourishing fits the purpose of sport (development, advancement, performance), can reduce the stigma surrounding engaging with sport psychology, and is a protective factor which can have a positive impact on resilience. It works to build upon important facets of a person's well-being rather than 'fixing' problems and has the potential to prevent problems from arising to begin with. We ask that you embrace your sport psychologist, encourage a mental health literate environment, and encourage others to do the same. As arguably one of the most influential stakeholders, if you are flourishing and encouraging others to do the same, others are likely to follow suit. Look after your own mental health, promote the mental health of those around you, and embrace a mental health literate culture which leans into flourishing rather than views mental health and psychology through a suspicious lens. This step will take you closer to a flourishing self and team, which can only have a positive impact on performance – with the added benefit of improved well-being and enjoyment in life!

Cultivating culture through a psychologically informed environment

An integral component of MHL is cultural competency (Gorczynski et al., 2020). Each club or team has its own unique culture, which has evolved over years of influence from countless factors inside and outside of the club. This culture impacts each individual, including coaches and staff members, and their characteristics and past experiences will affect their interactions with different elements of the culture (Henriksen et al., 2010). MHL interventions include an integral focus on culture, in which psychologists focus on factors which may influence flourishing or mental ill-health. Addressing a club's culture can have important outcomes, including reduced stigma surrounding help-seeking behaviours in their athletes (Champ et al., 2018).

For example, one author was recently hired to support athletes within an elite football academy; the brief was to address the symptoms of mental ill-health which 'popped up' throughout the season, particularly with players who were injured. It took only a few days to recognize the stigma against mental ill-health in a culture which demonized raising an 'issue', despite the fact that many boys came from difficult backgrounds rife with 'issues'. It took several weeks to learn how this impacted the players, particularly the injured athletes with a higher incidence of mental ill-health symptomatology. In keeping with the club's cultural fear of problems, injured players were tucked away in back rooms with little interaction with teammates or coaches. These athletes were shunned until they were ready to produce on the pitch again. They did not *choose* to stay hidden, they were actively rejected, a reminder of the potential consequences of the sport. This isolation resulted in many incidences of depression and anxiety symptomatology which could have been preventable and had the potential to impact their recovery and return to play. The psychologist resolved to focus on a club-wide MHL intervention (proactive) with an acute focus on those individuals working alongside injured athletes as well as the athletes themselves (proactive and reactive). This allowed her to focus on the problems which had already arisen with the goal of preventing further mental ill-health and potentially improving injury outcomes. After three months, the immensely improved MHL of those closest to injured athletes (who wholeheartedly committed to the intervention), as well as the interventions with the athletes themselves, were reported to have a positive impact on those injured athletes. Mental health and mental ill-health improved as did their confidence, and those injured athletes who spent the majority of their time with physiotherapists and other injured athletes (who had a more intensive MHL intervention), were reportedly less phased out by the rejection from their peers than when the intervention had begun. In a culture which does not support mental health, had the sport psychologist begun with merely 'fixing' problem athletes with anxiety or depression symptomatology, it is unlikely the effects of any intervention would have made such an impact.

While it is impossible to develop a culture which is appropriate for every individual, it is crucial to cultivate culture with intention; this will likely attract the athletes and staff which fit into a club's specific culture, in turn meeting its needs. This is a tactic commonly utilized in the USA's National Football League, most famously the New England Patriots. Facilitating mental toughness, a sought-after predictor of performance, is often focused on the individual; despite this, a significant factor in influencing the mental toughness of athletes is the environment, culture, and context in which they train, compete, and live (Eubank et al., 2017). Establishing consistent messaging with aspects, such as values and expectations throughout a club results in less confusion, improved confidence in what is expected of the individual, and can have positive psychological and behavioural effects on both athletes and staff (Fletcher et al., 2012a).

While intentionally developing a club's culture may seem like an impossible job, it is important to note that a crucial function of a sport psychologist is to establish and maintain high-performance cultures (Henriksen, 2015). Sport psychologists work alongside coaches and relevant staff to build a mental health literate environment and culture which aims to be conducive to performance as well as protect against mental ill-health and promote flourishing, and we are often very excited for this task! One fundamental way we accomplish this is through implementing a psychologically informed environment. It is difficult to define a psychologically informed environment, as they are complex with many interacting parts. It is important to note that, while they are related, psychologically informed environments are distinct from mental health literate cultures: while MHL is concerned with mental health and mental ill-health, psychologically informed environments utilize a holistic focus to inform the performance environment on important psychological tools which might improve performance and well-being. For example, a psychologically informed environment is one tool we might employ as we strive for MHL. One way in which they have been defined within sport is highlighted by this adapted quote from Jackson (2020):

A psychologically informed environment is a (1) complex concept, that benefits from a (2) person-centred approach, that is underpinned with a (3) wellbeing focus, which not only covers performers but encompasses (4) support staff as well. It requires an on-going, (5) proactive and (6) evaluative feedback loop, which requires time and investment but is worth it when helping to give performers and support staff (7) meaning and purpose, as well as a sense of (8) growth and development.

Developing a psychologically informed environment for youth athletes

One context in which a psychologically informed environment is paramount is within youth sport. If you work within youth sport, you may be familiar with statements such as 'she hasn't got what it takes', 'he has an attitude problem', 'they don't appreciate the opportunity they have'. These thought processes often prompt coaches to ask the sport psychologist to 'fix it'; however, rather than 'fixing' the adolescent brain, we must examine how we can cultivate the environment to support athletes' development. Take a moment to reflect upon your own adolescent characteristics. At the age of 14, what stories do you remember? Perhaps you were reckless at times, self-conscious, or went against the rules to look cool in front of your friends. This is the nature of the adolescent brain, which is at a different stage of development compared to an adult.

We must accept that youth athletes are not the finished product and work with the adolescent brain, rather than thwarting its biological nature, to support the adolescent along their developmental journey and prepare them for elite sport or life after sport. One author experienced a challenge when entering a youth performance environment for the first time as a trainee sport psychologist. This challenge was that 80% of her work was reactive, one-to-one sessions with youth athletes, which had no influence upon the performance system. Though this had an impact for some athletes, a very small percentage of the system benefited from the support. Work was often done independently from the performance staff, which impacted the longevity of improvements experienced by the athlete; this was not the most effective way to support individual athletes or improve club-wide performance and well-being. Due to the nature of the adolescent brain, it is imperative the environment (and culture) supports work conducted at an individual level. In this author's experience, most of an athlete's time is spent with coaches, physiotherapists, and strength and conditioning coaches – not the sport psychologist! Therefore, the sport psychologist in question proceeded to develop an intervention in which the performance environment evolved to be more system-focused, with a multidisciplinary team (MDT) which understood specifically how to support the adolescent brain; empowering the MDT to breathe psychology into the system day-to-day.

In creating a psychologically informed environment, psychology can live past the work of the psychologist by existing within the MDT. While this is a long-term process which requires stakeholder buy-in, working proactively to establish an environmental source of performance, well-being, and organizational support can reduce the reactive work required by coaches, psychologists, and other performance staff.

Role clarity and approach

As a profession, sport psychologists can occupy multiple psychological approaches to their practice as well as differing philosophical underpinnings (Keegan, 2015). To cover merely the philosophical models predominantly used by sport psychologists would perhaps require multiple chapters or a book in itself; however, it is an important factor to consider when working with or hiring a sport psychologist. We believe the first conversation with an incoming sport psychology consultant should consider their approach to practice. This is important to ensure congruence between the work carried out by the sport psychologist and the underlying values and philosophy of the practitioner (Lindsay, 2007; McDougal et al., 2015) As an example, one might sit down with a sport psychologist who predominantly focuses on performance – their chief goal as a practitioner is to utilize psychological interventions to enhance sporting performance. On the other hand, a different sport psychologist might employ a holistic approach, working towards developing the athlete both in *and* out of sport. And others may lean towards one end of the scale, with a scattering of mental health workshops throughout the year, for example. It is important, therefore, to understand the approach that your potential sport psychologist might take and reflect upon how their approach might bring you closer to your needs and goals as a coach.

A large body of research has examined the pivotal position role clarity has on athlete satisfaction (Eys et al., 2003), performance (Bray & Brawley, 2002), self-efficacy (Eys & Carron, 2001), and judgement of coaches' competency (Bosselut et al., 2012). Role clarity is a result of understanding one's own formal and informal expected behaviours within a group (Katz & Khan, 1978). Lack of clear expectations set from either party at the beginning of the consultancy process can result in confusion or misinformed expectations from either the coach or sport psychologist. We stress that this is the responsibility of *both* the sport psychologist and coach to outline the responsibilities and expectations of the work required, and therefore the role of the sport psychologist. There is always the potential for review throughout the consultancy process or on an annual/seasonal basis to address concerns or modifying expectations or roles which can be agreed upon collectively between each party. Beginning your work on the same page and understanding the *proactive,* and at times *reac-*

tive, nature of the sport psychologist's work serves to develop psychologically informed environments (Cotterill, 2018). It may also provide the opportunity to educate the sport psychologist about other stakeholders' roles, reducing an unnecessary waste of resources amongst staff which can direct the team towards a collective vision and goal (Fletcher, 2011). It should be noted that not all coaches will be involved in the recruitment process of securing a sport psychologist within their team and/or support staff: recruitment has predominantly been the responsibility of the head of sport science or health. While we do not expect this to change in the future, we do recommend that coaches are involved in the recruitment process, as they have the potential to play an essential role in determining whether the sport psychologist is a good 'fit', as the manager or coach(es) or are likely to understand the culture and values of the team and be at the forefront of influencing these factors. Coaches entering a new club or environment with a sport psychologist already embedded within the support staff are in luck! Sport psychologists can be massive resources (and allies) who can aid in newly recruited coaches' understanding of the team or organization, their culture, and how a coach can best approach developing players and athletes with minimal 'teething' issues. Finally, if one is 'in the market' for a sport psychologist, it may be useful to reflect upon your own expectations and needs for you, your team, athlete(s), and/or organization. These can include: (a) Why am I hiring a sport psychologist? (b) Who will the sport psychologist support, and why? (c) What am I trying to achieve in hiring a sport psychologist?

Summary

To summarize, we argue that the assumption 'The sport psychologist's sole role is to reactively fix individual athletes' is, for the most part, not true. Though reactive work with individual athletes is an integral aspect of the role of a sport psychologist, we believe it should not be relied on as their sole role. To work effectively within a performance environment, we must work proactively, supporting the growth of a mental health literate, positive performance culture for athletes and staff alike to thrive and flourish. Finally, coaches can enhance their own, and others', opportunities to flourish by promoting holistic development, as well as viewing sport psychology through a lens of curiosity and opportunity. Finally, we stress the importance of understanding the role of the sport psychologist and how values and philosophy of practice can impact service delivery. Of course, this does not outweigh the importance of the sport psychologist understanding the role of the coach, their philosophy, and the power of working collaboratively.

References

Aoyagi, M. W., Portenga, S. T., Poczwardowski, A., Cohen, A. B., & Statler, T. (2012). Reflections and directions: The profession of sport psychology past, present, and future. *Professional Psychology: Research and Practice, 43*(1), 32. https://doi.org/10.1037/a0025676

Birrer, D., Wetzel, J., Schmid, J., & Morgan, G. (2012). Analysis of sport psychology consultancy at three Olympic Games: Facts and figures. *Psychology of Sport and Exercise, 13*(5), 702–710. https://doi.org/10.1016/j.psychsport.2012.04.008

Bosselut, G., Heuzé, J. P., Eys, M. A., Fontayne, P., & Sarrazin, P. (2012). Athletes' perceptions of role ambiguity and coaching competency in sport teams: A multilevel analysis. *Journal of Sport and Exercise Psychology, 34*(3), 345–364. https://doi.org/10.1123/jsep.34.3.345

Bray, S. R., & Brawley, L. R. (2002). Role efficacy, role clarity, and role performance effectiveness. *Small Group Research, 33*(2), 233–253. https://doi.org/10.1177/104649640203300204

Champ, F. M., Nesti, M. S., Ronkainen N. J., Tod, D. A., & Littlewood, M. A. (2018) An exploration of the experiences of elite youth footballers: The impact of organizational culture. *Journal of Applied Sport Psychology, 32*(2), 146–167, https://doi.org/10.1080/10413200.2018.1514429

Cotterill, S. (2018). Working as a sport psychology practitioner in professional cricket: Challenges, experiences, and opportunities. *The Sport Psychologist, 32*(2), 146–155. https://doi.org/10.1123/tsp.2017-0010

Eubank, M., Nesti, M., & Littlewood, M. (2017). A culturally informed approach to mental toughness development in high performance sport. *International Journal of Sport Psychology, 48*(3), 206–222. https://doi.org/10.7352/IJSP.2017.48.206

Eys, M. A., & Carron, A. V. (2001). Role ambiguity, task cohesion, and task self-efficacy. *Small Group Research, 32*(3), 356–373. https://doi.org/10.1177/104649640103200305

Eys, M. A., Carron, A. V., Bray, S. R., & Beauchamp, M. R. (2005). The relationship between role ambiguity and intention to return the following season. *Journal of Applied Sport Psychology, 17*(3), 255–261. https://doi.org/10.1080/10413200591010148

Fletcher, D., & Arnold, R. (2011). A qualitative study of performance leadership and management in elite sport. *Journal of Applied Sport Psychology, 23*(2), 223–242. https://doi.org/10.1080/10413200.2011.559184

Fletcher, D., Hanton, S., Mellalieu, S. D., & Neil, R. (2012a). A conceptual framework of organizational stressors in sport performers. *Scandinavian Journal of Medicine & Science in Sports, 22*(4), 545–557. https://doi.org/10.1111/j.1600-0838.2010.01242.x

Fletcher, D., Hanton, S., & Wagstaff, C. R. D. (2012b) Performers' responses to stressors encountered in sport organisations. *Journal of Sports Sciences, 30*(4), 349–358. https://doi.org/10.1080/02640414.2011.633545

Giges, B., & Petitpas, A. (2000). Brief contact interventions in sport psychology. *The Sport Psychologist, 14*(2), 176–187. https://doi.org/10.1123/tsp.14.2.176

Gorczynski, P., Currie, A., Gibson, K., Gouttebarge, V., Hainline, B., Castaldelli-Maia, J. M., Mountjoy, M., Purcell, R., Reardon, C. L., Rice, S., & Swartz, L. (2020). Developing mental health literacy and cultural competence in elite sport. *Journal of Applied Sport Psychology, 1*–15. https://doi.org/10.1080/10413200.2020.1720045

Henriksen, K. (2015). Developing a high-performance culture: A sport psychology intervention from an ecological perspective in elite orienteering. *Journal of Sport Psychology in Action, 6*(3), 141–153, https://doi.org/10.1080/21520704.2015.1084961

Henriksen, K., Stambulova, N., & Roessler, K. K. (2010). Holistic approach to athletic talent development environments: A successful sailing milieu. *Psychology of Sport and Exercise, 11*, 212–222. https://doi.org/10.1016/j.psychsport.2009.10.005.

Jackson, P. (2020). The psychologically informed environment (P.I.E). Retrieved from https://medium.com/@petejackson/the-psychologically-informed-environment-p-i-e-59e3b7814c35

Katz, D., & Kahn, R. L. (1978). *The Social Psychology of Organizations.* New York: Wiley.

Keegan, R. (2015). *Being a Sport Psychologist.* New York: Macmillan International Higher Education.

Keyes, C. L. M. (2002). The mental health continuum: From languishing to flourishing in life. *Journal of Health and Social Behaviour, 43*, 207–222. https://doi.org/10.2307/3090197

Keyes, C. L. M., Dhingra, S. S., & Simoes, E. J. (2010). Change in level of positive mental health as a predictor of future risk of mental illness. *American Journal of Public Health, 100*, 2366–2371. https://doi.org/10.2105/AJPH.2010.192245

Kingston, K., Lane, A., & Thomas, O. (2010). A temporal examination of elite performers sources of sport-confidence. *The Sport Psychologist, 24*(3), 313–332. https://doi.org/10.1123/tsp.24.3.313

Li, C., Martindale, R., & Sun, Y. (2019). Relationships between talent development environments and mental toughness: The role of basic psychological need satisfaction. *Journal of Sports Sciences, 37*(18), 2057–2065. https://doi.org/10.1080/02640414.2019.1620979

Lindsay, P., Breckon, J. D., Thomas, O., & Maynard, I. W. (2007). In pursuit of congruence: A personal reflection on methods and philosophy in applied practice. *The Sport Psychologist, 21*(3), 335–352. https://doi.org/10.1123/tsp.21.3.335

McCann, S. (2008). At the Olympics, everything is a performance issue. *International Journal of Sport and Exercise Psychology, 6*(3), 267–276. https://doi.org/10.1080/1612197X.2008.9671871

McDougall, M., Nesti, M., & Richardson, D. (2015). The challenges of sport psychology delivery in elite and professional sport: Reflections from experienced sport psychologists. *The Sport Psychologist, 29*(3), 265–277. https://doi.org/10.1123/tsp.2014-0081

McGinty-Minister, K. L., Champ, F. M., Eubank, M. E., & Littlewood, M. A. (2021). Psychological flourishing and mental ill-health in english premier league football academies. Under Review.

Nesti, M. (2004). *Existential Psychology and Sport: Theory and Application.* London: Routledge.

Petitpas, A. J., Giges, B., & Danish, S. J. (1999). The sport psychologist-athlete relationship: Implications for training. *The Sport Psychologist, 13*(3), 344–357. https://doi.org/10.1123/tsp.13.3.344

Reardon, C. L., Hainline, B., Aron, C. M., Baron, D., Baum, A. L., Bindra, A., ... & Derevensky, J. L. (2019). Mental health in elite athletes: International Olympic Committee consensus statement (2019). *British Journal of Sports Medicine, 53*(11), 667–699. http://dx.doi.org/10.1136/bjsports-2019-100715

Schinke, R. J., Stambulova, N. B., Si, G., & Moore, Z. (2018). International society of sport psychology position stand: Athletes' mental health, performance, and development. *International Journal of Sport and Exercise Psychology, 16*(6), 622–639. https://doi.org/10.1080/1612197X.2017.1295557

Vealey, R. S. (2001). Understanding and enhancing self-confidence in athletes. *Handbook of Sport Psychology, 2*, 550–565.

World Health Organisation. (2003). *Investing in Mental Health.* Geneva: WHO.

16 Is Goal-Setting an Effective Way to Improve Athletic Performance?

Laura C. Healy and Desmond McEwan

Is goal-setting an effective way to improve athletic performance?

When it comes to enhancing sport performance or learning new skills, goal-setting is a widely used technique. Indeed, it has been shown that of all mental skills techniques, goal-setting is the most commonly used amongst coaches and their athletes (Burton & Weiss, 2008; Weinberg et al., 2000). As a result, coaches and athletes are increasingly aware of techniques such as setting S.M.A.R.T goals (i.e. Specific, Measurable, Assignable, Realistic, and Time-related; Doran, 1981) as a perceived way to improve their performance. However, despite this increasing familiarity with *how* to set goals, the question remains as to whether the techniques adopted by coaches and athletes are actually effective in bringing about changes to their desired outcomes, such as learning a new routine, gaining a personal best or winning a major championship. As such, within this chapter, we will explore the evidence in relation to goal-setting and sport performance. In doing so, we aim to determine (a) whether it is indeed a myth that goals enhance performance and (b) if the current ways in which coaches set goals with their athletes are appropriate or could be improved.

Origin of the myth

Athletes and coaches have been using goals to improve their performance for a number of years – consider Roger Bannister setting the goal to run a sub

4-minute mile during the 1950s. However, the first instances of applying theories of goal-setting to athletic performance came in the 1980s. Specifically, Locke and Latham (1985) suggested that Goal- Setting Theory (GST), which they had developed and tested within other performance contexts such as business and organizations, could apply to sport. Locke and Latham (1985) argued that goal-setting should work at least as, if not more, effectively in sport settings than in organizational contexts, as individual performance was easier to measure in sporting environments.

GST is based on four key tenets: (1) goal-setting directs attention and effort towards goal-related activities; (2) goals can energize an individual within a task, with more challenging goals resulting in higher effort; (3) goals can foster persistence on a task; and (4) goal-setting encourages the adoption of task-relevant strategies and knowledge, thus impacting action (Locke & Latham, 1990, 2002, 2019). Based on these tenets, and their research in organizational and laboratory settings, Locke and Latham (1985) proposed a series of hypotheses as to how goal-setting would be effective in sport contexts. In addition to the key tenets outlined in GST, these included recommendations for the types of goals to set (such as setting specific, difficult goals that were predicted to lead to better performance than 'do-your-best' or no goals) and that using a combination of short- and long-term goals would be better for performance. Furthermore, Locke and Latham (1985) proposed that feedback was vital for goal-setting, as it provides information about progress towards the goal. In addition, they suggested that commitment to the goal was important for difficult goals and could be facilitated by coaches asking an athlete to accept a goal, showing support for goal pursuit, using incentives and rewards, and by allowing athletes to participate in goal-setting, training, and selection procedures. For complex or long-term tasks, goal attainment can be facilitated by planning how to approach the goal. Finally, Locke and Latham (1985) proposed that sport competition can lead to enhanced performance, as it allows for the setting of higher, more difficult goals, and may increase the extent to which athletes are committed to their goals.

Locke and Latham's (1985) application of GST to sport and exercise settings provoked a large volume of research that examined the effects of goal-setting in such environments (Weinberg & Weigand, 1993). However, these early investigations revealed mixed results, with many papers finding null results of the impact of goal-setting on performance (e.g. Hall et al., 1987; Weinberg et al., 1990). Locke (1991) suggested that these findings were the result of methodological flaws, including failed manipulations of the 'do your best' goal conditions, participants not accepting assigned goals, specific goals not being sufficiently difficult, participants starting from different baseline positions, failing to measure or control for goal commitment, self-efficacy, or the effects of competition between participants on their goal pursuit. Weinberg and Weigand (1993) challenged some of these aspects, highlighting that the lack of support for the goal-setting-performance relationship within sport and exercise settings could not solely be attributed to such flaws in research design. Furthermore, they suggested that research needed to establish the kinds of goals that are most effective for different individuals in a range of tasks and under a variety of environmental conditions (e.g. training or competition).

In an attempt to provide clarity on the discrepancies between Locke and Latham's (1985) hypotheses and the research in sport and exercise contexts, Kyllo and Landers (1995) conducted a meta-analytical review of the sport and exercise-based goal-setting literature. They examined the evidence for three specific hypotheses: (1) difficult goals would result in larger performance gains than easy, 'do your best' or no goal comparison groups; (2) specific goals would result in greater performance gains than vague, general, 'do your best' or no goal comparisons; and (3) short-term goals used in combination with long-term goals would result in larger performance gains than when only long-term goals were employed. Their review included 36 studies with 136 separate effect sizes. While they found support that goal-setting was an effective technique for enhancing sport and exercise performance, there was limited support for their three hypotheses. Indeed, the only conclusive finding from the studies reviewed was that in sport and exercise contexts, moderately difficult goals yielded greater performance effects than difficult or easy goals. Kyllo and Landers suggested that this was due to a difficult goal having a low probability of success, whereas with an easy goal there is low incentive value of success.

Since this early work (i.e. Kyllo & Landers, 1995; Locke, 1991; Locke & Latham, 1985; Weinberg & Weigand, 1993), research in this area continued to burgeon. However, it remains unclear the extent to which goal-setting, along with some of the specifics of GST, can lead to performance benefits when used by coaches and their athletes. In particular, some of the nuances (i.e. the type of goal-setting practice that works for different athletes in different situations) that research have demonstrated to be important may not be fully reflected in applied goal-setting practice. As such, within the remainder of this chapter, we will review the evidence both in support of, and against, the use of goal-setting in an attempt to provide pragmatic yet evidence-based recommendations for how coaches and athletes can most effectively use goal-setting.

But goals work!

Goal-setting is widely used by athletes, suggesting that they perceive them to be useful in enhancing their performance (Weinberg et al., 2000). The popularity of goal-setting within applied sport psychology might be due to its perceived simplicity (e.g. merely specifying the improvements that the athlete needs to make) compared to other mental skills that require relatively more effort and skill (e.g. imagery, arousal regulation). Athletes may set different types of goals— we will illustrate the three common categories of goals using golf as an example. *Process goals* focus on improving technique or strategy such as when the golfer seeks to improve their swing technique. *Performance goals* focus on improving one's personal standards, such as when the golfer aims to decrease their handicap or average score per round. *Outcome goals* target specific results, such as reaching a certain world ranking or winning a major competition.

Despite some of the early work that demonstrated null effects of goal-setting (e.g. Hall et al., 1987; Weinberg et al., 1990), several studies over the last few decades across a range of athletic populations found that it can be a useful way to improve performance. For example, Giannini et al. (1988) demonstrated that individuals who set competitive goals (i.e. performance compared to others) showed greater basketball performance relative to those who were instructed to simply do their best on the task. Later, Kingston and Hardy (1997) found that golfers who set process goals or performance goals showed greater improvements in performance over the course of the year-long intervention compared to golfers who did not engage in goal-setting. In complement to that quantitative work, Vidic and Burton (2010) interviewed collegiate tennis players following an eight-week goal-setting intervention—the athletes suggested that goal-setting was helpful in facilitating their performance. More recent work by Neumann and Hohnke (2018) with elite basketball players demonstrated that those who were given a specific performance goal (namely, to improve their shooting percentages at a baseline session by 15%) performed better at a follow-up session compared to participants in a 'do-your-best' condition.

Significant effects on variables beyond individual performance have also been observed within this area of research. For example, McCarthy et al. (2010) showed improved positive affect amongst multisport athletes who took part in a season-long intervention focused on self-set, specific, and difficult (but realistic) performance goals. In addition, qualitative feedback from athletes suggests that goal-setting also fosters athlete motivation and confidence (Vidic & Burton, 2010). From a group perspective, team goal-setting interventions have also been found to improve athletes' engagement with their team (Palao et al., 2016), perceptions of cohesion (Senécal et al., 2008), and teamwork (McEwan & Beauchamp, 2020). In summary, on its face, it would seem that goal-setting can benefit a range of positive individual- and group-level outcomes, and thus coaches should be encouraged to incorporate goal-setting into their coaching strategies (whether with individual athletes or a team as a whole).

So, what is the problem?

Although there is evidence in support of goal-setting being an effective performance-enhancement technique within sport and exercise settings (Kyllo & Landers, 1995), it could be argued that this research presents a simplistic overview of how athletes and coaches might approach the goal-setting process. Early research in the area (e.g. Hall et al., 1987; Kyllo & Landers, 1995; Locke, 1991; Weinberg & Weigand, 1993; Weinberg et al., 1990) has shown equivocal findings. Furthermore, there is a lack of contemporary studies investigating the four key tenets of GST within sport settings. Thus, it may be that other theoretical perspectives should be considered to ensure that applied guidelines for coaches and athletes result in the most effective goal-setting practices. For instance, it has been noted within applied research that goal-setting practice may be ineffective if coaches rely on simplistic goal-setting processes that fail to acknowledge the wider social and motivational choices of athletes, such as the reasons why they choose to pursue certain goals (Maitland & Gervis, 2010). Furthermore, athletes may struggle to commit to the goal-setting process or follow principles such as setting specific goals, with coaches not always able to support them in such practices (Gillham & Weiler, 2013). In other words, simply relying on the notion that goal-setting is effective and only using the principles of GST or S.M.A.R.T goals may not be the most beneficial goal-setting approach for coaches and their athletes.

Research that fails to support GST

While some studies have provided support for GST, the findings from several studies do not align with these principles. For instance, Weinberg et al. (1994) examined the effect of a season-long goal-setting intervention with a university Lacrosse team. Twenty-four players from the squad were randomly allocated to either a goal-setting or a 'do-your-best' group. Performance in both groups was assessed by recording each game of the season, with an expert who was unaware of the goal-setting conditions reviewing the video and recorded statistics in relation to key offensive and defensive outcomes. When examining the differences between the goal-setting and the 'do-your-best' group, there were no significant differences in the targeted outcomes. The authors suggested that this was a result of the small sample size, which may have impacted the statistical findings. However, it is worthwhile to note that while the goal-setting group outperformed the 'do-your-best' group in several performance indicators at the end of the season, only five participants (21%) reached their individual goal. As such, it is difficult to claim that the factors implemented that aligned with GST, such as setting difficult, specific goals over the short- and long-term, lead to successful performance enhancement.

Other studies in sport and exercise contexts have also failed to support the recommendations of GST. For instance, Tenenbaum et al. (1999) found similar performance improvements in young female runners regardless of whether they were assigned to an easy, difficult/realistic or improbable/unattainable goal conditions. A goal-setting intervention with volleyball players showed no significant improvements for targets that had been selected by the players (Zetou et al., 2008). Furthermore, Pierce and Burton (1998) found that the benefits of goal-setting were moderated by the goal-setting styles of athletes, with some athletes experiencing performance improvements but others showing lower performance following a goal-setting intervention. These studies support Weinberg and Weigand's (1993) argument that goal-setting practices may need to be individualized to include aspects such as the preferences, abilities, and situations of individual athletes.

Recent research in physical activity contexts has also challenged key principles of GST. In particular, a meta-analysis showed that specific goals were no more effective than vague goals in increasing physical activity (McEwan et al., 2016). This may particularly be the case for those who are in the early stages of becoming physically active, for whom physical activity may be a complex task and who may find specific goals too challenging. Recent studies support this notion and have shown that open goals – where individuals are encouraged to 'see how well you can do' – can result in higher levels of goal attainment and more positive psychological experiences than S.M.A.R.T. goals when used with inactive individuals (Hawkins et al., 2020; Swann et al., 2020a). While this might not be relevant for coaches working with elite athletes, given the diverse nature of coaching, there may be scenarios where using open goals, rather than specific, challenging goals, result in greater achievements for some participants. Furthermore, it would be beneficial if the critical lens which has been applied to goal-setting in physical activity contexts (e.g. Swann et al., 2020b) could also be used to examine goal-setting practices of coaches and athletes in sport settings.

Athlete goal-setting preferences

An often-overlooked aspect within goal-setting is the preference of the athletes pursuing the goals. However, theoretical and empirical approaches demonstrate that this is an important factor to consider as it can influence how successful goal-setting is in enhancing performance. The Competitive Goal-Setting Model (CGS-3; Burton & Weiss, 2008) is one theoretical approach that suggests that athletes may have different preferences for the type of goals they set. An athlete's goal-setting style is likely to be determined by a combination of their disposition for judging their competence based either on their own improvement in performance or on how they perform in relation to important others (Dweck, 1999) and their perceptions of their own ability. Within this theory, three distinct goal-setting styles are proposed. For those athletes with a performance-oriented style, success is likely to be defined in relation to their own learning and improvement. Therefore, the goals they set are likely to be challenging with the aim being to increase their competence. Based on the theory, it is expected that athletes with this style would favour process goals, followed by performance goals, with outcome goals being their least preferred style. The other two goal-setting styles proposed within the CGS-3 model are success-oriented and failure-oriented goal-setting styles. Athletes with one of these styles define their success based on competitive outcomes (i.e. winning) or their performance in comparison to others. Thus, athletes with either of these styles are likely to prefer to set outcome goals, followed by performance and process goals.

Understanding the goal-setting style of athletes may be important for coaches, as it will affect not only the goals that they are likely to prefer but also the effectiveness of goal- setting programmes. Specifically, Burton and Weiss (2008) propose that while athletes with either a performance- or success-oriented style would experience performance improvements from goal-setting interventions, those with a failure-oriented style may experience decreased performance. As such, it may be important for coaches to consider if, based on their athletes' personal goal-setting style, whether goal-setting is the most appropriate mental skill to adopt with all of their athletes.

There is limited empirical evidence that has directly tested the predictions of the CGS-3 model. However, there is research which demonstrates that athletes may have preferences for different types of goals, with those who had high belief in a range of different types of goals (e.g. short-term, psychological, competitive goals) reporting higher career success, goal commitment and trait sport confidence, as well as setting goals more frequently (Burton et al., 2010). Further research has found broad support for the profiles proposed within the CGS-3 model and demonstrated that those with a performance-oriented goal-setting style reported more positive outcomes associated with goal-setting (Burton et al., 2013).

While more studies are needed to determine the role of athlete preferences within goal-setting, it seems important that coaches are aware that athletes may have different goal-setting styles. As such, it is plausible that goal-setting will not automatically be a useful technique for all athletes in all situations; at the very least, that the exact type and content of goals that should be set will vary from athlete to athlete and situation to situation. This appears to run counter to many applied recommendations (e.g. that goals should always be S.M.A.R.T.), and certainly is somewhat contradictory to Locke and Latham's (1985, 2019) proposals within GST.

Athlete motivation for goals

An additional aspect of goal-setting which has received little acknowledgement within applied recommendations for coaches and athletes is the role of the motives underpinning goal pursuit. While it has readily been accepted that setting goals can motivate individuals to pursue them, less acknowledgement has been given to the underlying reasons why individuals may be striving for such outcomes (Deci & Ryan, 2000). Addressing this, Sheldon and Elliot (1999) proposed the Self-Concordance Model (SCM), where they suggested that the motives underpinning goal pursuit could predict the effort with which an individual would pursue a goal, the likelihood they would attain the goal, and the impact of goal attainment on their psychological well-being. Grounded in Self-Determination Theory, or SDT (Deci & Ryan, 2000), it was proposed that the motives for goals can be broadly split into two distinct types. Autonomous goal motives relate to trying to achieve a goal for reasons of personal importance, perceived benefits, or the enjoyment goal pursuit provides. For example, an athlete might choose to work towards their goal of obtaining a personal best in an event, because they enjoy the challenge of performing their best. Controlled goal motives, on the other hand, are associated with striving for goals because of internal (e.g. to avoid feelings of guilt or anxiety) or external (e.g. extrinsic rewards such as winning; expectations of others such as coaches) pressures. The type of motives underpinning goal pursuit are largely independent of whether the goals are assigned by an important other (such as a coach), participatively set or self-set; in other words, an athlete may choose to accept a goal set by their coach as they understand the benefits associated with goal attainment thus pursue the goal with autonomous motives.

Within sport contexts, autonomous goal motives have consistently been associated with positive outcomes, such as goal attainment (Ntoumanis et al., 2014a; Smith et al., 2007), flexible goal pursuit (Healy et al., 2016; Ntoumanis et al., 2014b), and well-being (Healy et al., in press, 2014). Conversely, controlled motives have been largely found to be unrelated to goal attainment, negatively associated with well-being and positively associated with ill-being (Gaudreau & Braaten, 2016; Healy et al., 2014). Autonomous and controlled goal motives are not opposites of each other; recent research has demonstrated that athletes can pursue goals with different combinations of both autonomous and controlled motives (Healy et al., in press, 2016). This research found that while high levels of controlled goal motives may not be detrimental to goal management and well-being when accompanied by high levels of autonomous goal motives, the most beneficial combination is when autonomous motives are high and controlled motives are low.

This line of research demonstrates the importance that athletes are pursuing their goals with the most adaptive motives, in order to experience benefits not just for goal attainment but also their well-being. However, it also challenges the myth addressed within this chapter, as it could be argued that goals pursued with lower levels of autonomous, and higher levels of controlled motives, may not lead to benefits for athletic performance. In order words, goal-setting is less likely to be an effective way of improving performance in sport if they are not pursued with autonomous motives that have been shown to lead to successful goal attainment. Such considerations are not readily acknowledged with applied recommendations for coaches and athletes, potentially undermining the impact that goal-setting programmes may have within sport contexts.

Role of coaches

It will not come as a surprise to learn that coaches play a vital role in the success of goal setting programs. However, their role is considerably broader than just setting goals for their athletes (by either assigning goals or working collaboratively with athletes to develop their own goals). For instances, it is acknowledged within GST that feedback is a crucial part of the goal-setting process. Research has shown that when coaches struggle to find time to provide feedback to athletes on their goal progress, the effectiveness of goal-setting programmes is limited (Gillham & Weiler, 2013). The way that coaches provide feedback may also be important. For instance, applying findings of research conducted outside of the sport context suggests that the level of commitment an athlete has to their goal can impact whether it is more beneficial for coaches to highlight either the progress made towards goal attainment or the work still required to achieve the goal (Koo & Fishbach, 2008). Specifically, when individuals are less committed to their goals, highlighting how much progress they have already made can enhance adherence to the goal. Conversely, when goal commitment is high, emphasizing what is still required to achieve the goal increases adherence. While untested in sport, this may be an important consideration for coaches when using goals with their athletes.

As well as providing feedback and supporting athletes directly in their goal pursuits, coaches can also have an impact on the motives with which athletes pursue their goals. Specifically, several studies have demonstrated that when coaches use an interpersonal style that is more autonomy supportive – offering athletes choices, providing rationale for activities, acknowledging athletes' perspectives (Mageau & Vallerand, 2001) – athletes are more likely to pursue their goals with autonomous motives (Healy et al., 2014; Smith et al., 2010; Smith & Ntoumanis, 2014). Conversely, when coaches adopt a controlling interpersonal style, where they coerce athletes to perform and behave in a given way through controlling feedback, punishment, intimidation, and excessive personal control (Bartholomew et al., 2010), athletes are more likely to pursue their goals with controlled motives. Given the importance of pursuing goals with the most adaptive motives, this research demonstrates that coaches need to be aware of how their everyday engagements with athletes might indirectly affect the success of goal-setting. As such, it is necessary that coaches are supported to use more autonomy-supportive behaviours when interacting with their athletes. Athletes may also be inclined to align their personal goals to those they perceive their coach to be pursuing (Maitland & Gervis, 2010). While the implications of this have not been directly examined within the literature, it is plausible that such approaches may lead to athletes pursuing goals that are not personally important to them (i.e. with controlled motives), thus limiting the progress they may make towards these goals and leading to poorer well-being.

Is goal-setting an effective way to improve athletic performance?

It was not our intention within this chapter to suggest that goal-setting is not effective in enhancing athletic performance; indeed, we have provided ample evidence that this remains an effective and popular tool for athletes that can lead to a range of beneficial outcomes including performance enhancement. However, as demonstrated through the information presented, there is greater nuance to goal-setting as a technique than perhaps some coaches and athletes realize. Thus, in order to ensure that the effects of goal-setting are maximized by coaches and athletes, it is our suggestion that applied recommendations should go beyond the commonly known principles of GST (Locke & Latham, 2019) and setting S.M.A.R.T. goals. Such aspects may include considering the appropriate difficulty level for goal-setting in sport. While it may be argued that their work is somewhat dated, there is no robust evidence to challenge Kyllo and Landers' (1995) finding that goals of a moderate difficulty might be more effective than difficult goals in sport settings. Other key considerations may include the goal-setting preferences and motives of athletes. While the evidence presented generally suggests that goal-setting is a useful technique, there may be some athletes in specific situations for whom it is not effective, and the use of other mental skills would be a more appropriate way of enhancing performance. Equally, the types of goals set should be considered based on the specific athlete at that specific time. This may include thinking if process, performance, or outcome goals (or a combination of these types) would be more effective, as well as acknowledging that different benefits may come from specific, 'do your best' or open goals depending on the specific needs of the athlete. Finally, we have shown that coaches can both explicitly (i.e. through their engagement in the goal-setting process, providing feedback on progress) and implicitly (i.e. through their own goal pursuits and their use of autonomy supportive and controlling interpersonal behaviours) impact goal pursuit in their athletes. Thus, coaches could consider how their own involvement in goal-setting can bring about the most adaptive outcomes for their athletes.

Applied recommendations for coaches

We recognize the importance of providing applied recommendations for coaches based on our review of the literature in order for them to support their athletes in the pursuit of important goals. In doing so, it is necessary to reflect that the simplicity of the S.M.A.R.T acronym has no doubt contributed to its popularity as a tool for goal-setting. However, as we have demonstrated within this chapter, this simplicity may not result in the most beneficial goal-setting for performance enhancement in sport. Given the nuances of effective goal-setting that we have highlighted, rather than provide formula that coaches can follow when goal-setting with their athletes, we propose that there are some key questions that coaches could ask themselves, and their athletes, in order to set the most optimal goals:

- Who is the athlete?
  - What are their views on goal-setting?
  - What are their preferences for the types of goals set?
  - How do they feel about the targets that are being set?
  - How committed are they to the goal, and how might that impact how I need to support them?
- What motives are underpinning the pursuit of the goal?
  - How can I encourage the athlete pursue their goals with higher autonomous and lower controlled motives?
- What is an appropriate level of difficulty based on this athlete at their current stage?
  - Is a goal with moderate or high difficulty most suitable?
  - Would a specific, 'do your best' or open goal be more beneficial for this athlete in this goal?
- How am I going to support them as a coach?
  - When will I provide feedback?
  - What kind of feedback would be most appropriate for this athlete at this point?
  - How sure am I that the athlete is not aligning their goals to their perception of my goals as a coach?
  - How can I adapt my behaviour with this athlete in order to facilitate effective goal pursuit?

These questions are not intended to be a comprehensive list of what would work with every athlete. Indeed, given the evidence we have presented within the chapter, it would remiss to propose that a 'one-size-fits-all' approach to goal-setting in sport exists. However, if coaches can reflect upon the key themes presented within this chapter, and consider some of the questions posed, then it is anticipated that coaches and their athletes can have the most optimal experience in goal-setting, resulting in goal-setting indeed being an effective tool for enhancing athletic performance.

References

Bartholomew, K. J., Ntoumanis, N., & Thøgersen-Ntoumani, C. (2010). The controlling interpersonal style in a coaching context: Development and initial validation of a psychometric scale. *Journal of Sport and Exercise Psychology, 32*(2), 193–216. https://doi.org /10.1123/jsep.32.2.193

Burton, D., & Weiss, C. (2008). The fundamental goal concept: The path to process and performance success. In *Advances in Sport Psychology* (3rd ed, pp. 339–375, 470–474). Champaign, IL: Human Kinetics.

Burton, D., Gillham, A., Weinberg, R., Yukelson, D., & Weigand, D. (2013). Goal setting styles: Examining the role of personality factors on the goal practices of prospective olympic athletes. *Journal of Sport Behavior, 36*(1), 23–44.

Burton, D., Pickering, M., Weinberg, R., Yukelson, D., & Weigand, D. (2010). The competitive goal effectiveness paradox revisited: Examining the goal practices of prospective olympic athletes. *Journal of Applied Sport Psychology, 22*(1), 72–86. https://doi.org/10.1080/104132 00903403232

Deci, E. L., & Ryan, R. M. (2000). The "what" and "why" of goal pursuits: Human needs and the self-determination of behavior. *Psychological Inquiry, 11*, 227–268.

Doran, G. T. (1981). There's a S.M.A.R.T way to write management's goals and objectives. *Management Review, 70*, 35–36.

Dweck, C. S. (1999). *Self-theories: Their Role in Motivation, Personality, and Development* (pp. xiii, 195). East Sussex, UK: Psychology Press.

Gaudreau, P., & Braaten, A. (2016). Achievement goals and their underlying goal motivation: Does it matter why sport participants pursue their goals? *Psychologica Belgica, 56*(3), 244–268. https://doi.org/10.5334/pb.266

Giannini, J. M., Weinberg, R. S., & Jackson, A. J. (1988). The effects of mastery, competitive, and cooperative goals on the performance of simple and complex basketball skills. *Journal of Sport and Exercise Psychology, 10*(4), 408–417. https://doi.org/10.1123/jsep.10.4.408

Gillham, A., & Weiler, D. (2013). Goal setting with a college soccer team: What went right, and less-than-right. *Journal of Sport Psychology in Action, 4*(2), 97–108. https://doi.org/10.1080/2 1520704.2013.764560

Hall, H. K., Weinberg, M. S., & Jackson, A. (1987). Effects of goal specificity, goal difficulty, and information feedback on endurance performance. *Journal of Sport and Exercise Psychology, 9*(1), 43–54. https://doi.org/10.1123/jsp.9.1.43

Hawkins, R. M., Crust, L., Swann, C., & Jackman, P. C. (2020). The effects of goal types on psychological outcomes in active and insufficiently active adults in a walking task. *Psychology of Sport and Exercise*, 101661. https://doi.org/10.1016/j.psychsport.2020.101661

Healy, L. C., Ntoumanis, N., & Arthur, C. A. (in press). Goal motives and well-being in student athletes: A person-centered approach. *Journal of Sport & Exercise Psychology*.

Healy, L. C., Ntoumanis, N., & Duda, J. L. (2016). Goal motives and multiple-goal striving in sport and academia: A person-centered investigation of goal motives and inter-goal relations. *Journal of Science and Medicine in Sport, 19*(12), 1010–1014. https://doi.org/10.1016/j.jsam s.2016.03.001

Healy, L. C., Ntoumanis, N., Zanten, J. J. C. S. V. van, & Paine, N. (2014). Goal striving and well-being in sport: The role of contextual and personal motivation. *Journal of Sport and Exercise Psychology, 36*(5), 446–459. https://doi.org/10.1123/jsep.2013-0261

Kingston, K. M., & Hardy, L. (1997). Effects of different types of goals on processes that support performance. *The Sport Psychologist, 11*(3), 277–293. https://doi.org/10.1123/tsp.11.3.277

Koo, M., & Fishbach, A. (2008). Dynamics of self-regulation: How (un)accomplished goal actions affect motivation. *Journal of Personality and Social Psychology, 94*(2), 183–195. https://doi.org/10.1037/0022-3514.94.2.183

Kyllo, L. B., & Landers, D. M. (1995). Goal setting in sport and exercise: A research synthesis to resolve the controversy. *Journal of Sport and Exercise Psychology, 17*(2), 117–137. https://doi.org/10.1123/jsep.17.2.117

Locke, E. A. (1991). Problems with goal-setting research in sports: And their solution. *Journal of Sport and Exercise Psychology, 13*(3), 311–316. https://doi.org/10.1123/jsep.13.3.311

Locke, E. A., & Latham, G. P. (1985). The application of goal setting to sports. *Journal of Sport Psychology, 7*(3), 205–222. https://doi.org/10.1123/jsp.7.3.205

Locke, E. A., & Latham, G. P. (1990). *A Theory of Goal Setting & Task Performance.* New York: Prentice Hall.

Locke, E. A., & Latham, G. P. (2002). Building a practically useful theory of goal setting and task motivation: A 35-year odyssey. *American Psychologist, 57*(9), 705–717. https://doi.org/10.1037/0003-066X.57.9.705

Locke, E. A., & Latham, G. P. (2019). The development of goal setting theory: A half century retrospective. *Motivation Science, 5*(2), 93–105. https://doi.org/10.1037/mot0000127

Mageau, G. A., & Vallerand, R. J. (2001). The coach-athlete relationship: A motivational model. *Journal of Sports Sciences, 21*, 883–904. https://doi.org/10.1080/0264041031000140374

Maitland, A., & Gervis, M. (2010). Goal-setting in youth football. Are coaches missing an opportunity? *Physical Education & Sport Pedagogy, 15*(4), 323–343. https://doi.org/10.1080/17408980903413461

McCarthy, P. J., Jones, M. V., Harwood, C. G., & Davenport, L. (2010). Using goal setting to enhance positive affect among junior multievent athletes. *Journal of Clinical Sport Psychology, 4*(1), 53–68. https://doi.org/10.1123/jcsp.4.1.53

McEwan, D., & Beauchamp, M. R. (2020). Teamwork training in sport: A pilot intervention study. *Journal of Applied Sport Psychology, 32*(2), 220–236. https://doi.org/10.1080/10413200.2018.1518277

McEwan, D., Harden, S. M., Zumbo, B. D., Sylvester, B. D., Kaulius, M., Ruissen, G. R., Dowd, A. J., & Beauchamp, M. R. (2016). The effectiveness of multi-component goal setting interventions for changing physical activity behaviour: A systematic review and meta-analysis. *Health Psychology Review, 10*(1), 67–88. https://doi.org/10.1080/17437199.2015.1104258

Neumann, D. L., & Hohnke, E. (2018). Practice using performance goals enhances basketball free throw accuracy when tested under competition in elite players. *Journal of Human Sport and Exercise, 13*(2), 296–304. https://doi.org/10.14198/jhse.2018.132.05

Ntoumanis, N., Healy, L. C., Sedikides, C., Duda, J., Stewart, B., Smith, A., & Bond, J. (2014a). When the going gets tough: The "Why" of goal striving matters. *Journal of Personality, 82*(3), 225–236. https://doi.org/10.1111/jopy.12047

Ntoumanis, N., Healy, L. C., Sedikides, C., Smith, A. L., & Duda, J. L. (2014b). Self-regulatory responses to unattainable goals: The role of goal motives. *Self and Identity, 13*(5), 594–612. https://doi.org/10.1080/15298868.2014.889033

Palao, J., Garcia de Alcaraz, A., Hernández Hernández, E., & Ortega, E. (2016). A case study of applying collective technical-tactical performance goals in elite men's volleyball team. *International Journal of Applied Sports Science, 28*, 68–78. https://doi.org/10.24985/ijass .2016.28.2.68

Pierce, B. E., & Burton, D. (1998). Scoring the perfect 10: Investigating the impact of goal-setting styles on a goal-setting program for female gymnasts. *The Sport Psychologist, 12*(2), 156–168. https://doi.org/10.1123/tsp.12.2.156

Senécal, J., Loughead, T. M., & Bloom, G. A. (2008). A season-long team-building intervention: Examining the effect of team goal setting on cohesion. *Journal of Sport & Exercise Psychology, 30*(2), 186–199. https://doi.org/10.1123/jsep.30.2.186

Sheldon, K. M., & Elliot, A. J. (1999). Goal striving, need satisfaction, and longitudinal well-being: The self-concordance model. *Journal of Personality and Social Psychology, 76*(3), 482–497. https://doi.org/10.1037/0022-3514.76.3.482

Smith, A., Ntoumanis, N., & Duda, J. (2007). Goal striving, goal attainment, and well-being: Adapting and testing the self-concordance model in sport. *Journal of Sport and Exercise Psychology, 29*(6), 763–782. https://doi.org/10.1123/jsep.29.6.763

Smith, A., Ntoumanis, N., & Duda, J. (2010). An Investigation of coach behaviors, goal motives, and implementation intentions as predictors of well-being in Sport. *Journal of Applied Sport Psychology, 22*(1), 17–33. https://doi.org/10.1080/10413200903403190

Smith, A. L., & Ntoumanis, N. (2014). An examination of goal motives and athletes' self-regulatory responses to unattainable goals. *International Journal of Sport Psychology, 45*(6), 538–558.

Swann, C., Hooper, A., Schweickle, M. J., Peoples, G., Mullan, J., Hutto, D., Allen, M. S., & Vella, S. A. (2020a). Comparing the effects of goal types in a walking session with healthy adults: Preliminary evidence for open goals in physical activity. *Psychology of Sport and Exercise, 47*, 101475. https://doi.org/10.1016/j.psychsport.2019.01.003

Swann, C., Rosenbaum, S., Lawrence, A., Vella, S. A., McEwan, D., & Ekkekakis, P. (2020b). Updating goal-setting theory in physical activity promotion: A critical conceptual review. *Health Psychology Review,* 1–17. https://doi.org/10.1080/17437199.2019.1706616

Tenenbaum, G., Spence, R., & Christensen, S. (1999). The effect of goal difficulty and goal orientation on running performance in young female athletes. *Australian Journal of Psychology, 51*(1), 6–11. https://doi.org/10.1080/00049539908255328

Vidic, Z., & Burton, D. (2010). The roadmap: Examining the impact of a systematic goal-setting program for collegiate women's tennis players. *The Sport Psychologist, 24*(4), 427–447. https://doi.org/10.1123/tsp.24.4.427

Weinberg, R., & Weigand, D. (1993). Goal setting in sport and exercise: A reaction to locke. *Journal of Sport and Exercise Psychology, 15*(1), 88–96. https://doi.org/10.1123/jsep.15.1.88

Weinberg, R., Bruya, L., & Jackson, A. (1990). Goal setting and competition: A reaction to Hall and Byrne. *Journal of Sport and Exercise Psychology, 12*(1), 92–97. https://doi.org/10.1123/ jsep.12.1.92

Weinberg, R., Stitcher, T., & Richardson, P. (1994), Effects of a seasonal goal-setting program on lacrosse performance. *The Sport Psychologist, 8*(2), 166–175. https://doi.org/10.1123/tsp .8.2.166

Weinberg, R., Yukelson, D., Burton, D., & Weigand, D. (2000). Perceived goal setting practices of olympic athletes: An exploratory investigation. *The Sport Psychologist, 14*(3), 279–295. https://doi.org/10.1123/tsp.14.3.279

Zetou, E., Papacharisis, V., & Mountaki, F. (2008). The effects of goal-setting interventions on three volleyball skills: A single-subject design. *International Journal of Performance Analysis in Sport, 8*(3), 79–95. https://doi.org/10.1080/24748668.2008.11868450

17 Clutch Plays, Clutch Performances, and Clutch Performers

Separating Myth from Reality

Matthew J. Schweickle and Patricia C. Jackman

The notion that certain athletes have an ability to increase their performance during the most pressurized moments in sport is an appealing concept to athletes, coaches, and fans alike. Improving one's performance during pressure circumstances is known as clutch performance (Otten, 2009). Athletes with a perceived propensity for delivering clutch performances often hold a significant position in sporting folklore. For example, Michael Jordan has been described as 'the most clutch player in NBA history' (Wallace et al., 2013, p. 643), an unsurprising assertion for basketball fans familiar with Jordan's famous, game-winning moments, such as 'The Shot' against the Cleveland Cavaliers in the 1989 Finals series or 'The Last Shot' against Utah Jazz to win the 1998 NBA Finals Series. Indeed, players with reputations as clutch performers seem to appear in almost every sporting code, such as Derek Jeter in Major League Baseball, widely referred to as 'Mr November'; Tom Brady in the National Football League; or Cristiano Ronaldo's reputation for scoring in knockout games and major championships. Despite the widely held belief that certain athletes can consistently flourish under pressure, the statistical evidence supporting this idea is lacking, and on the whole suggests that clutch performers are a statistical myth. However, this assertion must be weighed against the definitional issues that are present within this field, as well as the lack of consensus over what exactly constitutes a clutch performance, and therefore a clutch performer. That is, asserting whether clutch performers are indeed a myth, or reality, largely depends on what we consider a clutch performer to be. This chapter aims to explore these issues, as well as providing recommendations to coaches on how clutch performances may be facilitated, based on the best available evidence.

Clutch plays and clutch performances

What is a clutch performance?

Whilst clutch performance is a growing area of research, and has garnered much media attention, a number of issues have been highlighted in how the concept is defined. The term 'in the clutch' was first used in a 1929 *New York Times* article to describe when a batter in baseball hits a safe 'blow' at an opportune moment (Safire, 2005). Although the term originated almost a century ago, a recent systematic review of clutch performance (Schweickle et al., 2020) suggested that there remains 'conceptual confusion surrounding what clutch performance is, and is not' (p. 20) due to the existence of multiple definitions of clutch performance. For example, from the 27 studies reviewed by Schweickle et al. (2020), 10 different definitions were provided for clutch performance. Furthermore, over a quarter of the studies failed to provide any definition of clutch performance within their research. This lack of clarity over what constitutes a clutch performance is important to consider when assessing the validity of evidence for clutch performance, and whether clutch performers are indeed a myth.

The aforementioned definitional issues, and their impact on how we examine clutch performance, are highlighted in the discrepancies between the two most widely used definitions of clutch performance provided by Otten (2009) and Hibbs (2010). Otten (2009) defines clutch performance as 'any performance increment that occurs under pressure circumstances' (p. 584). Hibbs (2010), meanwhile, defines clutch performance as:

> *when a participant in competitive sport succeeds at a competitive-related, challenging task during a clutch situation, is aware that the performance occurs during a clutch situation, possesses the capacity to experience clutch situation-related stress, cares about the outcome of the contest, and succeeds primarily due to skill rather than luck or cheating. (p. 55)*

Within this definition, Hibbs (2010) also introduces the notion of a clutch *situation*, defined as 'a point in a competitive sport where the success or failure of the participants has a significant impact on the outcome of the contest' (p. 48). Notably, these two definitions diverge on the two fundamental aspects of clutch performance: pressure and performance. In regard to pressure, Otten (2009) suggests that clutch performances occur under *pressure circumstances*. This relatively broad description by Otten (2009) suggests that clutch performance can, therefore, occur in *any* pressure circumstance, which contrasts with Hibbs (2010), who delineates that clutch performances only occur in situations that have a *significant impact on the outcome of the contest*, such as situations that present a 'psychological challenge' (p. 52). Therefore, this definition by Hibbs (2010) introduces the idea that an outcome is required for clutch performance. The second aspect on which these definitions diverge is the level of performance required. Otten (2009) calls for an *increased* or *superior* performance, suggesting that athletes must raise their performance to be considered clutch performance. Hibbs (2010), however, specifies that participants must *succeed* at a challenging task, noting that 'clutch performances are not preternatural events, but cases where a competitor manages to perform in according with their ability despite the pressure associated with the circumstances' (p. 56). As such, there is confusion over what level of performance improvement, if any, is required to classify a performance as clutch. It is therefore fundamental to consider the discrepancies in how these core aspects of clutch performance are defined when attempting to separate myth from reality in regards to clutch performances and clutch performers.

Evidence for clutch plays and clutch performances

Research examining clutch performance has focused on isolated moments, such as certain plays, within a performance (e.g. improved performance in the 30 seconds of the game), or to overall performances (e.g. improved performance across an entire game). For the sake of parsimony, the remainder of this chapter will refer to an isolated moment of performance within an event as a clutch play and the entirety of the performance across an event as a clutch performance.

Experimental research examining sport-specific skills in basketball and golf has suggested that athletes can improve their performance when placed under manipulated pressure circumstances. In a golf-putting task, Gray et al. (2013) found that participants who had a clutch play displayed better putting kinematics (e.g. swing amplitude), as opposed to participants who performed worse under the same pressure conditions. McEwan et al. (2012) also examined clutch plays in a golf-putting task, demonstrating that those who warmed up under a higher pressure manipulation were more likely to succeed in a subsequent one-off, high-pressure putt. Lastly, Otten (2009) examined clutch performance in a basketball free-throw task. The results demonstrated that participants who improved their free throw percentage in response to a pressure manipulation displayed higher levels of perceived control, confidence, and implicit knowledge (i.e. skill occurs largely independent of conscious thinking). Importantly, these experimental studies all demonstrated that whilst some participants improved their performance under a pressure manipulation, and therefore achieved a clutch play, the performance of other participants decreased. This divergence in performance under a pressure manipulation suggests that psychological factors are important for explaining individual variations in clutch plays and clutch performance.

In comparison to experimental research, which focuses on specific task performance, qualitative research on clutch performance has primarily examined athletes' perceptions of their own performance over the course of an event. That is, whilst athletes' have knowledge of their objective performance (e.g. winning an event, personal best), the primary indicator they rely on is their own recall and subjective perception of their performance. A number of studies by Hill et al. have reported a range of coping strategies that appear to facilitate clutch performance in elite athletes (Hill et al., 2017; Hill & Hemmings, 2015) and elite referees (Hill et al., 2016). Broadly speaking, some of the key coping strategies identified included: pre- and post-shot routines (e.g. imagery, deep breathing, trigger words, reviewing previous shots); cognitive restructuring (e.g. reappraising stressors, focusing on the process); simulated practice (e.g. practicing under pressure); proactive coping (e.g. referees researching the teams they were to officiate, mentally rehearsing); emotion-focused coping (e.g. deep breathing, centring); drawing on informational social support (e.g. utilizing sport psychologists or mentors); and having a task/process-focus (e.g. check-listing behaviours). Indeed, the evidence presented by Hill et al. (Hill & Hemmings, 2015; Hill et al., 2016, 2017) suggests that there are a number of coping strategies that may be deliberately implemented, and practiced, both ahead of a performance (e.g. simulated practice) and during the performance (e.g. cognitive restructuring).

Several recent qualitative studies have reported that there appears to be a distinct psychological state that underlies clutch plays and clutch performance, termed as *clutch state* (Swann et al., 2016, 2017a, b, 2019; Jackman et al., 2017, 2020). Clutch states are characterized by 12 features: absence of negative thoughts; absorption; altered sensory perceptions; automaticity of skills; confidence; deliberate focus; enhanced motivation; enjoyment; heightened arousal; heightened awareness; intense effort; and perceived control (Swann et al., 2016, 2017a, b, 2019; Jackman et al., 2017, 2020). As depicted in the Integrated Model of Flow and Clutch states (Swann et al., 2017b), clutch states occur through a series of steps in certain contexts. Specifically, clutch states are proposed to occur in pressured situations, and through a series of sequential steps, which include an initial appraisal of the situation as a challenge; the identification of fixed goals; and a conscious decision to increase effort and intensity. Lastly, whilst these states are suggested to be intrinsically rewarding, they are also reported as exhausting, suggesting that clutch states involve athletes pushing themselves to their mental or physical limits.

In sum, the research presented suggests that there is relatively strong evidence to support the occurrence of clutch plays and clutch performance. Whilst there are a number of experimental studies that provide support for clutch plays, the strongest available evidence stems from qualitative interview studies. The fact that the majority of evidence comes from qualitative research is important to note, as this is primarily based on athletes' perceptions of their own performance, an aspect that is often overlooked when trying to decipher whether clutch performers exist.

The statistical myth of clutch performers

A clutch performer, also referred to as having a clutch ability, is a term used to describe an athlete who is known for delivering clutch performances (Hibbs, 2010). The notion that some athletes seem to 'step up' in circumstances where others choke[1] (e.g. Gröpel & Mesagno, 2019) has long fascinated sport fans and media alike (e.g. West & Libby, 1969). Research into whether such clutch performers existed, beyond fan and media perceptions, began in baseball during the 1970s (Cramer, 1977). Indeed, research into clutch performers was exclusively conducted in baseball until the last decade, when researchers also began to explore the existence of clutch performers in basketball (e.g. Wallace et al., 2013) and tennis (e.g. Jetter & Walker, 2015). A common thread in research that has examined the existence of clutch performers is the shared methodological approach, as all of these studies have adopted an archival approach. As such, these studies have sought evidence of statistically significant improvements in performance when athletes were under pre-identified, situation-specific pressure circumstances, including finals and the last moments of a game. For example, Ruane (2005) examined the performance of baseball batters compared to their career average, when their teammates were in a scoring position. Alternatively, in basketball, Wallace et al. (2013) examined shooting performance during the 4th quarter of NBA playoff games, when compared with the previous three quarters from the same game.

The majority of research examining the existence of clutch performers has found little evidence that such performers exist. In a recent systematic review, Schweickle et al. (2020) highlighted that out of the 10 studies that directly examined the existence of clutch performers in baseball, basketball, or tennis, 8 provided no evidence of their existence. For example, in baseball pitching, Birnbaum (2009) indicated that performance variation during pressure situations was more likely a product of other performance factors, such as run support. Meanwhile, it was suggested that variations in batting performance were more likely to simply be a product of random variation (Brooks, 1989; Cramer & Palmer, 2008; Deane & Palmer, 2006; Ruane, 2005), or general hitting quantity (Cramer, 1977). As previously mentioned above in basketball, Wallace et al. (2013) showed that most players were statistically average during the 4th quarter of NBA playoffs games, when compared with the previous three quarters of the same game. Wallace et al. (2013) stated that this offered no evidence for the existence of clutch performers, as performance did not improve, but rather was maintained.

In contrast to the aforementioned research, two studies did provide support for the notion of clutch performers. Jetter and Walker (2015) demonstrated that higher ranked tennis players were more likely to win Grand Slam tournaments (i.e. higher pressure tournaments) compared to other tournaments, and were also more likely to perform well in pressure situations (i.e. tie-breaks) within those tournaments. This finding was taken to suggest that higher-ranked players were also more likely to be clutch performers. Solomonov et al. (2015), meanwhile, examined the performance of notable 'clutch players' during the last 20 games of the 2005–2006 NBA season, including players, such as Kobe Bryant, Steve Nash, Allen Iverson, and LeBron James. Compared to their non-clutch teammates, these clutch players scored more points, made more assists, and drew more fouls during the final, high-pressure moments of the game (i.e. 5 minutes remaining when the game was within a 6-point score differential; Solomonov et al., 2015). An interesting finding, however, was that no improvement was observed in field goal percentage. That is, the improved performance output of these players was primarily a result of taking more shots and exerting more effort, rather than any improvements in skill execution. Indeed, this finding has important implications for how we evaluate clutch performers, as discussed below.

Are clutch performers therefore a myth?

Whilst the statistical evidence for clutch performers is lacking, this does not necessarily mean such performers are a myth. Specifically, this is because there remain issues in how we measure, conceptualize, and define clutch performers.

Measurement issues

A fundamental limitation of the collective research base about clutch performers is that the evidence is entirely archival (Schweickle et al., 2020). A key limitation of archival designs is that an athlete's experience of pressure cannot be measured directly. Instead, archival designs have used certain in-game circumstances to represent 'objective' pressure situations, which act as a proxy measure of pressure. Underlying such archival approaches is the notion that athletes in such situations experience pressure categorically (i.e. athletes experience pressure in certain situations, and less/no pressure in others) and uniformly (i.e. all athletes experience increased pressure in certain situations, whilst all athletes in other situations do not). This assumption, however, overlooks a central tenet of the concept of pressure: that pressure has a subjective component (Baumeister, 1984). Accordingly, the psychological experience of athletes in the same situations may differ and what is considered a pressure situation to some athletes may not be for others. As such, it is difficult to make conclusions on the existence of clutch performers using designs that cannot directly measure perceptions of pressure, which is a fundamental aspect of clutch performance (Hibbs, 2010; Otten, 2009; Schweickle et al., 2020).

Conceptual issues

To evaluate whether clutch performers exist, archival studies have examined whether athletes *increased* their performance in 'objective' pressure situations. Questions have been raised, however, over whether increased performance is necessary for clutch performance. Solomonov et al. (2015), who reported that clutch performers in the NBA increased metrics of effort (i.e. shots taken, points scored, fouls drawn) but showed no increases in skill execution (i.e. field goal percentage) during pressure situations, made the observation that 'it should not be expected that players will become markedly better at shooting over the course of the final few minutes of the game', as 'the "ceiling effect" alone might explain the relative stability in the players hit rate' (p. 137). Indeed, this observation raises two important questions. First, would we expect highly trained, elite athletes to significantly improve their skill execution in certain situations? Second, if such athletes did exist and possessed such a capability, one may then ask: is it desirable to work with athletes who are only motivated to reach this new level of performance when the game hangs in the balance? By extension, would it not be more desirable for such an athlete to perform at this increased performance level earlier in the contest, reducing the possibility for the game to be so close at the finish? In defining clutch performance, Hibbs (2010) noted this issue, stating that 'clutch performances are not preternatural events, but cases where a competitor manages to perform in accordance with their ability despite the pressure associated with the circumstances' (pp. 55-56). As such, questions remain over whether clutch performances require an increase in skill level, or whether an increase in effort, or even simply maintenance of performance, may instead be more appropriate to categorize clutch performers.

Studies examining the existence of clutch performers have relied on objective performance indicators. Such indicators have included batting averages (e.g. Brooks, 1989), free-throw percentage (Worthy et al., 2009), or winning matches (e.g. Jetter & Walker, 2015). When using objective performance indicators, however, there appears to be ambiguity in terms of what barometer these objective performance indictors should be compared against. For example, studies examining clutch performers have compared the performance against career averages (Cao et al., 2011); previous season performance (e.g. Birnbaum, 2008); performance within the same season (e.g. Birnbaum, 2009); performance within the same game (e.g. Wallace et al., 2013); and projected performance (i.e. judged against performances that had not yet occurred; Deane & Palmer, 2006). As such, it seems unclear how objective performance should actually be assessed and what it should be compared against when evaluating the existence of clutch performers. Meanwhile, the strongest evidence for individual clutch performances comes from qualitative research. Primarily, this research has relied on subjective performance, that is, the athlete's recollection of their performance. Indeed, athletes may be in a stronger position to assess their own performance, as this assessment may consider performance factors overlooked in statistics (e.g. coming back from injury, performing a leadership role within the team, tactical instructions from the coach, against their own perceptions of pressure). Therefore, it may be the case that claiming clutch performers are a myth, based solely on statistical evidence, overlooks the important role that subjective assessments of performance have played within clutch performance research.

Rethinking the clutch performer

The clutch performer has been traditionally conceptualized and measured within the literature as an athlete who statistically increases their performance during pre-identified situations used to represent pressure. As discussed, however, a number of issues have been highlighted with this approach, namely: the lack of measurement validity surrounding pressure; whether clutch performers require an increase in their performance; and the use of solely objective performance data. Rethinking what characteristics constitute a clutch performer, however, could alter the extent to which we consider clutch performers a myth or reality.

As a starting point in rethinking the clutch performer, a move away from judgement based solely on performance outcomes (e.g. game-winning shot) and objective increases in performance may be beneficial. Perhaps one of Michael Jordan's most famous quotes is '26 times I've been trusted to take the game-winning shot and missed. I've failed over and over again in my life. And that is why I succeed' (Forbes, 2015). Indeed, one may consider if part of being a clutch performer is having the willingness (see discussions surrounding *confidence, challenge appraisal,* and *perceived contro*l below) to take the shot, regardless of the outcome. For example, mental toughness, which refers to the capacity to strive towards achieving ones goals, despite challenges and adversity (Hardy et al., 2014), has been associated with more frequent, and longer, clutch states (Jackman et al., 2020). Placing a focus on the process, rather than the outcome, also aligns with evidence presented by Hill et al. (2016), which suggested that a task/process focus may facilitate clutch performances. Rethinking what constitutes a clutch performer may also be beneficial from a coaching perspective, as intervening and influencing an athlete's performance processes is often much more achievable, and controllable, than changing their overall performance outcomes. In sum, whilst clutch performers may be a 'statistical myth', a rethink of what it means to be a clutch performer could potentially open up avenues for it to be considered a reality.

How can coaches facilitate clutch performances?

Despite the questions raised over the existence and conceptualization of clutch performers, there is relatively strong evidence for the occurrence of individual clutch performances. Based on the extant literature, a number of key factors that appear central to promoting clutch performances can be identified, including confidence; challenge appraisal; perceived control; and practicing under pressure. Of note, these are not isolated factors, but are all interrelated.

Confidence

Unsurprisingly, confidence appears to play a key role in the occurrence of clutch performance. There are a number of strategies that can be employed to increase confidence in athletes. First, Swann et al. (2017a) highlighted that whilst some athletes described having a pre-existing confidence under pressure, others gave themselves a 'forced confidence' (p. 2277) during the performance, by drawing on self-talk to establish a sense of confidence and belief. When using self-talk to enhance confidence, athletes should use phrases that are positive and approach-focused (e.g. 'I want to win') rather than negative and avoidance-focused (e.g. 'I don't want to lose'; Karageorghis & Terry, 2011). Second, previous performance accomplishments are considered to be the most powerful source of self-efficacy, which refers to confidence people have in specific situations (Bandura, 1986). Maher et al. (2018) reported that successful warm-up and early-game form was associated with increased confidence during clutch performances. Coaches may therefore consider how warm-up or early-game strategies may be manipulated to increase athlete confidence (e.g. using warm-up drills in which it is likely the athlete will be successful), or focus on highlighting previous successes prior to performances. Lastly, the use of imagery, such as recreating images of successful performances in one's mind, has been reported as a source of confidence prior to clutch performances (Hill et al., 2016). By implementing such techniques, coaches and athletes may be able to increase confidence, and hence promote clutch performances.

Perceived control

The concept of perceived control refers to ones perceptions of their capacity to be able to cope and attain goals under stress (Cheng et al., 2009). Importantly, this may not actually refer to the amount of *actual* or *objective* control one has over a situation but rather the *perception* that they have control (Skinner, 1996). Hill et al. (2016) reported that having a task or process focus often led to perceptions of control. That is, focusing on aspects that the athlete can control (e.g. their process) rather than aspects out of their control (e.g. the outcome), increased their subjective sense of control of the situation. This notion is captured in the relatively simple instruction to focus on 'controlling the controllables'

(Karageorghis & Terry, 2011, p. 114). Indeed, an appraisal of a situation as a threat, which is not conducive to clutch performances, may occur when an athlete focuses on factors they cannot control (e.g. the referee, other players, the weather; Jones et al., 2009). Lastly, individuals who experienced clutch states in exercise reported a sense of 'exerting control' (p. 93), in that they tried to increase their sense of control, but did not necessarily feel totally *in* control (Swann et al., 2019). Indeed, this finding may suggest that increases in ones perceived control can be a conscious decision. In sum, perceived control plays an important role in clutch performance. Coaches and athletes may attempt to facilitate such perceptions of control by increasing confidence (Otten, 2009), focusing on the task or process (Hill et al., 2016), or making conscious efforts to exert control (Swann et al., 2019).

Challenge appraisal

The importance of challenge appraisal during demanding sporting situations is widely recognized (see Jones et al., 2009 for review). Given that clutch performance and choking often occurred under the same circumstances, Hill et al. (2017) noted that 'the psychological response/appraisal of that pressure is likely to have determined the performance outcome' (p. 144). Similarly, Hill and Hemmings (2015) reported that the effectiveness of certain coping strategies may be affected by the appraisal of the situation, noting that 'the same coping strategy can have both a positive and negative effect, depending on the situation and the athlete's appraisal of that stressor' (p. 533). Meanwhile, Swann et al. (2016, 2017b, 2019) identified that challenge appraisal was part of the process of occurrence for clutch states. Specifically, this challenge appraisal emerged from an awareness of situational demands and the importance of performing in that situation for the outcome of the event or achievement of goals. Indeed, this challenge appraisal was described as a 'relatively sudden process of 'switching on' in response to appraisal of demands' (Swann, 2017b, p. 393). As such, employing strategies that encourage athletes to appraise pressure situations as a challenge, rather than a threat, is important to facilitating clutch performances.

The Theory of Challenge and Threat States in Athletes proposes three interrelated determinants for appraising situations as a challenge: (1) high self-efficacy (i.e. situation-specific confidence); (2) a sense of perceived control; and (3) an approach goal orientation (Jones et al., 2009). Self-efficacy can be increased via the use of several strategies, such as performance accomplishments; vicarious experiences; verbal persuasion; imagery experiences; and controlling physiological and emotional responses (Bandura, 1986; Schunk, 1995; Treasure, 1996). Perceived control, meanwhile, may be facilitated by focusing on the task or process (i.e. the controllables; Hill et al., 2016), or making conscious efforts to exert control (Swann et al., 2019). Last, goal orientation refers to the motives an athlete sets for participating in sport (Jones et al., 2009). An approach goal orientation is when an athlete's motive is to demonstrate competence against one's self or others (e.g. a coach may say '"We want to beat this rival team to show we are more talented than them'). Approach goal orientations facilitate challenge appraisals (Adie et al., 2008). Meanwhile, avoidance goal orientations, which reflect a drive to avoid incompetence compared to one's self or others (e.g. 'We don't want to lose to this rival team, as it will show everyone they are better than us'), are a predictor of threat appraisals (Adie et al., 2008). As such, to encourage challenge appraisals, coaches should focus on increasing athlete's self-efficacy and confidence, and also perceived control and set goals with an approach orientation rather than an avoidance orientation.

Performance under pressure

Evidence suggests that practicing under pressure may facilitate clutch performances. Hill and Hemmings (2015) reported that simulating pressure situations in training offered an opportunity for athletes to practice their coping strategies and pressurized skill execution, and subsequently was considered to facilitate clutch performance. Similarly, in a qualitative investigation by Maher et al. (2018), basketball players reflected that using pressure situations at training helped to improve their free-throw performance in games. More broadly, a meta-analysis by Low et al. (2020) of pressure training for performance domains, which included sport and law enforcement, reported that pressure training reported a large, positive effect on improving performance under pressure ($g = 0.85$). Indeed, McEwan et al. (2012) even demonstrated that, compared to those who warmed-up under low pressure, warming-up under higher pressure conditions resulted in better performance in a subsequent one-off, high-pressure putt. This finding suggests there may be some short-term, immediate benefits of practicing under pressure, in addition to longer term effects.

To successfully implement pressure training, coaches should consider both the environment the training occurs in and how pressure is manipulated. First, practicing under pressure should take place in a facilitative environment. Such an environment may be characterized by a strong coach–athlete relationship and encouragement when making mistakes (Fletcher & Sarkar, 2016). It is important that such training is viewed by athletes as an opportunity to learn, or practice, coping strategies. Second, coaches should consider how they increase pressure. Whilst pressure is inherently subjective (e.g. Baumeister, 1984), there are a number of common sources of pressure that are *likely* to increase the experience of pressure for athletes, including reward contingency (i.e. rewards or punishments based on the level of performance); an evaluative audience (i.e. others actively watching a performance); presence of comparative co-actors (i.e. competition with others); the extent to which the performance reflects important features of the self (i.e. performing a task in which the athlete expects to be sufficient or capable at, and places value in); and the likelihood that one will not have a second chance (i.e. knockout tournaments, finals, only having one-shot; Baumeister & Showers, 1986). When attempting to manipulate such sources of pressure, Low et al. (2020) recommends that coaches should utilize stressors that are inherent to the task. For example, utilizing monetary rewards may not be a feasible strategy to replicate regularly, whereas using competitive games (e.g. small-sided game where score is kept) or reduction of chances (e.g. shoot-out competition) may be more easily replicable and more relevant. For example, Kegelaers et al. (2019) implemented an 8-session pressure training interventions in basketballers. An example from the first week of the intervention for increasing pressure in a game simulation was:

> *two minutes left; referee; 5 points back log; both teams in penalty; both teams have 2 time-outs remaining; intervention groups starts with possession; play against man-to-man defence; athletes have to run full court length for each point behind at the end of the game.* (p. 7)

As seen, in this pressure manipulation, Kegelaers et al. (2019) drew on a range of sources of pressure, such as punishments (e.g. sprints and court runs); competition (e.g. incentivized game simulation); and reduction in number of chances (e.g. only two minutes remaining). In sum, introducing pressure simulations into training programs appears to be a robust strategy to develop athlete's coping strategies under pressure, and as a consequence promote future successful performance under pressure.

Conclusion

There is a long-standing interest in the idea of the clutch performer. Despite compelling evidence that athletes may have clutch plays or clutch performances, the statistical evidence for clutch performers remains limited. Indeed, many researchers consider the clutch performer a myth. Whilst future research remains needed, by rethinking what constitutes a clutch performer, and moving towards a conceptualization that focuses on the subjective performance of the athlete, and their process, rather than the outcome, there remains the possibility that clutch performers may yet still be a reality. In sum, athletes and coaches should reflect on what they expect from themselves, and their players, respectively, when under pressure. Meanwhile, to facilitate individual clutch performances, coaches may focus on strategies that promote confidence, perceived control, and challenge appraisal in the athletes they work with and could also consider implementing simulated pressure situations during training.

Note

1 Choking is defined as "an acute and considerable decrease in skill execution and performance when self-expected standards are normally achievable, which is the result of increased anxiety under perceived pressure" (Mesagno & Hill, 2013, p. 274).

References

Adie, J. W., Duda, J. L., & Ntoumanis, N. (2008). Achievement goals, competition appraisals, and the psychological and emotional welfare of sport participants. *Journal of Sport & Exercise Psychology, 30*, 302–322. https://doi.org/10.1123/jsep.30.3.302

Bandura, A. (1986). *Social Foundations of Thought and Action: A Social Cognitive Theory.* Hoboken, NJ: Prentice Hall.

Baumeister, R. F. (1984). Choking under pressure: Self-consciousness and paradoxical effects of incentives on skillful performance. *Journal of Personality and Social Psychology, 46*(3), 610–620. https://doi.org/10.1037/0022-3514.46.3.610

Baumeister, R. F., & Showers, C. J. (1986). A review of paradoxical performance effects: Choking under pressure in sports and mental tests. *European Journal of Social Psychology, 16*, 361–383. https://doi.org/10.1177/1368431009355866

Birnbaum, P. (2009). Players being "clutch" when targeting 20 wins. *The Baseball Resarch Journal, 38*, 44–48.

Brooks, H. (1989). The statistical mirage of clutch hitting. *The Baseball Resarch Journal, 18*.

Cao, Z., Price, J., & Stone, D. F. (2011). Performance under pressure in the NBA. *Journal of Sports Economics, 12*(3), 231–252. https://doi.org/10.1177/1527002511404785

Cheng, W. N. K., Hardy, L., & Markland, D. (2009). Toward a three-dimensional conceptualization of performance anxiety: Rationale and initial measurement development. *Psychology of Sport and Exercise, 10*(2), 271–278. https://doi.org/10.1016/j.psychsport.2008.08.001

Cramer, R. D. (1977). Do clutch hitters exist? *Baseball Research Journal, 6*, 74–79.

Cramer, R. D., & Palmer, P. (2008). Clutch hitting revisited. *The Baseball Resarch Journal, 37*, 85–88.

Deane, B., & Palmer, P. (2006). Still searching for clutch pitchers. *The Baseball Resarch Journal, 35*, 124–125.

Fletcher, D., & Sarkar, M. (2016). Mental fortitude training: An evidence-based approach to developing psychological resilience for sustained success. *Journal of Sport Psychology in Action*, *7*, 135–157. https://doi.org/10.1080/21520704.2016.1255496

Forbes. (2015). *Forbes Quotes*. Forbes.Com. https://www.forbes.com/quotes/11194/#:~:text =Twenty-six times I've, that is why I succeed.

Gray, R., Allsop, J., & Williams, S. E. (2013). Changes in putting kinematics associated with choking and excelling under pressure. *International Journal of Sport Psychology*, *44*(4), 387–407. https://doi.org/10.7352/IJSP2013.44.387

Gröpel, P., & Mesagno, C. (2019). Choking interventions in sports: A systematic review. In *International Review of Sport and Exercise Psychology*, *12*(1), 176–201. https://doi.org/10.1 080/1750984X.2017.1408134

Hardy, L., Bell, J., & Beattie, S. (2014). A neuropsychological model of mentally tough behaviour. *Journal of Personality*, *82*, 69–81. https://doi.org/10.1111/jopy.12034

Hibbs, D. (2010). A conceptual analysis of clutch performances in competitive sports. *Journal of the Philosophy of Sport*, *37*(1), 47–59. https://doi.org/10.1080/00948705.2010 .9714765

Hill, D. M., Carvell, S., Matthews, N., Weston, N. J. V., & Thelwell, R. R. C. (2017). Exploring choking experiences in elite sport: The role of self-presentation. *Psychology of Sport and Exercise*, *33*, 141–149. https://doi.org/10.1016/j.psychsport.2017.09.001

Hill, D. M., & Hemmings, B. (2015). A phenomenological exploration of coping responses associated with choking in sport. *Qualitative Research in Sport, Exercise and Health*, *7*(4), 521–538. https://doi.org/10.1080/2159676X.2014.981573

Hill, D. M., Matthews, N., & Senior, R. (2016). The psychological characteristics of performance under pressure in professional rugby union referees. *The Sport Psychologist*, *30*(4), 376–387. https://doi.org/10.1123/tsp.2015-0109

Jackman, P. C., Crust, L., & Swann, C. (2017). Systematically comparing methods used to study flow in sport: A longitudinal multiple-case study. *Psychology of Sport & Exercise*, *32*, 113–123. https://doi.org/10.1016/j.psychsport.2017.06.009

Jackman, P. C., Crust, L., & Swann, C. (2020). The role of mental toughness in the occurrence of flow and clutch states in sport. *International Journal of Sport Psychology*, *51*(1), 1–27. https://doi.org/10.7352/IJSP.2020.51.001

Jetter, M., & Walker, J. K. (2015). Game, set, and match: Do women and men perform differently in competitive situations? *Journal of Economic Behavior and Organization*, *119*, 96–108. https://doi.org/10.1016/j.jebo.2015.07.017

Jones, M., Meijen, C., McCarthy, P. J., & Sheffield, D. (2009). A theory of challenge and threat states in athletes. *International Review of Sport and Exercise Psychology*, *2*(2), 161–180. https:// doi.org/10.1080/17509840902829331

Karageorghis, C. I., & Terry, P. C. (2011). *Inside Sport Psychology*. Human Kinetics.

Kegelaers, J., Wylleman, P., Bunigh, A., & Oudejans, R. R. D. (2019). A mixed methods evaluation of a pressure training intervention to develop resilience in female basketball players. *Journal of Applied Sport Psychology*, *33*, 151–172. https://doi.org/10.1080/10413200 .2019.1630864

Low, W. R., Sandercock, G. R. H., Freeman, P., Winter, M. E., Butt, J., & Maynard, I. (2020). Pressure training for performance domains: A meta-analysis. *Sport, Exercise, and Performance Psychology*. https://doi.org/10.1037/spy0000202

Maher, R., Marchant, D., Morris, T., & Fazel, F. (2018). Managing pressure at the free-throw line: Perceptions of elite basketball players. *International Journal of Sport and Exercise Psychology*, *818*, 1–17. https://doi.org/10.1080/1612197X.2018.1536159

McEwan, D., Schmaltz, R., & Ginis, K. A. M. (2012). Warming up with pressure improves subsequent clutch performance on a golf-putting task. *Advances in Physical Education, 2*(4), 144–147. https://doi.org/10.4236/ape.2012.24025

Mesagno, C., & Hill, D. M. (2013). Definition of choking in sport: Re-conceptualization and debate. *International Journal of Sport Psychology, 44*(4), 267–277. https://doi.org/10.7352/IJSP2013.44.267

Otten, M. (2009). Choking vs. clutch performance: A study of sport performance under pressure. *Journal of Sport & Exercise Psychology, 31*(5), 583–601. https://doi.org/10.1123/jsep.31.5.583

Ruane, T. (2005). In search of clutch hitting. *The Baseball Resarch Journal, 34,* 29–36.

Safire, W. (2005). Go To! *The New York Times.* https://www.nytimes.com/2005/05/08/magazine/go-to.html

Schunk, D. H. (1995). Self-efficacy and education and instruction. In J. E. Maddux (Ed.), *Self-efficacy, Adaptation, and Adjustment: Theory, Research, and Application* (pp. 281–303). New York: Plenum Press.

Schweickle, M. J., Swann, C., Jackman, P. C., & Vella, S. A. (2020). Clutch performance in sport and exercise : A systematic review. *International Review of Sport and Exercise Psychology,* 1–28. https://doi.org/10.1080/1750984X.2020.1771747

Skinner, E. A. (1996). A guide to constructs of control. *Journal of Personality and Social Psychology, 71*(3), 549–570. https://doi.org/10.1037//0022-3514.71.3.549

Solomonov, Y., Avugos, S., & Bar-Eli, M. (2015). Do clutch players win the game? Testing the validity of the clutch player's reputation in basketball. *Psychology of Sport and Exercise, 16,* 130–138. https://doi.org/10.1016/j.psychsport.2014.10.004

Swann, C., Crust, L., Jackman, P., Vella, S. A., Allen, M. S., & Keegan, R. (2017a). Performing under pressure: Exploring the psychological state underlying clutch performance in sport. *Journal of Sports Sciences, 35*(23), 2272–2280. https://doi.org/10.1080/02640414.2016.1265661

Swann, C., Crust, L., Jackman, P., Vella, S. A., Allen, M. S., & Keegan, R. (2017b). Psychological states underlying excellent performance in sport: Toward an integrated model of flow and clutch states. *Journal of Applied Sport Psychology, 29*(4), 375–401. https://doi.org/10.1080/10413200.2016.1272650

Swann, C., Jackman, P. C., Schweickle, M. J., & Vella, S. A. (2019). Optimal experiences in exercise: A qualitative investigation of flow and clutch states. *Psychology of Sport and Exercise, 40,* 87–98. https://doi.org/10.1016/j.psychsport.2018.09.007

Swann, C., Keegan, R., Crust, L., & Piggott, D. (2016). Psychological states underlying excellent performance in professional golfers: "Letting it happen" vs. "making it happen." *Psychology of Sport and Exercise, 23,* 101–113. https://doi.org/10.1016/j.psychsport.2015.10.008

Treasure, D. C. (1996). Relationship between self-efficacy, wrestling performance, and affect prior to competition. *The Sport Psychologist, 10,* 73–83.

Wallace, S., Caudill, S. B., & Mixon, F. G. (2013). Homo certus in professional basketball? Empirical evidence from the 2011 NBA playoffs. *Applied Economics Letters, 20*(7), 642–648. https://doi.org/10.1080/13504851.2012.727965

West, J., & Libby, B. (1969). *Mr. Clutch: The Jerry West Story* (3rd ed.). Hoboken, NJ: Prentice-Hall.

Worthy, D. A., Markman, A. B., & Maddox, W. T. (2009). Choking and excelling at the rfree throw line. *The International Journal of Creativity & Problem Solving, 19*(1), 53–58.

18 Caring Coaching

Examining the Notion of 'cruel to be kind' and Other Caring Myths

Colum Cronin

Sport coaches have often been caricatured as dominant, demonstrative, and dictatorial. In popular culture, this strong, disciplinarian, and sometimes abusive trope is shared in films and documentaries. For example, an analysis of 19 sport films revealed 346 incidents of emotionally abusive coaching (Kerr, Stirling, & Bandealy, 2016). In 68.2% of these incidents, the coach was depicted enacting this abuse, which included yelling, name calling, threatening athletes, demanding excessive exercise, and throwing objects. What these films reveal, perpetuate at times, and critically question to some extent, is the pervasive myth that to be a coach is to be powerful, to be demanding, and the cliché that coaches need to be 'cruel to be kind'.

Early leadership literature, much like coaching in popular culture, similarly focused on dominant leaders. For Carlyle (1846), these great men, including prophets, priests, poets, and military generals, such as Napoleon Bonaparte, offered hero-worshipers alluring ways to understand and participate in the world. This concept of the inspirational leader influenced trait research, which argued that specific traits demarcate leaders as individuals to follow. Typically, such traits included being tall, athletic, well-educated, and intelligent men (Stogdill, 1948). This led to the dominant view of the powerful, authoritative, and male[1] leader who knows best. Emboldened by military notions of command and control, the 'great man' trope remains a part of sport today. Contemporaneous sporting terms, such as drills and formations, help coaches prepare their followers for battles and suggest coach's roles remain tied to notions of dominant great leaders. Here the image of a single powerful leader, often in the form of a coach or performance director, is operationalized as someone to follow. Indeed, research has recognized that the sport coach can be a powerful individual who has control over athletes' bodies, sporting experiences, and careers (Denison, Mills, & Konoval, 2017; Denison & Mills, 2014; Gearity & Mills, 2012).

Unfortunately, the powerful 'great man' coach has not always provided a healthy or positive influence on participants. The charismatic coach may have complete control of playing time, schedules, and staff, and from this position can enact disciplinary actions that may be harsh or extreme (Cushion & Jones, 2006; Gearity, 2012). Furthermore, coaches have been the source of abusive behaviours including physical, psychological, sexual, and neglectful mistreatment (Lang, 2021). Furthermore, the power that coaches wield often means that they are enable to enact harm, free from scrutiny. Here the view of the coach as an inherently 'great' individual who is the fount of knowledge and the gatekeeper of selection, sporting improvement and successful careers is undesirable, because it dogmatically situates the coach as almost beyond reproach. If questioned, abusive and inappropriate behaviours may be euphemistically justified under the guise of 'tough love', 'team and character building', or for the long-term benefit of athletes. It is here then, that the myth of a coach being 'cruel to be kind' is enacted. This discourse reinforces the fable that coaches always know best, are to be obeyed, and are the sole determinants of good practice in sport. The discourse further establishes the narrative that to be a coach is to be hard, cold, and detached from athletes in order to push them beyond where they would wish to go. This view of the coach is, however, dangerous from a safeguarding perspective, potentially undesirable for performance (Fisher, Larsen, Bejar, & Shigeno, 2019), and an inaccurate portrayal of what it means to be a coach (Cronin & Armour, 2015).

In response to the above practices and discourses, this chapter deconstructs the myth of being 'cruel to be kind' in coaching. It does so by firstly demonstrating how a great man view of coaching is naïve to the social-interactional aspects of coaching. In this section, coaching is redefined as a relational activity, and this raises the question of what type of relationships would help athletes flourish. Subsequently, the chapter proceeds to define what constitutes a caring relationship and explores how such relationships dismantle the myth of the cold and controlling coach who is 'cruel to be kind'.

Coaching as a relational activity

For some time now, coaching research has moved on from the 'great man' and all powerful stereotype of leadership. Indeed, this early theory has been critiqued for failing to recognize the relationship between leaders such as coaches and followers (Miller & Cronin, 2013). Additionally, the environmental influence on the development of leaders' traits, knowledge, and skills were underplayed by this early conception of leadership as an inherent and universal state. Indeed, conceptions of the coaching process have long recognized that coaches and athletes work together within situated social contexts. For example, Chelladurai's (1990) multidimensional model of leadership recognized that performance and satisfaction in sport contexts is influenced by the interaction of coaches and athletes. Similarly, Smoll and Smith (1989) used observation of coaches as a basis to propose a mediated model of sport leadership. The mediational model somewhat recognizes the complexity of coaching by highlighting how coaching practice is influenced by the characteristics of athletes such as age, gender, and self-esteem. Although, somewhat static compared to more contemporary research (e.g. Corsby & Jones, 2015; Cronin, Whitehead, Webster, & Huntley, 2019; Jones, Bailey, & Thompson, 2013), the mediational model recognized that successful coaching is not about a divine inspiration but involves and is in response to athletes' needs. Notwithstanding the relational view within the model, Smoll and Smith (1989) still recognized the prevailing mythos that many coaches 'believe that they are expected to win, and that successful coaches are (and should be) punitive' (p. 1535). Here then, Smoll and Smith (1989) not only described coaching as an interactional and situated process, but they also acknowledged that the contrasting view of the coach as an outcome-focused, commanding, and disciplining actor was widespread and enduring.

Over the last 30 years, human-focused research, including that from the sport sciences, have further examined relationships in sport coaching. For instance, Jowett et al. have studied the interactions between coaches and athletes. This research has identified that in contrast to the cold, and detached myth of the sport coach, closeness, commitment, and communication between coaches and athletes are key facets that lead to enhanced performances (Jowett, 2007; Jowett & Meek, 2000; Jowett, O'Broin, & Palmer, 2010). Other research has also established that coaches should facilitate the human needs for autonomy and relatedness to others (e.g. Cronin et al., 2018). Here then is a direct challenge to the 'cruel to be kind' fabrication, which posits that athletes need to be motivated through harsh disciplining practices such as running laps or experiencing physical and psychological 'beastings'. Further existential psychology has also advocated a pedagogy that considers athletes freedoms, choices, responsibilities, use of their time, and enables them to attune to and navigate their world (Ronkainen, Aggerholm, Ryba, & Allen-Collinson, 2021; Champ, Ronkianen, Littlewood, & Eubank, 2020; Ronkainen, Allen-Collinson, Aggerholm, & Ryba,

2020). Thus, within these more recent conceptions of learning, the role of the coach is not to dictate but to work alongside, empower, and support athletes on their journey.

Sociological conceptions of sport coaching research have also recognized coaching as a relational and interaction process. While instances of coaches misusing their power have been frequently analysed (e.g. Gearity, 2012), conversely, researchers have also described examples of caring coach–athlete relationships. For example, Annerstedt and Lindgren (2014) provide a case study of a successful elite adult coach: Bengt Johansson. The case study characterizes Johannsson's coaching as dialogical, empathetic, and respectful. This careful approach to coaching may be perceived by readers as unproductive, but Johannsson appears to simultaneously derive hard work, facilitate dedication, and achieve high performance standards from athletes through caring relationships. Additionally, from an American context, Knust and Fisher (2015) report on the care practices of 12 NCAA Division 1 coaches. These elite adult coaches reported caring for their athletes in ways that are patient, holistic, and nurturing. In both the above studies, it is emphasized that coaches are part of pedagogical relationships with athletes. Accordingly, coaches should not see athletes as resources to be manipulated and controlled, because the role of the coach is to work with athletes and couple their sporting knowledge with care by talking to participants, listening, and helping them learn. To that end, the next section will clarify what it means to be a caring coach.

What is care?

In sport coaching and other areas such as nursing, education, and social work, Nel Noddings ethic of care has been the predominant theoretical framework used by researchers (Cronin & Armour, 2018). Informed by the feminist writing of Carol Gilligan (1993), Noddings considered care a nurturing act. Gilligan's (1993) treatise, In Another Voice, argued that caring relations are widely undervalued in comparison to relationships based on principles such as justice, rule-based procedures, and authority. Of course, readers may also note how leadership informed by great man theory might similarly value authority, rules, and the leader's view of justice. Gilligan contrasts the prioritization of these characteristics over caring acts, such as compassion, empathy, and dialogue. With this dichotomy in mind, Noddings (1984) argued that care is an undervalued aspect of relationship. To evidence her argument, Noddings cites the low esteem afforded to caring professions such as childcare and nursing.

Noddings (2005a) also argues that pedagogical relationships should be based upon caring relations where both the carer (i.e. the coach) and cared for (i.e. the athlete) share understandings through dialogue. Such relationships have been identified in a number of sporting contexts including Australian Football League, U.K. basketball, and U.K. football (Agnew & Pill, 2021; Cronin & Armour, 2018; Daniels & Cronin, 2019). Here, the perception of the cold, detached, and rule-based sport coach has been questioned. Instead of a great man approach to coaching, these examples describe coaches listening to athletes, empathizing with their needs, and collaboratively working together. This once more emphasizes coaching as a relational and a two-way interactional process (Cronin & Armour, 2015), not one focused on cruel or dehumanizing treatments that coaches determine is for the greater good of athletes.

A nurturing relationship is focused on the needs of the cared for. This is an important point because supporting, the needs of others makes caring relationships, provides a moral and pedagogically rationale. Specifically, Noddings (2005a) highlights that carers need to provide sustained attention to the cared for. This is termed engrossment. In sport coaching, this period of engrossment enables coaches to understand athletes' needs (Cronin & Amrour, 2018). Here, empathetic observation by coaches can enable them to infer the needs of athletes. Additionally, through genuine dialogue, athletes can express their needs to coaches who are authentically listening. Subsequent to understanding the needs of athletes, coaches as carers could ensure their actions are motivated by meeting these needs either alongside or instead of their own individual desires, that is, motivation is displaced towards the needs of the cared for. Through engrossment and motivational displacement, coaches are able to both understand and work towards the needs of athletes. This provides a strong basis for coaching practice based on a moral ethic of care (Cronin & Armour, 2018). Additionally, understanding and working towards the needs of athletes provides a productive basis to develop the sporting potential of athletes. This is because understanding the athlete's strengths, weaknesses, fears, and motives may be a precursor to helping them flourish as a performer (Fisher, Larsen, Bejar, & Shigeno, 2019).

Engrossment and motivational displacement are two key tenets of a caring relationship and somewhat refute the myth that the role of the coach is to dictate athletic development. Rather, from a caring perspective, it is the needs of the athletes that should be the basis of coaching practice (Cronin & Armour, 2018). Furthermore, Noddings (2005a) argues that caring relationships should be genuinely dialogical two-way relationships. Here Noddings emphasizes that caring relationships should be reciprocal, in that the cared for (i.e. athletes) should have opportunities to contribute to the relationship and to recognize the care provided. This reciprocity is important because it recognizes the human rights of the cared for and asserts their autonomy to receive or reject care. In addition to engrossment and motivational displacement, reciprocity therefore enables a moral ethic of care. Furthermore, reciprocal relationships, where athletes contribute to the relationship and work with the coach, are likely to be productive in sporting terms (Cronin & Armour, 2018; Fisher, Larsen, Bejar, & Shigeno, 2019). This is because a coach–athlete relationship, where athletes contribute to the coaching process by providing input, critical thinking, and a commitment to a partnership, is desirable. That said, while such relationships appear obvious, the tenets of engrossment, motivational displacement, and reciprocity appear undervalued in contrast to the normative portrayal and myth that the authoritarian, loud, and demonstrative coach knows best.

Developing caring coaching

Caring relationships that include Noddings's focus on engrossment, motivational displacement, reciprocity, and needs-based relationships have been developed across a range of sporting contexts. Cronin and Armour (2018) provide examples from high performance athletics and basketball. In recreational youth sport environments, Newton et al. (2007) compared the impact of care on young people and highlighted that caring coaching held much promise for positive experiences and future sport participation. Since then, Fry & Gano-Overway (2010) explored care in youth sport and reported that a caring climate was associated with reports of 'higher enjoyment, more positive attitudes towards their coaches/teammates, greater commitment to soccer, and engage in more caring behaviors towards their coaches/teammates' (p. 1533). More recently, Gano-Overway and Guivernau (2018) summarized caring strategies for coaches through the SCENE acronym (i.e. support athletes, connect with athletes, empower athletes, nurture care in athletes, and establish a safe environment). Subsequently, Fry, Gano-Overway, Guivernau, Kim, and Newton (2020) have also provided a text of practical strategies to develop caring sporting climates. Simple suggestions, such as getting to know athletes through buddy breaks, interacting with friends and families, providing feedback for all players at tryouts/trials, involving athletes in session design and evaluation, developing connections in and outside of sporting contexts with players, and sharing leadership opportunities, provide actionable examples of caring coaching, and further dispel the myth of the coach who has to motivate through demanding and cruel activities. Thus, in providing evidence of coaching relationships built on listening, collaborating, and striving to meet athletes' needs, this chapter rejects the myth that coaches have to be cruel to be kind, aloof, or dictatorial.

More myths. Care involves dependency, and soft servitude

In critiquing the notion that coaches need to be cruel to be kind, it is also important to consider some other myths about care in coaching. To this end, the following section considers if care leads to dependent athletes, and if caring means 'being soft' and serving athletes' desires.

Dependence and care

At first glance, care can be associated with one person, the 'cared for', being considered dependent, weak, or inferior to 'the carer'. This conception of care can lead to an overly paternalistic relationship wherein the carer assumes all decision-making and the cared for develops a subservient, dominated, or co-dependent perspective. In such relationships, power could be used malevolently. Yet, Noddings's reciprocity concept makes clear that to care does not involve paternalistic control but respect for the autonomy of the other. Related to this, Van Manen (1982) argues that a pedagogical relationship 'involves the anticipatory and reflective capacity of fostering, shaping, and guiding the child's emancipatory growth into adulthood: what you should be capable of, *how you should have a mind of your own*' (author's emphasis) (p. 293). Thus, Van Manen (1982), similar to Noddings, emphasizes learner independence. This, of course, does not mean that controlling coaches should be replaced by absent coaches or controlling athletes. Rather, caring coaching involves respect from both parties for the autonomy of the other, an interdependent view of autonomy. Cronin and Armour (2018) provide an example of this from a high performance athletics coach, Terry. In this text, Terry describes how 'you educate athletes to independently cope and bring them up in a way so that they can do without the coach. Having said that, an athlete occasionally needs a pair of eyes to watch, or a sounding board ... I constantly encourage a dialogue' (p. 65). In essence, viewing autonomy as relational and interdependent is helpful as both a mechanism for supporting others, whilst simultaneously securing support for the athletes own autonomy. This once again rejects the view that coaches should dominate athletes, and athletes should depend on them entirely for support.

Similarly, it also rejects the idea of the coach becoming wholly redundant, in which athletes are left to flounder alone. Rather an interdependent view of autonomy is consistent with a caring coach where once again, coaching is seen as a collaborative and respectful partnership.

Care as soft servitude

Having established that coaching is not about great men, dominating and dictating demanding training programmes, but an interdependent relationship, there is the potential for caring coaching to be seen as 'soft'. Here the misconception may be that to care is to serve and to satisfy the desires of the athlete. This position is neither accurate nor desirable. To care is to serve the *needs* of the other, not necessarily their *wants*. For Noddings (2005b), needs may include basic and universal concerns, such as food and shelter. Beyond these, educators such as coaches may also infer the needs of athletes through a predetermined sport curriculum. While focused on athletes' needs, this is, however, a precarious act. Indeed, without engrossment through observation or dialogue, there is the potential for the curriculum to be divorced from the actual needs of the athlete. Thus, Noddings (2005b) encourages carers to establish genuine dialogue so that the cared for can express their needs. With genuine dialogue, involving authentic and empathetic listening, coaches may be able to ensure that they are not providing overly soft or overly hard training sessions, but ones that will help athletes grow within a web of care (Cronin & Armour, 2018). Thus, physically and psychologically challenging sessions can be a part of caring coaching if accompanied and informed by genuine care which clarifies that exercises and performance schedules are needed, and not merely wanted.

Crucially, Noddings (2003, p. 61) encourages individuals to distinguish between needs and wants through four criteria.

1. The want is fairly stable over a considerable period of time and/or it is intense.
2. The want is demonstrably connected to some desirable end or, at least, to one that is not harmful; furthermore, the end is impossible or difficult to reach without the object wanted.
3. The want is in the power (within the means) of those addressed to grant it.
4. The person wanting is willing and able to contribute to the satisfaction of the want.

These four criteria reassert that coaches should be engrossed in their athletes to understand and differentiate between wants and needs. Second, these points reinforce the reciprocal nature of a caring relationship by clarifying that the cared for (i.e. the athlete) should also contribute to meeting their own needs. Furthermore, needs rather than wants require the assistance of the carer (i.e. the coach). The role of the coach is therefore not to enforce and determine how every athlete develops, but to understand what an athlete needs and, where necessary, work alongside athletes to help them flourish, in ways and to the extent that the athlete is willing. As they do this, coaches should also be mindful of their own limitations. As Noddings (2003) notes, caring includes acting within your own capability and coaches may need to draw on the expertise of other professionals to support athletes. Furthermore, engrossment and motivational displacement are emotionally laborious and there is the potential for coaches to become overwhelmed in an attempt to meet the needs of athletes (Cronin & Armour, 2018). For the coach then, determining what is an athlete *need* and what is a *want*, is a crucial act. Doing so will develop caring relationships that are not soft and based on servitude, but that are relevant to desirable aims and which recognize the responsibility and capacity of the coach and athlete to work together. Without such consideration, there is potential for coaches to become swamped in a myriad of needless servitude.

Conclusion

For many, the cliché of the authoritarian coach remains a misconception of the coach's role or an all too frequent experience. Here faith has been placed in the stereotype of great man leadership, and oppressive coaching actions that are often justified, because the powerful coach knows best. This chapter, however, has demonstrated that the myth of the dominating coach is misplaced because effective coaching is fundamentally a relationship between coaches and athletes. Furthermore, the coach–athlete relationship often involves others such as parents and support staff. Each of these individuals brings knowledge, insight, and power to the coaching process. Thus, illustrating that moral and effective coaching is less about a controlling leader and more of a relational process. Accordingly, the chapter has provided examples of caring relationships between coaches and athletes through periods of observation and listening (engrossment), working in response to athletes' needs (motivational displacement), and working alongside athletes (reciprocity). In defining and explaining what constitutes a caring relationship, the chapter has also addressed two other myths; (1) that care leads to dependency and (2) that caring involves servitude. Rather caring coaching, as informed by Noddings's work, is exemplified as a moral and productive relationship, because it enables individuals to flourish, in their own right.

Note

1 Of course, such gendered notions of leadership reflect the thinking of the time, but are nonetheless incorrect.

References

Agnew, D., & Pill, S. (2021). Creating caring environments: An exploration of football managers and coaching. *Sports Coaching Review*, 1–20. doi:10.1080/21640629.2021.1896209

Carlyle, T. (1846). *On heroes, Hero-worship, & the Heroic in History: Six Lectures.* New York: Wiley and Putnam.

Champ, F. M., Ronkianen, N. J., Littlewood, M. A., & Eubank, M. (2020). Supporting identity development in talented youth athletes: Insights from existential and cultural psychological approaches. *Journal of Sport Psychology in Action, 11*, 219–232. doi:10.1080/21520704.2020 .1825027

Chelladurai, P. (1990). Leadership in sports: A review. *International Journal of Sports Psychology, 21*(4), 328–354.

Cronin, C., & Armour, K. (2018). *Care in Sport Coaching: Pedagogical Cases.* London: Routledge.

Cronin, C., & Armour, K. M. (2017). 'Being' in the coaching world: New insights on youth performance coaching from an interpretative phenomenological approach. *Sport, Education and Society, 22*(8), 919–931. doi:10.1080/13573322.2015.1108912

Cronin, C., Walsh, B., Quayle, L., Whittaker, E., & Whitehead, A. (2019). Carefully supporting autonomy: Learning coaching lessons and advancing theory from women's netball in England. *Sports Coaching Review, 8*(2), 149–171. doi:10.1080/21640629.2018.1429113

Cronin, C., Whitehead, A. E., Webster, S., & Huntley, T. (2019). Transforming, storing and consuming athletic experiences: A coach's narrative of using a video application. *Sport, Education and Society, 24*(3), 311–323. doi:10.1080/13573322.2017.1355784

Cushion, C., & Jones, R. (2006). Power, discourse and symbolic violence in professional youth soccer: The case of Albion FC. *Sociology of Sport Journal, 23*(2), 142–161. doi:10.1123/ ssj.23.2.142

Daniels, L., & Cronin, C. (2019). Athletes' views on care in coaching: Perspectives of women footballers in the U.K. *Applied Coaching Research Journal, 3*(1), 34–39.

Denison, J., & Mills, J. P. (2014). Planning for distance running: Coaching with Foucault. *Sports Coaching Review, 3*(1), 1–16. doi:10.1080/21640629.2014.953005

Denison, J., Mills, J. P., & Konoval, T. (2017). "Sports' disciplinary legacy and the challenge of 'coaching differently. *Sport, Education and Society, 22*(6), 772–783. doi:10.1080/13573322.2 015.1061986

Fisher, L. A., Larsen, L. K., Bejar, M. P., & Shigeno, T. C. (2019). A heuristic for the relationship between caring coaching and elite athlete performance. *International Journal of Sports Science & Coaching 14*, 126–137. doi:10.1177/1747954119827192

Fry, M. D., & Gano-Overway, L. (2010). Exploring the contribution of the caring climate to the youth sport experience. *Journal of Applied Sport Psychology, 22*(3), 294–304. doi:10.1080/10413201003776352

Fry, M., Gano-Overway, L., Guivernau, M., Kim, M.-S., & Newton, M. (2020). *A Coach's Guide to Maximizing the Youth Sport Experience.* New York: Routledge.

Gano-Overway, L. A., & Guivernau, M. (2018). Setting the SCENE: Developing a caring youth sport environment. *Journal of Sport Psychology in Action, 9*(2), 83–93. doi:10.1080/2152070 4.2017.1343214

Gearity, B. (2012). Coach as unfair and uncaring. *Journal for the Study of Sports and Athletes in Education, 6*(2), 173–200. doi:10.1179/ssa.2012.6.2.173

Gearity, B., & Mills, J. P. (2012). Discipline and punish in the weight room. *Sports Coaching Review, 1*(2), 124–134. doi:10.1080/21640629.2012.746049

Jones, R. L., & Corsby, C. (2015). A case for coach Garfinkel: Decision making and what we already know. *Quest, 67*(4), 439–449. doi:10.1080/00336297.2015.1082919

Jones, R. L., Bailey, J., & Thompson, I. (2013). Ambiguity, noticing, and orchestration: Further thoughts on managing the complex coaching. In P. Potrac, W. Gilbert, & J. Denison (Eds.), *Routledge Handbook of Sports Coaching* (pp. 271–283). London: Routledge.

Jowett, S. (2007). Interdependence analysis and the 3 + 1 Cs in the coach-athlete relationship. In S. Jowett, D. Lavallee, S. Jowett, & D. Lavallee (Eds.), *Social Psychology in Sport* (pp. 15–27). Champaign, IL: Human Kinetics.

Jowett, S., & Meek, G. A. (2000). A case study of a top-level coach-athlete dyad in crisis. *Journal of Sports Sciences, 18*(1), 51–52. doi:10.1080/026404100365289

Jowett, S., O'Broin, A., & Palmer, S. (2010). On understanding the role and significance of a key two-person relationship in sport and executive coaching. *Sport & Exercise Psychology Review, 6*(2), 19–30.

Kerr, G., Stirling, A., & Bandealy, A. (2016). Film depictions of emotionally abusive coach–athlete interactions. *Sports Coaching Review, 5*(1), 87–101. doi:10.1080/21640629.2016.1175149

Lang, M. (2021). *Routledge Handbook of Athlete Welfare.* London: Routledge.

Miller, P. K., & Cronin, C. (2013). Rethinking the factuality of 'Contextual' factors in an ethnomethodological mode: Towards a reflexive understanding of action-context dynamism in the theorization of coaching. *Sports Coaching Review, 1*(2), 106–123. doi:10.1080/216406 29.2013.790166

Newton, M., Watson, D. L., Gano-Overway, L., Fry, M., Kim, M.-S., & Magyar, M. (2007). The role of a caring-based intervention in a physical activity setting. *The Urban Review, 39*(3), 281–299. doi:10.1007/s11256-007-0065-7

Noddings, N. (1984). *Caring: A Feminine Approach to Ethics and Moral Education.* Berkeley, CA: University of California Press.

Noddings, N. (2003). *Happiness and Education.* Cambridge: University of Cambridge Press.

Noddings, N. (2005a). *The Challenge to Care in Schools: An Alternative Approach to Education* (2nd ed.). New York: Teachers College Press.

Noddings, N. (2005b). Identifying and responding to needs in education. *Cambridge Journal of Education, 35*(2), 147–159. doi:10.1080/03057640500146757

Purdy, L., Potrac, P., & Jones, R. L. (2008). Power, consent and resistance: An autoethnography of competitive rowing. *Sport, Education and Society, 13*(3), 319–336. doi:10.1080/13573320802200693

Ronkainen, N. J., Aggerholm, K., Ryba, T. V., & Allen-Collinson, J. (2021). Learning in sport: from life skills to existential learning, Sport, Education and. *Sport, Education and Society, 26*(2), 214–227. doi:10.1080/13573322.2020.1712655

Ronkainen, N., Allen-Collinson, J., Aggerholm, K., & Ryba, T. V. (2020). Superwomen? Young sporting women, temporality and learning not to be perfect. *International Review for the Sociology of Sport*, 1–17. doi:10.1177/1012690220979710

Smoll, F. L., & Smith, R. E. (1989). Leadership behaviors in sport: A theoretical model and research paradigm. *Journal of Applied Social Psychology, 19*(18), 1522–1551. doi:10.1111/j.1559-1816.1989.tb01462.x

Stogdill, R. M. (1948). Personal factors associated with leadership: A survey of the literature. *The Journal of Psychology, 25*(1), 35–71. doi:10.1080/00223980.1948.9917362

Van Manen, M. (1982). Phenomenological pedagogy. *Curriculum Inquiry, 12*(3), 283–299. Retrieved from http://www.jstor.org/stable/1179525

19 Psychological Resilience in High-Performance Athletes

Elucidating Some Common Myths and Misconceptions

Jolan Kegelaers and Mustafa Sarkar

Introduction

Michael Jordan winning his second three-peat after losing his father and being absent from the game of basketball for almost two years. Michael Phelps winning six medals in his final Olympics after publicly struggling with substance abuse and mental health issues. Or Liverpool F.C. winning the Premier League after a 30-year drought. Elite sport is rife with stories of high-profile athletes overcoming significant hardships and adversities on their way to exceptional achievements. It has even been argued that performances are often made more memorable because of the challenges athletes have to overcome (Russell, 2015). Those athletes who are able to reach such exceptional achievements despite experiencing adversity are commonly lauded for their exceptional *resilience* by fans and the media alike.

Following such popular interest, the notion of psychological resilience has also gained considerable attention as a scientific construct within sport psychology research over the past decade or so. Studies have shown that in order to reach the highest level of athletic expertise, athletes continuously – and often voluntarily – expose themselves to a wide range of potential stressors and adversities. Such stressors might be related to athletic performance (e.g. defeat, injuries), but can also include organizational (e.g. selection issues, team conflicts) and personal (e.g. long periods from home, family conflict) stressors (Sarkar & Fletcher,

2014). In order to continue optimal athletic development, athletes have to be able to withstand or overcome these stressors. As such, it seems no surprise that resilience has been identified as one of the essential psychological characteristics for athletic success (e.g. Rees et al., 2016).

But what exactly *is* psychological resilience? The study of resilience has often been criticized for its conceptual and theoretical unclarities (Bryan, O'Shea, & MacIntyre, 2019; Fletcher & Sarkar, 2013) and its conflation with other constructs of interest (e.g. mental toughness, growth; Brown, Sarkar, & Howells, 2020; Galli & Gonzalez, 2015). Not only are such unclarities limiting our understanding of the construct, they may also contribute to the status of resilience as a buzzword and perpetuate a number of myths, misunderstandings, and colloquialisms within the applied field (Bryan, O'Shea, & MacIntyre, 2019). As such, the aim of this chapter is to draw on recent advances in resilience research to highlight some of these common resilience myths and to explore how they might be re-examined or reframed.

Myth 1: Resilience reflects a stable personality trait

At its core, resilience implies (a) the exposure to some type of stressor or adversity and (b) the attainment of some type of positive functioning (e.g. performance, well-being) in response to this stressor (Fletcher & Sarkar, 2013; Luthar, Cicchetti, & Becker, 2000). However, debate exists around how we can explain that some individuals are capable of demonstrating such positive functioning in the face of adversity whereas others do not. One common explanation is that resilience is best conceptualized as a *trait*. Such a trait perspective proposes that resilience encompasses an innate personality characteristic – or constellation of characteristics – which remains relatively stable over time (Jacelon, 1997). This perspective can be traced back to the early work of Block and Block (1980), who coined the term *ego resiliency*. Drawing on psychodynamics, they defined ego resiliency as a personality parameter reflecting general resourcefulness, flexibility of functioning under stress, and sturdiness of character. In line with this early work, some researchers in sport have, indeed, suggested that resilience reflects a personality trait (e.g. Vitali, Bortoli, Bertinato, Robazza, & Schena, 2015).

Although intuitive, several issues exist with regard to the conceptualization of resilience as purely a trait. First, it has been demonstrated that resilience is, in fact, a contextual phenomenon (Fletcher & Sarkar, 2013; Luthar et al., 2000). This means that individuals who demonstrate resilience in one area of their life will not necessarily demonstrate resilience in other areas as well. Second, resilience has also been recognized as a temporally dynamic phenomenon, showing fluctuations over time (Hill, Den Hartigh, Meijer, De Jonge, & Van Yperen, 2018; Luthar et al., 2000). In other words, research has shown that an individual who is able to demonstrate resilience at one point in time will not necessarily demonstrate such resilience again at a different point in time. Clearly, both the context-specific and temporally dynamic nature of resilience do not match up with the proposed universal and static nature of resilience as a trait. Furthermore, a trait conceptualization also suggests there is limited opportunity for resilience to develop (IJntema, Burger, & Schaufeli, 2019), which is in direct contrast to a growing body of literature underlining the potential for resilience development (e.g. Joyce et al., 2018; Robertson, Cooper, Sarkar, & Curran, 2015).

Given these criticisms, scholars have increasingly highlighted that trait conceptualizations of resilience are no longer reasonable or valid. Consequently, current scientific consensus has shifted towards a conceptualization of resilience as a *process* (Bryan et al., 2019; Fletcher & Sarkar, 2013). In contrast to the trait approach, the process conceptualization recognizes that resilience is a dynamic state-like construct which is dependent upon time and context, and which is malleable for change. Such a process results from complex person–environment interactions, whereby several risk and protective factors – sometimes also referred to as resilient qualities or facilitative resources (cf. Bryan et al., 2019) – interact with each other over time to contribute to a given outcome. This process nature is captured in a recent resilience definition based on an extensive review of the literature within sport and work settings: 'A dynamic process encompassing the capacity to maintain regular functioning through diverse challenges or to rebound through the use of facilitative resources' (Bryan et al., 2019, p. 77). In order to further distinguish between trait and process perspectives, some researchers have called for a careful use of language and terminology and proposed the use of 'demonstrating resilience' (i.e. the process) rather than 'being resilient' (i.e. implying a trait).

Myth 2: Resilience is solely the responsibility of the individual

Erroneous resilience as trait conceptualizations might also hold an important ethical implication. Scholars have highlighted that such an approach risks shifting the blame towards the individual for not being able to effectively adapt to stressors (Fergus & Zimmerman, 2005; Oliver, 2017). Placing the onus of adapting to stressors squarely on the individual fails to take into account the role of environmental or situational influences. Indeed, within the context of sports, protective factors have been identified at both the personal (e.g. challenge appraisals, optimism, positive personality) and environmental (e.g. motivational climate, coach–athlete relationship) level (for more comprehensive reviews of personal and environmental protective factors, see Bryan et al., 2019; Galli & Gonzalez, 2015). In fact, one of the factors which has most consistently been associated with resilience actually reflects the amount of perceived and available social support (e.g. Fletcher & Sarkar, 2012; Galli & Vealey, 2008). In other words, rather than focussing on personal qualities, resilience might in many cases require turning to one's environment and eliciting the available support from important others (e.g. partner, coach, parents) within this environment. This has the important implication that in order to understand and influence resilience, we should also pay attention to the protective resources – as well as the risks – present within the environment around the individual (Taylor, 2019). Or to put it in a common proverb 'when a flower doesn't bloom, you change the environment in which it grows, not the flower'.

Myth 3: Resilience only occurs in the face of major adversity or negative life events

As highlighted by the examples provided in the beginning of this chapter, the notion of resilience in sport might evoke images of athletes overcoming major adversities on their way to exceptional athletic success. Within general psychology, resilience has also often been considered in light of major significant negative or even traumatic life experiences (e.g. parental divorce, environmental disaster, terrorism; Masten, 2014). However, a recent review of the resilience literature in sport highlighted that, in fact, resilience might be more common in relation to relatively small to moderate adversities, with reasonably short durations (Bryan et al., 2019). Fortunately, major and potentially traumatic life adversities are relatively rare in performance domains, such as sports. In reality, athletes will more often be confronted with 'everyday' hassles (e.g. performance slumps). Nevertheless, such relatively small adversities still hold the potential for disruption and require some form of adaptation, and thus, resilience (Russell, 2015).

Furthermore, Fletcher and Sarkar (2013) critiqued the negative value-laden connotation associated with the term adversity and argued that 'ostensibly positive life events – that are *not* typically associated with a higher probability of undesirable outcomes – can also be relevant in defining resilience' (p. 14).

Events which are generally labelled positive (i.e. normative and desirable) can still be perceived as stressful by the individual and hold potential for disruption. For example, Kegelaers, Wylleman, Blijlevens, Boonstoppel, and Hendriks (2020) found that athletes were also required to demonstrate resilience in face of seemingly positive events, such as being a tournament favourite. Similarly, participating in the Olympics – undoubtedly the pinnacle of many athletes' careers – can still be highly stressful and require resilience from the athletes (Wylleman, Reints, & Van Aken, 2012). As such, Fletcher and Sarkar (2013) advocated for the more neutral term stressors – over adversity – to highlight the potential need for resilience in relation to both perceived negative and positive life events.

Myth 4: Resilience is limited to a small number of 'special' people

Some early psychological research considered resilient outcomes as extraordinary and often used colourful terms such as 'invincible' or 'invulnerable' to describe individuals who demonstrated resilience (Masten, 2014). Such labels exemplify a common notion that resilience is somehow a unique quality, only possessed by a limited group of 'special' people. Similar ideas may have also found entry into sports. For example, former Arsenal coach Arsene Wenger commonly referred to the 'special resilience' of his players. In contrast to such popular views of resilience, research has demonstrated that resilience is actually a rather common phenomenon, which represents basic human adaptational processes that can easily be witnessed in everyday live. In this regard, resilience has sometimes been described as 'ordinary magic' (Masten, 2014) or 'a capacity in every soul' (Richardson, 2002, p. 315). A recent large review study found that resilience is, in fact, the most commonly observed trajectory following potentially traumatic events (Galatzer-Levy, Huang, & Bonanno, 2018). Although some scholars have somewhat nuanced this claim (Infurna & Luthar, 2018), the key message remains that resilience is something everybody is able to demonstrate over time, rather than being a quality unique to some 'special' individuals.

Myth 5: Resilience is always characterized by continued optimal functioning and a lack of (negative) emotions

Popular notions of resilience might suggest images of athletes who are able to 'push through', who remain unfazed and unaffected, and who refuse to give up even in the face of extreme adversity. Although resilience has often been considered as the ability to maintain a stable level of functioning under stress (Bonanno, 2012), it is recognized that, in fact, several resilience pathways exist (Masten, 2014). In this regard, Fletcher and Sarkar (2016) differentiated between two broad resilience pathways; i.e. *robust resilience* and *rebound resilience*. Robust resilience is typically manifested by both the general absence of negative consequences and the ability to maintain functioning under stress exposure. It is clear that the ability to demonstrate such robust resilience can be very relevant for high-performance athletes (e.g. maintain functioning during stressful competitions). However, it is not always possible to maintain functioning under severe stressors (e.g. following injuries). In fact, in certain cases blatantly refusing to give up goals in the name of resilience might actually compromise one's personal health and well-being. For example, Smith (2013) demonstrated that mistaken notions of resilience as just pushing through – embedded within typically masculine stereotypes in sport such as 'strength' and 'toughness' – might in some cases actually lead to unhealthy and maladaptive behaviours (e.g. refusal to seek help) in response to adversity. In contrast, more positive perspectives on resilience in such circumstances might revolve around shifting goals, finding meaning, adapting, and ultimately growing from adversity. Thus, another pathway of resilience can reflect a temporary period of deterioration in functioning followed by a relatively quick return to – or growth past – previous levels of functioning (Gucciardi et al., 2018). Such restorative processes in response to stress have been labelled rebound resilience (Fletcher & Sarkar, 2016).

In this regard, it is also important to highlight that resilience does not imply that individuals are not psychologically affected by adversity and demonstrate an absence of (negative) emotions. Research has demonstrated that positive emotions and a sense of optimism are, overall, associated with increased resilience (e.g. Gonzalez, Newton, Hannon, & Smith, 2018; Martin-Krumm, Sarrazin, Peterson, & Famose, 2003). However, in many instances, it might be expected and completely within the norm to experience negative emotions following stressors or adversity. In such instances, an overemphasis on positive emotions – a phenomenon colloquially also referred to as *toxic positivity* – might be maladaptive as it denies, minimizes, or oppresses basic human emotional experiences. Indeed, research has demonstrated that the process of resilience is often accompanied by a period of agitation and psychological distress (e.g. Galli & Vealey, 2008). In fact, such psychological struggles can act as an important catalyst for restored or even higher levels of functioning (i.e. resilient outcomes) following adversity (Richardson, 2002).

Myth 6: Resilience is only relevant at the individual level

When looking at the literature, it is clear to see that the vast majority of studies have focussed on resilience within individual athletes (Bryan et al., 2019; Galli & Gonzalez, 2015). This might create the notion that demonstrating resilience is a uniquely individual process. However, a small but growing body of work has found evidence for the occurrence of resilience within larger collectives as well, including sport teams (Morgan, Fletcher, & Sarkar, 2017) and organizations (Fasey, Sarkar, Wagstaff, & Johnston, 2020; Wagstaff, Fasey, & Sarkar, 2020). For example, Morgan, Fletcher, and Sarkar (2013) defined team resilience as: 'the dynamic psychosocial process which protects a group of individuals from the potential negative of stressors they collectively encounter' (p. 557). In parallel with individual resilience, this definition highlights that team resilience reflects a dynamic, temporal, and contextual process (Gucciardi et al., 2018). Furthermore, such team resilience does not simply reflect the sum of the individual resilient qualities of the different team members but also emerges from collective promotive factors inherent to the team's structure.

Although a comprehensive review of team resilience is beyond the scope of this chapter (for a review, see Morgan et al., 2017), some key team-level resilience characteristics and processes have been identified. For example, Morgan et al. (2013) identified four main characteristics of resilient teams: a strong group structure, a shared mastery approach, social capital, and collective efficacy. In addition to these team-level characteristics, a number of psychosocial processes might equally be conducive for team resilience, including transformational leadership, shared team leadership, team learning, positive emotions between team members, and a social or team identity (Kegelaers, Wylleman, Blijlevens, et al., 2020; Morgan, Fletcher, & Sarkar, 2015).

Myth 7: Resilience cannot be developed

The notion that resilience cannot be developed would seem to be the logical conclusion of a number of other myths highlighted earlier in this chapter. Considering resilience as a relatively stable personality trait, limited to only a few special individuals, leaves little room for development or improvement (IJntema et al., 2019). In sports, it might not be uncommon for coaches to believe athletes 'either have it or don't'. As stated earlier, however, this is in direct contrast to research demonstrating the potential for resilience development. Within the context of high-performance sport, recent studies have started to outline potential strategies and interventions to develop resilience in athletes. For example, scholars have proposed strategies based around life skills training (e.g. Cox, Neil, Oliver, & Hanton, 2016), rational emotive behaviour therapy (REBT) techniques (e.g. Deen, Turner, & Wong, 2017), or therapeutic counselling (e.g. Gonzalez, Detling, & Galli, 2016). One of the more comprehensive resilience training programmes for athletes was outlined by Fletcher and Sarkar (2016) in their Mental Fortitude programme. In line with process conceptualizations of resilience, the authors suggest that resilience training should take into account the complex interaction between personal qualities, appraisals, and environmental characteristics. Programmes should be set up holistically, focusing on three distinct aspects: (a) promoting a challenge mind-set (i.e. a positive appraisal of challenges and their own thoughts, emotions, and resources), (b) developing personal resilient qualities (i.e. promotive psychological traits, skills, or outcomes), and (c) creating a facilitative environment (i.e. balancing challenge and support) (Fletcher & Sarkar, 2016).

Building upon Myth 2, coaches play an important role in creating such a facilitative environment to develop resilience through their day-to-day work (Kegelaers, 2019). Recent research has examined how resilience is fostered within the daily practice environment in both athletes (e.g. Sarkar & Hilton, 2020; White & Bennie, 2015) and teams (e.g. Kegelaers, Wylleman, Blijlevens, et al., 2020; Morgan, Fletcher, & Sarkar, 2019). In line with the notions of robust and rebound resilience (Fletcher & Sarkar, 2016), coaches can develop resilience both proactively (i.e. prior to a stressor) and reactively (i.e. in response to a stressor). For example, Kegelaers and Wylleman (2019) found that coaches tried to foster resilience proactively by developing a positive motivational climate, promoting life balance, and anticipating and preparing for setbacks. Reactively, coaches tried to promote a challenge mind-set and encourage reflective behaviours following adversities.

A key aspect of the coach's ability to foster resilience also relates to the quality of the coach–athlete relationship (Kegelaers & Wylleman, 2019; Sarkar & Hilton, 2020). For example, Moen, Hrozanova, Stiles, and Stenseng (2019) demonstrated that the quality of the coach–athlete working alliance contributed to developing athlete resilience, which in turn mediated athlete burn-out. Such a quality relationship might strengthen athlete buy-in into shared goals and mediate the effectiveness of other resilience-building strategies highlighted above (Kegelaers & Wylleman, 2019; Moen et al., 2019). Furthermore, through a quality relationship, coaches can act as a source of social support, which in turn functions as a buffer against the negative effects of stress (Fletcher & Sarkar, 2012).

Researchers have also considered the role of challenge in the development of resilience. In line with theoretical suggestions (e.g. Fletcher & Sarkar, 2016; Galli & Gonzalez, 2015), coaches often use specific training strategies – labelled *planned disruptions* – to increase pressure within controlled practice environments, as a way to strengthen athletes' resilience under real-life stress conditions (Kegelaers & Wylleman, 2019; Kegelaers, Wylleman, Blijlevens, et al., 2020). Kegelaers, Wylleman, and Oudejans (2020) found that coaches use such planned disruptions to (a) expose and familiarize athletes to increased pressure, (b) create awareness about typical responses under stress, and (c) let athletes develop, train, and gain confidence in their own coping repertoire. Experimental studies have already demonstrated that such pressure training interventions are effective to increase performance under pressure (Low et al., 2020). In relation to resilience, one planned disruptions intervention study within female basketball found that participants reported increased awareness about their own strengths and weaknesses, emerging leadership, improved communication channels, and better action plans (i.e. shared mental models) for high- pressure situations (Kegelaers, Wylleman, Bunigh, & Oudejans, 2019). Although the use of planned disruptions has theoretical and applied support, a note of caution is warranted when applying such pressure training as the risk exists of creating aversive or even abusive training conditions when implemented incorrectly (Howells & Wadey, 2020). As such, coaches should be careful to frame their approach appropriately, balance increased pressure with sufficient support, and provide ample opportunities for debriefing and reflection (Fletcher & Sarkar, 2016; Savage, Collins, & Cruickshank, 2017).

Concluding remarks

This chapter aimed to elucidate a number of common myths surrounding the construct of resilience in high-performance sports. In sum, the current state of the research has demonstrated that resilience reflects a process that emerges over time as a result of dynamic person–environment interactions. Such a dynamic process reflects basic human adaptation and can be characterized by both an increase in negative emotions and a temporary decrease in functioning. Furthermore, such resilience processes are not only present in individuals but can also be observed within sport teams and organizations. Finally, the conceptualization of resilience as a process has the important implication that it can be developed over time. Within sports, coaches especially might have a crucial role in creating a facilitative environment to foster resilience in their athletes. We hope that with this chapter, coaches and practitioners might shift their understanding of resilience as a buzzword to that of a robust scientific construct with important practical implications.

References

Block, J. H., & Block, J. (1980). The role of ego-control and ego-resiliency in the organisation of behavior. In W. A. Collins (Ed.), *The Minnesota Symposia on Child Psychology* (Vol. 13, pp. 39–101). Hillsdale, NJ: Lawrence Erlbaum Associates.

Bonanno, G. A. (2012). Uses and abuses of the resilience construct: Loss, trauma, and health-related adversities. *Social Science and Medicine, 74*(5), 753–756. https://doi.org/10.1016/j.socscimed.2011.11.022

Brown, D. J., Sarkar, M., & Howells, K. (2020). Growth, resilience, and thriving: A jangle fallacy? In R. Wadey, M. Day, & K. Howells (Eds.), *Growth Following Adversity in Sport: A Mechanism to Positive Change* (pp. 59–72). London: Routledge.

Bryan, C., O'Shea, D., & MacIntyre, T. (2019). Stressing the relevance of resilience: A systematic review of resilience across the domains of sport and work. *International Review of Sport and Exercise Psychology, 12,* 70–111. https://doi.org/10.1080/1750984X.2017.1381140

Cox, H., Neil, R., Oliver, J., & Hanton, S. (2016). PasSport4life: A trainee sport psychologist's perspective on developing a resilience-based life skills program. *Journal of Sport Psychology in Action, 7*(3), 182–192. https://doi.org/10.1080/21520704.2016.1240733

Deen, S., Turner, M. J., & Wong, R. S. K. (2017). The effects of REBT, and the use of credos, on irrational beliefs and resilience qualities in athletes. *The Sport Psychologist, 31*(3), 249–263. https://doi.org/10.1123/tsp.2016-0057

Fasey, K. J., Sarkar, M., Wagstaff, C. R. D., & Johnston, J. (2020). Defining and characterizing organizational resilience in elite sport. *Psychology of Sport and Exercise.* https://doi.org/doi.org/10.1016/j.psychsport.2020.101834

Fergus, S., & Zimmerman, M. A. (2005). Adolescent resilience: A framework for understanding healthy development in the face of risk. *Annual Review of Public Health, 26,* 399–419. https://doi.org/10.1146/annurev.publhealth.26.021304.144357

Fletcher, D., & Sarkar, M. (2012). A grounded theory of psychological resilience in Olympic champions. *Psychology of Sport and Exercise, 13*(5), 669–678. https://doi.org/10.1016/j.psychsport.2012.04.007

Fletcher, D., & Sarkar, M. (2013). Psychological resilience: A review and critique of definitions, concepts, and theory. *European Psychologist, 18*(1), 12–23. https://doi.org/10.1027/1016-9040/a000124

Fletcher, D., & Sarkar, M. (2016). Mental fortitude training: An evidence-based approach to developing psychological resilience for sustained success. *Journal of Sport Psychology in Action, 7*(3), 135–157. https://doi.org/10.1080/21520704.2016.1255496

Galatzer-Levy, I. R., Huang, S. H., & Bonanno, G. A. (2018). Trajectories of resilience and dysfunction following potential trauma: A review and statistical evaluation. *Clinical Psychology Review, 63,* 41–55. https://doi.org/10.1016/J.CPR.2018.05.008

Galli, N., & Gonzalez, S. P. (2015). Psychological resilience in sport: A review of the literature and implications for research and practice. *International Journal of Sport and Exercise Psychology, 13*(3), 243–257. https://doi.org/10.1080/1612197X.2014.946947

Galli, N., & Vealey, R. S. (2008). "Bouncing back" from adversity: Athletes' experiences of resilience. *The Sport Psychologist, 22*(3), 316–335. https://doi.org/10.1123/tsp.22.3.316

Gonzalez, S. P., Detling, N., & Galli, N. A. (2016). Case studies of developing resilience in elite sport: Applying theory to guide interventions. *Journal of Sport Psychology in Action, 7*(3), 158–169. https://doi.org/10.1080/21520704.2016.1236050

Gonzalez, S. P., Newton, M., Hannon, J., & Smith, T. W. (2018). Examining the process of psychological resilience in sport: Performance, cortisol, and emotional responses to stress and adversity in a field experimental setting. *International Journal of Sport Psychology, 49*(2), 112–133.

Gucciardi, D. F., Crane, M., Ntoumanis, N., Parker, S. K., Thøgersen-Ntoumani, C., Ducker, K. J., … Temby, P. (2018). The emergence of team resilience: A multilevel conceptual model of facilitating factors. *Journal of Occupational and Organizational Psychology, 91*, 729–768. https://doi.org/10.1111/joop.12237

Hill, Y., Den Hartigh, R. J. R., Meijer, R. R., De Jonge, P., & Van Yperen, N. W. (2018). Resilience in sports from a dynamical perspective. *Sport, Exercise, and Performance Psychology, 7*, 333–341. https://doi.org/10.1037/spy0000118

Howells, K., & Wadey, R. (2020). Nurturing growth in the aftermath of adversity. In R. Wadey, M. Day, & K. Howells (Eds.), *Growth Following Adversity in Sport: A Mechanism to Positive Change*. London: Routledge.

IJntema, R. C., Burger, Y. D., & Schaufeli, W. B. (2019). Reviewing the labyrinth of psychological resilience: Establishing criteria for resilience-building programs. *Consulting Psychology Journal, 71*(4), 288–304. https://doi.org/10.1037/cpb0000147

Infurna, F. J., & Luthar, S. S. (2018). Re-evaluating the notion that resilience is commonplace: A review and distillation of directions for future research, practice, and policy. *Clinical Psychology Review, 65*, 43–56. https://doi.org/10.1016/j.cpr.2018.07.003

Jacelon, C. S. (1997). The trait and process of resilience. *Journal of Advanced Nursing, 25*(1), 123–129. https://doi.org/10.1046/j.1365-2648.1997.1997025123.x

Joyce, S., Shand, F., Tighe, J., Laurent, S. J., Bryant, R. A., & Harvey, S. B. (2018). Road to resilience: A systematic review and meta-analysis of resilience training programmes and interventions. *BMJ Open, 8*(6), 1–9. https://doi.org/10.1136/bmjopen-2017-017858

Kegelaers, J. (2019). *A coach-centered exploration of resilience development in talented and elite athletes*. Published doctoral dissertation. Brussels: VUBPRESS.

Kegelaers, J., & Wylleman, P. (2019). Exploring the coach's role in fostering resilience in elite athletes. *Sport, Exercise, and Performance Psychology, 8*(3), 239–254. https://doi.org/http://dx .doi.org/10.1037/spy0000151

Kegelaers, J., Wylleman, P., Blijlevens, S., Boonstoppel, A., & Hendriks, M. (2020). Coaches' perspective on team resilience during major international competition. *International Journal of Sport Psychology, 51*(3), 221–246. https://doi.org/10.7352/IJSP.2020.51.221

Kegelaers, J., Wylleman, P., Bunigh, A., & Oudejans, R. R. D. (2019). A mixed methods evaluation of a pressure training intervention to develop resilience in female basketball players. *Journal of Applied Sport Psychology*, 1–22. https://doi.org/10.1080/10413200.2019.1630864

Kegelaers, J., Wylleman, P., & Oudejans, R. R. D. (2020). A coach perspective on the use of planned disruptions in high-performance sports. *Sport, Exercise, and Performance Psychology, 9*(1), 29–44. https://doi.org/http://dx.doi.org/10.1037/spy0000167

Low, W. R., Sandercock, G. R. H., Freeman, P., Winter, M. E., Butt, J., & Maynard, I. (2020). Pressure training for performance domains: A meta-analysis. *Sport, Exercise, and Performance Psychology*. https://doi.org/10.1037/spy0000202

Luthar, S. S., Cicchetti, D., & Becker, B. (2000). The construct of resilience: A critical evaluation and guidelines for future work. *Child Development, 71*(3), 543–562. https://doi .org/10.1111/1467-8624.00164

Martin-Krumm, C. P., Sarrazin, P. G., Peterson, C., & Famose, J. P. J. P. (2003). Explanatory style and resilience after sports failure. *Personality and Individual Differences, 35*(7), 1685–1695. https://doi.org/10.1016/S0191-8869(02)00390-2

Masten, A. S. (2014). *Ordinary Magic: Resilience in Development.* New York: The Guilford Press.

Moen, F., Hrozanova, M., Stiles, T., & Stenseng, F. (2019). Working alliance in the coach-athlete relationship and athlete burnout: The mediating role of athlete resilience. *International Journal of Sport Psychology, 49,* 1–19. https://doi.org/10.7352/IJSP.2018.49.

Morgan, P. B. C., Fletcher, D., & Sarkar, M. (2013). Defining and characterizing team resilience in elite sport. *Psychology of Sport & Exercise, 14*(4), 549–559. https://doi.org/10.1016/j.psychsport.2013.01.004

Morgan, P. B. C., Fletcher, D., & Sarkar, M. (2015). Understanding team resilience in the world's best athletes: A case study of a rugby union World Cup winning team. *Psychology of Sport and Exercise, 16,* 91–100. https://doi.org/10.1016/j.psychsport.2014.08.007

Morgan, P. B. C., Fletcher, D., & Sarkar, M. (2017). Recent developments in team resilience research in elite sport. *Current Opinion in Psychology, 16,* 159–164. https://doi.org/10.1016/j.copsyc.2017.05.013

Morgan, P. B. C., Fletcher, D., & Sarkar, M. (2019). Developing team resilience: A season-long study of psychosocial enablers and strategies in a high-level sports team. *Psychology of Sport and Exercise, 45*(May), 101543. https://doi.org/10.1016/j.psychsport.2019.101543

Oliver, D. (2017). When "resilience" becomes a dirty word. *British Medical Journal, 358,* 1–2. https://doi.org/10.1136/BMJ.J3604

Rees, T., Hardy, L., Güllich, A., Abernethy, B., Côté, J., Woodman, T., … Warr, C. (2016). The Great British medalists project: A review of current knowledge on the development of the world's best sporting talent. *Sports Medicine, 46*(8), 1041–1058. https://doi.org/10.1007/s40279-016-0476-2

Richardson, G. E. (2002). The metatheory of resilience and resiliency. *Journal of Clinical Psychology, 58*(3), 307–321. https://doi.org/10.1002/jclp.10020

Robertson, I. T., Cooper, C. L., Sarkar, M., & Curran, T. (2015). Resilience training in the workplace from 2003 to 2014: A systematic review. *Journal of Occupational and Organizational Psychology, 88*(3), 533–562. https://doi.org/10.1111/joop.12120

Russell, J. S. (2015). Resilience. *Journal of the Philosophy of Sport, 42*(2), 159–183. https://doi.org/10.1080/00948705.2015.1009838

Sarkar, M., & Fletcher, D. (2014). Psychological resilience in sport performers: A review of stressors and protective factors. *Journal of Sports Sciences, 32*(15), 37–41. https://doi.org/10.1080/02640414.2014.901551

Sarkar, M., & Hilton, N. (2020). Psychological resilience in Olympic medal winning coaches: a longitudinal qualitative study. *International Sport Coaching Journal, 7,* 209–219.

Savage, J., Collins, D., & Cruickshank, A. (2017). Exploring traumas in the development of talent: What are they, what do they do, and what do they require? *Journal of Applied Sport Psychology, 29*(1), 101–117. https://doi.org/10.1080/10413200.2016.1194910

Smith, B. (2013). Disability, sport and men's narratives of health: A qualitative study. *Health Psychology, 32*(1), 110–119. https://doi.org/10.1037/a0029187

Taylor, R. A. (2019). Contemporary issues: Resilience training alone is an incomplete intervention. *Nurse Education Today, 78*(March), 10–13. https://doi.org/10.1016/j.nedt.2019.03.014

Vitali, F., Bortoli, L., Bertinato, L., Robazza, C., & Schena, F. (2015). Motivational climate, resilience, and burnout in youth sport. *Sport Sciences for Health, 11*(1), 103–108. https://doi.org/10.1007/s11332-014-0214-9

Wagstaff, C. R. D., Fasey, K. J., & Sarkar, M. (2020). Resilience in teams and organizations. In D. Hackfort & R. J. Schinke (Eds.), *The Routledge International Encyclopedia of Sport and Exercise Psychology. Volume 1: Theoretical and Methodological Concepts* (pp. 550–564). London: Routledge. https://doi.org/10.4324/9781315187259-40

White, R. L., & Bennie, A. (2015). Resilience in youth sport: A qualitative investigation of gymnastics coach and athlete perceptions. *International Journal of Sports Science and Coaching, 10*, 379–394. https://doi.org/10.1260/1747-9541.10.2-3.379

Wylleman, P., Reints, A., & Van Aken, S. (2012). Athletes' perceptions of multilevel changes related to competing at the 2008 Beijing Olympic Games. *Psychology of Sport and Exercise, 13*(5), 687–692. https://doi.org/10.1016/j.psychsport.2012.04.005

20 The Coach–Athlete Relationship

What Are we Missing from the Sociocultural Context?

Christopher R. D. Wagstaff

Scholars from diverse disciplines including pedagogy, sociology, philosophy, and psychology have for many years attempted to conceptualize the coaching process and coaching effectiveness in terms of relationships with athletes (see Jowett, 2017; Lyle, 2018). While these attempts have been somewhat helpful in terms of capturing what coaches do, and what promotes effective relationships between coaches and athletes, these approaches often have been accused of lacking practical utility, clarity, and specificity (see Cushion, 2007; Jowett, 2017). Indeed, many contemporary conceptual approaches to coaching practice idealize the *process* of coaching and the *characteristics* of coach–athlete relationships in clean, reductionist and, ultimately, limited ways. To elaborate, within much of the sport psychology coaching literature there has been an over-reliance on conceptualizations of coach–athlete relationships that seemingly exist in relative isolation from other sociocultural dynamics and are readily quantifiable. Typically inclusive of positivistic methods and assumptions, these reductionist approaches to coach–athlete interactions are, by their very nature, overly mechanistic guides that falsely portray complex dynamics as measurable, causally derived and thus controllable (cf. Cushion, Armour, & Jones, 2006). I have myself perpetuated such issues in my own work (e.g. Wagstaff, Arthur, & Hardy, 2020) and am aware of the limitations of this reductionism. Nevertheless, while authors have defended such measurement pursuits as 'a necessary foundation' with the alternative being 'a wasted effort' (Jowett, 2017, p. 154), the outcome is coach–athlete knowledge that remains 'divorced from the gritty realities of practice' (Jones et al., 2012). More pertinently for the present chapter, such approaches perpetuate a myth that coach–athlete transactions exist within a bubble – or vacuum – devoid of wider sociocultural influence. In the following pages, I will attempt to challenge this myth using literature from the fields of coaching sociology and pedagogy and organizational sport psychology.

Sport psychology researchers have rightly acknowledged the important role of the partnership that exists between coaches and place less emphasis on the coaching process or coach effectiveness. Within this work, valuable insights into the commitment, cooperation, communication, co-orientation, conflict and communication have been developed that have enhanced our insight into inter-personal relationships in this most-important-of-all sport dyads. These valuable contributions aside, some 15-years ago, Bowes and Jones (2006) noted that because social encounters like coaching, consist of non-linear relationships, they defy such unproblematic representations. Later, drawing from pedagogical the-ory, Jones and Wallace (2005) went further, arguing that such models can never grasp the functional complexities that lie behind and between their composite 'building blocks'. There is some justification in Jowett's (2017) assertion that 'at its simplest form, coaching concerns two people: the coach and the athlete. These two people form a unique dyadic relationship that holds a great deal of power and allows its members to achieve their individual and relationship goals …' and that 'Coaches and athletes are inseparable entities within the context of coaching' (p. 154). Indeed, such coach–athlete-centred approaches may offer a reasonable basis from which to understand the process and practice of the two stakeholder groups at the centre of much of the research and practice in sport. Yet, such approaches offer little in terms of the ways in which this relationship is located in and influenced by the sociocultural context. The coach–athlete, like many relational constructs within sport, can be – and regularly is – examined within a vacuum, but it is vital that we consider the many sociocultural factors and associated dynamics that influence this construct.

Another reason for the potential deficiency in accurately understanding the complexities surrounding the coach–athlete relationship – and one often noted by coaching sociologists and pedagogists – lies in the dominant pursuit of knowledge-for-action instrumental strategies (see Jones & Wallace, 2005). This knowledge-for-action has been driven by a fervour amongst coach developers to develop and prescribe 'good practice', leading to 'cut corners' and an eliding of the complex nature of coach–athlete transactions. Put simply, the oversimplifi-cation of coach–athlete relationships as standalone and 'clean' has led to unreal-istic conceptions (Jones & Wallace, 2005), the dissatisfaction of many coaches with professional development programmes as the advice given is simply not considered actionable (see Bowes & Jones, 2006) and many tensions and contradictions that characterize practice (Jones, Armour, & Potrac, 2003, 2004; Saury & Durand, 1998). Indeed, while many coach pedagogists might be accused of overindulging in a focus on the coach in the coach–athlete relationship, sadly, the approach to coach–athlete relationships represented within the extant sport psychology literature has typically elided the peculiarities, intricacies, and ambiguities of the *environment* in which these dynamic take place (cf. Bowes & Jones, 2006; Jones & Wallace, 2005). Certainly, coaching scholars have pointed to the complex and chaotic nature of coaching contexts (Jones, Bailey, & Thompson, 2013) and have pointed to the importance of sociocultural influences on coaching (Cushion & Jones, 2006), while others have called for holistic (Lyle, 2002; Cassidy, 2010) or integrative (Côté & Gilbert, 2009) approaches that better capture personal or contextual influences, yet little of this work has been fully incorporated into conceptual perspectives on the *coach–athlete relationship*.

The argument for sociocultural influences on the coach–athlete interactions

In this section of the chapter, I offer several arguments that attempt to dispel the myth of the coach–athlete bubble. Specifically, I offer four justifications: Coaches and athletes transact within and with their social context; Coach–athlete relationships are influenced by organizational systems in which they exist; Coach–athlete relationships are influenced by other key stakeholders; Coach–athlete relationships are socially constructed and influenced by power, cultural, emotional labour, and micropolitics.

Coaches and athletes transact within and with their social context

For many years, researchers have highlighted that social interaction lies at the heart of the coaching process (e.g. Jones, Armour, & Potrac, 2004). Furthermore, scholars from across the research landscape agree that coach–athlete relationships are not limited to isolated conversations between coach and athlete (Dorsch et al., 2020; Jowett & Cockerill, 2002; Mageau & Vallerand, 2003) and are dependent on a complex web of cultural relations (Cushion & Jones, 2006). Hence, coaching has come to be seen as a social process, comprising a series of negotiated outcomes between structurally influenced agents within an ever-changing environment (Cushion, Armour, & Jones, 2003; Poczwardowski,

Barott, & Henschen, 2002). It follows that the coach–athlete relationship should be viewed as a dynamic interaction between coaches, athletes, *and* the sociocultural context (Côté, Salmela, & Russell, 1995; Cushion, Armour, & Jones, 2006; Dorsch et al., 2020; Saury & Durand, 1998; Smith & Smoll, 1996). Such assertions are not particularly new, yet, despite researchers increasingly recognizing the many influences on coaches and athletes, sociological analyses have arguably remained underdeveloped within the coach–athlete literature. Moreover, while Cushion and Jones (2006) noted some time ago that 'gaps remain in our understanding of the social dynamics that construct and affect the relationships between coach, player, and club' (p. 143), arguably these dynamics remain under-researched, poorly understood, and consequently remain a notable absence from the coach–athlete field.

Within the integrative approaches to coaching, a tripartite approach is proposed that notes the importance of coaches' knowledge, athlete outcomes, and coaching contexts. To elaborate, Côté and Gilbert (2009) argued that an appreciation of the nuanced settings coaches operate within is critical to understanding effective coaching. Indeed, the authors drew on teaching research in going so far as to intimate that the coaching context is the determining concept for understanding coaching effectiveness. Sadly, while researchers (Lyle, 2002; Trudel & Gilbert, 2006) have developed classifications of coaching contexts (e.g. recreational sport, developmental sport, and elite sport), much of the current work examining coaching contexts has been focused on differentiating between the skills and knowledge demands across these forms of coaching. In turn, elided within this literature are the factors that influence the social, cultural, and psychological dynamics of the coach and athletes (as well as other stakeholders) or the heavy body of work that highlights the important transactions between coach, athlete, and context.

Coach–athlete relationships are influenced by organizational systems in which they exist

In line with the observation that coach–athlete relationships exist within and are influenced by social contexts, of relevance to this chapter is the body of work that has emerged under the rubric of organizational sport psychology (e.g. Fletcher & Wagstaff, 2009; Wagstaff, 2016, 2019). When describing the emergence of organizational sport psychology, scholars have frequently referred to a passage from Hardy, Jones, and Gould's (1996) seminal sport psychology text; borrowing from Shaw's (1981) work on social environments. Hardy et al.

concluded their book by noting that 'elite athletes do not live in a vacuum; they function within a highly complex social and organizational environment, which exerts major influences on them and their performances' (pp. 239-240). Allied with Hardy et al.'s vacuum analogy of the environments in which elite sport performers prepare and perform, there are many dangers of what I would label a 'myth of individualism' (Wagstaff, 2016, p. 3), wherein individual 'talent' is revered at the detriment of systemic functioning. Moreover, contemporary sport organizations, particularly those at the elite level, are characterized by complexity, turbulence, and volatility (Wagstaff, 2016) and are often precarious places to be employed as a coach (Wagstaff, Gilmore, & Thelwell, 2015, 2016). These high-change contexts have given way to organizations that seek to establish systems that instantly and consistently deliver success (Wagstaff, 2016) resulting in a growth in integrated technological, medical, and scientific expertise within sport systems to support their pursuit of competitive edge (Wagstaff, Gilmore, & Thelwell, 2016). The result of such change has been the creation of isomorphic institutions characterized by coordinated policies and processes, hierarchically structured bodies, with democratized authority, and largely shared collective goals. Given this changing landscape, it is perhaps understandable that scholars have increasingly emphasized the value of measuring and controlling the interaction of coaches and athletes for performance enhancement. Yet, seeking such knowledge without actually locating athletes and coaches in these complex systems of social and cultural influence risks reductionism and infers that coach and athlete, and their transactions, are unimpacted by the environment in which they operate, despite substantial research evidence indicates that they are. Indeed, within the organizational sport psychology literature, scholars have noted that influence of precarious employment (Gilmore et al., 2018; Wagstaff, Gilmore, & Thelwell, 2015), the need to coach through substantial organizational change (Wagstaff, 2016), and the deleterious effects of such change on relationships and performance for a variety of stakeholders (Wagstaff, Gilmore, & Thelwell, 2016).

The sociocultural contexts in which coaches and athletes interact are complex and chaotic

Given the different relationships, interests, goals, and expectations they must relate to, it has been suggested that coaches must work to orchestrate a complex social context and operate on or near 'the edge of chaos' (Bowes & Jones, 2006). In their important work, Bowes and Jones, attempted to portray a realistic conception of coaching that better accounts for the intricacy and dynamism that is endemic within it by exposing and explaining some of the invisible social contexts and cognitive constraints that drive coaches' behaviour. Specifically, they highlighted the value of complexity theory located within a structural framework of interactive relational schemas as offering a valuable scaffold to understand the ambiguous and personal nature of coaching (Jones, Armour, & Potrac, 2004). Later, Jones et al. have extended these descriptions of complexity and chaos with assertions that coaching should be seen as an act of orchestration.

Acknowledging the sea of relationships (cf. Wagstaff, Fletcher, & Hanton, 2012) within the sport environment, through the orchestration metaphor (Jones & Wallace, 2005, 2006), allows coaches to notice the complexity of their social context and prioritize efforts to make the most of their limited agency. Proponents of the coach-as-orchestrator metaphor explain it as akin to steering, as opposed to controlling, a dynamic interactive process and involving much 'behind the scenes string pulling' towards desired objectives; of constant analysis, evaluation and scrutiny to keep things going; and of maintaining detailed oversight of the minutiae of each coaching situation. While this position is articulated as one of influence and not control, the coach-as-orchestrator does to some degree carry linguistic implications of control, hierarchy, power, and challenges to dispersed influence in the coach–athlete relationship. Hence, while I value the fundamental sociocultural arguments of orchestration, I do not believe the orchestration metaphor offers a complete solution to the 'bubble' myth in part because it perpetuates the focus on individual actors within what is a complex system. Nevertheless, I do also appreciate that is helps to be somewhat pragmatic when attempting to understand sociocultural complexity and accept that the orchestrator metaphor was developed as a step towards making sense of coaching rather than a *fait accompli*.

Coach–athlete relationships are influenced by other key stakeholders

There are key social network considerations that influence relational dynamics pertinent to the coach–athlete relationship (see Ronglan, 2011). That is, both coaches and athletes must navigate and optimize relationships with other coaches and athletes, support staff, as well as athletes' parents. I would add to this list, managers or performance directors, agents, media, fans, administrators, and executives, Moreover, and in line with the myth of individualism alluded to earlier, scholars have argued that recurrent success in elite sport is not dependent on the talent (i.e. embodied competence) of individual performers but how effectively these individuals build and maintain working relationships with a systematic collective of social agents (e.g. coaches, managers, other performers, support staff, administrators, agents), supports (e.g. scientific, medical, and technological expertise), networks (e.g. personal social support), and bodies (e.g. sport organizations, commercial sponsors) to optimize day-to-day engagement and productivity in preparation for and performance at major competitions (see Wagstaff, Fletcher, & Hanton, 2012).

Again, these observations above are not entirely new with scholars having noted for some time that the coach–athlete relationship exists within a larger social network of parents and friends (see Brustad & Partridge, 2002; Jowett & Timson-Katchis, 2005; Smith & Smoll, 1996). Yet, again, such issues remain largely elided from coach–athlete conceptualizations and education. Taking the coach–athlete–parent relationship as an example, Smith and Smoll (1996) argued that regular meetings between coaches and parents can build lines of communication and enable an uninhibited flow of information exchange. Indeed, parents might have a legitimate expectation for information to be shared with them rather than their child, particularly when athletes are very young. In another notable exploration of the social networks that influence the coach–athlete relationship, Jowett and Timson-Katchis argued that dyadic relationships originate, mature, and are sustained within a larger social network. Moreover, they noted that evidence exists to support the notion that 'third parties' or network members (e.g. parents, siblings, friends) can emerge as robust predictors of relationship quality. Indeed, parents have consistently been reported to engage in direct conflict with coaches, other athletes, and their own athlete-children, with such acts hindering relationship closeness (Jowett & Timson-Katchis, 2005; Lauer, Gould, Roman, & Pierce, 2010; Weiss & Fretwell, 2005) and triggering intra-team conflict (Partridge & Knapp, 2016). Finally, a recent scoping review (Wachsmuth, Jowett, & Harwood, 2018) found 'external factors' including organizational stressors, discrimination, inequality, and stereotyping to be prominent antecedents of coach–athlete conflict in sport. Such observations do raise questions regarding why such sociocultural influences remain conspicuously absent from coach–athlete research in general.

In terms of athletes' relationships, most will be associated or linked to an established group of other athletes, sharing training and competitions. In many cases, the athletes will spend substantial time together with each other as a training squad, meaning that relationships develop not only between coach and athletes but between teammates. Noting the recent use of Wenger's 'community of practice' (CoP) in relation to sport coaching, and for understanding social interaction and exchange within a team, Ronglan (2011) argued that as a CoP, team members will engage in actions and interact with each other to negotiate the meaning of their participation within the enterprise. It follows that, rather than viewing the coach–athlete dyad as the basic relation, the whole community within the sport organization is seen as the fundamental unit for negotiation of meanings and the transfer of knowledge. In this vein, Ronglan (2011) argued that 'CoPs have the potential to hold several master–apprentice relations, where players can learn from each other as much as they learn from the coach' (p. 160). In doing so, Ronglan argued that face-to-face interactions between athletes and coaches are always situated in a culture marked by certain norms, values, and practices. Furthermore, this process of negotiation leads to the development of routines, norms, narratives, and a common language that act as cultural artefacts (cf. Wagstaff & Burton-Wylie, 2018). In this manner, athletes develop a sense of mutual experience and shared repertoire which act as resources for understanding the organizational culture (Galipeau & Trudel, 2006; Light, 2006). Ultimately, these factors will influence the coach–athlete transactions in an on-going and iterative manner.

Coach–athlete relationships are socially constructed and influenced by power, cultural, emotional labour, and micropolitics

Further to the arguments presented so far that the coach–athlete transactions involve the relationship between the coach, the athlete, *and* the environment, Cushion (e.g. 2010a, b) has argued that coaching practice is socially constructed and deeply embedded within social and cultural contexts. Cushion's work, among that of others, has demonstrated that knowledge between coaches and their athletes is produced within distinct sociocultural contexts, serves particular interests, and carries certain values. Unfortunately, such perspectives have not yet permeated the coach–athlete relationship literature. Hence, and in contrast to cognitive-behavioural conceptualizations of the coach–athlete relationship, the social constructivist approach, patronized by Cushion and others, offers another approach that explains how such phenomena are shaped by the environment and culture through interaction, shared values, knowledge, skills, structured relationships, and symbolic systems (see Cushion, 2011).

Support for the social constructivist lens on coach–athlete relationships comes from several sources. Cushion and Jones (2006) noted that dominant values and behavioural schema were uncritically accepted by the coaches, who defended their agency by stating 'it is the tradition, really' (p. 148). Moreover, aggressive coaching behaviour characterized by harsh and abusive language was not actively resisted and viewed by players as 'natural' (p. 158). These observations serve to highlight the processes and practices that shape the environment in which coaches and athletes transact, are embedded, and in which they develop and negotiate social identities. In turn, sport is far from being a unified context, and that it is necessary to consider the nuance of each environment within the bounds of time when trying to understand the relationships between coaches and athletes (see, for a review, Ronglan, 2011). In line with the potential contribution of the social constructivist approach to debunking the myth of the coach–athlete bubble, several additional considerations (viz. power, culture, emotional labour) are pertinent to consider.

Power. Researchers studying coaching and power relations in professional football (e.g. Cushion & Jones, 2006; Potrac, Jones, & Armour, 2002) have highlighted how context and culture dictate coaches' behaviour. That is, coaches have reported past experiences and expectations that led them to adopt a largely authoritarian and prescriptive approach to ensure they are seen to be 'doing the job properly'. For example, Cushion and Jones (2006) examined the coach–athlete relationship in terms of power, structure, and accompanying discourse within the existing social milieu. The authors reported how sense was made of aggressive and belligerent coaching practices in football through traditional institutional discourse about how best to prepare young players for professional sport. To this end, Cushion and Jones viewed interactions between coach and athlete to take place in and be influenced by their environment, and as inextricably tied to 'issues of power and power difference' (Snyder & Kiviniemi, 2001, p. 133). Similarly, and some time earlier, d'Arripe-Longueville, Fournier, and Dubois (1998) interviewed judo coaches and noted how aggressive and seemingly 'uncaring' acts toward athletes were influenced by their understanding of the culture and demands of the sport. While such acts would likely have a negative impact on the coach–athlete relationship, such behaviours are poorly captured by current models. Potrac and Jones (2011) concluded their commentary on power in coaching by noting that the interplay between coach, athlete, and context has largely been grounded in a somewhat simplistic and functionalist account of human relations and that if scholars are to better prepare individuals for the realities of practice, a more in-depth understanding of the multiplicities, workings, and potential consequences of power is essential.

Culture. Organizational culture has been identified as having a significant influence on performance outcomes at the Olympic Games, talent development, organizational functioning, and as a source of strain for athletes (see for reviews, McDougall et al., 2020; Wagstaff & Burton-Wylie, 2018). Recently, several programmes of research examining the sociocultural dynamics of sport organizations have begun instigated with salient observations for this chapter. For instance, in a recent programme of research, Feddersen, Morris, Littlewood, & Richardson (2020) noted that power is a critical social process that might be ever-present and manifest in conflicts and power plays. Moreover, systemic power (e.g. formal authority to reward or punish) and informational power (e.g. tacit feeling of oneness and belonging) characterized how a sport organization sought to implement top-down change and how individuals and subunits mobilized coalitions to support or obstruct the sports organization's agenda, respectively. It follows that in such scenarios, coaches might be perceived as 'part of the establishment' against which athletes come into conflict, adding hitherto unacknowledged influences on the coach–athlete relationship. Elsewhere, Champ et al. (2020) examined how the organizational cultural experiences of elite youth footballers shaped their identity development and behaviour, with the traditional masculine culture of professional football dominating the environment and influencing the behaviour of the actors within. Champ et al.'s observations were in line with those of Cushion and Jones (2006), who explored coaching practice, and Roderick (2006), who explored the lived experiences of youth apprentices. That is, coaches demonstrated an authoritarian management style; demonstration of power, dominance, and control; and punishments for not adhering to orders were all dominant cultural features that influenced the identity and development of youth players. Champ et al. concluded that the coaches in their study held hegemonic beliefs which they were typically reluctant to change, and in turn, these individuals act as key socializing agents. In addition to this, the coaches also wanted to survive within this social context and therefore most need to embody the cultural norms and demonstrate successful performance outcomes.

Emotional labour. Coaches and athletes are not able to choose freely the images of the self that they would have others accept; instead, they must conduct themselves in ways that are in congruence with the roles, statuses, and relationships that are accorded by the social order (Branaman, 1997). Moreover, to meet performance expectations in sport requires frequent and variable emotional transactions between athletes and multidisciplinary sports science and medicine teams (Hings et al., 2018). As such, coach and athlete behaviour are likely to be consistently influenced by the social context within which they operate as well as the dominant norms regarding behaviour and emotion in that environment. Hence, another consideration regarding the myth being debunked in this chapter relates to the performative and emotionally demanding nature of the coach–athlete relationship and the complex norms that guide expectations of coach and athlete behaviour. To elaborate, researchers have noted the requirements for (Hings et al., 2018; Potrac & Jones, 2011; Ronglan, 2011; Wagstaff, Fletcher, & Hanton, 2012) and consequences of (Larner et al., 2017; Hings et al., 2018) monitoring emotion display rules and engaging in emotion labour.

Many coaching sociologists have noted the need of coaches to manage, mutate, falsify, augment, or suppress their emotional expressions to perform their role and for organizational goals. In turn, this performative 'front' (Goffman, 1959) may lead these individuals to experience issues related to the inauthenticity of the self, self-worth management, scepticism, and exhaustion. For instance, in a sample including coaches and athletes (Larner et al., 2017) surface acting served as an important mechanism through which burnout mediated the relationship between the frequency of organizational stressors and turnover intentions. Researchers examining the emotional labour in coach samples have noted that emotional labour, coach burnout, job satisfaction, and turnover intention (Larner et al., 2017; Lee & Chelladurai, 2018) albeit using somewhat linear and reductionist questionnaire designs. Elsewhere, in a programme of research on coach stress using qualitative interviews, Thelwell et al. (Thelwell et al., 2017, Thelwell, Wagstaff, Chapman, & Kenttä, 2017) noted that athletes were able to detect when a coach was experiencing strain and that both athletes and coaches shared a perception of the coach as less effective at such times, as reflected by performance expectations, perceptions of competence, and lack of awareness. Such observations are pertinent to the current chapter, given findings support the emerging view that coach stress affects their own and athlete performance. In line with the dominant norms regarding emotional expression, there are salient challenges to complementarity and closeness that are socially influenced outside the coach–athlete relationship.

Micropolitics. The term micro-politics has been used to describe the political interactions that take place between individuals and groups within organizational contexts as they seek to use their resources of power and influence to further their interests (Hoyle, 1982). The micropolitics of sport organizations is relevant to the coach–athlete relationship as these contexts consist of an intricate system of historically and socially constructed hierarchies (Fletcher, Hanton, Mellalieu, & Neil, 2012). Moreover, sport environments have been the focus of numerous studies in which researchers have noted their importance for sport psychologists attempting to integrate potential stakeholders, micropolitics, and culture (e.g. McCalla & Fitzpatrick, 2016), developing micropolitical literacy in professional soccer (Huggan et al., 2014), and a critical appreciation of the day-to-day realities of sport psychology practice (Rowley et al., 2018). In their seminal work in this developing line of inquiry (Potrac & Jones, 2009b) began to question the governing discourse that sporting environments are or should be always characterized by functionality, collaboration, and trust. Indeed, in a follow-up article, Potrac and Jones (2009a) noted that a newly appointed coach acted to gain acceptance and 'buy in' from the players and later to displace a dysfunctional assistant coach who threatened his agenda. The coach did this by forging and re-forging alliances with contextual stakeholders and extensive 'face-work' (see section on emotional labour), where he carefully considered how to behave and manage the impressions of others towards preferred ends. Furthermore, Jones, Bailey, and Thompson (2013) reported the reflections of Jake, a trampoline coach being introduced to orchestration:

> When I looked through a micro-political lens I could understand better the organisational (e.g. working with other coaches, administrators and parents) and social issues experienced by myself and the gymnasts. It made it somewhat clear that being a good coach (pedagogy-wise) was not enough; if I could not influence the social and organisational contexts to function adequately, then my technical expertise was obstructed. (p. 279)

Such reflections can be interpreted to support the notion that the micro-political climate within a sport organization represents a potentially pivotal factor in determining the nature of coach–athlete interactions. Nevertheless, such micro-political considerations are elided by current coach–athlete relationship theory and research. It follows that better incorporating micropolitics into such work would go some way to dispelling the 'bubble' myth and better support coaches and athletes.

Recommendations for coaches

I reiterate from earlier in this chapter that there is some justification in assertions that coaching has at its center two inseparable and intertwined actors: the coach(es) and athlete(s). These two stakeholder groups form a unique dyadic relationship that holds a great deal of power in the pursuit of goals. Yet, the prevailing approaches within the literature offer little in terms of the ways in which this relationship is located in and influenced by the sociocultural context. The body of evidence presented in this chapter indicates that this omission is problematic and arguably serves to perpetuate the myth that the coach–athlete relationship exists in a bubble. Hence, I am moved to disagree with Jowett's (2017) other assertions that 'the effectiveness and success of coaching reside within the coach and the athlete and the unit relationship they develop' (p. 154). Put simply, it is more complex than that; the coach–athlete relationship does not exist in a bubble but is shaped by a multitude of social, cultural, historical, and psychological influences. As Finkelstein (2002) put it, 'I understand that as researchers we need to simplify very complex processes to study them carefully, but what are we left with when we remove the messiness, the back-and-forth, the reality?' (p. 77).

While there may be little direct translation of the arguments outlined here into changes in practice, and my comments might present more questions than answers, it is important to highlight potential blockages to effective knowledge transfer. First, we must recognize that the coach–athlete relationship transcends the individual and dyad by being fundamentally a system phenomenon. As a complex adaptive system (CAS), a sport organization is seen as comprising individuals, dyads, teams, and departments who transact in intricate ways with each other and the physical and sociocultural environment. Moreover, these stakeholders must respond to both external pressures (e.g. from environment or from other CASs or stakeholders) and internal pressures that are generated as the individuals struggle with interdependency and resulting conflicting constraints (e.g. when the needs of one person or group conflict with those of another). These tensions, when spread across a network of interactive and interdependent individuals, generate system-wide emergent learnings, capabilities, innovations, and adaptability. Therefore, the ambition to operate 'cleanly' in such an environment is somewhat unrealistic precisely, because such situations are relatively uncontrollable, incomprehensible, and imbued with contradictory values that coexist in some tension (Jones & Wallace, 2005). A more comprehensive framework is needed which better represents the complex reality within which coaches and athletes operate and transact. To fully capture and appreciate these complexities is difficult; to ignore them is wrong.

Conclusion

My intention here has not been to lambast the extant coach–athlete relationship literature. On the contrary, I believe there has been some valuable work conducted that has contributed to better understanding of these dyadic interactions and the characteristics that define effective relationships. My intent here has been to highlight opportunities for this work to better acknowledge the rising tide of evidence that indicates the importance of sociocultural influences on the coach–athlete relationship beyond the dyad. I do not deny the existence of dyadic coach–athlete relationships, or their value, but do feel that too much of the research on the coach–athlete relationship has been characterized as a dyadic phenomenon with little acknowledgment of the wider social environment in which this relationship exists. While there is value in understanding the dyadic interactions of two of the most prominent stakeholder groups within sport (i.e. coaches and athletes), the almost exclusive examination of this dyad in isolation is a fundamental limitation of the coach–athlete relationship literature that has served to precipitate and perpetuate the myth that this relationship exists within a bubble. For the reasons outlined in this chapter, I believe scholars and practitioners should better acknowledge the sociocultural complexity of the coach–athlete relationship and avoid clean, reductionist approaches that perpetuate the myth.

References

Bowes, I., & Jones, R. L. (2006). Working at the edge of chaos: Understanding coaching as a complex interpersonal system. *The Sport Psychologist, 20*, 235–245.

Branaman, A. (1997). Goffman's social theory. In C. Lemert & A. Branaman (Eds.), *The Goffman Reader* (pp. x1v–1xxxii). Oxford: Blackwell.

Cassidy, T. (2010). Holism in sports coaching: Beyond humanistic psychology. *International Journal of Sports Science & Coaching, 5*(4), 439–501.

Champ, F., Ronkainen, N., Nesti, M. S., Tod, D., & Littlewood, M. (2020). Through the lens of ethnography: Perceptions, challenges, and experiences of an early career practitioner-researcher in professional football. *Qualitative Research in Sport, Exercise and Health, 12*(4), 513–529.

Côté, J., & Gilbert, W. (2009). An integrative definition of coaching effectiveness and expertise. *International Journal of Sports Science & Coaching, 4*(3), 307–323.

Côté, J., Salmela, J. H., & Russell, S. (1995). The knowledge of high-performance gymnastic coaches: Methodological framework. *The Sport Psychologist, 9*(1), 65–75.

Cushion, C. J. (2007). Modelling the complexities of the coaching process. *International Journal of Sports Science & Coaching, 2*(4), 395–401.

Cushion, C.J. (2010a). The coaching process in elite youth soccer: The players' experiences. In B. Drust, T. Reilly, & M. Williams (Eds.), International Research in Science and Soccer: The Proceedings of the First World Conference on Science and Soccer (pp. 207–213). London: Routledge.

Cushion, C. J. (2010b). Understanding the coaching process in elite youth soccer. In B. Drust, T. Reilly, & M. Williams (Eds.), International Research in Science and Soccer: The Proceedings of the First World Conference on Science and Soccer (pp. 213–220). London: Routledge.

Cushion, C. (2011). Coach and athlete learning. In R. L. Jones, P. Potrac, C. Cushion, & L. T. Ronglan (Eds.), *The Sociology of Sports Coaching* (pp. 166–178). London: Routledge.

Cushion, C. J., & Jones, R. L. (2006) Power, discourse and symbolic violence in professional youth soccer: The case of Albion FC. *Sociology of Sport Journal, 23*(2), 142–161.

Cushion, C. J., Armour, K. M., & Jones, R. L. (2003). Coach education and continuing professional development: Experience and learning to coach. *Quest, 55*, 215–230.

Cushion, C. J., Armour, K. M., & Jones, R. L. (2006). Locating the coaching process in practice: Models 'for' and 'of' coaching. *Physical Education and Sport Pedagogy, 11*(1), 83–89.

d'Arripe-Longueville, F., Fournier, J. F., & Dubois, A. (1998). The perceived effectiveness of interactions between expert French judo coaches and elite female athletes. *The Sport Psychologist, 12*(3), 317–332.

Dorsch, T. E., Smith, A. L., Blazo, J. A., Coakley, J., Côté, J., Wagstaff, C. R. D., ... & King, M. Q. (2020). Toward an integrated understanding of the youth sport system. *Research Quarterly for Exercise and Sport,* 1–15.

Feddersen, N. B., Morris, R., Littlewood, M. A., & Richardson, D. J. (2020). The emergence and perpetuation of a destructive culture in an elite sport in the United Kingdom. *Sport in Society, 23*(6), 1004–1022.

Fletcher, D., & Wagstaff, C. R. (2009). Organizational psychology in elite sport: Its emergence, application and future. *Psychology of Sport and Exercise, 10*(4), 427–434.

Fletcher, D., Hanton, S., Mellalieu, S. D., & Neil, R. (2012). A conceptual framework of organizational stressors in sport performers. *Scandinavian Journal of Medicine & Science in Sports, 22*(4), 545–557.

Galipeau, J., & Trudel, P. (2006). Athlete learning in a community of practice: Is there a role for a coach? In R. L. Jones (Ed.), *The Sports Coach as Educator: Re-conceptualising Sports Coaching* (pp. 77–94). London: Routledege. Gilmore et al., 2018

Goffman, E. (1959). *The Presentation of Self in Everyday Life*. New York: Doubleday.

Hardy, L., Jones, J. G., & Gould, D. (1996). *Understanding Psychological Preparation for Sport: Theory and Practice of Elite Performers*. Hoboken, NJ: Wiley.

Hings, R. F., Wagstaff, C. R., Anderson, V., Gilmore, S., & Thelwell, R. C. (2018). Professional challenges in elite sports medicine and science: Composite vignettes of practitioner emotional labor. *Psychology of Sport and Exercise, 35*, 66–73. Hings et al., 2018;

Hoyle, E. (1982). Micropolitics of educational organisations. *Educational Management Administration and Leadership, 10*(2), 87–98.

Huggan, R., Nelson, L., & Potrac, P. (2015). Developing micropolitical literacy in professional soccer: A performance analyst's tale. *Qualitative Research in Sport, Exercise and Health, 7*(4), 504–520.

Jones, R. L., & Wallace, M. (2005). Another bad day at the training ground: Coping with ambiguity in the coaching context, *Sport, Education and Society, 10*(1), 119–134.

Jones, R. L., & Wallace, M. (2006) The coach as orchestrator. In R. L. Jones (Ed.), *The Sports Coach as Educator: Re-conceptualising Sports Coaching* (pp. 51–64). Stanford, CA: Thomson Learning.

Jones, R. L., Armour, K. M. & Potrac, P. (2003). Constructing expert knowledge: A case study of a top-level professional soccer coach. *Sport, Education and Society, 8*(2), 213–229.

Jones, R. L., Armour, K. M., & Potrac, P. (2004). *Sports Coaching Cultures: From Practice to Theory*. London: Routledge.

Jones, R. L., Bailey, J. & Thompson, I. (2013). Ambiguity, noticing, and orchestration: Further thoughts on managing the complex coaching context. In P. Potrac, W. Gilbert, & J. Denison (Eds.), *The Routledge Handbook of Sports Coaching* (pp. 271–283). London: Routledge.

Jowett, S. (2017). Coaching effectiveness: The coach–athlete relationship at its heart. *Current Opinion in Psychology, 16,* 154–158.

Jowett, S., & Cockerill, I. M. (2002). Incompatibility in the coach-athlete relationship. In I. M. Cockerill (Ed.), *Solutions in Sport Psychology* (pp. 16–31). London: Routledge.

Jowett, S., & Timson-Katchis, M. (2005). Social networks in sport: Parental influence on the coach-athlete relationship. *The Sport Psychologist, 19*(3), 267–287.

Larner, R. J., Wagstaff, C. R. D., Thelwell, R. C., & Corbett, J. (2017). A multistudy examination of organizational stressors, emotional labor, burnout, and turnover in sport organizations. *Scandinavian Journal of Medicine & Science in Sports, 27*(12), 2103–2115.

Lauer, L., Gould, D., Roman, N., & Pierce, M. (2010). Parental behaviors that affect junior tennis player development. *Psychology of Sport and Exercise, 11*(6), 487–496.

Lee, Y. H., & Chelladurai, P. (2018). Emotional intelligence, emotional labor, coach burnout, job satisfaction, and turnover intention in sport leadership. *European Sport Management Quarterly, 18*(4), 393–412.

Light, R. (2006). Situated learning in an Australian surf club. *Sport, Education and Society, 11*(2), 155–172.

Lyle, J. (2002). *Sports Coaching Concepts: A Framework for Coaches' Behaviour.* London: Routledge.

Lyle, J. (2018) The transferability of sport coaching research: A critical commentary, *Quest, 70*(4), 419–437.

Mageau, G. A., & Vallerand, R. J. (2003). The coach–athlete relationship: A motivational model. *Journal of Sports Sciences, 21,* 883–904.

McCalla, T., & Fitzpatrick, S. (2016). Integrating sport psychology within a high-performance team: Potential stakeholders, micropolitics, and culture. *Journal of Sport Psychology in Action, 7*(1), 33–42.

McDougall, M., Ronkainen, N., Richardson, D., Littlewood, M., & Nesti, M. (2020). Three team and organisational culture myths and their consequences for sport psychology research and practice. *International Review of Sport and Exercise Psychology, 13*(1), 147–162.

Partridge, J. A., & Knapp, B. A. (2016). Mean girls: Adolescent female athletes and peer conflict in sport. *Journal of Applied Sport Psychology, 28*(1), 113–127.

Poczwardowski, A., Barott, J. E., & Henschen, K. P. (2002). The athlete and coach: Their relationship and its meaning. Results of an interpretive study. *International Journal of Sport Psychology, 33*(1), 116–140.

Potrac, P., & Jones, R. L. (2011). Power in coaching. In R. L. Jones, P. Potrac, C. Cushion, & L. T. Ronglan (Eds.), *The Sociology of Sports Coaching* (pp. 135–150). London: Routledge.

Potrac, P., & Jones, R. L. (2009a). Micro-political workings in semi-professional soccer coaching, *Sociology of Sport Journal, 26*(4), 557–577.

Potrac, P., & Jones, R. L. (2009b). Power, conflict and co-operation: Towards a micro-politics of coaching, *Quest, 61*(2), 223–236.

Potrac, P., Jones, R. L., & Armour, K. M. (2002). It's all about getting respect: The coaching behaviours of an expert English soccer coach. *Sport, Education and Society, 7*(2), 183–202.

Potrac, P., Jones, R. L., Gilbourne, D., & Nelson, L. (2012). 'Handshakes, BBQs, and bullets': Self-interest, shame and regret in football coaching. *Sports Coaching Review, 1*(2), 79–92.

Roderick, M. (2006). *The Work of Professional Football: A Labour of Love?* London: Routledge.

Ronglan, T. L. (2011). Social interaction in coaching. In R. L. Jones, P. Potrac, C. Cushion, & L. T. Ronglan (Eds.), *The Sociology of Sports Coaching* (pp. 151–166). London: Routledge.

Rowley, C., Potrac, P., Knowles, Z. R., & Nelson, L. (2020). More than meets the (rationalistic) eye: A neophyte sport psychology practitioner's reflections on the micropolitics of everyday life within a rugby league academy. *Journal of Applied Sport Psychology, 32*(3), 315–333.

Saury, J., & Durand. M. (1998). Practical knowledge in expert coaches: On-site study of coaching in sailing, *Research Quarterly for Exercise and Sport, 69*(3), 254–266.

Smith, R. E., & Smoll, F. L. (1996). *Way to Go, Coach! A Scientifically-proven Approach to Coaching Effectiveness*. Palo Alto, CA: Warde.

Snyder, M., & Kiviniemi, M. (2001). Getting what they came for: How power influences the dynamics and outcomes of interpersonal interaction. In A. Lee-Chai & J. Bargh (Eds.), *The Use and Abuse of Power: Multiple Perspectives on the Causes of Corruption* (pp. 133–155). Oxfordshire, UK: Taylor & Francis.

Thelwell, R. C., Wagstaff, C. R. D., Chapman, M. T., & Kenttä, G. (2017a). Examining coaches' perceptions of how their stress influences the coach–athlete relationship. *Journal of Sports Sciences, 35*(19), 1928–1939.

Thelwell, R. C., Wagstaff, C. R. D., Rayner, A., Chapman, M., & Barker, J. (2017b). Exploring athletes' perceptions of coach stress in elite sport environments. *Journal of Sports Sciences, 35*(1), 44–55.

Wachsmuth, S., Jowett, S., & Harwood, C. G. (2018). On understanding the nature of interpersonal conflict between coaches and athletes. *Journal of Sports Sciences, 36*(17), 1955–1962.

Wagstaff, C. R. D. (2016a). Coaching through organizational change: the influence of leadership succession events. In *The Psychology of Sports Coaching: Research and Practice* (pp. 68–83). London: Routledge.

Wagstaff, C. R. D. (Ed.). (2016b). The organizational psychology of sport: An introduction. In C. R. D. Wagstaff (Ed.), *The Organizational Psychology of Sport: Key Issues and Practical Applications* (pp. 1–7). London: Routledge.

Wagstaff, C. R. D. (Ed.). (2016c). *The Organizational Psychology of Sport: Key Issues and Practical Applications*. London: Routledge.

Wagstaff, C. R. D. (2019). A commentary and reflections on the field of organizational sport psychology. *Journal of Applied Sport Psychology, 31*(1), 134–146.

Wagstaff, C. R. D., & Burton-Wylie, S. (2018). Organizational culture in sport: A conceptual, definitional, and methodological review. *Sport and Exercise Psychology Review, 14*(2), 32–52.

Wagstaff, C. R., Arthur, C. A., & Hardy, L. (2018). The development and initial validation of a measure of coaching behaviors in a sample of army recruits. *Journal of Applied Sport Psychology, 30*(3), 341–357.

Wagstaff, C. R. D., Fletcher, D., & Hanton, S. (2012). Positive organizational psychology in sport: An ethnography of organizational functioning in a national sport organization. *Journal of Applied Sport Psychology, 24*(1), 26–47.

Wagstaff, C. R. D., Gilmore, S., & Thelwell, R. C. (2015). Sport medicine and sport science practitioners' experiences of organizational change. *Scandinavian Journal of Medicine & Science in Sports, 25*(5), 685–698.

Wagstaff, C. R. D., Gilmore, S., & Thelwell, R. C. (2016). When the show must go on: Investigating repeated organizational change in elite sport. *Journal of Change Management, 16*(1), 38–54.

Weiss, M. R., & Fretwell, S. D. (2005). The parent-coach/child-athlete relationship in youth sport: Cordial, contentious, or conundrum? *Research Quarterly for Exercise and Sport, 76*(3), 286–305.

Index

INDEX